MEXICO CITY

JULIE MEADE

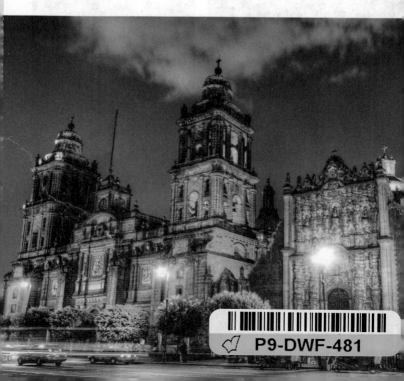

P9-DWF-481

CONTENTS

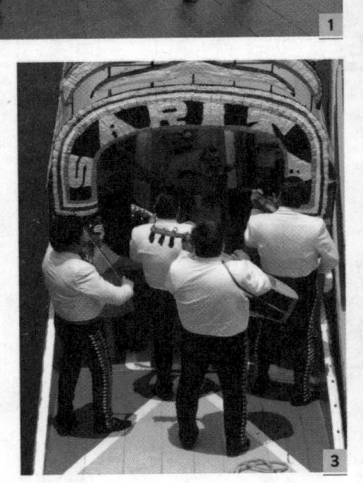

1 Traditional dancers in the Zócalo (page 73)

2 Sculptures at the Templo Mayor (page 72)

3 Mariachis playing in the traditional *trajineras* of Xochimilco (page 103)

4 Facade of the Catedral Metropolitana (page 74)

5 Museo Memoria y Tolerancia at Plaza Juárez (page 165)

6 The pedestrian street Madero in the Centro Histórico (page 36)

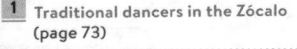

MAPS

Neighborhoods

Day Trips

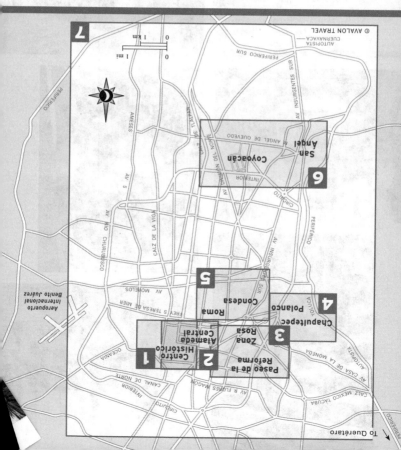

DISCOVER
MEXICO CITY

Mexico City occupies a piece of land that seems destined for conflict and grandeur. Blanketing a broad alpine valley, it was once Tenochtitlán, an island city that was the most populous in the Americas—and by some estimates, the world—during the 15th century.

Razed during the Spanish conquest, Tenochtitlán's ruins lie beneath the modern metropolis, which covers 1,480 square kilometers and has a population over 21 million.

6

Amid the urban sprawl, there are lovely residential enclaves, architectural landmarks, and a multitude of cultural treasures, from dazzling pre-Columbian artifacts to artist Frida Kahlo's childhood home. For those who love to eat, there is no better place to explore Mexico's varied palate. The city's famous food scene runs the gamut from relaxed street-side taco stands to elegant fine dining.

Mexico City defies expectations. It's a city of contrasts, where baroque palaces rise above streets noisy with traffic, old-fashioned coffee shops filled with seniors sipping *café con leche* stand beside generic convenience stores, and contemporary art galleries adjoin hole-in-the-wall bakeries and auto-repair shops. Travelogues and photo essays struggle to capture the true essence of a place so vast and multifaceted. Many of the descriptors most closely associated with the capital—crime, pollution, poverty—belie a city that is beguilingly low-key and friendly, rarely gruff, and invariably worth the effort it takes to explore. In this and every way, Mexico City is a place you must experience to understand. Come expecting one city and you'll likely find another, but the contrasts, both jarring and delightful, define this mad metropolis, one of the most singular and marvelous places on Earth.

10 TOP
EXPERIENCES

1 **Museo del Templo Mayor:** Mexico City's tumultuous history is visible at the ruins of the Templo Mayor, a great temple-pyramid that was destroyed during the 16th-century Spanish siege of Tenochtitlán. The museum showcases artifacts recovered from the archaeological site (page 72).

2 **Palacio de Bellas Artes:** With its grand marble facade and opulent art deco interior, the incomparable Palacio de Bellas Artes is one of Mexico's most striking buildings, as well as a keynote arts institution (page 83).

3 **Museo Nacional de Antropología:** Take a grand tour of the many pre-Columbian cultures in Mexico through artifacts and art. The most impressive rooms are dedicated to the people who lived in Teotihuacán and in what is today Mexico City (page 89).

4 **Museo Frida Kahlo:** A superbly talented painter and a beloved icon the world around, Frida Kahlo is celebrated at this lovely and intimate museum housed in her childhood home (page 96).

5 **Teotihuacán:** Admire the views from the top of two spectacular temple-pyramids at the country's most-visited archaeological site, a day trip just outside the city limits (page 237).

>>>

6 **Cantina Culture:** These relaxed neighborhood bars are quintessential to Mexico City. Spend a few hours enjoying the convivial atmosphere with a shot of good tequila in hand (page 149).

>>>

7 **Classic Cuisine:** Mexico City's tremendous food scene is reason alone to visit the city. You'll find ace eats in every price range and in every neighborhood, from old cantinas and street-front *taquerías* to fine dining (page 109).

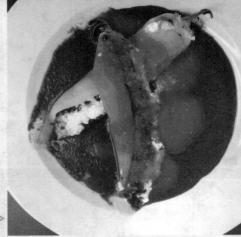

>>>

8 **Traditional Markets:** The city's colorful and atmospheric markets are where locals shop for everything from home goods to used LPs. If you only have time to visit one, make it Mercado de la Merced (page 197).

<<<

9 **Pulque:** This fizzy fermented beverage, made from the sap of the maguey cactus, is a capital tradition. As the younger generation discovers this drink, it's experiencing a deserved revival (page 146).

>>>

10 **Contemporary Art:** With the opening of new museums and the continued excellence of many long-running galleries, there's never been a better time to be an art lover (page 171).

EXPLORE
MEXICO CITY

THE BEST OF MEXICO CITY

>DAY 1:
THE CENTRO HISTÓRICO

- **Metro:** Zócalo

Mexico City's **Zócalo,** one of the largest public squares in the world, is located in the same open square that once stood at the center of the Mexica city of Tenochtitlán. Take a moment to feel the power and history of this grand plaza, then stop in to the northern wing of the **Palacio Nacional,** where Diego Rivera's breathtaking murals chronicle life in the pre-Columbian city, during the Spanish conquest, and through the ensuing centuries of industrialization.

To the north of the plaza, you can visit the remains of Tenochtitlán's holiest site, a twin temple-pyramid that adjoined the city's central plaza, at the fascinating **Museo del Templo Mayor.** Though much of the temple was destroyed by the Spanish and then buried for centuries beneath the colonial city, its base was uncovered in the 1970s, along with hundreds of artifacts, now held in the on-site museum. It's one of the Centro's most moving sights.

Palacio Postal is an architectural jewel.

BEST PEOPLE-WATCHING

With more than 20 million people living in the greater Mexico City region, it's easy to find a place to watch the crowds roll by.

MORNINGS AT CAFÉ JEKEMIR

There's a mix of seniors, students, and neighborhood locals sipping espressos at this old-timey café in the Centro. From the outdoor tables, watch passersby on the pedestrian street Regina.

FRIDAY NIGHT IN THE PLAZA GARIBALDI

You'll always find grandly dressed mariachi bands strolling this historic plaza, but it truly comes to life in the evenings.

SATURDAY AT THE TIANGUIS CULTURAL DEL CHOPO

You'll find a pierced-and-tattooed crowd at this unique Saturday-morning punk-rock market, originally founded in conjunction with the nearby Museo Universitario del Chopo as an informal album exchange for music lovers.

SATURDAY NIGHT IN THE ROMA NORTE

Stroll along the Roma's central avenue Álvaro Obregón on a Saturday night, when crowds often spill from the barroom into the street.

SUNDAYS ON PASEO DE LA REFORMA

People from every age group, neighborhood, and walk of life come together on Sundays to pedal, skate, or stroll along the grand Paseo de la Reforma, which is closed to automobile traffic from 8am to 2pm.

ANY HOUR, ANY DAY AT THE BASÍLICA DE SANTA MARÍA DE GUADALUPE

At the shrine to the Virgen de Guadalupe in northern Mexico City, mass is held every hour from 6am to 8pm, drawing throngs of worshippers from across Mexico and Latin America, many arriving in costume, as part of a bicycle tour, or on their knees.

Have lunch at **El Cardenal,** just a block from the Zócalo, widely considered one of the best traditional Mexican restaurants in the city. After lunch, head east along Madero, stopping to see the current show in the **Palacio de Cultura Banamex** and making note of two iconic buildings just before the Eje Central, the **Casa de los Azulejos** and the **Palacio Postal.** Take a turn around the **Palacio de Bellas Artes,** one of the city's flagship cultural institutions, where the gorgeous art deco interiors are as opulent as its elaborate marble facade. It's worth the admission fee to ascend to the top floors of the building, where there are interesting murals by Diego Rivera, David Alfaro Siqueiros, and Rufino Tamayo, as well as contemporary art galleries.

Dusk is the perfect time to start a tour of the Centro's many cantinas. Begin by sipping a tequila at the grandest old joint, **Bar La Ópera,** on Cinco de Mayo. Next, head to **Salón Corona** for tasty tacos and mugs of beer. If you're up to it, make one last stop to old-time cantina **Tío Pepe,** another historic watering hole with an excellent atmosphere.

> ## DAY 2: CHAPULTEPEC AND THE CONDESA

- **Metro:** Chapultepec, followed by Sevilla

Set aside the morning to tour the **Museo Nacional de Antropología,** a vast and fascinating museum dedicated to pre-Columbian and modern-day cultures in Mexico. You won't have time to see the whole museum. Streamline your visit by focusing on the spectacular rooms dedicated to the Mexica people, as well as the Teotihuacán galleries. Back outside, take an hour or two to explore a bit of the surrounding **Bosque de Chapultepec** on foot, strolling past the multidisciplinary cultural center **Casa del Lago Juan José Arreola**, the pretty manmade lake beside it, and the industrial facade of the **Museo de Arte Moderno** as you make your way to the **Castillo de Chapultepec**, set atop a rocky outcropping overlooking the park and the Paseo de la Reforma. It's worth visiting for the views alone, though the legendary building and the history museum it houses offer an interesting glimpse into Mexico's past.

Just below the Castillo de Chapultepec are the main gates to the park. From here, take the Metro one stop from Chapultepec to Sevilla, then walk into the Roma Norte for a late lunch at **Contramar,** an ultra-popular, always-bustling seafood restaurant near the Glorieta de las Cibeles. There's often a wait around lunchtime, but the food and atmosphere are ace.

After lunch, spend a few leisurely hours watching dogs romp and children play in **Parque México.** Stroll along Avenida Amsterdam, snapping photos of the Condesa's distinctive art deco architecture and enjoying the people-watching in the many neighborhood cafes. Wrap up the day with a drink at one of the neighborhood's trendy bars, like the hip pool hall **Salón Malafama** or good-time standby **Pata Negra.**

>DAY 3: COYOACÁN

- **Metro:** Viveros

If you arrive in Coyoacán via the Metro stop Viveros, you can admire old country mansions and towering trees while walking into the heart of neighborhood via avenue Francisco Sosa. Peek into the rust-colored Moorish-inspired hacienda that is home to the **Fonoteca Nacional,** an interesting sound archive and gallery space. Down the road, take a breather in charming **Plaza Santa Catarina,** a quiet, cobbled square popular with locals and their dogs. Once you arrive in the center of town, spend some time people-watching in **Jardín Hidalgo** and **Jardín Centenario,** the two old-fashioned public plazas at the center of the neighborhood.

Jardín Hidalgo, the main square of Coyoacán

Grab a mocha at long-running coffee shop **Café El Jarocho,** then wander through the **Mercado Coyoacán,** where you can snack on a tostada or two (the market is famous for them) to tide you over till lunch. From there, it's a few blocks to the **Museo Frida Kahlo,** a moving museum dedicated to the life and legacy of its namesake artist. Walk back to the Jardín Centenario for a late lunch on the patio at **Los Danzantes,** and accompany your meal with a shot of their house brand of Oaxacan mezcal. If you want to extend the evening, drop in for a drink at nouveau cantina **La Bipo,** just a few blocks away.

>DAY 4:
SAN ÁNGEL AND UNAM

▪ **Metrobús:** La Bombilla, then CCU

Saturdays are a popular time to visit the colonial-era neighborhood of San Ángel, where the weekly **Bazaar Sábado** attracts some excellent artisan vendors, including some modern designers. From there, stroll through the neighborhood, stopping for a bite in one of the pretty restaurants around the **Plaza San Jacinto** or touring the wonderful **Museo de El Carmen,** housed in a colonial-era Carmelite monastery. Frida Kahlo and Diego Rivera fans will prefer a short walk out to the **Museo Casa Estudio Diego Rivera,** the former adjoined homes the couple shared in San Ángel.

From San Ángel, take the Metrobús along Insurgentes to the CCU stop, then spend the rest of the afternoon exploring the cultural center on the Universidad Nacional Autónoma de México (UNAM) campus. Have a very late lunch at contemporary Mexican restaurant **Azul y Oro,** then spend a few hours in the light-filled

Museo Universitario Arte Contemporáneo, one of the finest contemporary-art museums in Mexico City, opened in 2008. From there, wander into the northern section of the **Espacio Escultórico de la UNAM,** a massive outdoor sculpture garden built atop an expanse of volcanic rock in the 1960s. Head home early and prepare for your next-day departure or continue your travels with Day 5.

With More Time

DAY 5: TEOTIHUACÁN
• **Metro:** Line 6 to Terminal Autobuses del Norte, then a local **bus** to Teotihuacán

Have a hearty breakfast in or near your hotel, slather on some sunscreen, and pack a big bottle of water before making your way to the Terminal Autobuses del Norte, the first stop in your journey to the ruins at **Teotihuacán.** Mexico's most famous and most visited archaeological site is just 30 kilometers outside the city, and buses depart the city for the pyramids every 15 minutes.

Though little is known about its people, Teotihuacán was once the most powerful city-state in Mesoamerica, evidenced by its massive installations and visionary city planning. Today, you can get a small glimpse into the past by walking along Teotihuacán's grand central avenue and climbing to the top of its massive pyramids. After touring the ruins, cool off with a bite in quirky restaurant **La Gruta,** though you may prefer to relax after getting back to town. After all the stairs and sun, make it an easy but classic pick for dinner: *tacos al pastor,* the city's signature dish. You can try some of the best at **El Huequito** in the San Juan, or at **El Califa** in the Condesa. Crash to sleep with plans to return.

MEXICO CITY WITH KIDS

Mexico City is large, loud, and relentlessly urban, yet it's a remarkably agreeable place to visit with your family. Here, children are treated with respect and kindness, graciously welcomed at most restaurants and hotels, and often granted free admission to museums and other cultural institutions. Even more compelling, the capital's rich history and diverse local culture make it a truly magical and eye-opening place to visit—at any age. A few smaller and boutique properties do not accept children, but **Suites del Ángel** is a good and economical choice for a family, with small sitting rooms that can be converted to a second bedroom. Just around the corner, the ultra-posh **St. Regis** has a children's center with arts and crafts, story time, and other kid-centric activities on-site.

>FRIDAY: CENTRO HISTÓRICO

The Centro Histórico is a magical neighborhood, filled with old palaces, bustling with visitors, and buzzing with years of history. Start with breakfast in the historic dining room at **Café de Tacuba,** then walk down to the **Zócalo,** where you'll often find brightly dressed *concheros* (also called "Aztec dancers") performing a rhythmic dance to the beat of a drum.

For older children, Diego Rivera's extensive murals inside the **Secretaría de Educación Pública,** or SEP, north of the Zócalo, provide an engaging look into Mexican history and popular culture—as well as Rivera's communist political

traditional dancers in the Zócalo

The Alameda Central is Mexico City's oldest urban park.

views. There are often free English-speaking tour guides wandering through the plaza, who can help provide context and background for Rivera's work.

Have lunch at **Balcón del Zócalo,** a fun Mexican restaurant with gorgeous views of the cathedral and plaza, then walk down Cinco de Mayo to the **Dulcería de Celaya,** one of the oldest and most charming sweet shops in the city. From there, it's an easy stroll along the pedestrian avenue Madero to the **Torre Latinoamericana.** Take the elevator to the 44th-floor observation deck, which affords tremendous vistas of the city in every direction, including the snow-capped volcanoes Popocatépetl and Iztaccíhuatl to the south.

From there, cross the Eje Central to the Alameda, peeking into the **Palacio de Bellas Artes.** You can tour the opulent main theater, where on most Wednesday and Sunday evenings, the colorful **Ballet Folklórico de México de Amalia Hernández** performs traditional Mexican folk dances—a good reason to return to Bellas Artes a few days later.

Finally, let the kids stretch their legs along the paved paths in the **Alameda Central,** Mexico City's oldest urban park, which was remodeled and expanded in 2012. On warm days, children often run through the park's many attractive fountains while their parents relax on park benches. Wrap up the day with a sugar-topped churro and creamy hot chocolate, the signature combination at old-fashioned **Churrería El Moro,** in business since 1935 and open 24 hours, 365 days a year.

> SATURDAY: XOCHIMILCO

Though you can visit **Xochimilco** any day of the week, it is most festive on the weekends, when local families and revelers come

the canals at Xochimilco

her namesake museum. Housed in an old, beautiful hacienda, the **Museo Dolores Olmedo** contains a large collection of work by Frida Kahlo and Diego Rivera, among other modern artists, as well as her collection of pre-Columbian artifacts. It's particularly delightful to wander the grounds, where peacocks and *xoloscuintle* (Mexican hairless dogs), Olmedo's favored pet, roam freely.

›SUNDAY: CHAPULTEPEC

Closed to automobile traffic every Sunday, the **Paseo de la Reforma** fills with cyclists, roller-bladers, pedestrians, and dog walkers. Get an early start on the day to ride a bike (or simply stroll) along Reforma, checking out the many famous monuments, like the **Ángel de la Independencia,** as you make your way to the **Bosque de Chapultepec**'s main entrance.

to float along the old **canals,** a small remnant of the vast system of waterways that once ribboned the Valley of Mexico. You can take the light rail from Metro Tasqueña all the way to Xochimilco, though lighter traffic on Saturday mornings can make taxi or Uber an easy option too.

Enlist the kids to help pick out a *trajinera*, one of the colorful flat-bottomed boats typical to Xochimilco, and plan to spend a few hours exploring the canals. The main tourist corridor is often jammed with boaters, giving it a light-hearted atmosphere, though you may also want to ask the driver to go farther into the canals, to see the floating gardens, or *chinampas*, where people still live and grow food. Order quesadillas and other snacks from the vendors paddling by in canoes, and consider commissioning one of the floating mariachi bands for a tune.

Back on dry land, take a taxi (or the train to La Noria) to visit the former home of philanthropist and art collector Dolores Olmedo, now

Families flock to the Bosque de Chapultepec on Sundays, when museums are free and the footpaths are filled with vendors selling balloons, balls, tacos, fresh fruit, and bubbles, among other treats. At the base of the Cerro de Chapultepec, a small motorized train will take you up the hill to the **Castillo de Chapultepec;** it has marvelous views of the park and the Paseo de la Reforma, while the period rooms bring the opulence of 19th-century Mexico City to life.

Save Chapultepec's children's museum for tomorrow; instead stop by the **Casa del Lago Juan José Arreola,** a wonderful cultural center that often has concerts and special workshops for kids. And even small children will enjoy the

outdoor art exhibit along the
Paseo de la Reforma

children's museum **Papalote Museo del Niño** is open on most Mondays throughout the year (check the website for an updated calendar)—and noticeably less crowded during the week than on a Saturday or Sunday. Take a taxi into Chapultepec's Segunda Sección to spend the morning at this big, interactive museum, where your kids will get a chance to practice their budding language skills (all exhibits are in Spanish).

eye-catching interactive exhibits and video installations at the **Centro Cultural Digital,** just outside the main gates. From there, you can walk through Chapultepec along the Paseo de la Reforma, where there are often interesting photo exhibitions hanging along the famous green fence that encircles the park.

Cross the Paseo de la Reforma to **Los Panchos** for a casual lunch of tacos, quesadillas with handmade tortillas, and *carnitas*.

>MONDAY: CHILDREN'S MUSEUM AND CONDESA

Though the Bosque de Chapultepec is closed to visitors, the

From there, it's easiest to take an Uber ride, as taxis rarely circle the park; alternatively, the Metro stop Constituyentes is a five-minute walk, and with just one transfer you can arrive at Metro Sevilla, on the north edge of the Condesa neighborhood. Spend the afternoon wandering in and around **Parque México,** visiting the duck pond and the playground, and watching local kids ride bikes and kick soccer balls in the outdoor amphitheater **Foro Lindbergh.** Stop in for a double-scoop cone at throwback ice-cream parlor **Nevería Roxy,** and wrap up the day with a plate of tacos at **El Tizoncito,** which has been serving capital families for decades.

MEXICO CITY: PAST AND PRESENT

Mexico City's streets tell the story of its past, with institutions, architecture, and landmarks that are testament to 500-plus years of culture and change.

>DAY 1:
CENTRO HISTÓRICO

In the 1970s, the ruins of the **Templo Mayor,** a twin temple-pyramid at the heart of Tenochtitlán, were unearthed after more than four centuries under the city floor. After an extensive excavation that demolished a number of colonial-era buildings beside the Catedral Metropolitana, the archaeological site was opened to the public, alongside the fascinating **Museo del Templo Mayor,** which contains dozens of pre-Columbian artifacts recovered from the site.

Though they haven't received permission to continue demolitions, archaeologists surmise that even more ruins lie beneath the 17th-century palaces on the street República de Guatemala, as evidenced recently at the **Centro Cultural de España,** a contemporary cultural center overseen by the Spanish government. In a planned expansion of the space, belowground construction unearthed Mexica ruins, believed to have been part of a *calmécac,* a school for young Mexica nobles. The ruins are on display in the onsite **Museo del Sitio,** in the center's basement, a lovely complement to its avant-garde program of music and art events. After your visit,

Templo Mayor

BEST MURALS

CENTRO HISTÓRICO

The city's most famous mural is Diego Rivera's series *Epic of the Mexican People in Their Struggle for Freedom and Independence,* in the north patio of the **Palacio Nacional.** A few blocks north, at the headquarters of the **Secretaría de Educación Pública,** Rivera covered the walls of two adjoining patios with elaborate depictions of Mexican history and culture.

At the **Antiguo Colegio de San Ildefonso,** find interesting murals by Rivera, David Alfaro Siqueiros, Fermín Revueltas Sánchez, and Jean Charlot, among others, in addition to extensive works by José Clemente Orozco in the main patio.

ALAMEDA CENTRAL

See monumental works by some of Mexico's modern-art masters at the **Palacio de Bellas Artes,** including David Alfaro Siqueiros's *Nueva Democracia* (New Democracy), commemorating the Revolution of 1910. Cross the Alameda to see one of Rivera's most entertaining works in the **Museo Mural Diego Rivera.**

POLANCO

There are several murals by Siqueiros inside the **Museo Sala de Arte Público David Alfaro Siqueiros,** a nonprofit gallery. Different artists periodically re-paint the building's facade.

SOUTHERN MEXICO CITY

The three-dimensional mural covering the arts space **Poliforum Siqueiros** astonishes in its proportions, colors, and ambition. Inside, Siqueiros's *La Marcha de la Humanidad* covers the walls and ceiling of an entire room.

CIUDAD UNIVERSITARIA

Juan O'Gorman designed the giant volcanic-stone mosaic that covers the facade of the **Biblioteca Central.** Next door, a famous work by Siqueiros adorns the Rectoría.

grab a coffee and a snack on the rooftop cafe, which overlooks the cathedral.

During the pre-Columbian era and throughout most of the last four centuries, canals linked central Mexico City to the farming communities in the southern Valley of Mexico, with a major waterway terminating in what is today the old Merced commercial district. Today's **Mercado de la Merced** remains one of the largest and most important markets in the city. You can walk to the Merced from the Zócalo, but it's faster to take the Metro just one stop from Pino Suárez to La Merced. Before boarding, take note of the Templo Ehécatl-Quetzalcóatl, inside the Metro station; this unusual round Mexica pyramid was uncovered by transit workers during construction of the subway line. Plans for the station were altered to accommodate the temple; today, in a delightful mix of old and new, the pyramid is on display in an open-air plaza within the station.

Take your time wandering through the towering stacks of fruits and vegetables, home supplies, and crafts for sale at the Mercado de la Merced, making your way down the circuitous aisles to neighboring **Mercado Sonora,** known for its herbal remedies, witchcraft supplies, and live animals. Finish up the day with a late lunch at chile-pepper-centric, Merced-inspired restaurant **Roldán 37,** or try food based on pre-Columbian culinary traditions at long-running **Restaurante Chon,** both located in the old Merced commercial district.

>DAY 2: CHAPULTEPEC

The **Museo Nacional de Antropología** is a must for any visitor to the city, but those with an interest in pre-Columbian cultures could easily spend a full day in this spectacular museum. Set aside time for the rooms dedicated to the cultures of the Valley of Mexico, which include, among other treasures, the famous Piedra del Sol, a basalt monolith carved with Mexica calendar glyphs. It's also worth checking out the recently remodeled second-floor ethnographic exhibits, which cover the dress, customs, language, and culture of Mexico's diverse cultures and ethnic groups.

Museo Nacional de Antropología

The museum's greater home, the **Bosque de Chapultepec,** is itself a site of great historic importance: Its springs provided fresh water to the city of Tenochtitlán, and later the capital of New Spain, via an aqueduct that ran along what is today the Avenida Chapultepec. Though little is left, you can visit the site of the springs where the Mexica emperors came to bathe, today known as the **Baños de Moctezuma.** Just beside it, amateur anthropologists will enjoy spotting the pre-Columbian reliefs carved onto the walls of the Cerro de Chapultepec. Although there are no ruins on the top of Cerro de Chapultepec, it is interesting to tour the Castillo de Chapultepec and look down on the greenery.

>DAY 3: COYOACÁN AND ANAHUACALLI

Take a day away from the bustle of the central districts to explore the historic neighborhood of Coyoacán, home of beloved artist Frida Kahlo, who with her husband, Diego Rivera, collected pre-Columbian art and artifacts. Have breakfast at Casa del Pan Papalotl, then visit the **Museo Frida Kahlo** to see the home where the artist grew up, a selection of her work, and a small selection of her collection of pre-Columbian arts and crafts.

Admission to the Museo Frida Kahlo includes entrance to the **Museo Anahuacalli,** a surprisingly under-visited museum that houses Diego Rivera's wonderful collection of pre-Columbian art and artifacts in a wholly unique and inspiring pyramid-shaped, volcanic-stone building. For around US$8, the Fridabús will shuttle you between the two. When you're returned to Coyoacán, enjoy some food with pre-Columbian roots at the bar and restaurant **Corazón de Maguey,** in the Jardín Centenario, accompanied by a flight of mezcal.

>DAY 4:
TLATELOLCO AND SAN JUAN

During the 15th and 16th centuries, Tlatelolco was inhabited by Nahuatl-speaking people, allied with but separate from the people of Tenochtitlán. When the Spanish launched their final attack on the Mexica during the summer of 1521, the remaining residents of Tenochtitlán fled to Tlatelolco, where they were eventually overcome. Today, the ruins of Tlatelolco are located in the **Plaza de las Tres Culturas,** in the Tlatelolco neighborhood. The interesting site contains the foundations of what were once towering religious and ceremonial buildings, including the Tlatelolco's Templo Mayor, and adjoined by Ex-Convento de Santiago Tlatelolco, originally constructed with the stones of the destroyed city in the early 16th century.

Have Uber pick you up at the ruins site, as it's a bit too far (and a bit too rough) to walk from Tlatelolco back to the Centro. Get off near the Alameda to grab a quick bite at casual **Fonda Santa Rita,** or head to the one-of-a-kind **Mercado San Juan** for a plate of imported cheese and charcuterie from one of the market's remarkably fancy deli counters. Next, set aside a few hours to learn more about Mexico's traditional cultures at the wonderful **Museo de Arte Popular.** The museum's exquisite collection of handicrafts from across the country includes some pre-Columbian art, which helps illuminate the aesthetic roots of today's artisan traditions.

>DAY 5:
CIVILIZATIONS IN THE VALLEY OF MEXICO

One of the finest ruin sites in the country, the city of **Teotihuacán** is a must-see for anyone interested in anthropology and pre-Columbian civilizations. If you've visited Teotihuacán in the past, take a trip to the smaller and lesser-known settlement of **Cuicuilco,** located in the south of the city, near the Line 1 Metrobús stop at Villa Olímpica. Flourishing just before the rise Teotihuacán, the city of Cuicuilco was largely destroyed in a lava flow from a nearby volcano, but its remains include an interesting circular pyramid.

From there, it's a quick Metrobús ride to the main campus of the Universidad Nacional Autónoma de México (UNAM), where the many architectural and artistic treasures include the **Biblioteca Central,** adorned with a lava-stone mural by Juan O'Gorman. Alternatively, head just a bit farther south to **Tlalpan,** a more off-the-beaten-path neighborhood, which maintains a quiet, distinctly nontouristy feeling.

A DAY OF DESIGN

Historically, Mexico City has had a vibrant and unique aesthetic. Today, contemporary art and design still flourish in the capital, making the city a destination for design-centric travelers.

>MORNING

Make a reservation for the 10:30am tour at the **Casa Luis Barragán,** near Tacubaya. The former home of the famed architect—widely considered one of the most influential voices in modern Mexican design—was mostly left as it was when Barragán lived there, showcasing not only his talent as an architect but his charmingly minimalist personal style. Note the saturated colors and use of light, two of Barragán's signatures.

Right next door to the Casa Luis Barragán, the lesser-known **Archivo Diseño y Arquitectura** is located in a lushly landscaped and beautifully remodeled midcentury home. In the galleries upstairs, guest curators are invited to create exhibitions exploring themes in industrial and applied design, often drawing from the impressive collection of more than 2,500 design pieces in the archive's collection. Just across the street, a large unmarked turquoise building is home to **Labor,** one of the more interesting contemporary galleries in the city. The gallery moved to its current location in 2011 and represents a range of international artists, including Mexican sensation Pedro Reyes.

Archivo Diseño y Arquitectura

>AFTERNOON

It's a short walk from the Casa Luis Barragán across Avenida Parque Lira and into the San Miguel Chapultepec neighborhood. This attractive residential community, wedged between the historic neighborhood of Tacubaya and the Bosque de Chapultepec, is the location of some of the city's most renowned contemporary-art galleries, giving the otherwise sleepy area a hint of posh.

Cancino, a place for pizza and people-watching

Order a thin-crust pizza in the garden at **Cancino,** where the neighborhood's gallery-goers often lunch. Cross the street to visit **Kurimanzutto,** one of the city's preeminent art spaces, co-owned by Mexico's best-known living artist, Gabriel Orozco. Walk just a few blocks north to the long-running **Galería de Arte Mexicano,** which represents many important national artists, from Olga Costa to Francisco Toledo.

Though the doors are usually closed at both of these galleries, ring the doorbell to see the current exhibits. Next, rest your legs with an espresso at artsy **Café Zena,** where you can thumb through a design magazine (they sell them) at the big communal table.

You can take the Metro from Constituyentes to Auditorio in Polanco (it's just one stop), though it's easier to hop an Uber for the short ride across the park. Polanco's toniest avenue, Presidente Masaryk, is lined with designer shops from many of the world's celebrated labels (Dolce & Gabbana, Gucci), but it's much more fun to browse the Mexican-owned boutiques in the neighborhood, like famous silver shop **Tane,** or high-end Puebla-based Talavera shop **Uriarte Talavera.**

>EVENING

If all that window-shopping works up an appetite, drop in for supper at **Eno,** a stylish Mexican deli with salads, sandwiches, and *tortas,* as well as a nice selection of beer and wine. Or make a memorable night of it at upscale **Dulce Patria,** where chef Martha Ortiz creates unique and colorfully plated Mexican dishes. Top off the evening with a tour of the fantastic midcentury **Camino Real Mexico City,** staying for a drink in the hotel's swanky lobby bar.

MARKET SATURDAY

Several interesting weekly markets set up in the Roma on Saturday mornings, making it the perfect day to visit this excellent shopping district.

>MORNING

There's often a wait for Saturday brunch at **Sobrinos,** where black-vested waiters rush trays of *café con leche* and baskets of sweet breads to local families filling the bustling old-fashioned dining room. From there, walk a few blocks east to the **Mercado de Cuauhtémoc,** a weekly vintage market held in the Jardín Dr. Ignacio Chávez, on the border of the Roma and the Colonia Doctores. Though not as well known as the antiquities markets in La Lagunilla and the Plaza del Ángel, this weekly flea has some funky booths and, often, excellent finds for sharp-eyed shoppers. Look for watches, midcentury home accessories, and antique toys, though you may have to sift through some flotsam to find them.

After the market, take your treasures out for a coffee at the wonderfully unpretentious yet high quality café **El Cardinal,** on Córdoba in the Roma. After that, walk along the Roma's main corridor, Álvaro Obregón, which is filled with creaky old bookshops, hip cocktail bars, and 19th-century mansions. Take a look inside the art gallery and bookshop at multidisciplinary cultural center **Casa Lamm,** and pick up a jar of honey or guava-chile salsa at **Delirio.**

Next, walk south along Orizaba,

Mercado El 100

wandering past the shaded fountains in the **Plaza Luis Cabrera** on your way to the **Mercado El 100,** which sets up in the Plaza del Lanzador every Saturday morning. At this small open-air market, you'll find locally produced and largely organic products, from spirulina powder to freeze-dried mango, as well as lead-free clay cookware and plates.

The Plaza Luis Cabrera, in the heart of the Roma neighborhood, is a popular gathering spot.

>AFTERNOON

Do like the local crowd and set aside a few hours for lunch—though first you'll face the near-impossible task of deciding where to eat. If there are tables available, try inspired Mexican spot **Fonda Fina,** grab a sidewalk table at hopping oyster bar **La Docena,** or, if you don't have reservations for **Máximo Bistrot Local,** line up for a spot at the communal table at **Lalo,** the more casual cousin to chef Eduardo Garcia's famous restaurant.

After lunch, wander along the shady street Colima, stopping in to its funky skate shops and boutiques, like **180° Shop** and **Goodbye Folk,** and seeing what's on show in galleries, like **Galería OMR.** Top off the afternoon at **Mercado Roma,** a next-generation market and food court, which can pack to standing-room-only during the lunch hour. Since you probably aren't hungry, better to head upstairs to the **Biergarten,** spending an hour or two enjoying the sunshine with a Mexican-made craft beer. Order some bar snacks and linger, or head back into the heart of the Roma to have a proper dinner at hipster hot spot **Mog,** a popular Asian café on Álvaro Obregón.

>EVENING

Wrap up the evening with a drink at one of the neighborhood's best bars, like tiny **Félix** or cocktail-centric **Licorería Limantour.**

PLANNING YOUR TRIP

WHEN TO GO

There is no high season or low season for travel to Mexico City. At over 2,200 meters (over 7,000 feet) above sea level, the city's altitude tempers its tropical latitude, creating a temperate and sunny climate year-round. The short **summer rainy season** (June-Oct.) brings showers, but these are usually isolated to bursts in the afternoon and evening. If you're averse to crowds or traffic, consider visiting during **Semana Santa** (the Easter holidays) or **Christmas,** when locals leave town and the city is noticeably quieter. Note that during these weeks, many restaurants, bars, and attractions also close.

ENTRY REQUIREMENTS

All foreign nationals visiting Mexico must have a valid **passport.** For citizens of most countries, a 180-day **travel permit,** known as the *forma migratoria multiple* (FMM), is issued automatically upon entry. Hold on to your stamped FMM; you will need to return it at the airport on your way home. When entering or leaving Mexico, children must be accompanied by their parents or, if unaccompanied or traveling with another adult, present an officially notarized

a view of the Polanco neighborhood from the Bosque de Chapultepec

DAILY REMINDERS

- **Monday:** Most public museums and cultural sights close, and Chapultepec park shuts its gates (though cyclists can pass through the Primera Sección). This makes Monday a good day to stroll the Roma and Condesa, shop markets like La Merced and the Mercado San Juan, day trip to the pyramids at Teotihuacán, or visit one of the few museums that open every day, like the Museo Soumaya or the Museo del Juguete Antiguo México.

- **Wednesday:** The last Wednesday of every month, dozens of museums and cultural centers extend their hours as a part of the Noche de Museos event. Many offer free admission and special events like concerts or movie screenings.

- **Saturday:** San Ángel's popular Bazaar Sábado craft market takes place, as do two smaller outdoor markets in the Roma: the Mercado de Cuauhtémoc, a vintage market, and the Mercado El 100, which focuses on local and organic products.

- **Sunday:** Many museums and cultural centers are free, though free admission often applies only to Mexican nationals or visa-holding foreign residents of Mexico. As a result, the most famous museums often fill to capacity. Some smaller spaces, like the rarely crowded Museo Jumex and Museo Soumaya, do allow foreign nationals free entry on Sundays. In the Centro, the La Lagunilla art and antiquities market takes place. The central stretch of the Paseo de la Reforma closes to car traffic, making it a great day to stroll this historic avenue. On the last Sunday of the month, the Paseo de la Reforma and several other major avenues close to create bike paths throughout the city as part of the Ciclatón. Thousands of cyclists attend the event.

and translated letter from their parents authorizing the trip.

TRANSPORTATION

Most foreign visitors arrive in Mexico City via the **Aeropuerto Internacional Benito Juárez,** the city's main hub. Recently, both major airlines and low-cost carriers have begun offering service to smaller regional airports like **Toluca** and **Puebla,** which may add a bit of travel time but can be cheaper, particularly for travel within Mexico.

Getting around Mexico City on public transportation is cheap, easy, efficient, and generally safe. Easy-to-use transport options include buses, microbuses, Metro, Metrobús, and light rail, though most visitors find the **Metro** and **Metrobús** systems get them everywhere they want to go. Secure radio taxis are an easy and inexpensive way to get around, as is Uber, which is growing in popularity. Within each neighborhood, walking is the best way to see everything. Given the horrendous traffic, expensive car rentals, and accessibility of public transit, driving is not recommended for short trips to the city.

RESERVATIONS

It is generally not necessary (or even possible) to make reservations for cultural sights and museums in Mexico City. During regular weekday hours, most museums have no wait. The one exception is the **Casa Luis Barragán,** which can only be visited via pre-booked guided tour. Reservations are required, and should be made at least a few days in advance. Though not required, also consider buying tickets online a day or two in advance for the **Museo**

a line outside Museo Frida Kahlo

Frida Kahlo, where there may be a wait at the ticket counter.

Reservations for the city's most famous **restaurants** are a must. For world-renowned restaurants like **Pujol** or **Máximo Bistrot Local,** book as early as possible—at least a month before you plan to go. Newer restaurants generating a lot of buzz, like **Huset** or **Fonda Fina,** often require advance reservations as well, particularly on weekends. Call at least a few days ahead. Note that *comida,* or lunch, is considered the most important meal of the day in Mexico, so a 2pm reservation on Saturday or Sunday can be one of the toughest to get.

A number of popular **bars** accept reservations. Some require them—particularly in tony neighborhoods like Polanco. Reservations are a must at **Jules Basement** and, though not required, highly recommended at live music venues, like **Parker &** **Lenox.** Increasingly, both bars and restaurants accommodate online reservations via Twitter or Facebook.

If you are flexible about where you're staying (and especially if you are planning to stay in a budget hotel), it's fine to make **hotel reservations** a day or two before your arrival. However, if you want to stay in the Roma or the Condesa, and especially if you have your heart set on one of the popular small hotels in those areas (like **Condesa DF** or the **Red Tree House**), book your hotel reservation as soon as you plan your trip. It's also worth planning ahead if you will be visiting during a major holiday like Independence Day, popular vacation seasons like the winter holidays, or during a big event, like Pope Francis's 2016 visit to the capital, when hotels in the Centro Histórico were booked to capacity.

WHAT'S NEW?

- **A new name:** In 2016, the city's government officially changed its name to Ciudad de México, replacing its previous moniker, the Distrito Federal—though it's unlikely that locals will stop referring to their city as "El D.F." anytime soon.

- **More art:** In November 2013, one of Latin America's most important art collectors opened **Museo Jumex,** which quickly became known as one of the city's best places to see contemporary art. After a three-year renovation, public photography gallery **Centro de la Imagen** reopened in October 2015 with dramatically upgraded gallery spaces. Visiting the Casa Luis Barragán became even more worthwhile when the **Archivo Diseño y Arquitectura** opened next door in 2012 and contemporary art gallery **Labor** relocated to a midcentury house across the street in 2013.

- **More eats:** Mexico City's reputation as a food capital has been duly established. Today, the **Roma neighborhood** is the locus of avant-garde dining and nightlife, home to recently opened hot spots **La Docena, Huset, Yuban, Lalo,** and **Mercado Roma.** In 2015, the chef from Nicos, a beloved foodie destination in the Claveria neighborhood, opened **Fonda Mayora** in the Condesa, while the chef from Casa Oaxaca in Oaxaca city debuted **Guzina Oaxaca** in Polanco in 2014.

- **Chic sleeps:** Design-centric **Hotel Carlota,** just steps from the Paseo de la Reforma, opened in 2015.

- **Bicycles galore:** The Ecobici bicycle-share program continues to expand across the city, with dozens of stations opening in neighborhoods like **San Miguel Chapultepec** and **Polanco.** Thanks to Ecobici, new bike lanes across the city, and a crop of cool new bicycle shops, you'll see a lot more pedaling around the capital.

- **Eye candy:** The annual autumn event **Design Week Mexico** continues to reach larger audiences and include more participants every year. The **Material Art Fair,** which runs at the same time as the city's most important art fair, Zsona MACO, but focuses on emerging artists, was inaugurated in 2014. New boutiques, like **Taxonomía,** show off the best in Mexican design. The beautiful art deco building **Barrio Alameda** opened in 2015; it's filled with three stories of design shops, galleries, and restaurants.

- **Fast times:** After a two-decade hiatus, **Formula One Grand Prix** returned to Mexico in 2015. Plans are in the works for several more championship events at the Autódromo Hermanos Rodríguez.

PASSES AND DISCOUNTS

With little exception, museums and cultural institutions in Mexico City have low admission prices. On top of that, museums often offer discounted or free admission on Sunday, and some have permanent discounts for children, seniors, educators, and people with disabilities. Increasingly, discounted admission, including free Sunday admission, applies only to Mexican nationals. There are no citywide passes for cultural centers, museums, or transportation.

GUIDED TOURS

Tour group **Eat Mexico** (www.eat-mexico.com) offers excellent tours of street food, markets, and other *taquerías*. Among other options, they offer tours of **La Merced** market or the gourmet-centric **Mercado San Juan** and its environs.

The Mexican government's **Instituto Nacional de Antropología e Historia** (INAH), or National Institute of Anthropology And History, offers guided tours of the city sights it oversees, including the Museo Nacional de Antropología, as well as cultural trips to destinations around central Mexico. The trips, operated under the name Turismo Cultural INAH, usually include transportation, a Spanish-speaking guide, and entrance fees (special trips can be arranged with English-speaking guides for groups). For more information, visit the INAH office in the Museo Nacional de Antropología (55/5553-2365 or 55/5215-1003, www.tci.inah.gob.mx).

CALENDAR OF EVENTS

FEBRUARY

Mexico City's biggest contemporary-art fair, **Zsona MACO** (México Arte Contemporáneo) (www.zsonamaco.com), is held over five days in early February in the Centro Banamex in Lomas de Sotelo, bringing a high-quality roster of exhibitors from the surrounding city and overseas. It's posh and well-attended event, and a good anchor for art lovers planning a trip to the city.

MARCH AND APRIL

One of the country's biggest and most respected arts events, **Festival del Centro Histórico de la Ciudad de México** (http://festival.org.mx) is held in public plazas, museums, and concert venues across the Centro Histórico every March and April. It's a great way to take an unofficial tour of the Centro's historic theaters and museums, with concerts, art exhibits, culinary events, and activities for children.

Semana Santa (Easter week or Holy Week) is celebrated with enormous solemnity and tradition.

The holidays officially begin on Domingo de Ramos, or Palm Sunday, when hand-woven palm crosses are sold outside the city's churches. The main reason to visit (or avoid) Mexico City during the Easter holidays is to experience a notably quieter metropolis. Traffic is subdued, museums are nearly empty, and you'll rarely need restaurant reservations—though many shops, restaurants, and bars close for the week.

Día de la Independencia bell in the Zócalo

SEPTEMBER

Mexico officially commemorates its independence from Spain on September 16; however, the keynote **Día de la Independencia** festivities in Mexico City take place on the evening of September 15, when thousands of revelers crowd the Zócalo. At 11pm, the president of the republic appears on the balcony of the Palacio Nacional, reenacting independence hero Miguel Hidalgo's cry for independence, including "Viva México!"—also known as El Grito—to a crowd that echoes

Aztec dancers gather in front of the Basílica de Santa María de Guadalupe on December 12.

his shouts. Fireworks and parties follow. There is a military parade through the Centro and along the Paseo de la Reforma the next day.

DECEMBER

The Virgin of Guadalupe miraculously appeared to Saint Juan Diego on the hill of Tepeyac on December 12, 1531. Today, the **Día de Nuestra Señora de Guadalupe** is one of the most important religious holidays across Mexico and Latin America. On the days leading up to the 12th, pilgrims can be seen walking through the city toward the Basílica de Santa María de Guadalupe in northern Mexico City, often setting off fireworks as they go, and thousands of pilgrims pack the area around the basilica.

NEIGHBORHOODS

Centro Histórico

Map 1

The heart and soul of Mexico City, the Centro Histórico is the oldest district in the capital, built in the 16th century atop what was once the Mexica city of Tenochtitlán. The blocks surrounding the **Zócalo** are dense with impressive architecture, museums, and landmarks, including such iconic sites as the pre-Columbian ruins of the **Templo Mayor,** the **Catedral Metropolitana,** and the **Palacio Nacional.**

TOP SIGHTS
- Museo del Templo Mayor (page 72)
- Mercado de la Merced (page 75)

TOP RESTAURANTS
- El Cardenal (page 108)
- Azul Histórico (page 108)
- Bar La Ópera (page 111)
- Casino Español (page 114)

TOP NIGHTLIFE
- Miralto (page 143)
- El Marrakech Salón (page 145)

TOP SHOPS
- Remigio (page 195)
- Dulcería de Celaya (page 196)
- Mercado Sonora (page 197)

TOP HOTELS
- Downtown Hotel (page 218)
- Hotel Catedral (page 220)
- Hotel Isabel (page 221)

GETTING THERE AND AROUND
- Metro lines: 1, 2, and 8
- Metro stops: Zócalo, Allende, Pino Suárez, Isabel la Católica, Merced
- Metrobús lines: 4
- Metrobús stops: Eje Central, El Salvador, Isabel la Católica, Museo de la Ciudad, Circunvalación

CENTRO HISTÓRICO WALKING TOUR

Total distance: 2.75 kilometers (1.7 miles)
Total walking time: 2 hours

Walking is the best way to explore any neighborhood in Mexico City, but especially the Centro Histórico. Each block yields a multitude of treasures: **colonial-era palaces, stone chapels, old public squares,** and **bustling pedestrian corridors.** While the colonial-era grandeur most quickly meets the eye, look closely and you'll find the remnants of another, older city buried beneath today's metropolis.

The Spanish destroyed the Mexica city of Tenochtitlán in the 16th century, building a European-style settlement atop the ruins—and, in many cases, using the stones from fallen Mexica temples to construct their own churches and palaces. Five hundred years later, Mexico's **pre-Columbian heritage** is embedded throughout the Centro Histórico—in its layout, in its place-names, and, quite literally, in its architecture.

1 The Spanish borrowed from Tenochtitlán's street plan when building their city. In fact, Mexico City's **Zócalo** was the site of a great open square at the center of the Mexica city. Take a moment to feel the power and history of this grand plaza, then stop in to the northern

the Zócalo

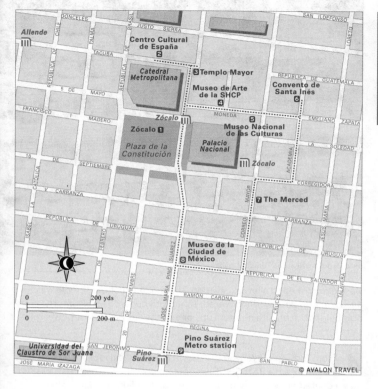

wing of the **Palacio Nacional,** where Diego Rivera's astonishing murals depicting the history of Mexico include a rendering of the city of Tenochtitlán.

2 Wander down Calle de Tacuba, just behind the cathedral. Here, a number of colonial-era buildings were demolished during the excavations of the Templo Mayor, though archeologists surmise that many more ruins lie beneath the many colonial-era mansions here. Among them, the **Centro Cultural de España,** overseen by the Spanish government, offers cinema, music, art, and educational events. In a planned expansion of the space, underground construction unearthed Mexica ruins, believed to have been part of the *Calmécac,* a school for young Mexica nobles. The ruins are on display in the on-site **Museo del Sitio,** in the center's basement.

3 Just as the cathedral stands beside the Zócalo, so did the Mexica's most important religious site adjoin the city's central square. The ruins of the **Templo Mayor,** a twin temple-pyramid at the heart of the Tenochtitlán, were rediscovered in the 1970s, when several city blocks

39

detail from a wall at the Templo Mayor

were demolished to allow excavation. Though much of the temple was destroyed, its base was uncovered, along with hundreds of artifacts, now held in the on-site museum. It's one of the Centro's most powerful sights.

4 From the Templo Mayor, turn down Moneda, and look for the **Museo de Arte de la SHCP,** an opulent colonial-era palace that is now a contemporary-art museum. After the building was damaged in the 1985 earthquake, construction workers uncovered the base of the **Templo de Tezcatlipoca,** which once stood beside the Templo Mayor. Today, the ruins, along with artifacts recovered from the site, are on display in the building's west wing.

5 Back along Moneda, the palace that today is home to the **Museo Nacional de las Culturas** (Moneda 13) was the city's first mint, while the first printing press in the Americas was originally installed in a little colonial-era building on the corner of Moneda and Licenciado Verdad.

6 From Moneda, head south along Academia, where you'll pass the beautifully restored 16th-century **Convento de Santa Inés** (Academia 13) and its adjoining temple. Across

Museo Nacional de las Culturas

the street, the oldest art school in the city, the **Academia San Carlos,** is open to the public.

7 Swing right onto Corregidora then continue south along Correo Mayor. The bustle of shops and street vendors indicates that you are now entering the **Merced,** a historic market district with roots to the pre-Columbian era. Before the Spanish conquest, a great causeway linked this urban district to the farming communities of Xochimilco and Chalco, making it a propitious spot for vendors. It was only in the early 20th century that the canal dried up entirely.

8 Head west on the street República de El Salvador until you reach the corner of Pino Suárez. Here, look for the massive serpent's-head stone embedded in the foundation at the **Museo de la Ciudad de México.** While the current building was commissioned in the 18th century, the foundation was likely laid by an early conquistador, who used this carved piece as a decorative cornerstone.

a unique serpent-head cornerstone at the Museo de la Ciudad de México

9 Another surprising discovery is just a few steps away, at the **Pino Suárez Metro station.** In the 1960s, during the building of the city's Metro, workers tunneled directly into the **Templo Ehécatl-Quetzalcóatl,** an unusual round pyramid. Plans for the station were altered to accommodate the temple; today, the pyramid is on display in an open-air plaza within the station.

Alameda Central   Map 2

On the western edge of the Centro Histórico, the Alameda Central is the city's oldest and most well-known urban park, flanked by the stunning **Palacio de Bellas Artes.** In the surrounding blocks, there are numerous fine colonial-era churches and several interesting museums, including the **Museo Franz Mayer** design museum and the **Museo de Arte Popular.** The **San Juan** neighborhood, to the south, is known for its top-notch street food and excellent gourmet market.

TOP SIGHTS
- Palacio de Bellas Artes (page 83)

TOP NIGHTLIFE
- Tío Pepe (page 145)
- Pulquería Las Duelistas (page 147)

TOP ARTS AND CULTURE
- Centro de la Imagen (page 163)
- Museo de Arte Popular (page 163)
- Museo Franz Mayer (page 165)
- Palacio de Bellas Artes (page 166)

TOP SPORTS AND ACTIVITIES
- Arena México (page 183)

TOP SHOPS
- La Lagunilla (page 198)
- FONART (page 198)
- Mercado San Juan (page 199)

GETTING THERE AND AROUND
- Metro lines: 1, 2, 3
- Metro stops: Bellas Artes, Hidalgo, Balderas, San Juan de Letrán, Garibaldi, Tlatelolco
- Metrobús lines: 3, 4
- Metrobús stops: Hidalgo, Balderas, Plaza San Juan, Eje Central

Paseo de la Reforma   Map 3

One of the capital's central arteries, the Paseo de la Reforma is also one of Mexico City's **most recognizable landmarks.** This monument-studded boulevard is lined with banks, high-rise office buildings, and luxury hotels. Many of Mexico City's historic neighborhoods flank its central stretch. Of these, the best known is the **Zona Rosa,** a big **shopping and entertainment district** and a major center for **gay nightlife,** especially along the street Amberes. It's a safe, friendly, and charming neighborhood with several pedestrian-only streets. The **San Rafael** neighborhood, on the north side of Reforma, has experienced a small renaissance as more young people and **galleries**

move in amid the auto shops and old coffee joints. The **Museo Universitario del Chopo** is particularly worthwhile.

TOP SIGHTS
- Monumento a la Revolución Mexicana (page 87)

TOP RESTAURANTS
- La Polar (page 120)
- La Especial de Paris (page 121)

TOP ARTS AND CULTURE
- Museo Universitario del Chopo (page 168)

TOP SPORTS AND ACTIVITIES
- Ciclatión (page 185)

TOP HOTELS
- El Patio 77 (page 223)
- Hotel Carlota (page 224)
- Casa de los Amigos (page 225)

GETTING THERE AND AROUND
- Metro lines: 1, 2
- Metro stops: Insurgentes, Cuauhtémoc, Revolución, San Cosme
- Metrobús lines: 1
- Metrobús stops: Insurgentes, Hamburgo, Reforma, Revolución, Buenavista

PASEO DE LA REFORMA WALK

Total distance: 3 kilometers (1.8 miles)
Total walking time: 45 minutes

The central stretch of the Paseo de la Reforma, which runs from the Centro Histórico through the Bosque de Chapultepec, is one of the city's main thoroughfares and filled with **signature landmarks.** A **wide, old-fashioned avenue** designed to resemble the grand boulevards of Europe, it was first commissioned by Hapsburg emperor Maximilian and completed by President Porfirio Díaz at the end of the 19th century. **Fashionable neighborhoods** cropped up quickly along Reforma, and the avenue remains one of the city's most exclusive addresses.

On **Sundays,** the avenue is **closed to automobile traffic,** so it's a wonderful time to take a stroll or rent a bike for a leisurely exploration of Reforma's many **monuments** and **public sculptures,** all the way to the main entrance of the **Bosque de Chapultepec.**

1 Occupying the enviable address Paseo de la Reforma 1, the art deco **Edificio El Moro**—better known to many as La Lotería, the home of the national lottery—was inaugurated in 1945. This elegant skyscraper, with its strip of windows running up the front facade, was once the

walking down the Paseo de la Reforma

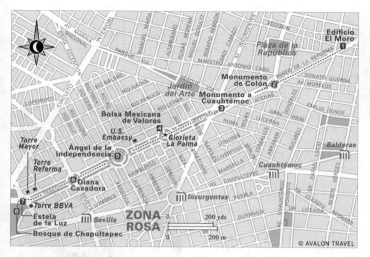

highest building in Mexico City. Beside it, a statue of King Carlos of Spain originally marked the start of Reforma; it has been replaced by a giant yellow modernist interpretation of a king on horseback by sculptor Sebastián.

2 About a half-kilometer west of La Lotería, the **Monumento de Colón** (Monument to Christopher Columbus), still stands—despite the best efforts of political protesters who'd like to take it down. It was cast in 1877 by French sculptor Charles Cordier.

3 Walk another 500 meters west to the **Monumento a Cuauhtemóc,** which stands at the intersection of Paseo de la Reforma and Insurgentes, a 19th-century tribute to the last Mexica emperor, who led the Mexica people in a last stand against the Spaniards before the fall of Tenochtitlán in 1519.

4 Just west of Insurgentes, the next traffic circle (with a palm tree at its center) is adjoined by the mirrored **Bolsa Mexicana de Valores,** the home of the Mexican stock exchange. This futuristic building is notable for its glassy, spherical entryway, joined by an unusual three-section skyscraper entirely covered in mirrors. The architect who designed it also created the spherical TAPO bus station, with which the stock exchange has some similarities.

5 Halfway up the block, the U.S. Embassy (blocked off by giant fences since 2001) is always thronged by visa applicants waiting for appointments. At the following intersection, one of the city's most iconic landmarks, the **Ángel de la Independencia,** was erected by President Porfirio Díaz as a tribute to Mexico's independence from Spain.

6 At the westernmost glorieta (traffic circle) before Chapultepec, the circular fountain is topped by a **statue of the Greek goddess Diana Cazadora** (Diana the Huntress), constructed in 1942. Diana's nudity created such a scandal that the sculptor, Juan Francisco Olaguíbel, was forced to add bronze undergarments. The bronze clothing was removed in 1967, in anticipation of the Mexico City Olympics in 1968.

7 Just east of the main entrance to the Bosque de Chapultepec are the city's three tallest buildings—the Torre Reforma, the Torre BBVA Bancomer, and the Torre Mayor—overlooking the park. Just outside the park's main entrance, Reforma's newest monument is the **Estela de la Luz** (Pillar of Light), a 104-meter, quartz-covered tower commemorating 2010's bicentennial of independence from Spain and the concurrent centennial of the Revolution of 1910. Its construction was mired in controversy, first by going massively over budget and later for overshooting its September 2010 construction deadline by 15 months and missing the anniversary celebrations altogether.

the Estela de la Luz (Pillar of Light) and the Torre Mayor

8 If you aren't worn out, continue your tour through the **Bosque de Chapultepec** (page 54).

SANTA MARÍA LA RIBERA WALK

Total distance: 3.5 kilometers (2.2 miles)
Total walking time: 1 hour

The San Rafael and the Santa María la Ribera show a different side of Mexico City. These **vibrant, working-class neighborhoods** are a bit rough around the edges, but their historic streets are in many ways emblematic of the capital's appeal, filled with **crumbling mansions, cheap eats,** and **lovely museums.** Though they remain off the beaten track, you can also find a few contemporary art galleries and boutiques in both neighborhoods.

1 Take the Metro to the San Cosme station, located on the Ribera San Cosme, a central artery that divides the San Rafael from the Santa María. Head west along the avenue, and note the **Casa de los Mascarones** (Ribera de San Cosme 71) just beside the Metro station; this gorgeous, 18th century baroque palace now houses the national university's foreign-language institute.

2 Detour south to see some of the San Rafael neighborhood, including the **Mercado San Cosme,** a low-key market on the Ribera

Mercado San Cosme

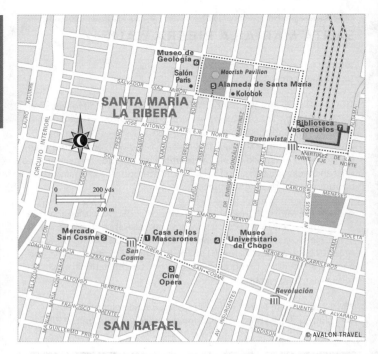

San Cosme, which is a great place to pick up a snack, like a quesadilla or tamal.

3 Continuing your detour, walk east to check out the grand **Cine Ópera** (Serapio Rendón 9), a dilapidated art deco movie house with an impressive facade, adorned by two towering stone statues. Abandoned in the 1990s, the building is reportedly under the control of Mexico's Institute of Fine Arts, though it continues to deteriorate.

4 Returning to the Ribera San Cosme, take Jaime Torres Bodet a few blocks north to the **Museo Universitario del Chopo,** one of the city's finest, most architecturally unique museums. The gothic-inspired iron-and-glass building, constructed in Germany, originally held the city's natural-history museum, which was later moved to Chapultepec; since

Museo Universitario del Chopo

Alameda de Santa María

1975, it has been a contemporary-art space operated by the national university.

5 From El Chopo, head into the heart of the Santa María la Ribera, walking north along the street Dr. Atl. Several blocks later, you will reach the tranquil **Alameda de Santa María,** the square at the heart of the neighborhood. Particularly impressive is the soaring, multicolor Moorish pavilion at the park's center; it had several homes, including a place in the Alameda Central, before being moved to the Santa María in 1910. Over the years, this historic plaza has been home to some quirky inhabitants. On one corner is long-running Russian restaurant **Kolobok** (Salvador Díaz Mirón 87), on another the **Salón Paris** (Jaime Torres Bodet 152), an old cantina where Mexican singer and songwriter José Alfredo Jiménez once worked.

6 Adjoining the plaza to the west, the historic **Museo de Geología** (Geology Museum) contains a woolly mammoth skeleton and is housed in a 19th-century mansion commissioned by Porfirio Díaz. Some find the building more intriguing than its contents.

7 Walk a few blocks east to Insurgentes from the Alameda, where you can hop the Metrobús south at Buenavista. Before departing, take a turn around the **Biblioteca Vasconcelos.** Just beside the Buenavista train station, it is a breathtaking public space, with unique "floating bookshelves" surrounding a central atrium.

Chapultepec and Polanco Map 4

The **Bosque de Chapultepec,** a vast urban forest, is filled with jogging paths and wooded glens for picnicking. It is also the site of many of the capital's most important cultural institutions, notably the spectacular **Museo Nacional de Antropología,** with its incredible collection of early art and artifacts from Mesoamerica. To the north of the park across the Paseo de la Reforma, posh Polanco is a top destination for **fine dining; upscale hotels,** and **top-quality shopping.**

TOP SIGHTS

TOP RESTAURANTS

TOP NIGHTLIFE

TOP ARTS AND CULTURE

TOP SPORTS AND ACTIVITIES

TOP HOTELS

GETTING THERE AND AROUND

- Metro lines: 1, 7
- Metro stops: Chapultepec, Juanacatlán, Constituyentes, Polanco, Auditorio

CHAPULTEPEC WALK (PRIMERA SECCIÓN)

Total distance: 3.75 kilometers (2.3 miles)
Total walking time: 1.5 hours

The Bosque de Chapultepec is a beautiful **urban park** and a place of great history and culture. On the weekdays, it's the perfect place to escape the city's chaos; the park is surprisingly quiet and refreshingly cool. On the weekends, it's a joyous jumble of humanity, as families from across the city come to relax, party, and play soccer amid the park's many meadows and wooded groves.

Chapultepec's remarkable landscape design includes dozens of **fountains, gardens,** and **winding, wooded footpaths,** which make it a delight to explore. If you are inspired by what you find in the Primera Sección—the most accessible and most visited section of the park—consider a trip to the Segunda Sección, a larger and more wild swath of parkland, filled with odd monuments and museums, including the children's museum and an old but perennially popular amusement park.

1 Chapultepec's main entrance is appropriately regal, marked by green wrought-iron gates and flanked by bronze lions, right on the Paseo de la Reforma. Before you enter, take a moment to visit the interesting

the entrance to the Bosque de Chapultepec

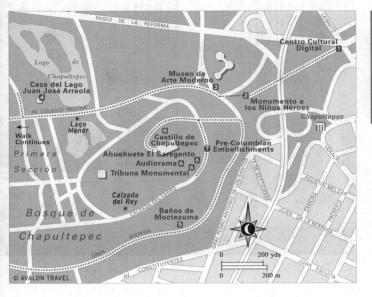

Centro Cultural Digital, located just below the **Estela de la Luz,** a contemporary monument commemorating Mexico's 200 years of independence. Admission is free, and the center often hosts fun, eye-catching exhibits in the two-story belowground space.

2 Once you've entered the park, the first thing you'll see is the massive six-pillar **Monumento a Los Niños Héroes,** which commemorates the six young army cadets who jumped to their death rather than surrender to the U.S. military during the 1847 American invasion of Chapultepec during the Mexican-American War.

Casa del Lago Juan José Arreola

3 Continue along the footpath past the backside of the **Museo de Arte Moderno** and its pretty sculpture garden, and onto the pedestrian street Colegio Militar.

4 Just ahead, one of the park's manmade lakes, the Lago Menor, is filled with ducks and paddle-boaters. Located on a grassy meadow beside the lake, the **Casa del Lago Juan José Arreola** is one of the city's oldest cultural centers, with workshops, artist

55

Monumento a Los Niños Héroes

residencies, movie screenings, and dozens of other ongoing art and cultural events—including many workshops designed for children and families. Wander in to see what's on display in the pretty galleries, and pick up a brochure to see what's ahead.

5 As Colegio Militar loops back toward the entrance to the park, look for the turnoff to the smaller footpath known as the Calzada del Rey, and head east. Just a bit south along this wooded route, you'll pass the remains of one of the many spring-fed pools constructed by Mexica emperor Moctezuma. After years of abuse, the **Baños de Moctezuma** have been reduced to little more than a sad, sunken pool encased in concrete—but the historic value is phenomenal.

6 Farther ahead, you'll pass the **Tribuna Monumental,** a giant outdoor amphitheater, which is adjoined by one of the oldest cypress trees in the park, known as **Ahuehuete El Saregento.** Though the tree is no longer living, its trunk tells us it has stood here for more than 550 years; its birth date suggests that this tree may be among

Ahuehuete El Saregento

the many cypresses planted by the emperor of Texcoco, Nezahual-cóyotl, in the 15th century.

Just behind the Tribuna Monumental, the **Audiorama** is a quirky little corner of the park built in the 1970s, where public speakers pump out an ongoing program of music; genres change from new age to traditional Mexican and so on, depending on the day of the week.

7 In the 15th century, Chapultepec's springs provided fresh water for the island community of Tenochtitlán via aqueduct, and it was a favorite retreat for Mexica emperor Moctezuma, who came to bathe in its pools. In 1966, excavations revealed **pre-Columbian embellishments** carved into the stones, just below the castle on the Cerro de Chapultepec. Though only fragments of these works remain intact, it's fascinating to spot these historic pieces amid the natural landscape.

8 Head up the Cerro de Chapultepec to end your walking tour at the **Castillo de Chapultepec,** a fascinating museum that offers lovely views of the greenery below.

the view from the Castillo de Chapultepec

Roma and Condesa   Map 5

These adjacent residential neighborhoods were quiet middle-class enclaves through most of the 20th century; today, they are the center of Mexico City's **hippest dining and nightlife.** The upscale Condesa's beautiful parks are worth visiting, especially **Parque México.** The neighborhood's art deco and modern apartment buildings make a pleasant backdrop for the slew of boutique hotels and stylish eateries. The youth-oriented Roma is edgier. Here, it's fantastic to simply ramble and admire the neighborhood's impressive **late-19th-century mansions** and gorgeous **eclectic architecture.** Window shop or pop into galleries, dine at one of the lauded restaurants, or sip mezcal in one of the area's hipster bars.

TOP SIGHTS
- Parque México (page 93)

TOP RESTAURANTS
- Máximo Bistrot Local (page 133)

TOP NIGHTLIFE
- Pata Negra (page 152)
- La Clandestina (page 152)
- M. N. Roy (page 153)
- Multiforo Alicia (page 154)
- Salón Malafama (page 155)

TOP SHOPS
- Librería Rosario Castellanos (page 204)
- Goodbye Folk (page 206)

TOP HOTELS
- Red Tree House (page 228)

GETTING THERE AND AROUND
- Metro lines: 1, 3, 9
- Metro stops: Insurgentes, Sevilla, Hospital General, Niños Héroes, Chilpancingo, Patriotismo
- Metrobús lines: 1
- Metrobús stops: Insurgentes, Álvaro Obregón, Sonora, Campeche

ROMA AND CONDESA WALK

Total distance: 3 kilometers (1.8 miles)
Total walking time: 1.75 hours

In a ramble through the attractive, walkable Roma and Condesa neighborhoods, you'll pass many eye-catching **old mansions, tree-filled parks,** and **public squares.** If you want to make a point of seeing some of the keynote designs and **architectural gems** in the area, here are a few of the most notable spots.

THE ROMA

Largely constructed during the Porfiriato era at the end of the 19th century, the northern blocks of the Colonia Roma are filled with impressive mansions, some beautifully preserved, others abandoned since the 1985 earthquake. The greatest concentration of historic architecture is along Avenida Álvaro Obregón and Calle Colima, as well as around the Plaza Río de Janeiro. Some wildly original, the neighborhood's buildings are a good example of 19th-century eclecticism, which incorporates elements from different eras, including art nouveau, art deco, and neocolonial styles.

art nouveau windows on a residential building in the Roma

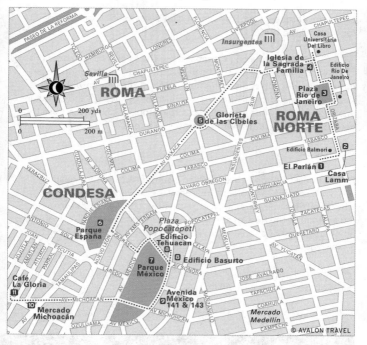

1 Start by walking along the Roma's main stretch, Álvaro Obregón; its notable structures include **El Parián** (Álvaro Obregón 130). This unusual building opened as a market in 1833 but was severely damaged in the 1985 earthquake; the building was eventually restored and reopened as a shopping center. Notice the beautiful carved stone details surrounding the doorways and windows.

2 Built by Lewis Lamm and completed in 1922, **Casa Lamm** is a beautiful mansion that was never occupied by its owner. Since the 1990s, the Casa Lamm has been a cultural center, with restored interiors and gardens open to the public. Just across the street, on the corner of Álvaro Obregón and Orizaba, **Edificio Balmori** (Orizaba 101) is a palace-like building with a sandstone facade and elegant French windows, originally constructed as residence apartments. The slightly sunken first floor is now filled with street-level boutiques.

3 Walk north along Orizaba to the **Plaza Río de Janeiro,** a favorite spot for dog walkers. Better known as La Casa de las Brujas (Witches' House) for its unusual peaked roof, the **Edificio Río de Janeiro** apartment building is located on the east side of the park. It was constructed by British architect Regis A. Pigeon in 1908, and it was among the first buildings constructed beside the Plaza Río de Janeiro, then called the Parque Roma. However, it didn't receive its distinctive deco facade until the 1930s.

4 Continue north along Orizaba to see the **Iglesia de la Sagrada Familia.** Officially inaugurated in 1925 (though construction began more than a decade earlier), this neo-gothic stone church with impressive Italian stained-glass windows was built for the Jesuits and continues in operation today (it's a popular spot for weddings). Note the **Casa Universitaria del Libro** (Orizaba 24) across the street.

CONDESA

5 Walk east along Puebla, crossing Insurgentes, and then heading south along Oaxaca until you reach the **Glorieta de las Cibeles,** where traffic circles around an attractive bench-filled plaza surrounding a statue of the Roman goddess Cybele in her carriage. The statue is an exact replica of a fountain in Madrid, and a gift to the city from the Spanish government in 1980.

6 From Glorieta de las Cibeles, continue south along Oaxaca until you reach **Parque España.**

Tree-filled Avenida Amsterdam in the Colonia Condesa is a popular route for walking and biking.

7 Circle south through the park, heading southeast along Sonora until you reach the **Parque México.** The Condesa was largely built in the 1920s, occupying land that was once a part of a hacienda owned by the Condesa de Miravalle, the neighborhood's eponymous countess. The Condesa's developers incorporated a former horseracing track into their street plan, creating the unusual oval-shaped Avenida Amsterdam, with Parque México in the middle. Parque México is a jewel of landscape architecture, with numerous art deco fountains in addition to a unique outdoor theater, Foro Lindbergh, at the center.

the Edificio Basurto

8 Avenida México, which circles the park, is the heart of Condesa's art deco district, and the address of many fine buildings. Designed by Francisco Serrano and built between 1942 and 1945, the **Edificio Basurto** (Avenida México 187) is a gem of art deco design, with a unique horseshoe-shaped lobby. At the time it was built, it was the tallest building in the city. Just across the street, the **Edificio Tehuacan** is another jewel of Mexican art deco, now a hotel.

9 Celebrated modern architect Luis Barragán constructed two family homes on the Avenida México in 1936. Located at **Avenida México 141** and **143,** they are both private homes, but their exteriors display Barragán's trademark style.

10 From the southeast edge of the park, head along Avenida Michoacán to the heart of the Condesa's bustling restaurant and nightlife district. Amid the many lovely early-20th-century mansions and modern apartment buildings, it's worth noting the **Mercado Michoacán** (Michoacán 82), a streamlined, modern food market that merits attention for its 20th-century design.

11 End your walk with a meal at **Café La Gloria,** one of the first cool restaurants to open in the Condesa.

ROMA AND CONDESA

Coyoacán and San Ángel   Map 6

Coyoacán's quiet colonial plazas and cobblestone streets offer a pleasant oasis within the city. Lined with restaurants and shops, the twin squares at the center of Coyoacán, **Jardín Centenario** and **Jardín Hidalgo,** receive a flurry of visitors cooling off with drinks or listening to live bands. Coyoacán is best known as the provenance of Mexican painter Frida Kahlo; her childhood home, now **Museo Frida Kahlo,** chronicles her life and work.

Upscale San Ángel is a colonial-era neighborhood and home to one of Mexico's best modern Mexican art museums, **Museo de Arte Carrillo Gil,** and a wonderful Saturday market, the **Bazaar Sábado.**

Wander any direction from the main plaza to find cobblestone streets with marvelous colonial-era homes and haciendas, now inhabited by Mexico City's wealthier denizens.

The Ciudad Universitaria is the main campus for the **Universidad Nacional Autónoma de México (UNAM),** the largest and most prestigious university in Mexico. The campus was named a World Heritage Site for its modernist architecture, engineering, and landscape design.

TOP SIGHTS

- Museo Frida Kahlo (page 96)
- Biblioteca Central (page 100)

TOP RESTAURANTS

- Corazón de Maguey (page 135)

TOP ARTS AND CULTURE

- Cineteca Nacional (page 174)
- Museo Universitario Arte Contemporáneo (page 177)

TOP SPORTS AND ACTIVITIES

- Viveros de Coyoacán (page 188)

TOP SHOPS

- Bazaar Sábado (page 210)
- Casa del Obispo (page 212)

GETTING THERE AND AROUND

- Metro lines: 3
- Metro stops: Coyoacán, Viveros
- Metrobús lines: 1
- Metrobús stops: La Bombilla, Dr. Galvez, Ciudad Universitaria

COYOACÁN WALK

Total distance: 4.5 kilometers (2.8 miles)
Total walking time: 2.5 hours

There are no Metro stations in central Coyoacán, nor any major avenues passing through the neighborhood's charming **colonial-era** *centro*. As a result, a visit to Coyoacán often begins with a stroll. End your walk at **Museo Frida Kahlo,** the artist's childhood home.

ALONG FRANCISCO SOSA

1 At a brisk pace, it takes 15-20 minutes to walk from **Metro Viveros,** on Line 3, to central Coyoacán, though considering how many lovely sights are dotted along the way, it's unlikely you'll make the journey so quickly. Departing the station, walk south along Avenida Universidad until you reach Avenida Francisco Sosa. Swing a left, and slow your gait: This historic, tree-lined avenue leads right into the heart of Coyoacán.

2 Within a block, you'll find the **Fonoteca Nacional,** an unusual public archive dedicated to documenting the unique music and sounds of Mexico. It's a fascinating project housed in Casa Alvarado, a brick-red 18th-century hacienda with strong Moorish and Andalusian influences. Wander through the lush gardens, where speakers play traditional music and sounds.

3 Take a small detour south along the street Tato Vasco to arrive in the **Callejón del Aguacate,** a historic and picturesque alleyway that is the subject of numerous legends and ghost stories. Whether or not

© AVALON TRAVEL

the alley is haunted, it is worth seeing this pretty corner of the neighborhood, marked by a small altar to the Virgin Mary on its corner.

4 Head back northeast to Francisco Sosa, then backtrack a half block to the **Plaza Santa Catarina,** a serene colonial-era plaza, where paper flags flutter between leafy trees and the picturesque **Iglesia de Santa Catarina,** built in the 18th century.

5 Just across the street, the **Casa de Cultura Jesús Reyes Heroles** (Francisco Sosa 202) is a multipurpose cultural center, set in another lovely hacienda; join locals relaxing in the pretty coffee shop in back.

JARDÍN HIDALGO AND THE PLAZA DE LA CONCHITA

6 As you approach **Jardín Centenario** from Francisco Sosa, you'll pass through two colonial-era archways that were once part of the massive Dominican convent that dominated central Coyoacán. Wander through the square, rest your legs on a bench overlooking its central fountain, or settle in for a drink at **Los Danzantes,** one of the many bars and restaurants that adjoin the plaza.

7 Just across the street, the **Jardín Hidalgo** is Coyoacán's central square, over which the historic **Parroquia de San Juan Bautista** presides. The first parish was built here in 1528, atop a native school (the ruins of which still lie below the cloister), though the current church was constructed several decades later.

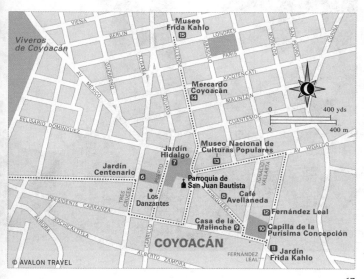

© AVALON TRAVEL

8 Behind the church, the small street Higuera cuts diagonally south-east from the Jardín Hidalgo. Stop into **Café Avellaneda** for a coffee to go, then continue down Higuera until you reach the end.

9 At the very end of Higuera, take note of the dark-red **Casa de la Malinche,** widely believed to be the former house Cortés shared with his lover and interpreter Malintzin, better known as La Malinche. Though many historians discredit these rumors, the home is certainly interesting, and now a city landmark.

10 Just across the street, the quiet Plaza de la Conchita is the setting for one of the earliest colonial-era churches in Mexico, the **Capilla de la Purísima Concepción.** This old baroque church is undergoing renovation and not open to the public, but you can admire its crumbling, ornate facade. According to archaeological evidence, this plaza may have been a central ceremonial space for pre-Columbian cultures in Coyoacán.

11 Walk through the plaza to the **Jardín Frida Kahlo,** a pretty public garden dedicated to the famous Coyoacán painter.

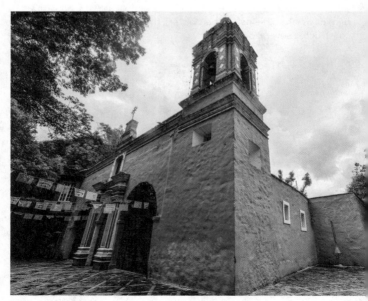

Iglesia de Santa Catarina

Museo Frida Kahlo

TO MUSEO FRIDA KAHLO

12 You can follow Higuera back to the plaza, but it's nicer to walk along the quaint and cobbled **Fernández Leal,** filled with the towering trees and country houses emblematic of residential Coyoacán.

13 Heading back toward the center of town via Hidalgo, you'll pass coffee shops and taco stands, as well as the **Museo Nacional de Culturas Populares,** a craft museum, where a large ceramic *árbol de la vida* (tree of life) is located in the central courtyard.

14 Continue along Allende, one of the neighborhood's main avenues, past locals sipping lattes at Café El Jarocho. A block farther, you'll likely notice a bit of bustle at the perennially popular seafood spot Jardín del Pulpo right on the corner of the **Mercado Coyoacán,** the neighborhood's municipal market. Wander amid flower vendors or stop to try one of Coyoacán's famous tostadas.

15 A few blocks farther, on the corner of Allende and Londres, Frida Kahlo's childhood home, now the **Museo Frida Kahlo,** is known as "Caza Azul" or "Blue House" for its striking cobalt color.

SIGHTS

The oldest and largest city in the Americas, Mexico's capital is a place of great tradition and history. It's also a dynamic and modern metropolis, with a vibrant local culture, lively youth scene, and an impressive number of museums and cultural institutions.

Ángel de la Independencia on the Paseo de la Reforma

Architecturally, the streets tell the story of the city's past. Founded by the Mexica in 1325, the remains of the great pre-Columbian city-state of Tenochtitlán are still subtly evident throughout modern Mexico City—in its street plan, in its place-names, and in the ruins embedded within the cityscape. After the conquest, Mexico City became the capital of New Spain, growing rich and splendid as the booming trade generated by Mexico's plentiful silver mines flooded the city with wealth and power. After three centuries of Spanish rule, the capital was left with some of the most impressive baroque architecture in the Americas, notable in the colonial neighborhoods of Coyoacán and San Ángel, but most especially in the Centro Histórico. Even neighborhoods like the San Rafael and the Roma, both built toward the end of the 19th century, display surprising opulence and architectural creativity.

These beautiful buildings are the backdrop to the world-class cultural institutions, museums, and vibrant culture that make Mexico City pulse. You'll find everything from the folkloric to the avant-garde, whether you are wandering through the national university campus or joining the throngs of visitors at the shrine to the Virgen de Guadalupe, one of the world's most visited Catholic pilgrimage sites.

HIGHLIGHTS

✪ **MOST EYE-OPENING SITE:** In the 1970s, remains of a massive pyramid-temple were discovered in the Zócalo. Today, those ruins are the cornerstone of the **Museo del Templo Mayor,** which provides an eye-opening vision of the city's history (page 72).

✪ **GRANDEST MARKET:** Since the pre-Columbian era, markets have been a mainstay of life in Mexico. **Mercado de la Merced,** with its long history of importance in the capital, is among the most interesting and atmospheric in the city (page 75).

✪ **CULTURAL HEART OF THE CENTRO:** In addition to its impressive architecture and breathtaking interiors, the **Palacio de Bellas Artes** is one of the city's premiere cultural institutions and home to some of the country's most important early-20th-century murals (page 83).

✪ **MOST AESTHETIC MONUMENT:** It's easy to appreciate the creative art deco elements adorning the **Monumento a la Revolución Mexicana.** Riding the glass elevator to its dome is a unique experience (page 87).

✪ **THE JEWEL OF MEXICO:** The astounding collection of pre-Columbian art and artifacts at the **Museo Nacional de Antropología** is one of the country's great cultural treasures (page 89).

✪ **BEST WINDOW INTO THE CITY'S PAST:** Explore the Bosque de Chapultepec and Mexican history at the **Castillo de Chapultepec,** an opulent castle originally built for Spanish royalty in the late 18th century. It now houses the **Museo Nacional de Historia** (page 90).

✪ **TOP SPOT FOR DESIGN LOVERS:** Home of one of 20th-century Mexico's most influential architects and interior designers, the **Casa Luis Barragán** is a must-see for designers (page 92).

✪ **NICEST NEIGHBORHOOD PARK:** Wander past art deco fountains, duck ponds, lush gardens, and dog walkers in **Parque México,** the heart of the Condesa neighborhood (page 93).

✪ **MOST MOVING MUSEUM:** Artist Frida Kahlo's childhood home is now the enchanting **Museo Frida Kahlo,** a museum dedicated to her life and legacy (page 96).

✪ **MOST RADICAL SPOT:** Covered in an impressive volcanic-stone mosaic, the **Biblioteca Central** sits at the center of Universidad Autónoma de México's dynamic modern campus (page 100).

❂ Museo del Templo Mayor

A twin temple-pyramid located in the heart of Tenochtitlán, the Templo Mayor was built around 1325 and was at the center of religious and political life for the Mexica people until the Spanish conquest of the city. After 1430, the structure was enlarged by successive Mexica rulers, reaching about 60 meters by the 16th century. Dual staircases led up its face to the two temples, one dedicated to Huitzilopochtli, the god of war and sun, and the other to Tlaloc, the god of rain and agriculture.

After the Spanish siege on Tenochtitlán, the Templo Mayor was razed. The pyramid's location was eventually forgotten, though archaeologists long suspected that it lay beneath the cathedral. On February 21, 1978, electric-company workers digging at the corner of República de Argentina and República de Guatemala uncovered an eight-ton monolith adorned with carvings of the moon goddess Coyolxauhqui. The magnitude of the discovery prompted a major excavation. After demolishing four city blocks, archaeologists uncovered the base of the Templo Mayor, along with a multitude of artifacts.

Open to the public, the archaeological site's footpath circles the base of the temple. It is accompanied by a fascinating museum, with an extensive collection of pre-Columbian pieces, the majority recovered during the Templo

Templo Mayor

Mayor's major excavation, including the Coyolxauhqui stone. Among the other magnificent artifacts, the museum contains a four-meter-long carved monolith dedicated to the goddess Tlaltecuhtli, discovered here in 2006.

MAP 1: Seminario 8, 55/4040-5600, ext. 412930, www.templomayor.inah.gob.mx; Tues.-Sun. 9am-5pm; US$5, free on Sun.; Metro: Zócalo

NEARBY:

- Appreciate the murals inside the **Antiguo Colegio de San Ildefonso** (page 76).
- See avant-garde art and performances at **Ex-Teresa Arte Actual** (page 160).
- Browse photos of the city's past at **Museo Archivo de la Fotografía** (page 161).
- Eat traditional Mexican cuisine at the elegant **El Cardenal** (page 108).
- Have lunch at **Casino Español**, an old-fashioned Spanish restaurant (page 114).
- Pick up a gift at **The Shops at Downtown**, located in a 17th-century palace (page 197).

The Zócalo

The Zócalo, also known as the Plaza de la Constitución, has been the heart of the metropolis since the founding of Tenochtitlán in 1325. Adjoining the city's most holy site, the Templo Mayor, the plaza was a place of ritual and celebration during the 14th and 15th centuries, in addition to being the site of an important market. The Mexica rulers' palaces lined the plaza, and causeways leading off the island radiated out from its four sides.

After the fall of Tenochtitlán, the Zócalo became the center of the Spanish city of Mexico, and it was known as the "Plaza Mayor" throughout the colonial era. It remained the center of government and religious activity; as today, the cathedral borders the plaza to the north and the government palaces run along the east side. Today, the empty square serves as a concert venue, protest site, and performance-art venue.

MAP 1: Plaza de la Constitución, bordered by Madero, Moneda, 16 de Septiembre, Corregidora, 5 de Febrero, República de Brasil, and Pino Suárez; free; Metro: Zócalo

Palacio Nacional

The deep-red facade of the Palacio Nacional stretches grandly across the eastern edge of the Zócalo. After the destruction of Tenochtitlán, the palace was comuseo fnstructed for Hernán Cortés, though it later became the official home for Spanish viceroys governing the colonies. After independence, it became the seat of government, and

Catedral Metropolitana

the bell from the church in Dolores Hidalgo, Guanajuato, was hung over the presidential balcony. It was this bell that war hero Miguel Hidalgo rang while issuing his famous battle cry, or *grito,* which heralded the start of the War of Independence.

The highlight of the Palacio Nacional is the spectacular murals painted by Diego Rivera in the north plaza and stairwell. A masterwork of composition and color, Rivera painted this chronicle of the history of Mexico between 1929 and 1951. The panel entitled "The Great City of Tenochtitlán" provides a detailed rendering of the Mexica city, viewed from today's Zócalo.

MAP 1: Plaza de la Constitución between Moneda and Corregidora, 55/3688-1602; Tues.-Sun. 10am-5pm; free; Metro: Zócalo

Catedral Metropolitana

Dominating the Zócalo to the north, the Metropolitan Cathedral is a mortar-and-stone representation of the central role of the Catholic church in Mexico's past and present. The first church was built on this site in 1524 and named a cathedral in 1534. It was a modest building, and New Spain's governors commissioned the construction of a bigger, grander church for the City of Palaces. The first stone of the new cathedral was laid in 1553, but it wasn't completed for 240 years.

Over the centuries, different architects and changing aesthetics left their mark on the cathedral, which mixes Renaissance, baroque, and neoclassical styles. It's also worth visiting the cathedral's two towers, where 25 multi-ton bells are still rung by hand. It's a blood-pumping ascent to the roof, but you're rewarded with gorgeous views of the Zócalo. Tours depart from inside the cathedral and run roughly every hour 10:30am-6pm.

MAP 1: Plaza de la Constitución between Monte de Piedad and Pino Suárez, 55/5208-3200, www.arquidiocesismexico. org.mx; daily 7am-7pm; free, US$1 to visit the bell towers; Metro: Zócalo

Sagrario

Adjacent the Catedral Metropolitana is the baroque Sagrario, or Tabernacle, which was built between 1749 and 1768 by Spaniard Lorenzo Rodríguez. The white sculpted-stone front of the Sagrario is offset by flanking walls made with blocks of deep-red *tezontle*, a volcanic stone. Inside, the bare, neoclassical altars (the originals were destroyed long ago by fire) don't compare to the magnificent exterior, though there is a replica of the Virgen de Guadalupe painting based on the original work in the Basílica de Santa María de Guadalupe, in the north of the city.

MAP 1: Plaza de la Constitución between Monte de Piedad and Pino Suárez; daily 7am-7pm; free; Metro: Zócalo

chillies for sale at Mercado de la Merced

Museo de la Ciudad de México

Three blocks south of the Zócalo, a colonial-era mansion is today the city museum. Historians surmise that one of the conquistadors built a home on this site shortly after the conquest: The building's cornerstone is a large carved serpent head, likely taken from the Templo Mayor after the building's destruction by the Spanish.

The current baroque facade was constructed by the Conde de Calimaya in the late 18th century, with a richly carved main portal that leads to a quiet patio. On the second floor, there is a small chapel to the Virgen de Guadalupe with three colonial-era religious paintings, as well as galleries exhibiting the museum's permanent collections of paintings and sketches of the city, along with rotating exhibits of contemporary work.

MAP 1: Pino Suárez 30, 55/5542-0487; Tues.-Sun. 10am-6pm; US$2, free on Wed.; Metro: Pino Suárez

✪ Mercado de la Merced

One of the largest retail markets in Mexico, the Mercado de la Merced is the centerpiece of a bustling commercial district known as the Antiguo Barrio de la Merced, covering several city blocks on the eastern edge of the Centro. Trade has taken place here since the days of Tenochtitlán, when a canal transported goods from the agricultural communities of Xochimilco and Chalco to Moctezuma's palaces, in what is now the Zócalo. A market was built on the former grounds of the Merced convent in the 1860s, though the current building was constructed in 1957, several decades after the canal finally dried up.

Wandering through the Merced is a feast for the senses and a bonanza for curious foodies. In the main market, you'll find stacks of banana leaves, baskets towering with dried chiles, bags of black *huitlacoche* (corn fungus), and bins of traditional Mexican herbs and spices. Farther inside, stalls sell kitchen supplies, woven baskets, piñatas, and handicrafts, while aromatic food stands offer everything from quick quesadillas to a full meal at rock-bottom prices. Adjoining the Merced is the interesting Mercado Sonora, which sells home goods, herbal medicines, live animals, and products for spells and witchcraft.

In 2014, the city government announced a 16-year plan to rehabilitate the rough-around-the-edges Merced neighborhood, which will include the planting of new trees, the introduction of Ecobici bicycle stations, and the construction of a gastronomy center. Today's market is generally safe, but take care walking the streets nearby.

MAP 1: Circunvalación between General Anaya and Adolfo Gorrión, Col. Merced Balbuena, 55/5522-7250; daily 6am-6pm; Metro: La Merced

Centro Cultural de España

Run by the Spanish government since 2002, this unique gallery, cultural center, and anthropology museum is located in a 17th-century baroque palace behind the Metropolitan Cathedral. Throughout the year, the center presents exhibitions of contemporary work by Mexican and Spanish artists, often featuring experimental proposals and installations, in addition to hosting workshops, readings, and performances on-site. There's a design shop on the first floor, as well as a lovely terrace bar and café, with charming views of the back of the cathedral.

During an expansion of the space in 2006, construction workers encountered remains from the city of Tenochtitlán beneath the building's foundation. Archaeological study suggests these structures housed a *calmécac*, a pre-Hispanic school from the 15th and 16th centuries. After the discovery, the CCE opened the Museo del Sitio, a small, interesting museum in the basement of the building, which showcases both the ruins and artifacts recovered from the site.

MAP 1: Guatemala 18, 55/5521-1925 or 55/5521-1926, http://ccemx.org; Tues.-Fri. 11am-9pm, Sat. 10am-9pm, Sun. 10am-4pm; free; Metro: Zócalo

Antiguo Colegio de San Ildefonso

The Antiguo Colegio de San Ildefonso was a Jesuit school from 1588 to 1767, shuttering when the Spanish crown expelled the Jesuits from New Spain. In the 19th century, under President Benito Juárez, it reopened as the Escuela Nacional Preparatoria, a prestigious secondary school.

In 1922, Secretary of Public Education José Vasconcelos hired a group of young Mexican artists to paint the walls of the school; it was the beginning the mural project that would become emblematic of early-20th-century Mexican art. Diego Rivera, José Clemente Orozco, David Alfaro Siqueiros, Fermín Revueltas Sánchez, Ramón Alva de la Canal, Fernando Leal, and Jean Charlot all painted different sections of the interior. Among the building's most important works, Orozco's murals cover three stories in the main patio.

In 1992, San Ildefonso became a museum and cultural center. In addition to the murals, it hosts rotating art exhibits, usually showing contemporary work from Mexico and around the world.

MAP 1: Justo Sierra 16, 55/5702-2991, www.sanildefonso.org.mx; Tues. 10am-7:30pm, Wed.-Sun. 10am-5:30pm; US$3, free on Tues.; Metro: Zócalo

Templo y Plaza de Santo Domingo

Surrounded by churches and palaces, the Plaza de Santo Domingo was the second most important public square in colonial Mexico City, after the Zócalo. On the north end, the Templo de Santo Domingo was constructed in 1530 as part of a Dominican convent, which included a hospital, libraries, and a cloister,

Plaza de Santo Domingo

largely destroyed during the 19th-century Reformation. Opposite the square, the palace housing the **Museo de la Medicina Mexicana** (Brasil 33, 55/5623-3147, daily 9am-6pm) was originally built in the 1730s as the Palacio de la Inquisición, home to the dreaded Inquisition in Mexico, an extension of the Spanish Inquisition.

Look for the dozens of professional scribes beneath the plaza's western archways. They have been producing typed documents for paying clients since the mid-19th century, and can help compose anything from a cover letter to a love note at their small kiosks, in addition to producing official forms and contracts.

MAP 1: Brasil at Belisario Domínguez, 55/5563-0479; Templo de Santo Domingo, hours vary; free; Metro: Zócalo

Secretaría de Educación Pública

Former Secretary of Public Education José Vasconcelos was the mastermind behind the public mural project in early-20th-century Mexico. During Vasconcelos's tenure, the offices of the Secretaría de Educación Pública (SEP) moved into two adjoining colonial-era buildings, where the department is still headquartered today. Both were extensively renovated, and fittingly, Vasconcelos hired Diego Rivera to outfit them with some of the

city's most elaborate murals. Painted between 1923 and 1928 and covering two three-story patios, Rivera's paintings adorn every free surface, from the elevator vestibules to the space above the door frames. On the top floor, *El Arsenal* depicts Rivera's wife, Frida Kahlo, holding a rifle.

On most days, there are knowledgeable English-speaking guides wandering the plaza; they can explain the history of the mural project and Rivera's artistic process, in addition to providing a primer on the personages and themes depicted in the paintings. Their services are provided by SEP, free of charge.

MAP 1: Argentina 28, 55/3601-1000; Mon.-Fri. 9am-5pm; free; Metro: Zócalo

Museo de Arte de la SHCP (Antiguo Palacio del Arzobispado)

Just east of the Zócalo, the former Palacio del Arzobispado (Archbishop's Palace) was built in the 1530s by Mexico's first archbishop, undergoing numerous renovations (and lavish expansions) during the 500 years after its founding. Today, it is an art museum run by the Finance Secretariat (Secretaría de Hacienda y Crédito Público, SHCP), with a sizable collection of Mexican art, much of which was donated to the government by artists or collectors in lieu of tax payments, including work by Diego Rivera and Rufino Tamayo, as well as contemporary artists.

The building suffered serious damage during the earthquake of 1985, and during renovation and retrofit of the space, a surprising discovery was made: Two meters beneath the palace's second courtyard, the foundations of the former Templo de Tezcatlipoca of Tenochtitlán were uncovered, including artifacts and painted murals. Today, the palace includes a viewing area for these ruins along the western wall.

MAP 1: Moneda 4, 55/3688-1248 or 55/3688-1710, www.shcp.gob.mx; Tues.-Sun. 10am-5pm; US$1; Metro: Zócalo

Plaza Loreto

A few blocks from the Zócalo, this modest public square is centered around a circular fountain designed by Manuel Tolsá in the 18th century. It is flanked by two historic churches, the Iglesia de Nuestra Señora de Loreto and the smaller Templo de Santa Teresa La Nueva. Perhaps the most striking aspect of the former is the dramatic angle at which its heavy baroque facade is sinking into the soft topsoil, creating something of a funhouse effect as you enter.

Facing the plaza to the south, the Sinagoga Histórica Justo Sierra (Justo Sierra 71, 55/5522-4828, http://sinagogajustosierra.com, Sun.-Fri. 10am-5pm, free) was the first synagogue in Mexico City, and today it is open to the public as a cultural center and museum. Visitors will notice the building doesn't resemble a typical synagogue: The founders, many of whom came from anti-Semitic environments in Europe, built their temple behind a colonial-era facade, intentionally keeping their religious activities out of the public eye.

MAP 1: Iglesia de Nuestra Señora de Loreto: San Antonio Tomatlán and Jesús María Loreto, 55/5702-7850; daily 10am-5pm; Templo de Santa Teresa La Nueva: Loreto 15, 55/5702-3204; daily 10am-5pm; free; Metro: Zócalo

Academia San Carlos

The Academia San Carlos was originally founded as a school of engraving and printmaking. Ten years later, in 1791, it opened at its current location and expanded its academic disciplines to include all manner of art, architecture, and sculpture. During the 18th and 19th centuries, most of the art produced in Mexico originated here. With the exception of the glass atrium added to the main courtyard in the 20th century, the school's building has barely changed during its 200-plus years in operation.

Since its founding, the academy only closed briefly during the War of Independence. Since 1910, the school has been run by UNAM, the national university, though the original building in the Centro Histórico is now home only to the university's graduate art programs. Visitors are allowed to tour the wonderful old building, as well as visit the school's galleries, which mount rotating exhibitions of Mexican art.

MAP 1: Academia 22, 55/5522-0630, www.artesvisuales.unam.mx; Mon.-Fri. 9am-2pm and 5pm-8pm; free; Metro: Zócalo

Iglesia de la Santísima Trinidad

Iglesia de la Santísima Trinidad

Popularly known simply as La Santísima, this church is a baroque masterpiece tucked away on a scruffy pedestrian backstreet, a couple of blocks east of the Zócalo. The first small hermitage was erected here in 1526, while the current building was constructed between 1755 and 1783. The main facade, decorated with busts of the 12 apostles and a symbol of La Santísima Trinidad (the Holy Trinity), is stunning, and the deep relief carvings on the side entrance are also exceptional. The original altarpiece is long gone, however, so don't worry if the church doors are closed when you stop by.

MAP 1: Emiliano Zapata at La Santísima; daily 8am-1:30pm and 5pm-6pm; free; Metro: Zócalo

Museo de la Cancillería (Oratorio de San Felipe Neri el Viejo)

The congregation of San Felipe Neri built its first church in Mexico City in 1684. In the 18th century, the church and adjoining chapels were embellished with churrigueresque-style details, which were fortunate to survive to the present day: In 1768, an earthquake toppled the rest of building. After years of disuse, the entire complex was renovated and is now the site of a small museum overseen by the Secretaría de Relaciones Exteriores (Secretary of Foreign Affairs), which exhibits portraits, books, and other artifacts, as well as contemporary artwork and cultural pieces from across the world.

Just to the east, another beautiful 18th-century chapel that was part of the Oratorio de San Felipe Neri is now home to the Biblioteca Miguel Lerdo de Tejada (República de El Salvador 49, 55/9158-9837, Mon.-Fri. 9am-5pm), a library with holdings in social sciences and humanities, and a collection of rare books from the 16th through 19th centuries.

MAP 1: República de El Salvador 47, 55/3686-5100, ext. 8327, http://imr.sre.gob.mx; Mon.-Fri. 10am-5pm; free; Metro: San Juan de Letrán or Isabel la Católica

Templo y Convento de Regina Coeli

Once part of a larger Conceptionist convent founded in 1573, the massive Templo de Regina Coeli dominates the eastern end of the pedestrian street Regina. Although the convent's remains aren't open to the public, the church continues to function as a Catholic parish, and it contains several wonderful 18th-century altarpieces inside its soaring nave. The principal altar, dedicated to the Regina Coeli and dating to 1671, has an oil painting of the Virgin in the center and a statue of San José with the baby Jesus above. The *estípite* columns, characteristic of the churrigueresque style of the church, are dazzlingly complex. It is generally open to the public in the mornings, though you might also find the doors open during afternoon mass.

MAP 1: Regina 3, 55/5709-2640; Tues.-Fri. 10am-1:30pm and 4pm-6pm, Sat. 10am-4pm; free; Metro: Isabel la Católica

Universidad Claustro de Sor Juana

During the late 17th century, beloved Mexican poet Sor Juana Inés de la Cruz wrote much of her remarkable, passionate verse from within the confines of her small room in the Convento de San Jerónimo in central Mexico City, a nunnery that was originally founded in 1585. By the middle of the 19th century, when it was closed by the Reform Laws, the convent had at least 200 permanent residents.

Today, the remains of the old convent have been beautifully restored

HIGH-SPEED SIGHTSEEING

double-decker tour bus from Capitalbus

Despite a rather efficient (if overcrowded) public-transportation system, getting from one place to another can be a challenge in Mexico City. An inexpensive, safe, and stress-free way to get the lay of the land, or to see a lot of sights in a limited time, is to take a bus tour of the city.

Capitalbus (www.capitalbus.mx) offers three sightseeing routes in its pink-and-white double-decker buses: Centro-Polanco, which stops at the Alameda Central and the Monumento a la Revolución Mexicana, among other stops; Reforma-Santa Fe, which travels along the Paseo de la Reforma; and Circuito Templos, which runs north to the Basílica de Santa María de Guadalupe. You can buy a ticket for 6, 24, or 48 hours, during which time you are allowed to ride any of the three lines and get on and off the bus, at official stops, as often as you like. All three lines run 10am-10pm, 365 days a year, and tickets cost US$7-14, depending on the length of time you choose. If you're staying in the Centro, there is a ticket and information kiosk near the Zócalo, on Montes de Piedad, just west of the cathedral.

Another option, also departing from the Zócalo but taking different routes through the city, **Turibus** (www.turibus.com.mx) makes frequent circuits through the major city neighborhoods on bright-red double-decker buses. Four main tours run 9am-9pm year-round, including the Downtown Tour, which goes from the Auditorio Nacional to the Centro Histórico via Reforma, stopping at many of the city's important museums (as well as a few malls and tourist traps, like the wax museum). The Southside Tour departs from the Roma and travels south through the Napoles and Del Valle neighborhoods to Coyoacán and UNAM, and finally to the southern reaches of Tlalpan. It takes over three hours to complete each of these tours nonstop (maybe more, depending on traffic); however, Turibus tickets are good all day, 9am-9pm, so you can get on and get off as many times as you wish. A one-day pass for the Turibus costs about US$10 Monday-Friday and about US$14 on the weekends.

and are occupied by a small, private university with an arts and cultural focus, called the Universidad Claustro de Sor Juana. Visitors are free to enter the ex-convent during the week to tour the tranquil main courtyard, around which the nuns' former cells are arranged. There is also a small contemporary art gallery open to the public, in what was once a bathing area for the nuns.

MAP 1: Izazaga 92, 55/5709-4066 or 55/5709-4126, www.ucsj.edu.mx; Mon.-Fri. 10am-6pm; free; Metro: Isabel la Católica

Palacio de Cultura Banamex (Palacio de Iturbide)

A massive baroque mansion with a burgundy-stone facade and elaborate sandstone carvings surrounding the windows and doorframes, the Antiguo Palacio de Iturbide was constructed between 1779 and 1785 for the family of Count San Mateo de Valparaiso. However, the palace is best known as the home of emperor Agustín de Iturbide, who lived there briefly during his short reign of Mexico during the tumultuous post-Independence era.

Banamex purchased the palace in 1964, and after a long renovation project, it became the home of the Fomento Cultural Banamex, a foundation dedicated to the promotion and exhibition of Mexican art; it was officially inaugurated as the Palacio de Cultura Banamex in 2004. Today, the foundation hosts high-quality exhibitions of painting, folk art, and craft in the palace's impressive courtyard; recent shows have included a review of silver design throughout Mexico's history, colonial painting, and a selection from the grand masters of popular art in Iberoamerica.

MAP 1: Madero 17, 55/1226-0247, www.fomentoculturalbanamex.org; daily 10am-7pm; free; Metro: Allende

Museo Nacional de Arte

The Mexican National Art Museum holds the most extensive collection of Mexican artwork in the country, with thousands of pieces from the very early colonial era to the mid-20th century. A tour of the museum chronicles the changing attitudes toward religion, government, and education over the course of many centuries, providing an engaging look at Mexican social history through works of art. Particularly interesting are the 19th-century rooms, which show the emergence of a Mexican national character in the wake of the country's independence, a marked transition from the European-style religious paintings that dominate the colonial-era galleries.

Completed in 1910, the building itself is a masterpiece of modernist architecture, designed by Italian architect Silvio Contri. The lavish interior unites architectural styles from classical to gothic, and is replete with curved marble staircases, gilded moldings, and elaborate iron lamps. In front, there is a bronze statue of King Carlos IV, one of the best-known works by Spanish architect Manuel Tolsá.

MAP 1: Tacuba 8, 55/8647-5430, ext. 5065 and 5067, www.munal.com.mx; Tues.-Sun. 10am-5:30pm; US$3 adults, US$1.50 students, free Sun.; Metro: Bellas Artes

Palacio Postal

On the site of what was once the Franciscan hospital, the central post office is one of the most distinctive architectural landmarks in the city, designed by Italian architect Adamo Boari (who also oversaw the Palacio de Bellas Artes across the street) and Mexican engineer Gonzalo Gorita. Officially inaugurated in 1902, the

Palacio Postal

palace was built with a mix of sandstone and *chiluca*, a very light, almost translucent stone, and it is covered with fine detail, including iron dragon light fixtures and elaborate stone carving around the windows and the top-floor arches. The spacious interior is filled with lavish detail, including gleaming cashier counters and old brass elevators. It's hard to believe this gorgeous palace was built for public use—but even today, it is a fully functioning post, where you can buy stamps or mail a postcard home.

MAP 1: Tacuba 1, 55/5510-2999, www. palaciopostal.gob.mx; Mon.-Fri. 8am-8pm, Sat. 8am-6pm; free; Metro: Bellas Artes

Torre Latinoamericana

Torre Latinoamericana

The iconic Torre Latinoamericana was the capital's tallest building at its inauguration in 1956. Though it long ago lost that distinction, the Latinoamericana is still one of the few skyscrapers downtown, giving its top floors one of the most privileged vantage points in the city. On the 44th floor of the building, an open-air observation deck affords stunning, panoramic views of the city from north to south and east to west. On clear days, the volcanoes Iztaccíhuatl and Popocatépetl may even be visible to the southeast. If you're feeling a little vertigo, take heart: The tower was specially designed to withstand Mexico City's seismic instability and soft topsoil, with a foundation reaching deep into the earth and a flexible structure that sways with ground movement. Indeed, the Torre Latinoamericana survived both the 1957 and 1985 earthquakes.

MAP 1: Eje Central Lázaro Cárdenas 2, 55/5518-7423, www.torrelatinoamericana. com.mx; daily 9am-10pm; US$6 adults, US$4 kids; Metro: Bellas Artes

✪ Palacio de Bellas Artes

The majestic Palacio de Bellas Artes (Palace of Fine Arts) is one of the city's finest buildings and a highly respected cultural institution that hosts live performances and art exhibitions overseen by the National Institute of Fine Arts. Overseen by Italian architect Adamo Boari, construction on the palace began in 1904 but halted when the Mexican Revolution erupted in 1910. Twenty years later, architect Federico Mariscal took over the project, completing the rooftop cupola and the building's interiors in art deco style. In the opulent main auditorium, a stunning Tiffany glass curtain was designed by Mexican artist Dr. Atl.

On the second and third floors, the Museo del Palacio de Bellas Artes (55/5521-9251, http://museopalaciode-bellasartes.gob.mx, Tues.-Sun. 10am-6pm) has hosted some of the most important art shows of the past decade, including a 2007 Frida Kahlo retrospective. Admission includes access to the Palacio's many murals, which include David Alfaro Siqueiros's *Nueva Democracia* (*New Democracy*) on the second level. On another wall, Diego Rivera's 1934 *El Hombre Contralor del Universo* (known as *Man at the Crossroads* in English) was originally commissioned by Nelson Rockefeller, though, famously, the American businessman canceled the project when Rivera included a likeness of Lenin in the piece.

interior view of the famous dome of the Palacio de Bellas Artes

Alameda Central

On the top floor, the **Museo Nacional de Arquitectura** exhibits building floor plans, photos, and other archived memorabilia related to Mexico City's historic buildings.

MAP 2: Corner of Av. Juárez and Eje Central, 55/5512-2593, www.palacio. bellasartes.gob.mx; Tues.-Sun. 10am-9pm; free to enter the lobby, US$4 admission to museum and mezzanine level; Metro: Bellas Artes

NEARBY:

- Take a leisurely stroll around **Alameda Central,** Mexico City's oldest urban park (page 84).
- Snack on carnitas at the low-key **Fonda Santa Rita** (page 115).
- Take in the best view of the city from **Miralto** bar (page 143).
- Explore three centuries of Mexican design at **Museo Franz Mayer** (page 165).
- Sip tequila at **Tío Pepe,** a historic cantina (page 145).

Alameda Central

Just west of Bellas Artes, the Alameda Central is the largest green space in the center of the city and the oldest public park in the Americas. Today, it is a tree-filled respite from the bustle of the Centro Histórico—despite being flanked by major avenues on all sides and serviced by two Metro stations and two Metrobús stops.

Inaugurated in the 16th century, the original Alameda was filled with poplars, or *alamos*—hence, the park's name. Throughout the centuries, it evolved from an exclusive strolling park to a bustling family-oriented

destination. La Alameda's popular spirit was celebrated by Diego Rivera in his famous work *Sundays on the Alameda Central*, located in the Museo Mural Diego Rivera on the west end of the park. The most prominent of the Alameda's many fountains and neoclassical statues is the Hemiciclo de Benito Juárez, a semi-circle of eight marble columns, facing Avenida Juárez on the south.

MAP 2: Bordered by Juárez, Hidalgo, Eje Central, and Paseo de la Reforma; Metro: Bellas Artes or Hidalgo

Plaza de San Juan

In the bustling neighborhood four blocks south of the Alameda, this pretty plaza was the site of a market during the colonial era. The square is closely associated with the El Buen Tono cigarette company, which once adjoined it. Founded by Frenchman Ernesto Pugibet in the late 19th century, El Buen Tono grew rapidly—eventually manufacturing 3.5 billion cigarettes per year—and the plant, employee housing, and warehouses overtook the neighborhood. Though much of the industrial complex has since been razed, there are vestiges of its presence: The adjoining artisan market, for example, was once part of the tobacco factory warehouses.

On the west side of the plaza, the pretty but often overlooked church Nuestra Señora de Guadalupe del Buen Tono (once the site of the chapel of the old San Juan convent, which was established in the early colonial era) was constructed by Pugibet for factory workers, and it was designed by well-known Mexican architect Miguel Ángel de Quevedo.

MAP 2: Buen Tono and Ayuntamiento; daily 24 hours; free; Metro: Salto de Agua or San Juan de Letrán

Templo San Hipólito

This church, on the corner of Hidalgo and Zarco, is said to have been founded by Hernán Cortés in remembrance of the Noche Triste, on June 30, 1520, when Cortés's forces fled the city of Tenochtitlán, resulting in major Spanish casualties. In 1559, the Spanish constructed a church on this site, right at the beginning of the causeway leaving the island and, for the following centuries, the outer limits of the city. A small plaque in a corner of the church courtyard commemorates the Noche Triste. The church was repeatedly rebuilt over the centuries, with much of the building dating to the 1730s. Today, the church is dedicated to Jude the Apostle, and on the 28th of every month, a special mass is celebrated in the saint's honor.

MAP 2: Av. Hidalgo 107, 55/5510-4796; daily 7am-7pm; free; Metro: Hidalgo

Centro Cultural Universitario Tlatelolco

Located right next to the ruin site in the Plaza de las Tres Culturas, this multipurpose cultural center is a nice accompaniment to the Tlatelolco archaeological site. Inside the center, the Museo de Sitio de Tlatelolco holds a permanent exhibit of around 400 pieces excavated from the ruins in 1944, which are divided into pre-Columbian and colonial-era exhibits. Also of interest to visitors, the center's Memorial de 68 is dedicated to the memory of the events on October 2, 1968, when the plaza was the site of a notorious and highly controversial massacre. Under circumstances still murky, several hundred student protesters were shot and killed by Mexican military (*guardias presidenciales*) just before the start of the Mexico City Olympics. For anyone who'd like to learn more about the summer of 1968 and the immense impact it had on Mexico City's psyche, this is a comprehensive introduction.

MAP 2: Corner of Eje Central Lázaro Cárdenas and Ricardo Flores Magón, 55/5782-7290, www.tlatelolco.unam.mx; daily 10am-6pm; free; Metro: Garibaldi or Tlatelolco

Plaza de las Tres Culturas

Several blocks north of the Plaza Garibaldi, the Plaza de las Tres Culturas (Plaza of the Three Cultures) in Tlatelolco is so named because it is surrounded by symbols of three distinct periods of Mexican history: ruins of an ancient temple, the renovated 16th-century Iglesia de Santiago Tlatelolco, and a 1960s-era apartment complex designed by architect Mario Pani.

Tlatelolco was a Mexica city-state, sister to the great Tenochtitlán. Here, the Mexica withstood the final Spanish siege before Cortés and his men were finally able to breach the city. The event is commemorated with a plaque in the middle of the Plaza de las Tres Culturas, with a famous inscription: "Heroically defended by Cuauhtémoc, Tlatelolco fell to the power of Hernán Cortés. It was neither a triumph nor a defeat. It was the painful birth of the mestizo nation that is the Mexico of today."

MAP 2: Eje Central Lázaro Cárdenas and Ricardo Flores Magón; Metro: Tlatelolco or Garibaldi

Zona Arqueológica Tlatelolco

Though it never reached the size or grandeur of neighboring Tenochtitlán, the city-state of Tlatelolco was a major settlement in the Valley of Mexico, home to the largest and most important market in Mesoamerica. Most of the city was destroyed immediately following the conquest, and a Franciscan church was built atop Tlatelolco's main temple-pyramid (as in the Zócalo, the first church was likely built using rubble from the fallen pyramid). The site was excavated in 1928 and again in 1944, uncovering both pre-Columbian and colonial-era artifacts.

Today, this small, nicely maintained site reveals the foundations of religious and ceremonial buildings from the former city, including the Templo Mayor of Tlatelolco. The temple to Ehécatl-Quetzalcóatl is an interesting half-round, half-rectangular structure, where a late-1980s excavation recovered the remains of 41 people and more than 50 offerings. The smaller Templo Calendárico displays 13 glyphs from the Mesoamerican calendar carved into each of its four facades.

MAP 2: Corner of Eje Central Lázaro Cárdenas and Ricardo Flores Magón, 55/5782-7290, www.tlatelolco.inah.gob. mx; daily 8am-6pm; free; Metro: Garibaldi or Tlatelolco

mariachi band in Plaza Garibaldi

Plaza Garibaldi

On weekend nights, Plaza Garibaldi comes to life as dozens of mariachi bands roam the square, playing traditional tunes to the crowd of revelers in a glorious cacophony. Garibaldi is a popular spot for locals and tourists after a few rounds of tequila. (If you want to commission a song, expect to pay at least US$10-15 per tune.)

The plaza is historic, if not notably atmospheric: It held a market during the colonial era and was inaugurated as a public space in 1850. In post-revolutionary Mexico, the area became a nightlife hub, filled with cabarets and nightclubs. It has since lost much of its madcap splendor, but it remains a vibrant part of the city.

Though a 2012 renovation made Garibaldi safer, there is a history of crime in the area, and some bars along the plaza make a business of cheating tourists. Stick to the Tenampa or other recommended establishments, and never wander on the backstreets around Garibaldi after dark.

MAP 2: Eje Central at República de Honduras; Metro: Garibaldi

Paseo de la Reforma Map 3

⊗ Monumento a la Revolución Mexicana

Mexico City's monument to the Revolution of 1910 wasn't originally designed as a war memorial. Surprisingly, this towering dome was built during the first phase of construction on a luxurious, neoclassical congressional building, commissioned by President Porfirio Díaz in the early 20th century. When the Revolution of 1910 broke out, the project was abandoned.

In 1933, Carlos Obregón Santacilia took over the project. He completed the volcanic-stone facade and added art deco finishes to each of the four corners, working with sculptor Oliverio Martínez. Crypts in the monument's feet hold the remains of Revolution heroes Venustiano Carranza, Francisco I. Madero, Francisco "Pancho" Villa, Plutarco Elias Calles, and Lázaro Cárdenas.

Leading up to the centennial of the Revolution, in 2010, the monument and surrounding plaza received a full renovation. Perhaps the most exciting new feature is the glass elevator that ascends from the ground floor to the monument's dome, where visitors can stroll beneath the vaulted roof, with a view of the city below.

The basement-level Museo Nacional de la Revolución (Mon.-Fri. 9am-5pm, Sat.-Sun. 9am-6:30pm), or National Museum of the Revolution, opened as a part of the renovation project. The permanent exhibit chronicles the major events and philosophies that drove different factions to action

Monumento a la Revolución Mexicana

during the Revolution of 1910, as well as a few period artifacts, like Pancho Villa's riding saddle and vintage guns.

MAP 3: Plaza de la República, Vallarta at Gomez Farías, 55/5592-2038 or 55/5591-1894, www.mrm.mx; Mon.-Thurs. noon-8pm, Fri.-Sat. noon-10pm, Sun. 10am-8pm; elevator/dome access US$3.50, museum US$2; Metro: Revolución

Biblioteca Vasconcelos

This huge, architecturally stunning public library, designed by Mexican architect Alberto Kalach, opened next to the Buenavista train station in 2006. Its unique layout features "floating" bookshelves that surround a towering central atrium, which is filled with comfortable chairs and desks for reading. Hanging from the roof in the middle of the space is the famous "whale" sculpture, *Matrix Móvil,* by artist Gabriel Orozco.

interior of Biblioteca Vasconcelos

Despite the overall beauty of the project, the library was mired in controversy for both its cost and unexpected construction issues after its opening. But critics cannot diminish the stunning design of the building, which also serves as an informal public space where locals and families roam through the stacks, take advantage of the free Internet-connected computers, or attend screenings of movies organized by the Cineteca Nacional. An on-site bookstore is run by Conaculta, the National Council for Culture and Arts.

MAP 3: Eje 1 Norte (Mosqueta), corner of Aldama, 55/9157-2800, www. bibliotecavasconcelos.gob.mx; daily 8:30am-7:30pm; free; Metro: Buenavista, Metrobús: Buenavista

La Alameda de Santa María

This tranquil, tree-filled park, located at the center of the Santa María la Ribera neighborhood, has an old-fashioned feeling. Its chief attraction is the gorgeous, brightly colored Moorish-style kiosk in the middle of the square, made entirely of iron, which was originally constructed for Mexico's pavilion at the World's Fair in 1886. It was moved to several locations around Mexico City before settling in its current location in the Santa María.

On the west side of the Alameda is UNAM's Museo de Geología, housed in a beautiful old mansion. The main gallery holds a reconstructed woolly mammoth skeleton, and glass cases showcase the museum's collection of fossils, stones, minerals, and meteorites. The opulent building was originally commissioned by Porfirio Díaz, and some visitors are more interested in the space itself than its contents: The sweeping art nouveau wrought-iron staircase in the entryway is a highlight of the space.

MAP 3: Dr. Atl and Salvador Díaz Mirón; La Alameda is open daily 24 hours; Museo de Geología, 55/5547-3900 or 55/5547-3948, Tues.-Sun. 10am-5pm; La Alameda is free; museum is US$1.50; Metro: Buenavista

Ángel de la Independencia

In the center of a busy traffic circle on the Paseo de la Reforma, the Ángel de la Independencia is a striking 36-meter-high column topped with a gold-plated bronze angel. It was inaugurated by President Porfirio Díaz on September 16, 1910, to commemorate the country's centennial of independence from Spain. One of the city's most recognizable landmarks, it is the site of frequent political rallies and spontaneous street celebrations whenever Mexico's national soccer team pulls off a victory. And, like many Mexican monuments, it's had its share of drama: In 1957, the bronze angel toppled from its perch during a major earthquake.

When crossing Reforma to the monument, use caution—there are no official crosswalks, and traffic flows from all four directions. Within the column's base, a small passageway contains three niches, which store the remains of 12 heroes from the independence struggle.

MAP 3: Paseo de la Reforma and Florencia; free; Metro: Insurgentes

Chapultepec and Polanco Map 4

TOP EXPERIENCE

✪ Museo Nacional de Antropología

The Museo Nacional de Antropología (National Anthropology Museum) is an educational and thought-provoking museum that provides an unparalleled look into the diverse cultures of pre-Columbian and modern-day Mexico. The massive two-story space is divided into 23 exhibition rooms and is filled with an astounding array of artifacts from pre-Columbian cultures in Mexico, including the Olmecs of the Gulf Coast, Teotihuacán, the post-Teotihuacán Toltecs, the Zapotecs and cultures of Oaxaca, the Mexica, and the Maya. Some key pieces among the collection include the colossal Olmec heads carved from giant monoliths, the carved lintel from Yaxchilan in the Maya room, and the Toltecs' towering stone warriors.

The galleries dedicated to the Valley of Mexico are the centerpiece of the museum. Here, some of the collection's most stunning artifacts are on display, including a stone sculpture of the goddess Coatlicue (originally found in Mexico City's Zócalo), a richly carved sacrificial urn called the Piedra de Tizoc, and the Piedra del Sol (also called the "Aztec calendar"), which illustrates the 20 signs and 13 numerals of the Mesoamerican calendar round.

If time allows, it's worth touring the less-visited second floor, where ethnography exhibits are dedicated

Museo Nacional de Antropología

to the native cultures of Mexico today, including the Huichol, Cora, Purépecha, and Otomí people. There are dioramas of typical dwellings, an excellent collection of textiles and handicrafts, and extensive wall text in Spanish and English that gives depth to the exhibits.

MAP 4: Paseo de la Reforma and Calzada Gandhi, 55/4040-5300, www.mna.inah. gob.mx; Tues.-Sun. 9am-7pm; US$5; Metro: Auditorio

NEARBY:

- Grab a bite to eat at Chapulín, a creative Mexican restaurant (page 122).
- Make a reservation to dine with a lakeside view at El Lago (page 126).
- See the changing murals on the facade of the Museo Sala de Arte Público David Alfaro Siqueiros (page 172).
- Visit the Museo Rufino Tamayo, Chapultepec's premiere contemporary art museum, and grab a bite at its lovely in-house café (page 171).

✪ Castillo de Chapultepec and the Museo Nacional de Historia

Overlooking the Paseo de la Reforma from the Cerro de Chapultepec, this opulent castle and Mexican history museum was originally built as a country house for Spanish royalty under Viceroy Bernardo de Gálvez in the late 18th century. Later, the castle was taken over by the government, serving as a military college for several decades after the War for Independence. During the 1847 U.S. Army invasion of Mexico City during the Mexican-American War, the *castillo* was the last bastion of defense. In an infamous moment in Mexican history, American forces overtook the castle, raising an American flag on its roof.

Castillo de Chapultepec

During the brief rule of Maximilian I in the 1860s, the emperor made the Castillo de Chapultepec his official residence, refurbishing it with grand salons, flowered terraces, and a rooftop garden. After Maximilian and Carlota were overthrown by Benito Juárez, the castle was converted to the Mexican presidential residence. Under President Porfirio Díaz, the castle's interior reached new heights of luxury.

Monumento a Los Niños Héroes

Progressive president Lázaro Cárdenas finally converted the castle to a public museum in 1939; it opened in 1944.

Today, the castle is home to the **Museo Nacional de Historia** (the National History Museum), with a permanent collection of paintings, documents, and artifacts documenting the changing eras in Mexican history. Equally interesting are the many rooms preserved in period furnishings. The gardens are well-tended, and the views of the Paseo de la Reforma from the terraces are postcard-worthy. **MAP 4:** Primera Sección, Bosque de Chapultepec, 55/5241-3100, www.mnh. inah.gob.mx; Tues.-Sun. 9am-5pm; US$5.50, free for children and seniors; Metro: Chapultepec

Monumento a Los Niños Héroes

At the foot of the Cerro de Chapultepec, this six-column monument commemorates the heroic defense of the Castillo de Chapultepec by six young soldiers against invading U.S. troops during the Mexican-American War. On September 13, 1847, when it was clear the Americans would take the castle, six military cadets—Juan de la Barrera, Juan Escutia, Fernando Montes de Oca, Vicente Suárez, Francisco Marquéz, and Agustín Melgar—wrapped themselves in Mexican flags and jumped to their deaths from the castle ramparts rather than surrender. Their deaths are honored by six tall columns, each topped with a black eagle. The Americans ultimately prevailed and flew their flag over Mexico City. **MAP 4:** Primera Sección, Bosque de Chapultepec, east of the castle; free; Metro: Chapultepec

Baños de Moctezuma

At the southern base of the Cerro de Chapultepec, behind the Niños Héroes monument, there are remains of one of the many spring-fed pools where Mexica emperors came to bathe, later used by the Spanish as a retreat during the colonial era. Time has not treated these historic landmarks very well; today, the baths are little more than a sad sunken pool, but the historic value is phenomenal. Up until the mid-20th century, water still rose here. Nearby, there are pre-Columbian carvings on the rocks around the base of the Cerro de Chapultepec.

MAP 4: Primera Sección, Bosque de Chapultepec, south of the castle; Metro: Chapultepec

✪ Casa Luis Barragán

Luis Barragán is considered one of Mexico's greatest modern architects and interior designers. Born in Guadalajara in 1902, he built a number of residences in his hometown before relocating to Mexico City, where his most famous work was completed. Barragán was known for integrating a clean modernist style with an innovative use of light, bright primary colors, and subtle Mexican vernacular elements.

Today, Barragán's former home and studio near Tacubaya, built between 1947 and 1948, is preserved as a museum. With its modern lines and clean spaces, the building is representative of Barragán's work, but it also provides an intimate look into the architect's life and personal aesthetics. Throughout the living quarters, Barragán's personal belongings, furniture, and art collection—which includes work by Miguel Covarrubias, Diego Rivera, and Henry Moore—are on display. In 1988, the home was named a national monument by the Mexican government, and in 2004, it was recognized as an UNESCO World Heritage Site.

Visitors must preregister for a guided tour of the three-story space, which takes you through the library, living rooms, study, patios, and garden. Make reservations well in advance, and note that you must buy a photo permit for about US$30 if you want to take photos of any kind. Though tour guides only speak Spanish, the visuals need little explanation. For those with an interest in modern architecture, it is one of the city's must-see spots.

MAP 4: Av. General Francisco Ramírez 12-14, 55/5515-4908 or 55/5272-4945, www.casaluisbarragan.org; guided tours by appointment only, Mon.-Fri. 10:30am, 11:30am, 12:30pm, 3:30m, and 4pm, and Sat.-Sun. 10:30am and 12pm; US$15; Metro: Constituyentes

Roma and Condesa Map 5

✪ Parque México

One of the prettiest urban respites in Mexico City, the Parque México is a big reason why the Condesa has become one of the nicest neighborhoods in the city. Much beloved by locals, the large, oval-shaped park, encircled by the tree-lined Avenida Amsterdam, was built in the center of what was once a horse track. Officially named the Parque San Martín (though no one ever calls it that), the Parque México provides a wonderful, surprisingly peaceful respite from the noise and traffic of the city, filled with footpaths, towering trees, and lush gardens. In addition to being a relaxing neighborhood spot, Parque México is known as a jewel of art deco landscape architecture.

Wander past its ponds and unusual fountains, and stop to admire the graffiti-covered outdoor auditorium **Foro Lindbergh,** where kids often ride bikes or kick soccer balls after school. During the week, Condesa locals come here to jog, walk their dogs, host scout meetings, or read; on the weekends, families come to stroll and play.

From Parque México, walk one block in any direction to Avenida Amsterdam, an oval-shaped avenue with a tree-filled pedestrian median. From Amsterdam, follow Michoacán four blocks west, across Nuevo León and Tamaulipas; you'll find yourself in the middle of the Condesa restaurant and café zone. Or, swing north on Nuevo León to visit **Parque**

lush foliage in the Parque México

ICONS OF 20TH-CENTURY ARCHITECTURE

Mexico City's unique cityscape has been shaped by a long tradition of creative architecture, from the baroque masterpieces of the colonial era to the showy design of its newest museums. During the 20th century, as Mexico City experienced unprecedented growth, a number of important architects left their mark on the city, creating some of its most iconic sights while influencing the aesthetics of their contemporaries.

Pedro Ramírez Vázquez (1919-2013) designed many of the city's iconic sights, including the Museo Nacional de Antropología, with its soaring central canopy and fountain; the Basílica de Santa María de Guadalupe, a circular church that displays the shroud bearing the Virgin of Guadalupe's image; the Museo de Arte Moderno, with its concrete facade and circular atrium; and the Estadio Azteca sports stadium. Together with Gonzalo Ramírez del Sordo, he also designed the Auditorio Nacional in Polanco.

Artist and architect **Juan O'Gorman** (1905-1982) began his career working for Carlos Obregón Santacilia, who designed the Monumento a la Revolución Mexicana with art deco touches. You're most likely to see O'Gorman's work, inspired by the functionalism of Le Corbusier, when you visit the city's south: He designed joined houses for Frida Kahlo and Diego Rivera that are now the Museo Casa Estudio Diego Rivera, and later he created the massive lava-rock mosaics on the UNAM's iconic Biblioteca Central.

Luis Barragán (1902-1988), among the most influential names in modern architecture, principally designed private residences, but there are many opportunities to see his work in Mexico City. His own home, the Casa Luis Barragán, is now a museum, but he also designed the Casa de los Amigos, a guesthouse and social-justice organization in the Tabacalera neighborhood; the home was once owned by muralist José Clemente Orozco. In Tlalpan, the Capilla de los Capuchinos is one of Barragán's public works, and with Jesús Reyes Ferreira and Mathias Goeritz, Barragán created the famous Torres Satelite, a public monument in one of Mexico City's biggest suburbs.

The Condesa derives its beauty from its ubiquitous art deco aesthetics, and **Francisco J. Serrano** (1900-1982) is one of the most famous names in Mexican art deco architecture. Notably, he designed the towering Edificio Basurto, built from 1942-1945, on Avenida México in the Condesa, as well as the Edificio México (123 Av. México). In Polanco, he built the Pasaje Comercial, an unusual shopping center in the "colonial californiano" style, on Presidente Masaryk.

Many of Mexico's great 20th-century architects shared an interest in functionalism, including **Mario Pani** (1911-1983), who was responsible for the city's first major projects in low-cost housing, designing the massive *mutlifamiliares* (multifamily apartment buildings) that are now emblematic of the city. His first project was the Centro Urbano Presidente Alemán in the Colonia Del Valle, and later the 101 towers of the Conjunto Urbano Nonoalco Tlatelolco, a massive housing project that included schools, shops, and hospitals. Disastrously, these buildings were badly damaged in the 1985 earthquake; one collapsed entirely.

Ricardo Legorreta (b. 1930) created several architectural gems in his native Mexico City, including the eye-catching Camino Real hotel in Polanco, with its saturated colors and unusual fountains. Later, he designed Plaza Juárez, as well as the adjoining Museo de Memoria y Tolerancia, right across the street from the Alameda Central.

Teodoro González de León (b. 1926) designed the concrete Museo Rufino Tamayo, together with Abraham Zabludovsky. In the 21st century, he was responsible for the renovation of the Centro Cultural Bella Época in the Condesa and the design of the light-filled Museo Universitario Arte Contemporáneo, the contemporary-art museum on UNAM's central campus.

España, a smaller but equally pretty park just a few blocks from Parque México.

MAP 5: Av. México, between Av. Sonora and Av. Michoacán; Metro: Chilpancingo, Metrobús: Sonora

Plaza Río de Janeiro

A nice place to start a stroll around the Roma neighborhood is the Plaza Río de Janeiro. Surrounded by beautiful old mansions, this low-key park rings a central fountain, with a rather incongruous replica of Michelangelo's *David* statue in the center. On the east side of the square, La Casa de las Brujas (Witches' House), as the Edificio Río de Janeiro is popularly known, is a red-brick castle, built in 1908, with notable art deco accents.

Plaza Río de Janeiro

A block north of the park, the Casa Universitaria del Libro (Orizaba 24, Mon.-Fri. 10am-3pm and 5pm-8pm) contains the offices of a small publishing house run by UNAM. There are frequent special events and speakers open to the public, as well as a small cineclub.

MAP 5: Durango and Orizaba; Metro: Insurgentes

Templo San Francisco Javier and Plaza Romita

Long before the 19th-century development of the Roma neighborhood, the land was a part of the small pre-Columbian settlement of Aztacalco. There, in 1530, Spanish settlers built a small chapel named Santa María de la Natividad to serve the community. Many centuries later, as the area began to develop, that chapel was the center of a subdistrict of the Roma neighborhood known as La Romita. Though the greater Roma was wealthy, La Romita became famous for its crime, thieves, and poverty. Luis Buñuel filmed part of his famous film *Los Olvidados,* about destitute children in Mexico, in La Romita.

Today, the area is less infamous, and the original 16th-century church still stands (having withstood a few renovations). It is one of the oldest buildings in the city, tucked off a side street and adjoining a tree-filled plaza.

MAP 5: Plaza Romita between Morelia and Guayamas, 55/5207-7700; Templo San Francisco Javier: daily 9am-noon; Plaza Romita: daily 24 hours; free; Metro: Niños Héroes

❂ Museo Frida Kahlo

Frida Kahlo produced a small body of work during her lifetime, yet her paintings are so unique and powerful that she is now one of the most recognizable names in modern art. The Museo Frida Kahlo is located in the house where Kahlo grew up, lived with her husband (artist Diego Rivera), and died. Known as the Casa Azul for its cobalt color, this wonderful museum is both an art gallery and a re-creation of the home when Kahlo and Rivera lived there. It's an absolute must for Kahlo fans.

The ground-floor galleries exhibit some of Kahlo's work—including a lovely portrait of her father, Guillermo—as well as some of her modern art collection. Perhaps the most moving rooms are upstairs, where visitors can see Kahlo's studio, with her wheelchair at the easel, as well as the bed where Kahlo spent so much time after a tragic trolley-car accident in her teenage years left her permanently disabled. Kahlo was a collector of traditional Mexican clothing and jewelry, which became a huge part of her public persona, as well as a key element in her artistic work. Many of her outfits are displayed throughout the museum.

Recently, the museum's collection became more robust after a remarkable discovery within its own walls. In 2002, the home's bathrooms were unsealed, revealing a treasure of

Museo Frida Kahlo

clothing, documents, toys, books, and other artifacts from the artists' lives. The collection was so extensive that the museum acquired the adjoining Porfiriato-era house to exhibit them. Advance tickets can be purchased via the museum's website (there is often a wait on weekends).

MAP 6: Londres 247, 55/5554-5999, www.museofridakahlo.org.mx; Tues., Thurs.-Sun. 10am-5:45pm, Wed. 11am-5:45pm; US$4.50 adults, US$2 students; Metro: Coyoacán

NEARBY:

- Visit **Museo Casa Leon Trotsky**, the former home of the Bolshevik revolutionary and friend of Frida Kahlo and Diego Rivera (page 99).
- Grab a mocha with Coyoacán old-timers at **Café El Jarocho** (page 137).
- Have a veggie breakfast at **Casa del Pan Papalotl** (page 135).
- Sip mezcal cocktails and sample bar snacks at **La Bipo** (page 156).
- Visit one of the popular seafood stalls or tostada stands at the **Mercado Coyoacán** (page 138).

Jardín Centenario

If you arrive in Coyoacán via Avenida Francisco Sosa, you will arrive first at the Jardín Centenario, a shady plaza that adjoins the neighborhood's main square, Jardín Hidalgo, to the west. At

the entrance to the square is a lovely arched entryway, built by hand in the 16th century; it was once a part of the cloister of the San Juan Bautista monastery and church. The centerpiece of the garden is a circular stone fountain featuring bronze sculptures of two coyotes, a reference to the neighborhood's Nahuatl name, "Place of Coyotes." The fountain has become a symbol of Coyoacán throughout the city. Both sides of the plaza are lined with restaurants and cafés, and there is often a friendly, upbeat vibe in the square, where students play guitars on a park benches, intellectuals converse over coffees, and locals stroll along the stone paths with their dogs.

MAP 6: Carrillo Puerto and Tres Cruces; Metro: Viveros

Jardín Hidalgo and Antiguo Palacio del Ayuntamiento

Jardín Hidalgo is Coyoacán's lovely central plaza, bordered to the east by the impressive Parroquia de San Juan Bautista, one of the oldest churches in the city. Larger than the adjoining Jardín Centenario, this sun-drenched esplanade features an iron kiosk with a stained-glass cupola, constructed in France in the 19th century. Filled with benches and constantly patrolled by shaved-ice carts, this plaza is a popular place for a weekend stroll.

Today, Coyoacán's main government offices are located in the **Antiguo Palacio del Ayuntamiento de Coyoacán** (Plaza Hidalgo 1), a rust-colored building constructed in 1755 and stretching across the entire north end of Jardín Hidalgo. Also known as the Casa de Cortés, the building is located on the site of what is believed to be one of Cortés's many former residences in Mexico.

Parroquia y Ex-Convento de San Juan Bautista

One of the oldest surviving Catholic churches in Mexico City, this baroque gem was built in 1589 by Dominicans, on land given to them by Hernán Cortés. Like many churches of its era, it was once part of a much larger monastery complex at the center of Coyoacán (stretching all the way to the arches at the entrance to adjoining Jardín Centenario). Later transferred to the Franciscans and remodeled by secular clergy in the 18th century, it retains its original hand-carved-stone facade. The interior of the church was thoroughly and beautifully reconstructed at the beginning of the 20th century, with the altars restored and recoated in gold leaf, and new frescos added to the walls. In one of the church's three naves, the Capilla del Rosario contains an ornate baroque retablo from the end of the 17th century, as well as a collection of 18th-century oil paintings.

MAP 6: Jardín Hidalgo (bordered by Carrillo Puerto, Caballocalco, and B. Domínguez); daily 8am-6pm; free; Metro: Viveros

Plaza y Capilla de la Conchita

The colonial-era street Higuera cuts diagonally southeast from the Jardín Hidalgo, terminating at the picturesque Plaza de la Conchita. The chapel here, one of the oldest in the city, was originally constructed in 1521 by order of Hernán Cortés. By some accounts, it was the very first Christian church in Mexico. Although officially known as Capilla de la Purísima Concepción, the chapel and surrounding garden are more commonly known by the

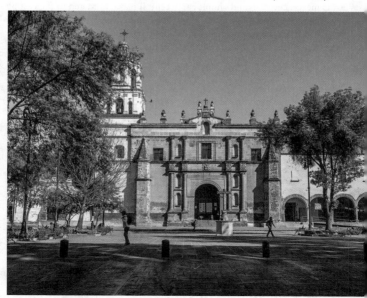

Parroquia y Ex-Convento de San Juan Bautista

affectionate nickname La Conchita (the Little Shell). According to archaeological evidence, this plaza may have been a central ceremonial space for pre-Hispanic cultures in Coyoacán.

On one corner of the Plaza de la Conchita, the brick-red Casa de la Malinche is said to be the house Cortés shared with his lover and interpreter Malintzin, better known as La Malinche. The story is likely apocryphal: Historians say the house was constructed many centuries after Cortés and La Malinche lived in the Valley of Mexico.

MAP 6: Higuera and Vallarta; Metro: Viveros

Plaza Santa Catarina

A few blocks west of Jardín Centenario along Avenida Francisco Sosa is a lovely cobblestone square, fronted by the bright-yellow Capilla de Santa Catarina and surrounded by restored colonial-era houses. On one side is the Casa de Cultura de Coyoacán (Francisco Sosa 202, 55/5658-7826), which often holds cultural events and art exhibits. Stop in to admire the rambling old hacienda, or enjoy the lush gardens in back, where there is also an attractive coffee shop with shaded tables. Back toward the center of Coyoacán, on Francisco Sosa, the Instituto Italiano di Cultura (Francisco Sosa 77, 55/5554-0044, www.iicmessico.esteri.it) often hosts art exhibits and other special events.

MAP 6: Francisco Sosa at Tata Vasco; Metro: Viveros

Museo Casa Leon Trotsky

During the 20th century, Mexico's leftist government offered asylum to political exiles from many different countries, including anti-Fascist intellectuals from Spain and Cold War exiles from the United States. Following a power struggle with Josef Stalin, Russian Marxist revolutionary Leon Trotsky left the Soviet Union in 1929, eventually coming to Mexico with his wife, Natalia, in 1937, at the invitation of Frida Kahlo and Diego Rivera.

Trotsky remained a vocal anti-Stalinist, hence his life was always in peril. In 1940, a Spanish Stalinist named Ramón Mercader gained Trotsky's confidence, then fatally wounded him with an ice axe while Trotsky was in his study. Today, visitors can visit the room in which Trotsky was killed; it has been left entirely untouched since the day he died. Other rooms in the house have been converted into galleries, exhibiting photographs of Trotsky, his wife Natalia, and Rivera and Kahlo, as well as many of the Bolshevik revolutionary's documents, personal effects, and furnishings.

MAP 6: Río Churubusco 410, 55/5658-8732 or 55/5554-0687, http://museocasadeleontrotsky.blogspot.com; Tues.-Sun. 10am-5pm; US$3; Metro: Coyoacán

memorial and tomb of Leon Trotsky

San Ángel

Map 6

✪ Biblioteca Central

Just outside of San Ángel, the Universidad Nacional Autónoma de México (UNAM), the country's oldest, largest, and most prestigious college, can trace its founding to the early colonial era. It was inaugurated as the national university in September 1910, and was granted its unique status as autonomous from the government in 1923. UNAM's main campus, built from 1949 to 1952 by more than 60 architects, engineers, and artists, is a UNESCO World Heritage Site. There are many architectural gems within UNAM's central campus, known as the Ciudad Universitaria, though none more iconic than the Biblioteca Central (Central Library). All four sides of this million-plus-title library

are covered in a dazzling mosaic made of colored volcanic stone. Designed by artist and architect Juan O'Gorman, the mural illustrates themes from Mexican history in four eras: pre-Hispanic, colonial, modern, and the present.

The library is a good place to start a tour of the Ciudad Universitaria. Just south of the library is the Rectoría, the campus's main administration building, whose south wall is covered with a three-dimensional mural by David Alfaro Siqueiros. Just below, Museo Universitario de Ciencias y Artes CU (Av. Insurgentes Sur 3000, 55/5622-0206, Mon.-Fri. 10am-7pm, Sat.-Sun. 10am-6pm) is a public museum that hosts free exhibits by predominantly Mexican artists. Across

Biblioteca Central

Insurgentes, the Estadio Olímpico is the home field for the Pumas soccer club, with a mosaic of the university's shield created in colored stones by Diego Rivera.

MAP 6: Circuito Interior, Ciudad Universitaria, 55/5622-1603, www. patrimoniomundial.unam.mx; daily 8:30am-9:30pm; free; Metro: Copilco, Metrobús: Ciudad Universitaria

Casa del Risco

The Centro Cultural Isidro Fabela, better known by its original name, Casa del Risco, is located in a 17th-century mansion, right in front of the Plaza San Jacinto in downtown San Ángel. Politician and judge Isidro Fabela donated the home, long a private residence and now a historic landmark, to the city in 1958, along with his collection of baroque European and colonial-era Mexican art and furnishings, including works by notable names from New Spain, like Miguel Cabrera. The seven rooms, distributed across three floors, are nicely restored and connected by outdoor breezeways. One of the most striking features of the museum is the large Mexican baroque wall fountain in the main courtyard, which is decorated with dozens of round Talavera ceramic plates, interspersed with hand-painted tiles and seashells. Admission is free.

MAP 6: Plaza San Jacinto 15, 55/5616-2711, www.museocasadelrisco.org; Tues.-Sun. 10am-5pm; free; Metro: Miguel Ángel de Quevedo

Plaza San Jacinto

The fine cobblestone plaza at the heart of San Ángel is ringed by cafés and restaurants. Although it's just a couple of blocks from a sea of traffic on Insurgentes and Avenida Revolución, wandering around the relaxed plaza

makes it easy to imagine San Ángel as a village far from Mexico City. On Saturdays, local artists sell work in the square, turning the plaza into a *jardín del arte* (art garden).

Iglesia de San Jacinto

Up San Jacinto street, on the west side of the plaza, the Iglesia de San Jacinto was once part of a Dominican monastery built between 1564 and 1614. Notable are the principal retablo inside and the carved stone *cruz atrial* (atrium cross) standing in front of the church. The beautiful walled gardens in front of the church are a favorite venue for weekend wedding parties.

MAP 6: Av. Madero at San Jacinto; Metro: Miguel Ángel de Quevedo, Metrobús: La Bombilla or Dr. Gálvez

Museo de El Carmen

A former Carmelite monastery, built between 1615 and 1626, is a fitting backdrop to the collection of Mexican colonial art and furniture at this wonderful museum. Including oil paintings, sculpture, and religious pieces from the 17th and 18th centuries, the large and interesting collection has been overseen by INAH (National Institute of Art and History) since the 1930s; the organization opened the museum here in 1955.

Once the religious and economic center of San Ángel, the convent housed an order of Carmelite nuns. While touring the museum, note the vestry (where priests' robes were hung), with its elaborate, gold-leaf carvings; the old bathroom and wash-basins with Talavera-tile bowls; and the beautiful crypt downstairs, where naturally mummified bodies were discovered and are now on display in a somewhat macabre exhibit. Next door, the adjoining church, Iglesia de El Carmen, with its three beautiful tile-covered domes, was built in 1624. MAP 6: Av. Revolución 9, 55/5616-2816, www.museodeelcarmen.gob.mx; Tues.-Sun. 10am-5pm; US$3.50 adults, free for students and teachers, free on Sun.; Metro: Miguel Ángel de Quevedo or Barranca del Muerto, Metrobús: La Bombilla or Dr. Gálvez

Greater Mexico City   Map 7

GREATER MEXICO CITY

Poliforum Siqueiros

On Insurgentes Sur, in the shadow of the 50-story World Trade Center de México, this eye-catching arts complex is covered with huge three-dimensional murals created by artist David Alfaro Siqueiros. Commissioned by ex-revolutionary Manuel Suárez, the mural was originally intended for a building in Cuernavaca, but the project was relocated to its present site in 1965, opening in 1977.

Inside, in the second-floor Foro Universal, Siqueiros created a massive, three-dimensional mural entitled *La Marcha de la Humanidad* (The March of Humanity), a tribute to men and women who fought to better society. It's generally open to the public 10am-6pm, and there are audio sessions at noon and 2pm on Saturdays and Sundays, when visitors can hear Siqueiros describe the inspiration for the work while the entire room rotates.

On the ground floor, the Espacio Arte Emergente often mounts rotating exhibits by contemporary artists, and there's a nice café, if you want to linger.

MAP 7: Insurgentes Sur 701, 55/5536-4520, www.polyforumsiqueiros.com; daily 9am-7pm; US$2 Foro Universal; gallery free; Metro: San Pedro de los Pinos or Eugenia, Metrobús: Poliforum

Basílica de Santa María de Guadalupe

At every hour of every day, there are pilgrims arriving at the Basílica de Santa María de Guadalupe in northern Mexico City. It was here, on December 12, 1531, that Saint Juan Diego had a vision of a dark-skinned, Nahuatl-speaking Virgin Mary, whose image miraculously appeared imprinted on his shroud. Since the 16th century, numerous chapels have been built on the site, most recently, the modern basilica, designed by architect Pedro Ramírez Vásquez in 1976. Here, you can get a closer look at Juan Diego's shroud, which hangs behind the altar, where a moving walkway helps prevent human traffic jams. It is particularly crowded on and around December 12, the anniversary of the date when the Virgin appeared to Juan Diego.

VIRGEN DE GUADALUPE: A NEW WORLD MARY

The Virgin of Guadalupe is one of the most powerful and well-known images in Mexico: a dark-skinned Virgin Mary, eyes cast downward, dressed in robes of green, white, and red and standing atop an angel. Synonymous with Mexican Catholicism and, for many centuries, Mexican nationalism, this mighty symbol's origins can be traced back to a hillside in northern Mexico City.

According to oral history, in December 1531, the image of a dark-skinned Virgin Mary first appeared to a Mexica man named Juan Diego Cuauhtlatoatzin, speaking to him in his native Nahuatl language and asking him to build a shrine in her honor on the hill at Tepeyac, previously the site of a Mexica pyramid dedicated to the goddess Tonantzin. Church authorities initially ignored Juan Diego's entreaties, but the Virgin appeared again, instructing him to gather roses in his cloak and carry them to the bishop to prove the validity of his story.

Following her instructions, Juan Diego visited the bishop a second time. He opened the cloak before the assembled clergymen, displaying a detailed image of the Virgin he had seen. The bishop was dazzled by the image, declaring it a miracle; construction of the church at Tepeyac began. Juan Diego lived the rest of his life on the hill at Tepeyac. Today, his shroud hangs in the modern **Basílica de Santa María de Guadalupe**.

The appearance of the Virgin of Guadalupe is believed to have been a watershed moment in the spread of Christianity to the New World. In the early colonial era, Spanish settlers and missionaries struggled to introduce native people to Catholicism; the story of the Nahuatl-speaking Virgin of Guadalupe inspired mass conversion in Mexico City. Later, she was credited with stopping the spread of an early measles epidemic, and miracles were thereafter repeatedly attributed to her beneficence. Declared the patroness of Mexico, she became a symbol of the New World. Indeed, the image would become synonymous with Mexico during the Mexican War of Independence, when leader Miguel Hidalgo used a banner with the image of the Virgin of Guadalupe as a flag to lead the Mexican army into battle against the Spanish.

While the significance of the icon is immense, details of the Virgin's origin story have long been debated. Little is known about the life of Juan Diego, who has been described as both a peasant and a Mexica nobleman. Neither the Virgin of Guadalupe nor Juan Diego is mentioned in the surviving early-colonial accounts from Mexico City. Numerous historians (and even some high-ranking church authorities) have questioned if Juan Diego existed at all.

Others point out that the many curiosities related to the shroud itself suggest the intervention of a divine power. According to some studies, the 47 stars in the image represent the exact constellations seen over Mexico on the night of the winter solstice 1531. The pigments are also of unknown origin, and unusual for the time period. Plus, no one can deny that the colors of the shroud have remained remarkably bright, despite several hundred years on display, the latest of which have allowed flash photography.

Controversies, however, have had little influence on the fervent following of the Virgen de Guadalupe. Her shrine is the second-most-visited Catholic pilgrimage site in the world, after the Vatican, with an estimated six million people visiting each year (including 300,000 visitors arriving on her feast day, December 12). The Catholic church has also embraced the Virgen de Guadalupe. Saint Juan Diego was canonized by Pope John Paul II on July 31, 2002. He is the first indigenous American saint.

You can reach the basilica via Metro La Villa, or take buses marked "La Villa" on the Paseo de la Reforma to the final stop, then walk to the church.

MAP 7: Plaza de las Américas 1, Col. Villa de Guadalupe, 55/5118-0500, www.virgendeguadalupe.org.mx; daily 6am-9pm; free; Metro: La Villa

Canals at Xochimilco

The Mexica city of Tenochtitlán, built atop Lake Texcoco, was ribboned with canals and surrounded by *chinampas*, or floating gardens. In the southern neighborhood of Xochimilco, a small segment of this once-massive canal system remains intact. Visitors to Xochimilco can explore the main canals on colorful *trajineras*

THE FLOATING GARDENS OF XOCHIMILCO

According to the Códice Ramírez, Xochimilco ("place where flowers grow") was originally founded on an island in the Lago de Xochimilco in AD 919 by a Nahuatl-speaking tribe that called themselves Xochimilcas.

Around the 13th century, the people living in Xochimilco and Chalco (today communities in southern Mexico City) developed an ingenious farming system atop the broad lakes of the Valley of Mexico. To help support a continual harvest in the area, the Xochimilcas built a network of floating gardens, or *chinampas*—cultivated, manmade islands that were assembled using reeds, tree limbs, and earth, some anchored to the lakebed through the roots of willow trees. Benefiting from the fertile soil beneath the lake, agriculture flourished on the *chinampas*.

After the Mexica people established Tenochtitlán in Lake Texcoco and exerted their dominance over the Valley of Mexico, they conquered Xochimilco and extended the *chinampas* to their own island city. Eventually, the *chinampas* became so numerous that they were divided by canals leading in and out of Tenochtitlán, and were tended by farmers who pushed along the lake in canoes. The hydroponic gardens were essential to the survival of Tenochtitlán, producing an estimated 100 million pounds of maize every year.

After the conquest and destruction of Tenochtitlán, the Spanish drained the canals to build roads in and out of Mexico City. As it was an important source of food, much of Xochimilco was left intact, but, over time, the expanding metropolis encroached on the community, and new farming techniques supplanted the traditional style. Of the estimated 40,000 *chinampas* found in Xochimilco at the beginning of the 18th century, only 15,000 were left when the 20th century began.

Canoe vendors began serving snacks to weekend visitors around 1920, followed by the first restaurants on the embarcaderos. Around this same time, traditional *trajineras*, poled barges used for transporting local cargo along the canals, were transformed into tour boats by the addition of seats, tables, tarp roofs, and colorful flower-covered facades. Today, it is a popular destination in the south of the city.

Vegetables and flowers continue to grow on the *chinampas* today, and floriculture is the region's principle source of income. **Mercado Xóchitl** (Av. 16 de Septiembre s/n, Col. Barrio El Rosario) in the center of town, **Mercado de Plantas Madreselva** (Calle Madreselva 3, next to the bosque de Nativitas) in the south of town, and **Mercado de Plantas y Flores Cuemanco** (Periférico Sur, Col. Cuemanco) next to the Parque Ecológico are the main plant markets. Native flora can be seen along the banks of the canals, including bulrushes, pepper trees, camphor, *jarilla*, *toloache*, and Mexican poppy.

(flat-bottomed rafts), where canoes paddle alongside you to sell handmade quesadillas, beer, and other snacks, while musicians float by, playing songs for commission. Alternatively, you can ask the boatman to take you to the *canales virgenes*, where people still live and grow food, offering an interesting look into traditional life in this neighborhood.

To reach Xochimilco by public transportation, take Metro Line 2 to Tasqueña, then take the Tren Ligero (light rail) to Xochimilco. Several *embarcaderos* (docks) are close to the Tren Ligero station, along Calle Violeta, off Avenida Cuauhtémoc. Embarcadero Nativitas is about a 30-minute walk. The price for a ride on a *trajinera* is about US$20 per hour. **MAP 7:** Calle Violeta, Xochimilco; boats daily 8am-8pm; US$20 per hour for a boat that holds up to 12 people; Tren Ligero: Xochimilco

Cuicuilco

Only a few round ruins remain in Cuicuilco, once a settlement of 20,000. The city was built in approximately 600 BC, and the ceremonial center was active 600-200 BC. The main religious site, an unusual 118-meter-long circular-shaped platform, was topped with a ceremonial altar. Volcán Xitle, which looms to the south, buried the base of the pyramid, along with the rest of the ceremonial center, with lava. Much of the lava has been removed, making it possible to see the construction of the pyramid.

The small site museum provides more information about Cuicuilco's inhabitants and displays some artifacts found at the site. Visitors can also walk along the footpaths in the small surrounding nature preserve. It's easiest to arrive via Metrobús, but you can also take a bus marked Cuicuilco from the Universidad Metro station.

MAP 7: Just south of the intersection of Insurgentes and Periférico Sur, Col. Isidro Fabela, 55/5606-9758; daily 9am-5pm; US$2.50; Metro: Universidad, Metrobús: Villa Olímpica

Tlalpan

Tlalpan is a lesser-known colonial-era settlement on the southern edge of the city. Tlalpan's heart is the Plaza de la Constitución, a lovely public square with swaying trees and iron benches. On the east side of the plaza is the 17th-century Iglesia de San Agustín de las Cuevas, surrounded by well-kept gardens. Behind the municipal building, on the south side of the plaza, Mercado de la Paz is a large market good for a quick bite. Cross the street to have a drink at La Jaliscience, a charming old cantina.

Next, follow Moneda east to the Capilla de las Capuchinas, designed by architect Luis Barragán.

Iglesia de San Agustín de las Cuevas in Tlalpan

Most visitors come by taxi, but the extension of the Metrobús has made it relatively easy, albeit time-consuming, to get to Tlalpan via public transport. From anywhere along Insurgentes, take a southbound Metrobús marked El Caminero past the university to the Fuentes Brotantes stop; the center of Tlalpan is a few blocks east.

MAP 7: Between Insurgentes Sur and Calz. De Tlalpan, Calvario and Av. San Fernando; Metrobús: Fuentes Brotantes

RESTAURANTS

With its multitude of aromatic taco stands, fine-dining restaurants, and mom-and-pop *fondas,* Mexico City is an unquestionably wonderful place to eat. These days, it's not uncommon for visitors to come to the city specifically to dine.

housemade salsas

The city's food culture spans classes, neighborhoods, and milieus. *Chilangos* are serious eaters, profoundly omnivorous, and discriminating even when snacking on the street. As a result, you will find good things to eat in every neighborhood and at every price point.

Quick bites at street stands and in neighborhood markets are ubiquitous, and, by many accounts, are among the best bites in the city. Tacos are a mainstay of the local diet, but you'll also see hundreds of other snacks for sale, including tamales, fresh fruit, seafood cocktails, smoked plantains, deep-fried quesadillas, and corn-flatbread-based snacks like *tlacoyos.* At some popular street stands, you can see a full pig being carved for *carnitas* as commuters rush past to the Metro.

Until recently, eateries in the capital were largely traditional places—family-style restaurants, small *fondas,* or taco joints—and happily, many of these old-school places continue to thrive. Recently, however, city residents with more disposable income, foodie tourists, and inventive chefs have brought Mexico City to the forefront of the world food scene with some excellent contemporary Mexican restaurants. There are also more Thai, Japanese, Italian, and Indian restaurants than ever before, and many Mexican restaurants are experimenting with a fusion of ingredients and preparations from other cultures.

✪ **BEST CLASSIC CUISINE:** Try *mole negro, chiles en nogada,* and other traditional Mexican dishes at **El Cardenal,** a beloved restaurant in the Centro Histórico (page 108).

✪ **COOLEST NEW-SCHOOL SPOT IN THE CENTRO:** The Centro's traditional atmosphere is well served by **Azul Histórico,** which offers creative contemporary Mexican food in a pretty courtyard (page 108).

✪ **MOST HISTORIC ATMOSPHERE:** With its opulent 19th-century ambience, bow-tied wait staff, and traditional menu, **Bar La Ópera** is the city's most charming cantina (page 111).

✪ **FINEST OLD-FASHIONED LUNCH:** An opulent colonial-era palace houses **Casino Español,** an elegant, old-fashioned Spanish restaurant (page 114).

✪ **BEST HOUSE SPECIALTY:** Cantina **La Polar**'s rich and hearty *birria* (goat stew) is legendary (page 120).

✪ **SWEETEST SPOT:** Since the 1930s, **La Especial de Paris** has been serving handmade ice creams and *nieves* in intense flavors like cacao and coconut (page 121).

✪ **TOP FOODIE DESTINATION:** Chef Enrique Olvera has garnered worldwide celebrity for the modernist Mexican food served in his Polanco restaurant **Pujol,** a must for food-obsessed travelers (page 122).

✪ **MOST EXCITING NEIGHBORHOOD CHEF:** Focused on local ingredients and inventive preparations, **Máximo Bistrot Local** is a cozy neighborhood gem (page 133).

✪ **BEST MEZCAL PAIRINGS:** Pair grasshopper-topped guacamole and crispy hibiscus tacos with a shot of artisanal mezcal at **Corazón de Maguey** (page 135).

✪ **BEST BITES FOR THE EARLY BIRD:** By the time it opens at 5:30am, regulars are already filing into **Fonda Margarita,** where fragrant daily specials are cooked in traditional clay pots (page 140).

PRICE KEY

$	Entrées less than US$10
$ $	Entrées US$10-20
$ $ $	Entrées more than US$20

Centro Histórico

Map 1

MEXICAN

Balcón del Zócalo $$

For first-time visitors to Mexico City, lunching at one of the many restaurants overlooking the Zócalo is a memorable must. While most of these touristy establishments offer surly service and overpriced steak, Balcón del Zócalo, on the top floor of the Zócalo Central hotel, offers a surprisingly nice menu of well-prepared Mexican food, a lovely plant-filled dining room, and, most important, a gorgeous view, overlooking the eastern wing of the cathedral.

MAP 1: Av. 5 de Mayo 61, 55/5130-5130, www.balcondelzocalo.mx; daily 7am-11pm; Metro: Zócalo

✪ El Cardenal $$

This classic spot serves traditional Mexican dishes from across the republic, in addition to seasonal specials, like Valencia-style salt cod at Christmas. With baskets of fresh breads and pitchers of hot chocolate, breakfast is a popular meal here, though you'll find many interesting options, from moles to Oaxacan-style *chiles rellenos,* on the lovely lunch and dinner menu. The original location on Palma occupies a beautiful French-style mansion, but there are several other branches, including in the Hilton Mexico City Reforma (Juárez 70, Centro, 55/5518-6632) and in San Ángel (Av. de la Paz 32, San Ángel, 55/5550-0293).

MAP 1: Palma 23, 55/5521-8815, www. elcardenal.com.mx; Mon.-Sat. 8am-6:30pm, Sun. 8:30am-6pm; Metro: Zócalo

Roldán 37 $$

Deep within the Merced commercial district, a pedestrian street leads to an old two-story home where chef Rómulo Mendoza's family once stored green chile peppers that were sold at city markets. Today, that home has been transformed into a lovely traditional restaurant, where Mendoza and his team serve what they describe as food "from the Merced." The specialty here is *chiles rellenos,* served in a wide variety of styles; they even serve drinks in a hollowed-out poblano pepper.

MAP 1: Roldán 37, 55/5542-1951; daily noon-7pm; Metro: Pino Suárez or Merced

Sanborns de los Azulejos $$

Owned by billionaire Carlos Slim, Sanborns has hundreds of locations across the city. It's not uncommon to see one Sanborns directly across the street from the one you're sitting in. The restaurant's ubiquity has made it an institution in the capital, and if there's one Sanborns you should visit, it's the Casa de los Azulejos. Occupying the patio of a gorgeous 16th-century palace adorned with hand-painted tiles, the dining room is perpetually packed with locals lingering over coffee.

MAP 1: Av. Madero 4, 55/5512-1331, www. sanborns.com.mx; daily 7am-11:30pm; Metro: Bellas Artes

✪ Azul Histórico $$

Chef Ricardo Muñoz Zurita's Azul Histórico is set in the tree-shaded courtyard of a colonial-era palace,

CLASSIC CUISINE

There is an astonishing diversity of places to eat in Mexico City. For visitors, exploring these contrasts is part of the fun, joining commuters for a plate of *carnitas* outside the Metro stop at lunchtime, then savoring a multicourse feast at an elegant restaurant for dinner.

PUESTOS AND TAQUERÍAS
In any neighborhood, you'll find a multitude of **puestos,** or street stands, often crowded around areas where there's lots of foot traffic, like outside a Metro station or office buildings. If you see a crowd around a *puesto,* it's a good bet that the food will be tasty.

A step up from balancing your plate in one hand and taco in the other, **taquerías** are simple sit-down eateries (sometimes with a bar and barstools only) that serve tacos and other snacks, while a **tortería** is the same, but for *tortas.* The Condesa is a good place to try some of the best *taquerías* in the city, including *tacos-al-pastor* temples El Tizoncito and El Califa.

cooking *tortas*

FONDAS, COMEDORES, AND CANTINAS
You can have a very inexpensive sit-down meal in the city's many **fondas** or **comedores,** small independent restaurants that usually serve breakfast, *almuerzo,* and *comida.* At many of these places, the main offering is an inexpensive afternoon *comida corrida:* a three- or four-course meal that usually includes a drink, soup, rice, entrée, and dessert. You'll see these casual eateries throughout the city, particularly in places where there are a lot of office workers. A wait for a table around 2pm is often an indication that you've found a good *fonda.*

Also casual, **cantinas** are bars that serve food in addition to drinks, with some boasting remarkably good kitchens. Many offer free *botanas* (snacks) when you order drinks, which, in some places, can become a filling meal after a few beers or tequilas. Some cantinas have become so popular for eating that they are more like restaurants than bars. One worth noting is La Polar, in the San Rafael, where the *birria* (goat meat) stew is famous.

RESTAURANTES
Restaurantes are the most formal designation for an eatery with table service, though there's a very wide diversity of restaurants worth visiting in Mexico City, from an incredibly casual spot like low-key Los Chamorros de Mérida in the Roma to a hot new neighborhood destination drawing hipsters and foodies, such as superlative Máximo Bistrot Local or newer Fonda Fina, both in the Roma, or an ultra-elegant fine-dining restaurant; Pujol in Polanco is the most famous and beloved restaurant in this category.

Azul Histórico

which it shares with the Downtown Hotel and the Shops at Downtown. Its charming yet relaxed atmosphere is well suited to a leisurely Sunday lunch and also goes perfectly with the restaurant's appealing menu of creatively rendered Mexican dishes. With heavy influence from Veracruz, Campeche, and other southern states, the menu includes dishes like *ceviche verde* and hibiscus-stuffed tacos, in addition to monthly specials that showcase more unusual dishes from across the republic.

MAP 1: Isabel la Católica 30, 55/5510-1316, www.azul.rest; Mon.-Sat. 9am-11:30pm, Sun. 9am-9pm; Metro: Zócalo

Café de Tacuba $$

Occupying two floors of a 17th-century mansion, this old-fashioned family restaurant has long been a keynote establishment in the Centro Histórico. The fun of eating here is enjoying the Old Mexico atmosphere in the dining room, with its tall wood-beamed ceilings, pretty frescos, and old oil paintings. Fittingly, the kitchen serves a range of traditional dishes, like chicken in *pipián* (a sauce of ground pumpkin seeds and spices), enchiladas, and *sopes* (round corn cakes topped with beans and cheese).

MAP 1: Tacuba 28, 55/5521-2048, www.cafedetacuba.com.mx; daily 8am-11:30pm; Metro: Allende

Limosneros $$

The low-lit, stone-walled dining room at Limosneros provides an elegant accompaniment to the restaurant's menu of beautifully prepared Mexican food. You'll find some unusual ingredients and preparations in dishes like squash flowers stuffed with cheese, mushrooms, and walnuts; rabbit "carnitas"; or soup with *quelites* (traditional Mexican greens). It's all nicely complemented by a small-batch mezcal or glass of Mexican wine from the restaurant's well-chosen list.

MAP 1: Ignacio Allende 3, 55/5521-5576, www.limosneros.com.mx; Mon. 1:30pm-10pm, Tues.-Sat. 1:30pm-11pm, Sun. 1pm-6pm; Metro: Allende

Zéfiro $$

The culinary school at the Universidad Claustro del Sor Juana operates one of the best-known chef-training programs in the country, with a course of instruction that focuses entirely on Mexican ingredients and preparations. At Zéfiro, the school's elegant student-run restaurant, you can taste the work of the Claustro's burgeoning chefs, who design the menu and helm the kitchen. Most diners come for the weekday four-course lunch, which changes monthly and often mixes traditional and contemporary flavors.

MAP 1: San Jerónimo 24, 55/5709-7983, http://elclaustro.edu.mx/claustronomia; Tues.-Fri. 1pm-5pm, Sat. 1pm-6pm; Metro: Isabel la Católica

Restaurante Chon $$

A down-to-earth eatery in the bustling Merced district, Restaurante Chon has a unique menu based largely on unusual and pre-Hispanic ingredients and recipes. Come here to try crocodile meat, *venado con huitlacoche* (venison with corn fungus), and *chinicuiles* (caterpillars) among other exotic dishes. (Note that based on seasonal availability, not all the dishes on the menu may be offered.) Despite its rather scruffy location, Chon's dining room is clean and relaxed, drawing tourists and locals alike.

MAP 1: Regina 160, 55/5542-0873; Mon.-Sat. 12:30pm-7pm; Metro: Merced or Pino Suárez

Hostería Santo Domingo $$

Opened in 1860, this Centro establishment is the oldest operating restaurant in the capital. Not surprisingly, it is a place of great tradition, with an atmosphere and menu typical of old family-style eateries throughout the country. The *hostería* is known for its *chiles en nogada* (poblano peppers stuffed with meat, dried fruits, and nuts, then bathed in a creamy walnut sauce), which are generally regarded as the city's best, though the menu also features excellent *mole poblano*, soups, and appetizers.

MAP 1: Belisario Domínguez 72, 55/5510-1434 and 55/5526-5276; Mon.-Sat. 9am-10pm, Sun. 9am-9pm; Metro: Allende

Café El Popular $

Chinese-owned bakeries were ubiquitous in Mexico City during the early 20th century. Owned by immigrants, these cafés originally served Chinese food and breads, but their menus gradually became more Mexican than international. Among the few survivors in this unique genre, old-fashioned Café El Popular has two locations on Cinco de Mayo—the more charming of which is the smaller spot to the east. It's a perfect place for breakfast accompanied by a *café con leche*, served in a glass tumbler at your table.

MAP 1: Cinco de Mayo 50 and 52, 55/5518-6081, www.cafeelpopular.com.mx; daily 24 hours; Metro: Bellas Artes

Coox Hanal $

Food from the Yucatán peninsula mixes native spices with European and Lebanese influences to create some of the most distinctive and delicious cuisine in Mexico. This long-running lunch spot opened in 1953, specializes in Yucatec food. During the early-afternoon lunch rush, it is always bustling with locals filling up on inexpensive specialties such as *sopa de lima* (lemon soup) or *papadzules* (tortillas stuffed with egg and covered in a pumpkin-seed sauce).

MAP 1: Isabel la Católica 83, 55/5709-3613, www.cooxhanal.com, daily 10:30am-6pm; Metro: Isabel la Católica

CANTINAS

✪ Bar La Ópera $$

This historic cantina has been in operation since 1895, and the old-fashioned interior is filled with French-inspired carved-wood panels, glittering mirrors, and globe lamps. Waiters in vests and bow ties attend to the evening crowd of locals and tourists, who come hoping to locate the bullet hole that Pancho Villa allegedly shot into the cantina's tin ceiling. Atmosphere trumps the food here, but Mexican snacks, like chorizo, guacamole, and *queso fundido* (a pot of melted cheese), are nicely done.

MAP 1: Av. Cinco de Mayo 10, 55/5512-8959, www.barlaopera.com; Mon.-Sat. 1pm-midnight, Sun. 1pm-6pm; Metro: Bellas Artes

Salón Corona $

This convivial family-owned cantina opened in 1928 and has since expanded to several locations beyond the original spot on Bolívar. It's a friendly, bustling place with good eats and cold drinks, perfect for watching a Sunday-afternoon soccer game or passing an evening with beer and bar snacks, like beef tacos in *mole verde* (green mole) and *tortas al pastor* (chile-rubbed pork sandwiches). If the tables are full, there's a second branch nearby, at Filomena Mata 18.

MAP 1: Bolívar 24, 55/5512-9007, www. saloncorona.com.mx; daily 8am-2am; Metro: Allende

TACOS, *TORTAS*, AND SNACKS

Casa del Pavo

Casa del Pavo $

If you like a throwback (and a bargain), this tiny sandwich shop seems to have changed nothing more than

its lightbulbs during its hundred-plus years in operation. The worn leatherette booths are often filled with seniors and students filling up on the namesake turkey, which is served in heaping *tortas* (sandwiches). Just a few doors down, La Rambla (Motolinia 38, 55/5512-9260) is another old-time *torta* shop with a notably vintage feel.

MAP 1: Motolinia 40, 55/5518-4282; daily 9am-8pm; Metro: Allende

Los Cocuyos $

When celebrity chef and adventurous eater Anthony Bourdain came to Mexico City for his television show *No Reservations,* his hosts quickly escorted him to this long-running street stand, where the specialty is beef tacos with a "nose to tail" approach. Despite its Hollywood connections, don't expect any glamour at this sidewalk joint. Call out your order over the vats of sizzling meats, then prepare to dine standing on the sidewalk.

MAP 1: Bolívar 56; daily 10am-5am; Metro: San Juan Letrán

SEAFOOD
El Danubio $$

El Danubio is often heralded as the best seafood restaurant in the Centro, and the pride of that moniker emanates throughout the dining room, which is decorated with autographs of the famous people who dined here. El Danubio has been in business since 1938, and food is old-fashioned yet delicious, with a strong Spanish influence. House specialties, like the *sopa verde* (green seafood soup) and *langostinos* (grilled crawfish) go equally well with a glass of Rioja or a shot of tequila.

MAP 1: Uruguay 3, 55/5512-0912, www. danubio.com; daily 1pm-10pm; Metro: San Juan Letrán

COFFEE TOWN

Mexico is a coffee-producing country, with high-quality beans cultivated in the southern states. In the capital, particularly in the Centro Histórico and the San Juan, the scent of roasting beans is a regular delight. Until recently, however, the cafés peddling Mexican beans were small and old-fashioned, hardly competition for the major chains.

The landscape has changed. With the introduction of enthusiastic roasters and brewers, coffee has become a highlight of a trip to the capital. Here are just some of the notable places to get your caffeine fix:

THE INDEPENDENTS
In addition to operating three coffee shops, the folks at **Buna Café Rico** (www.buna.mx) roast their own beans at a "coffee lab" in the Colonia Doctores. Taste their work at the spacious shop **B42** (Orizaba 42, 55/6724-5578), just north of the Plaza Río de Janeiro in the Roma, or at the **Mercado Roma** (page 129). **Espressarte** (Monterrey 151, 55/4171-1969) roasts carefully selected beans from Chiapas, Oaxaca, and other Mexican regions and uses French press, Chemex, and other brewing methods in their Roma shop; try the excellent cold brew. **Cucurucho** not only roasts beautiful Mexican coffees; the design in their shops is playful and contemporary. In the cool south Roma branch (Tonalá 183, 55/5264-1285), a whimsical mural covers the wall behind the espresso machine. **Café Avellaneda** (page 137) in Coyoacán is tiny, but it's regarded as one of the city's best new coffee roasters.

THE BREWERS AND BUYERS
Supporting small coffee farmers is a mission at **Drip Specialty Coffee** (Río Lerma 45, 55/5566-1432, www.dripspecialtycoffee.com), a little shop in the Cuauhtémoc where you can get espresso drinks, cold brew, or a Chemex. At **Cardinal** (page 134) in the Roma, caffeine lovers can expect high-quality Mexican beans, specially selected to complement their artisanal brewing methods, like siphon and Aeropress. At **Centro Café** (Galveston 21, 55/5575-2230) in the Napoles, each barista has a signature bean paired with a recommended brewing method; the staff can help you decide which "author" creates your drink.

THE BIG(GER) GUYS
Café Punto del Cielo (www.puntadelcielo.com.mx) is a Mexican-owned coffee franchise that sells Mexican beans and espresso drinks. You'll see their nice, modern shops throughout the capital, including a spacious branch just below the Monumento a la Revolución Mexicana (Av. Plaza de la República 48, 55/535-1595) and another in the Shops at Downtown (Isabel la Católica 30, 55/5538-1610). **Cielito Querido** is a chain of coffee shops selling only Mexican products, with a menu that mixes espresso drinks with traditional Mexican options, like *café de olla* (coffee boiled with cinnamon and raw cane sugar). Their shops, like the large branch in the Zona Rosa (Reforma 234, 55/5533-9905), all take design cues from traditional *rotulistas*, or sign painters, in Mexico.

THE OLD GUARD
Mexico's coffee culture got its start long ago, as evidenced by the many long-running cafes and roasters in the Centro Histórico. Though **Café Jekemir** (page 114) may not use newfangled extraction methods, this old shop has been roasting Mexican beans since the early 20th century, when it was founded by a Lebanese immigrant. Many locals stop in for a cup or a bag of beans. In the San Juan, **Café El Cordobés** (Ayuntamiento 18, 55/5510-2413) is another long-running spot, opened in 1937. **Café La Habana** (page 115), with its hand-pulled espresso machine, is a great place to try a *café con leche*, made with house-roasted coffee.

MIDDLE EASTERN
Al Andalus **$**

There was a large influx of Lebanese immigrants to Mexico in the early 20th century, and as a result, you'll find some fine Middle Eastern cuisine in the capital. Among the best, Al Andalus, tucked into the heart of what was once a predominantly immigrant district, is in a renovated two-story

colonial house, with professional, efficient service and a menu of excellent Middle Eastern specialties, like shawarma, hummus, and *kepa bola* (a mix of wheat, ground beef, and onion).
MAP 1: Mesones 171, 55/5522-2528; daily 9am-6pm; Metro: Pino Suárez

El Ehden $

Located on the second floor of a large mansion, tucked between the many textile merchants of Venustiano Carranza, this off-the-beaten-track Lebanese restaurant is a clean and simple spot, often filled with locals in the afternoon and evening. Stacks of warm pita accompany dishes like grilled lamb, *jocoque* (Middle Eastern-style strained yogurt), stuffed grape leaves, and other regional specialties. There are plenty of options for vegetarians.
MAP 1: Venustiano Carranza 148, 2nd fl., 55/5542-2320; daily noon-6pm; Metro: Zócalo

Productos Helus $

Even though it's hidden down a narrow passageway off a bustling street in the Merced district, it's easy to spot this wonderful Middle Eastern deli at lunch time, when a long line snakes out the door and into the street. As locals know, it's worth the wait for house-baked pita bread, olives, *kepes* (lamb meatballs), tahini, and a wide range of honey-drenched desserts. If you manage to snag one of five small tables inside, you can eat on the spot.
MAP 1: República del Salvador 157, 55/5542-2693, www.productoshelus.com.mx; Mon.-Sat. 9am-7pm; Metro: Pino Suárez

SPANISH
✪ Casino Español $$

Worth a visit for the Old World ambience alone, the Casino Español is an old-fashioned Spanish restaurant housed in a gorgeous early-20th-century mansion, with soaring ceilings, massive chandeliers, and stained-glass windows creating an opulent backdrop to the menu of delicious, traditional dishes like paella and *lechón* (suckling pig). There is a less formal café downstairs, popular for lunch with locals, but if you want the full experience, head to the more serious dining room upstairs, order a glass of Rioja, and make an afternoon of it.
MAP 1: Isabel la Católica 31, 55/5521-8894, www.cassatt.mx; daily 8am-6pm; Metro: Allende

COFFEE AND SWEETS
Café Jekemir $

Grab a sidewalk table at this always-bustling coffeehouse while recharging with some top-quality caffeine. This long-running café traces its roots back to the 1930s. Here, baristas churn out a steady stream of coffee and espresso drinks, all made from 100 percent Mexican beans for a crowd of neighborhood locals, students, and intellectuals. If you like what you sip, they also sell bags of whole beans and ground coffee.
MAP 1: Isabel la Católica 88 A-B, 55/5709-7086, http://cafejekemir.com; Mon.-Sat. 8am-9pm; Metro: Isabel la Católica

Churrería El Moro $

Hidden within the chaos of the Eje Central, this old-time café specializes in a very Mexican sugar fix: churros and hot chocolate, a match-made-in-heaven combination for a rainy afternoon. Peer into the window-front kitchen to see how the churros are swirled by hand into large crunchy rounds, 24 hours a day. The simple

1935-vintage atmosphere makes the experience all the sweeter: blue-and-white tiles on the walls, wood-beamed ceilings, and Formica tables provide a quintessentially Mexican backdrop for a quintessentially Mexican treat.

MAP 1: Eje Central 42, 55/5512-0896; daily 24 hours; Metro: San Juan Letrán

Pastelería Ideal $

Opened in 1927, Pastelería Ideal is a traditional Mexican bakery specializing in *pan dulce*, lightly sweetened rolls, pastries, buns, and empanadas that are meant to be accompanied by coffee or hot chocolate. Here, as in most old-fashioned bakeries in Mexico, you grab a tray and a set of tongs, select the bread and pastries you want from the shelves, then bring it all to the register, where they'll tally up the cost and bag it.

MAP 1: 16 de Septiembre 18, 55/5521-2233, http://pasteleriaideal.com. mx; daily 6:30am-9:30pm; Metro: San Juan Letrán

Alameda Central   Map 2

MEXICAN

La Cervecería de Barrio $$

A spinoff of the Condesa original (Vicente Suárez 38, 55/5212-1421), this casual-cool Mexican cantina serves fish tacos, seafood cocktails, ceviche-topped tostadas, and other snacks inspired by the many popular seafood joints throughout the city. Low-key and family-friendly, but stylish enough to feel special, it is a good place for a few drinks and a *fútbol* match, just across the street from the Alameda Central.

MAP 2: Avenida Juárez 64, 55/5512-4612, www.lacerveceriadebarrio.com.mx; Mon.-Tues. noon-midnight, Wed.-Sat. noon-2am, Sun. 1pm-8pm; Metro: Hidalgo or Bellas Artes

Café La Habana $

This spacious old coffeehouse has long been frequented by journalists working at the periodicals headquartered nearby. It's a wonderful spot to enjoy a traditional breakfast amid the rustling of newspapers and the whirl of ceiling fans, accompanied by one of the café's signature dark-roast drinks, which are prepared on an impressive old-fashioned, hand-pulled espresso machine. Adding to the café's legend, it is rumored Che Guevara and Fidel Castro planned the Cuban Revolution here.

MAP 2: Morelos 62, 55/5535-2620; Mon.-Sat. 7am-1am, Sun. 8am-11pm; Metro: Juárez

Fonda Santa Rita $

You'll only need to step inside this traditional *fonda* to see great promise for the traditional Mexican meal that awaits you: Heaping piles of *carnitas* are stacked in the window, cooks toast handmade tortillas on a giant *comal*, and chefs busily ladle pozole into bowls from the open kitchen. You can't go wrong with any of the economical, nicely prepared dishes here, and the simple, convivial dining room is a fun place for people-watching.

MAP 2: Independencia 11, 55/5512-4485; Sun.-Thurs. 8am-11pm, Fri.-Sat. 8am-midnight; Metro: Bellas Artes

STREET SNACKS

Mexico City has its own flavors, including a serious taste for *garnachas* (simple snacks). These quick bites, sold in parks and on street corners, might be the most distinctive aspect of the capital's food scene.

TACOS AL PASTOR

If one snack is emblematic of Mexico City, it's *tacos al pastor,* pork tacos cooked on a spit. They're typically seasoned with a spicy *adobado* rub and garnished with pineapple, cilantro, and onion (order *con todo,* if that's how you want them).

When: Late afternoon and evening

Where: El Huequito (page 118) in the Centro Histórico; El Trompito (page 120) in the Zona Rosa; El Califa (page 130) and El Tizoncito (page 131) in the Condesa.

TACOS DE GUISADO

Warm tortillas are stuffed with a variety of fillings, usually prepared and served in traditional clay pots. Fillings include *picadillo* (spiced ground beef), chile relleno (stuffed chile pepper), *tinga de pollo* (seasoned shredded chicken), hard-boiled egg, prickly pear, mushroom, or potato with chorizo.

When: Midmorning to early afternoon. Though they're normally a late breakfast or snack, they can make filling meals.

Where: On the southern pedestrian entrance to the Insurgentes traffic circle, at the corner of Insurgentes and Álvaro Obregón, and at El Jarocho (page 130) in the Roma; Tacos El Güero (page 131) and Tacos Gus (page 131) in the Condesa; La Poblanita de Tacubaya (page 123) in Tacubaya.

TLACOYOS

Dense, handmade, torpedo-shaped corn cakes are stuffed with beans, cheese, or *chicharrón* (pork rind), grilled until crunchy, then topped with nopal (prickly pear), cheese, onions, and salsa.

When: Morning-to-midafternoon.

Where: On street corners throughout the Centro Histórico and San Juan neighborhoods; outside the Mercado de Medellín (page 208) and at El Parnita (page 127) in the Roma.

TORTAS

These sandwiches are made on a *telera,* a flat white roll with a thin crust, and served with *chiles en vinagre* (pickled jalapeños). Usually warmed on a grill, the *telera* is brushed with refried beans and piled with meat, lettuce, tomato, and avocado. Popular fillings include *milanesa* (pounded and breaded beef) and eggs with chorizo. Vegetarians can order *tortas* filled with avocado, cheese, eggs, or beans.

When: Breakfast, lunch, and dinner.

Where: Outside Metro stops; on street corners throughout the city; Casa del Pavo (page 112) and La Rambla (page 112) in the Centro Histórico; El Cuadrilatero (page 117) in the San Juan neighborhood; Bravo Loncherías de México (page 119) in the Cuauhtémoc; Peltre Lonchería (page 129) in the Roma; L'Encanto de Lola (page 139) in San Ángel.

TACOS, TORTAS, AND SNACKS

El Caguamo $

A small street stand rarely gets as much press as El Caguamo, but once you sit down at this little seafood-only *puesto,* it becomes clear why it's been the subject of so much food-blog chatter. Though it's a small operation, the food here is deliciously prepared and incredibly fresh, drawing locals for ceviche-topped tostadas, deep-fried seafood quesadillas, and shrimp cocktails. Grab a barstool and order from the friendly chefs; they'll pass you a cup of shrimp-broth soup, gratis.

MAP 2: Ayuntamiento and López; daily 10am-6pm; Metro: San Juan de Letrán

PAMBAZOS

These popular sandwiches are made from a white roll (also called a *pambazo*) dipped in a mild guajillo chile sauce, stuffed with cooked potatoes and chorizo, and garnished with sour cream and lettuce.

When: All hours.

Where: At street stalls in *tianguis* (open-air markets); **Bravo Loncherías de México** (page 119) in the Cuauhtémoc; **Los Chamorros de Mérida** (page 129) in the Roma.

PLÁTANOS MACHOS

Plátanos machos (plantains) and *camotes* (sweet potatoes) are baked over mesquite coals, imparting a smoky flavor to these sweet, starchy treats. Served with sweetened condensed milk and cinnamon.

When: Early evening.

Where: Vendors roam central neighborhoods at dusk, listen for their distinctive low-pitched whistle.

TAMALES AND *ATOLE*

Tamales in *hoja de maíz* (corn husk) or *hoja de plátano* (banana leaf) are prepared as a breakfast food, often accompanied by *atole,* a warm, sweetened corn-based drink flavored with chocolate, rice, strawberry, or guava, or served natural and lightly sweetened.

When: Early mornings and dinnertime.

Where: Corner stands in the daytime; from circulating bicycles and outside traditional Mexican bakeries at night; outside churches on Sunday morning.

TORTA DE TAMAL

A stick-to-your-ribs variation on the typical *tamal* for breakfast, this is a *tamal* in corn husk, stuffed between a sliced *bolillo* (white-bread roll).

When: Early morning.

Where: Morning street-corner tamales vendors are the only place you'll find them.

ELOTES AND ESQUITES

Elotes are boiled ears of corn served on a stick, slathered in mayonnaise and sprinkled with chile powder, salt, and cheese. *Esquites* are loose corn kernels, sometimes cooked with the herb *epazote,* which are served in a small cup then topped with mayonnaise, cheese, chile powder, and lime juice.

When: Nighttime.

Where: Public squares, parks, outside churches, outside convenience stores; **Peltre Lonchería** (page 129) in the Roma.

QUESADILLAS

These fresh hand-pressed corn tortillas are stuffed with cheese and fillings, cooked on a griddle, and deep-fried in oil or lard (but some stands will skip the fryer if you request it). *Flor de calabaza* (squash flower) and *huitlacoche* (corn fungus) are popular fillings. Be aware that your quesadilla may only be filled with a *guisado* (filling) unless you specify that you'd like it *con queso* (with cheese).

When: Afternoon and evening.

Where: Parks and street corners; any restaurant.

El Cuadrilatero $

This popular neighborhood *tortería* is owned by former pro wrestler Super Astro, and the shop is decorated with *lucha libre* masks, posters, and other memorabilia from his career. The signature dish is La Gladiador, a 1.3-kilo *torta* stacked with egg, six kinds of meats, and cheese. Those who finish it in 15 minutes get the whole sandwich for free. Fortunately, any *torta* here will satisfy your appetite; try the *pierna adobado* (chile-rubbed pork), which is prepared fresh in-house.

MAP 2: Luis Moya 73, 55/5521-3060; Mon.-Sat. 7am-8pm; Metro: San Juan de Letrán

El Huequito $

Tacos al pastor are emblematic of the capital, and every *taquería* has its own secret recipe (and every local a favorite spot to get them). At El Huequito, you won't find the typical chile-rubbed *pastor,* but rather spit-roasted pork tacos that are doused in salsa and rolled into small tortillas. You can order a plate of tacos on the street, where the original stand is still in operation, or sit down in the adjoining dining room.

MAP 2: Ayuntamiento 21, 55/5518-3313, www.elhuequito.com.mx; daily 9am-10pm; Metro: San Juan Letrán

ASIAN
Café 123 $

Though just a few blocks from many prime tourist attractions, the western blocks of the street Articulo 123 feel rather rough and abandoned. It's a surprising setting for this quirky café, which shares an owner with the Roma's hit eatery Mog. In pleasant complement to its urban surroundings, the atmosphere is eclectic industrial-chic, and the appealing menu offers Asian-inspired soups, noodles, rice, pastries, and espresso drinks, principally attracting a young coffeehouse crowd.

MAP 2: Articulo 123 123, 55/5512-1772; Mon.-Wed. 9am-8pm, Thurs.-Sat. 9am-11pm; Metro: Hidalgo or Juárez

MARKETS
Mercado San Juan $

The San Juan Market is best known for its high-quality and unusual fish, meats, produce, and cheeses, but it is also a great place to nosh. Head to the market's famous cheesemongers, where you can order Spanish-style tapas, baguette sandwiches, or charcuterie and cheese plates; they'll even pour you a small glass of Spanish wine, on the house. The most famous is La Jersey (Local 147), but most cheese shops offer the same lunch specials.

MAP 2: Ernesto Pugibet between Luis Moya and Buen Tono; daily 7am-5pm; Metro: San Juan Letrán

Paseo de la Reforma   Map 3

MEXICAN
Fonda El Refugio $$

Originally founded in 1954 with the aim to preserve traditional Mexican cuisine, Fonda El Refugio was long considered one of the best traditional spots in the Zona Rosa. Under the current chef, the grandson of the restaurant's founder, the *fonda* expanded its menu to offer more vegetarian options, like enchiladas stuffed with *jamaica* (hibiscus flower). The atmosphere in the dining room pairs nicely with the food, as it's in a two-story colonial home decorated with traditional Mexican furnishings.

MAP 3: Liverpool 166, 55/5525-8128, http://fondaelrefugio.com.mx; daily 1pm-10:30pm; Metro: Insurgentes

Beatricita $

At the turn of the 20th century, a taco shop owned by Beatriz Muciño Reyes—nicknamed "La Beatricita"—was the rage in the capital. The *taquería* proliferated throughout the city, and though most branches have since closed, the Beatricita in the Zona Rosa maintains the legacy. Now a small *fonda*, La Beatricita offers tasty, inexpensive breakfast and lunch, served with a basket of handmade tortillas, so hot you can barely hold them.

MAP 3: Londres 190D, 55/5511-4213, http://beatricita.com; daily 10am-6pm; Metro: Insurgentes

Bravo Loncherías de México $

At this happening restaurant, *tortas*—warm sandwiches typically sold at small shops and street stands—get the star treatment, with fillings like melted cheese and *huauzontle* (a Mexican green) or pulled pork and onions, though there are also excellent starters and salads, all for reasonable prices. Accompany your lunch with one of the interesting beer cocktails or a glass of cucumber-mint juice, then wrap it up with *horchata* ice cream. (*Horchata* is a sweetened rice beverage.)

MAP 3: Río Sena 87, 55/5207-6276, http://lonchesbravo.mx; Mon.-Wed. 9am-11pm, Thurs.-Sat. 9am-2am, Sun. 9am-11pm; Metro: Insurgentes, Metrobús: Reforma

El Corral del Chivo $

Located in a pretty, tile-filled house on the west side of La Alameda in Santa María la Ribera, this casual *fonda* specializes in spicy, fragrant *birria*, a hearty soup made with goat meat, traditionally from the state of Jalisco. It's also a great place to try pozole, a hominy stew traditionally topped with lettuce, radishes, and chopped white onion. Freshly made tortillas are brought to your table directly from the griddle.

MAP 3: Jaime Torres Bodet 152-C, 55/5547-5609; daily 9am-11pm; Metro: Buenavista

Bravo Loncherías de México

CANTINAS
✪ La Polar $

This old-style cantina in the San Rafael neighborhood serves what is widely considered to be Mexico City's best *birria*, a stew of shredded lamb in a spicy broth, served with tortillas, onion, salsa, and avocado. A no-frills place with a loyal clientele, the cantina is often packed with crowds of locals enjoying the music by roving *norteña* and mariachi bands, accompanied by a mug of beer on tap.

MAP 3: Guillermo Prieto 129, 55/5546-5066, www.lapolar.com.mx; daily 7am-2am; Metro: San Cosme

TACOS, *TORTAS*, AND SNACKS
El Trompito $

There are few good places for a quick bite in the bustling blocks of the Zona Rosa proper, where the pedestrian corridors are clogged with a less-than-ideal mix of pricier chain restaurants and international fast-food joints. Fortunately, this hole-in-the-wall *taquería* will set you up with some legitimately delicious tacos at almost any hour of the day or night. Grab a bar stool and accompany your order of crispy *pastores* with a bowl of *frijoles charros* (stewed beans) and a cold beer.

MAP 3: Londres 119A, 55/5511-1015; daily 1pm-4am; Metro: Insurgentes

Taquería Lozano $

Just across the street from the PRI political party's headquarters, this bare-bones establishment specializes in *carnitas* (braised pork) tacos and *sesadillas,* quesadillas stuffed with *sesos* (brain) and fried in lard. When you place your order, take your pick from any part of the pig—*buche* (stomach), *trompo* (snout), or, believe it or not, *nana* (uterus)—or play it safer by ordering the tasty, light *maciza,* pulled meat, usually from the shoulder.

MAP 3: Héroes Ferrocarrileros 26, 55/5233-1920; Mon.-Sat. 9:30am-7pm; Metro: Buenavista

SEAFOOD
Boca del Río $

Trapped in another era, Boca del Río is an old-fashioned seafood palace in business since 1941, with a throwback decor and a menu straight from mid-century Mexico City. Walk past the stainless steel bar at the entrance and into the surprisingly spacious dining room with green-tile floors attended by waitresses in pink vests. The menu focuses on seafood, from deep-fried fillets to tacos, though most diners come for seafood cocktails. Preparations aren't particularly contemporary, but the experience is old-school perfection.

MAP 3: Ribera de San Cosme 42, 55/5535-0128, www.restaurantebocadelrio. com.mx; daily 11am-11pm; Metro: San Cosme

ASIAN
Rokai Izakaya Bistro $$$

On a quiet little street in the Cuauhtémoc neighborhood, this unassuming restaurant has a reputation for serving the best and most authentic Japanese food in the city, from ultrafresh sushi during the day and a set-course *omakase* (chef's menu) at night. Your supper might include ginger tofu, creatively plated ramen, or bone marrow. The menu changes daily, depending on seasonal produce and the day's catch. Inside, just 13 seats ring a clean blonde-wood bar; reservations are required.

MAP 3: Río Ebro 87, 55/5207-7543; Mon.-Sat. 1:30pm-5pm and 7pm-11pm, Sun. 1:30-11pm; Metro: Insurgentes

Nadefo $

Once you walk through the doors of this spacious Korean spot, it's hard to believe you're still in Mexico City. Here, a predominantly Korean crowd gathers around big tables, each with a central grill, lingering late into the evening over boisterous conversation and bottles of rice wine. The thing to order is cuts of raw meat (tongue, shrimp, and ribs are all excellent), which you cook tableside and top with one of the many condiments brought to the table.

MAP 3: Liverpool 183, 55/5525-0351; daily noon-11pm; Metro: Sevilla

MIDDLE EASTERN
Paprika $$

At this cozy restaurant helmed by chef Josefina Santacruz, you'll find many rich flavors inspired by the cuisines of the Middle East, North Africa, and India, yet the unique hybrid of spices and techniques creates something wholly original (and totally delicious) here. The menu lends itself to sharing, so order a bunch of plates, like the re-markably satisfying roasted eggplant with tomatoes, lamb meatballs, and lemon-kissed green beans—and then order some more.

MAP 3: Marsella 61, 55/5533-0303; Tues.-Sat. 1:30pm-11pm, Sun. 2pm-6pm; Metro: Insurgentes

Paprika

COFFEE AND SWEETS
Café Gran Premio $

This old-fashioned neighborhood coffee shop is a true throwback, pop-ulated by sundry locals and seniors dressed in ties and caps. During the daytime, many patrons seem to know each other (and the waitstaff) well, greeting each other as they come in and chatting casually between tables. The menu is limited to espresso drinks (made on a vintage machine), a few sweets, and tamales, but the people-watching is the most delectable part of the experience.

MAP 3: Antonio Caso 72, 55/5535-0934; Mon.-Sat. 8am-8pm; Metro: Revolución

Pandería Rosetta $

There was so much demand for the wonderful artisan bread made at Italian restaurant Rosetta that the owners opened a bakery across the street (Colima 179, 55/5207-2976). The bakery itself became so popular that there are now several branches across the city. For a sandwich, coffee, and perfectly flaky croissant, head to the pretty Juárez branch, set in a romantic old mansion with gold chandeliers, tile floors, and seating in a small garden.

MAP 3: Havre 73, 55/5207-7065, www. rosetta.com.mx; Mon.-Sat. 7am-8pm, Sun. 7:30am-6pm; Metro: Insurgentes

✪ La Especial de Paris $

In operation since 1921, this tiny ice-cream shop is easy to overlook along traffic-choked Insurgentes, but it is the surprising home of the best old-fash-ioned *nieves* in Mexico City. Every fla-vor here is elaborated by hand using natural ingredients, and options run from old-fashioned choices like Veracruz vanilla bean to more unique choices like ginger, cardamom, and cacao. Sit at the bar, order a cone, and listen to the friendly ice-cream scooper discuss the making of artisan sweets.

MAP 3: Insurgentes 117, 55/5591-1017; daily noon-8pm; Metro: Revolución

MARKETS
Mercado San Cosme $

Located on busy San Cosme, this old neighborhood market is friendly, uncrowded, and impeccably clean. It lacks the hustle and bustle of most of the city's shopping centers, yet still offers a broad selection of products, from piñatas to fruit to homemade yogurt. It's a great place to pick up a snack, like a quesadilla or *tamal,* or to have a full, inexpensive meal at one of the numerous small fondas offering daily *comida corrida.*

MAP 3: Ribera de San Cosme s/n, between Gabino Barredo and Altamirano, 55/6363-2923; daily 8am-8pm; Metro: San Cosme

Chapultepec and Polanco Map 4

MEXICAN
✪ Pujol $$$

Mexico City's top foodie mecca is this modernist Mexican fine-dining restaurant, one of the most celebrated places to eat in the country. Here, chef Enrique Olvera has made his name serving refined and innovative Mexican cuisine, using traditional ingredients in contemporary presentations. Diners can choose from one of two fixed-menu options, a 4-course dinner or the 13-course tasting menu, though the latter is the restaurant's signature. You may have to dodge a few bodyguard-driven SUVs parked outside the restaurant, which attracts a tony crowd, but Pujol is a memorable place to dine.

Pujol

MAP 4: Francisco Petrarca 254, 55/5545-4111, www.pujol.com.mx; Mon.-Sat. 2pm-4pm and 6:30pm-11:30pm; Metro: Polanco

Chapulín $$$

The InterContinental Presidente in Polanco is well-known for its fine in-house restaurants, and Chapulín, which opened in 2014, has continued that tradition with creative takes on traditional Mexican dishes. Try the shrimp ceviche with watermelon or turkey in *mole negro,* accompanied by a drink from the restaurant's extensive selection of small-batch mezcal, artisanal beer, and Mexican wine. The artistic, upscale dining room overlooks the surrounding forestland.

MAP 4: InterContinental Presidente Mexico City, Campos Eliseos 218, 55/5327-7700, ext. 5424, www.chapulin.rest; Mon.-Sat. 1pm-1am, Sun. 1pm-10pm; Metro: Auditorio

Dulce Patria $$$

In the ground floor of Las Alcobas hotel, this nouveau Mexican restaurant is vibrant in every way, from the magenta wine glasses set on each linen-topped table to the creative dishes that are, by design, as precious to look at as they are delicious. Run by chef Martha Ortiz, the menu reimagines Mexican recipes with inventive presentations, without losing their traditional elements, from the mole tasting pots to ceviches served with mango. The creative cocktails rival the all-Mexican wine list.

MAP 4: Anatole France 100, 55/3300-3999, www.dulcepatriamexico. com; Mon.-Sat. 1:30pm-11:30pm, Sun. 1:30pm-5:30pm; Metro: Polanco

Quintonil $$$

Quintonil's focus is on modern food with native Mexican ingredients (its name comes from the Nahuatl word for a type of *quelites*, wild herbs consumed since the pre-Columbian era). There is a daily tasting menu, but you can also order appetizers and main courses à la carte, like *chilacayotes* (yellow squash) in mole sauce or a ceviche of cactus and scallops with avocado and *xoconostle* (sour prickly-pear fruit).

MAP 4: Newton 55, 55/5280-2680, www. quintonil.com; Mon.-Sat. 1pm-5pm and 6:30pm-10:30pm; Metro: Polanco

Eno $$

Owned by famed Pujol chef Enrique Olvera, this small delicatessen has a nice menu of Mexican breakfasts, sandwiches, and salads, as well as a full coffee bar. Grab a seat at the shared wood table for *pan dulce* and hot chocolate in the morning or a turkey sandwich with *panela* cheese and avocado at lunch. Though the atmosphere is casual, Olvera's name and the quality draw a crowd: The place can get packed with afternoon lunchers in suit and tie.

MAP 4: Francisco Petrarca 258, 55/5531-8535, www.eno.com.mx; Mon.-Fri. 7am-10pm, Sat. 9am-10pm, Sun. 9am-5pm; Metro: Polanco

Guzina Oaxaca $$

Alejandro Ruiz, the chef behind the elegant restaurant Casa Oaxaca in the city of Oaxaca, brings his creative approach to cuisine to this lovely restaurant in Polanco. Try excellent renditions of typical Oaxacan plates, like tacos stuffed with grasshoppers, Oaxacan cheese, and the fragrant herb *hoja santa;* or the chef's signature *mole negro,* served with turkey, as is traditional. Casual but attractive, the restaurant subtly recalls Oaxacan aesthetics with details like embroidered throw pillows on the dining room's benches.

MAP 4: Presidente Masaryk 513, 55/5282-1820, www.guzinaoaxaca.com; Mon.-Sat. 8am-11pm, Sun. 8am-6pm; Metro: Auditorio or Polanco

La Poblanita de Tacubaya $

A thoroughly traditional Mexican restaurant with a surprisingly extensive menu, this family-style spot serves fantastic renditions of Mexican classics, from a simple but delicious taco filled with guacamole and *chicharrón* (pork rind) to elaborate *mole poblano* ladled over chicken breast. The *poblanita* in the name refers to the state of Puebla, and *poblano*-style food is the house specialty—though don't let that limit your order.

MAP 4: Luis G. Vieyra 12, 55/2614-3314, www.lapoblanita.com.mx; daily 9am-7pm; Metro: Juanacatlán

NEW WORLD FOODS

As much as Mexican food has changed over the past 500 years, many popular dishes trace their roots directly back to the pre-Columbian era. Today, Mexican chefs are using more indigenous ingredients, and foods that once seemed more adventurous, like bugs and worms, have become almost commonplace in the city's top restaurants. Here are a few of the New World foods you'll find on menus in the capital.

CHAPULINES
Grasshoppers, collected in the wild then fried until crispy. An excellent source of protein and deliciously salty, they add an acidic bite to guacamole and quesadillas. In 2013, Mexican artist Pedro Reyes developed a grasshopper hamburger (or "grasswhopper") as a part of his work *Entomofagia*, through which Reyes hoped to promote the environmental and health benefits of eating insects.

Where: In tacos at **Guzina Oaxaca** (page 123) in Polanco; in quesadillas at **La Casa de la Tlayuda** (page 128) and with guacamole at **Yuban** (page 128) in the Roma; mixed into melted cheese at **Corazón de Maguey** (page 135) in Coyoacán.

QUELITES
Quelites refers to any wild, indigenous greens—some better known, like *huauzontles* (a bitter broccoli-esque vegetable) and others less common, like *pápalo* (a perfumy, citrusy herb). In modern farming, many of these "weeds" are eradicated, but *quelites* have experienced a renewed popularity.

Where: In soup at **Limosneros** (page 110) in the Centro Histórico; in salad at **Quintonil** (page 123) in Polanco; with braised ribs at **Fonda Fina** (page 127) in the Roma. **Tacos Gus** (page 131) in the Condesa often makes tacos with quelites.

HUITLACOCHE
The soft black fungus that grows naturally on corn. It's not only edible, but delicious, with a mild mushroom-like flavor. It's generally in season from July to September. *Huitlacoche* has more nutritional properties—including essential amino acids—than the corn it grows on.

Where: At produce stands in the **Mercado San Juan** (page 199); in crepes at **Sobrinos** (page 128) in the Roma; in ravioli at **Los Danzantes** (page 135) in Coyoacán.

ESCAMOLES
Ant larvae, often fried in butter with the herb *epazote*, then folded into a warm tortilla. Frying them in butter enhances the mild nutty flavor of the larvae. *Escamoles* are generally a pricey delicacy, with a very short season making them scarce (they are harvested annually between March and April).

Where: When they are in season, you can find them at **Limosneros** (page 110) and **El Cardenal** (page 108) in the Centro, and in the **Mercado San Juan** (page 199) near the Alameda Central.

CHILACAYOTE
A squash that resembles a small watermelon (also known as "fig leaf" in English), *chilacayote* has a mild earthy flavor, like a summer squash or potato. *Chilacayote* is used throughout Mexico. There are dozens of indigenous names—*gueeto-xiu* in Zapoteco, *macuá* in Chinateco—for the squash.

Where: As a crystallized candy at **Dulcería de Celaya** (page 196) in the Centro Histórico; in mole at **Quintonil** (page 123) in Polanco.

CHINICUILES
A caterpillar commonly found in maguey and agave, they are often served baked or fried, then folded into a taco. Frying before serving gives the shells a crisp texture, complementing the caterpillars' pungent, savory flavor. These little caterpillars were often added to bottles of mezcal to prove that the drink was made from maguey.

Where: **Restaurante Chon** (page 111) and **El Cardenal** (page 108) in the Centro Histórico.

TACOS, *TORTAS,* AND SNACKS

El Turix $

El Turix does one thing, and it does it well: *cochinita pibil*, achiote-spiced pulled pork prepared in the Yucatec style. You can order it in soft tacos, in a *torta* (sandwich style), or on *panuchos* (thick, circular corn cakes from the Yucatán). This singularly focused spot has garnered a loyal following, and at the hour of the afternoon *comida*, there is often a line of expectant diners snaking out the door and around the block.

MAP 4: Emilio Castelar 212, 55/5280-6449; daily 11am-9pm; Metro: Auditorio

Los Panchos $

In business since 1945, Los Panchos has been catering to a loyal local clientele for generations. The atmosphere here is a bit more upscale than what you'd find at most *taquerías,* with a full bar and table service. The food, however, is traditional, homey, and generously served. Best known for the *carnitas* (braised pork), the extensive menu includes plenty of other options, from a fresh guacamole to huge *sopes* (thick corn cakes) topped with beans and cheese.

MAP 4: Tolstoi 9, 55/5254-5390, www.lospanchos.mx; Mon.-Sat. 8am-10pm, Sun. 8am-8pm; Metro: Chapultepec

SEAFOOD

Mi Gusto Es $$

A casual lunch-only eatery that originally opened in the Narvarte neighborhood, Mi Gusto Es is the place to go for Sinaloan-style seafood dishes, like perfectly prepared ceviche-topped tostadas, hot peppers stuffed with shrimp, and marlin flautas—all of which goes perfectly with an ice-filled bucket of beer. With its casual ambience, sidewalk tables, and snappy service, Mi Gusto Es is a fun place to eat, and easy on the pocketbook too.

MAP 4: Torcuato Tasso 324-M, 55/5254-5678, www.migustoes.com.mx; Sun.-Thurs. noon-7pm, Fri.-Sat. noon-8pm; Metro: Polanco

ASIAN

Dawat $$

As soon as you walk into this cozy Indian restaurant, the authentic smell of simmering spices promises a satisfying meal. The warm wood-floored dining room with white-clothed tables is far quieter than most Polanco establishments, but Dawat is nonetheless big on flavor, considered by many to have the best Indian food in the city, with a menu that includes biryanis, tandoor-oven-baked fish and meats, and curries. There are plenty of vegetarian options.

MAP 4: Séneca 31, 55/5281-8020, www.resdawat.com; Mon.-Sat. 1pm-11pm, Sun. 1pm-6pm; Metro: Polanco

FRENCH

Au Pied de Cochon $$$

Considered one of the best French restaurants in the capital, this high-end restaurant in the InterContinental Presidente has an extensive menu of classics, from foie gras to cassoulet. While the food is excellent, the most amazing thing about this long-running establishment is its operating hours: Au Pied de Cochon is open 24 hours a day. Come late and you'll likely see a posh crowd enjoying a post-party nosh.

MAP 4: InterContinental Presidente Mexico City, Campos Eliseos 218, 55/5327-7756, www.aupieddecochon.com.mx; daily 24 hours; Metro: Auditorio

ITALIAN
Cancino $

Right across the street from contemporary gallery Kurimanzutto, Cancino draws an artsy crowd. There are panini and salads on the menu here, in addition to the restaurant's signature thin-crust oven-baked pizzas—which lean experimental, with toppings like gorgonzola and pear. If you just want to rest your legs, there's a small coffee bar, La Ventanita, also inside the space, where you can get an espresso and a snack, to enjoy at the sun-dappled garden tables.

Cancino

MAP 4: Gobernador Rafael Rebollar 95, 55/4333-0770, www.archipielagocorp.com; Mon.-Wed. 8am-midnight, Sun. 8am-6pm; Metro: Juanacatlán

Non Solo Pasta $

Non Solo Pasta maintains a cozy, neighborhood-restaurant feeling, despite its high-end location. With more than a decade in operation, it is a reasonably priced spot for conversation accompanied by a glass of Chianti, a few Roquefort-topped bruschetta, and a nicely served plate of fettuccine with pesto. It's open late and rarely too crowded, so you can linger over drinks or coffee.

MAP 4: Julio Verne 89, 55/5280-9706, www.nonsolo.mx; Sun.-Tues. 12:30pm-1am, Wed.-Sat. 12:30pm-2am; Metro: Polanco

INTERNATIONAL
El Lago $$$

The opportunity to eat in the middle of Bosque de Chapultepec is the reason to book a reservation at this beautiful restaurant, where a sophisticated glass-walled dining room overlooks the Lago Mayor. With its elegant atmosphere, it's popular with well-heeled locals, many of whom come for romantic dinners or to celebrate birthdays or other special occasions. Breakfasts are particularly good here; it's a popular place for Sunday brunch.

MAP 4: Segunda Sección, Bosque de Chapultepec, 55/5515-9586, www.lago. com.mx; Mon.-Sat. 7:30am-11pm, Sun. 10:30am-4pm; Metro: Auditorio

COFFEE AND SWEETS
Bimmy $

This charming bakery, sweet shop, and café is owned by two chefs from Yokohama, Japan. A great place to stop for a light breakfast, it has beautiful baskets of picture-perfect European-style pastries—like croissants and lemon bread—as well as loaves of artisanal bread and a line of Asian-influenced sweets like green-tea cheesecake and curry bread. Everything here not only looks beautiful, it's freshly made and tasty.

MAP 4: Newton 186, 55/2624-3302, www. bimmymexico.com; Mon.-Fri. 8:30am-7pm, Sat. 8:30am-5pm; Metro: Polanco

Café Zena $

Though it's still a largely residential neighborhood, San Miguel Chapultepec's chic gallery-centric side is clearly noticeable in this artsy café, where one long table is shared by patrons having coffee, working on their laptops, or thumbing through magazines. Though Café Zena serves breakfast, lunch, and dinner (including a daily lunch special for about US$8, which includes a soup, main course, and dessert), many locals just stop in for an espresso or a beer.

MAP 4: Gobernador Protasio Tagle 66, San Miguel Chapultepec, 55/2614-1408, www.cafezena.com; daily 8am-8pm; Metro: Juanacatlán

Roma and Condesa   Map 5

MEXICAN
Merotoro $$$

The team behind the ultra-popular seafood spot Contramar opened this surf-and-turf restaurant in 2010, with a kitchen overseen by chef Jair Téllez, who comes to Mexico City by way of Baja California. With a focus on seafood and meat dishes, the food has drawn rave reviews from Mark Bittman of the *New York Times*, among others. The menu changes with the seasons. Try the namesake *mero*, or grouper, if it's available.

MAP 5: Amsterdam 204, 55/5564-7799, www.merotoro.mx; Mon.-Sat. 1:30pm-midnight, Sun. 1:30pm-6pm; Metro: Chilpancingo, Metrobús: Campeche

El Parnita $$

The simple menu at this trendy family-owned restaurant is composed entirely of *antojitos,* or little snacks. Mix and match to create a meal from the selection of shrimp tacos, ceviche-topped tostados, or *tlacoyos* (corn cakes) filled with cheese. As any *capitaleño* can tell you, the key to a good *antojito* is the salsa that accompanies it, and El Parnita doesn't stumble in this department. They serve three salsas daily, with changing recipes, though the ultra-spicy charred habanero salsa made is a mainstay.

MAP 5: Yucatán 84, 55/5264-7551, http://elparnita.com; Tues.-Thurs. 1pm-6pm, Fri.-Sat. 1pm-7pm, Sun. 1pm-6pm; Metro: Insurgentes or Chilpancingo, Metrobús: Sonora

Fonda Fina $$

A genuine love for traditional Mexican food is what drives the menu at this lovely Roma spot, a chef-driven homage to the city's many *fondas*. Here, dishes you'd find at a typical family-run restaurant in the capital—tamales, *sopes*, black-bean soup—are presented with thoughtfulness and creativity, while main courses, like braised ribs, are sophisticated and filling. The cozy dining room is often full during the lunch rush; make a reservation.

MAP 5: Medellín 79, 55/5208-3925; Mon.-Wed. 1pm-11pm, Thurs.-Sat. 1pm-midnight, Sun. 1pm-7pm; Metro: Insurgentes

Fonda Mayora $$

Classic Mexican dishes are served with warmth and elegance at this relaxed Condesa restaurant. At breakfast, you can order a cup of Oaxacan hot chocolate, a side of house-baked sweet bread, and an egg cooked inside a neatly folded leaf of *hoja santa* (a Mexican herb); at lunch, fill the table with prickly-pear salad, bone-marrow *sopes* (round corn cakes), and octopus *a la antigua*, based on an 18th-century Mexican recipe. Housemade tortillas are a perfect, chewy accompaniment to every meal.

MAP 5: Campeche 332, 55/6843-0595, www.fondamayora.com; daily 8am-7pm; Metro: Chilpancingo

Fonda Mayora

Sobrinos $$

Though it's been in operation for less than a decade, there is an old-fashioned charm to Sobrinos, where globe lamps, checkered floors, and an attentive white-coated waitstaff seem born of another era. The menu is likewise classic, with upscale "cantina-style" favorites like tacos, tostadas, and *tortas*. Breakfast, when you can get eggs scrambled with asparagus, *chilaquiles verdes*, or crepes with *huitlacoche*, might be the highlight. Don't miss the *conchas* with *nata*, a sugar-topped bread filled with cream.

MAP 5: Álvaro Obregón 103, 55/5264-6059, http://bajodelatintorera.com; Mon. 8am-1pm, Tues.-Thurs. 8am-midnight, Fri. 8am-12:45am, Sat. 9am-12:45am, Sun. 9am-6:30pm; Metro: Insurgentes, Metrobús: Álvaro Obregón

Yuban $$

This unique restaurant is inspired by the cuisine of the Zapotec culture, incorporating flavors and ingredients that aren't often found outside the state of Oaxaca. Start with fried grasshoppers and guacamole or a plate of marinated *quesillo*, a soft mozzarella-like cheese from Oaxaca; follow up with one of the restaurant's unusual moles. Everything goes splendidly, of course, with a shot of smoky small-batch mezcal—and in that department, Yuban's bar has got you amply covered.

MAP 5: Colima 268, 55/6387-0358, www.yuban.mx; Mon.-Wed. 1:30pm-midnight, Thurs.-Sat. 1:30pm-1:30am, Sun. 1:30pm-8pm; Metro: Insurgentes, Metrobús: Álvaro Obregón

Café Paris $

With zero pretension and plenty of ambience, this old-school cafeteria continues to serve economical Mexican meals in a classic diner setting. It's a good place for breakfast, with a range of typical options, like *huevos divorciados* (two fried eggs, one topped with green salsa and the other with red) and crunchy *chilaquiles verdes*. The highlight, however, is the *café con leche*, a strongly brewed dark-roast coffee mixed with scalding-hot milk, poured to your tastes at the table.

MAP 5: Córdoba 107, 55/5264-2312; Mon.-Sat. 7am-11pm, Sun. 8am-11pm; Metro: Insurgentes, Metrobús: Álvaro Obregón

La Casa de la Tlayuda $

A snack typical to the state of Oaxaca, *tlayudas* are large, thin corn tortillas, which are brushed with lard, folded in half, stuffed with beans and cheese, and toasted on a griddle. At this popular spot on Avenida Insurgentes, you

can get some of the best and most authentic *tlayudas* you'll find outside of Oaxaca, in addition to other regional specialties like empanadas filled with chicken and *amarillito* (yellow mole), cheese-and-grasshopper-stuffed quesadillas, or cured beef called *tasajo*.
MAP 5: Insurgentes 280, 55/6798-4764, www.casadelatlayuda.com; daily 12:30pm-10pm; Metro: Insurgentes, Metrobús: Álvaro Obregón

Los Chamorros de Mérida $

There are many classic, deliciously prepared snacks at this inexpensive Roma spot, including handmade *huaraches* topped with refried beans and crumbled cheese; *pambazos*, a potato-and-chorizo-stuffed sandwich on a soft roll; and, of course, the namesake *chamorros*, melt-in-your-mouth fried pork leg, which is plated with guacamole and *nopales* (cactus) or stuffed into *gorditas* (corn cakes) with *chicharrón* (pork rind). Sit down at one of sidewalk tables on a sunny afternoon to enjoy the Roma people-watching as you dine.
MAP 5: Mérida 124, 55/5264-0210, www.loschamorros.com.mx; daily 9am-6pm; Metro: Niños Héroes, Metrobús: Jardín Pushkin

Mercado Roma

Peltre Lonchería $

While its geometric turquoise-and-white decor is unapologetically contemporary, this low-key coffee shop and sandwich bar is unpretentious and inexpensive—much-appreciated qualities in the relentlessly trendy Roma. Overseen by the same chef behind the more upscale restaurant Nudo Negro (Zacatecas 139, 55/5564-5218), it's a good place for breakfast, where you can start the day with a plate of fresh fruit with housemade granola, savory *enfrijoladas* (tortillas drenched in bean sauce) topped with cream and avocado, and a tall glass of green juice.
MAP 5: Álvaro Obregón 85-A, 55/5207-3801, www.danielovadia.com.mx; Mon.-Fri. 7am-11pm, Sat. 8am-11pm, Sun. 8am-10pm; Metro: Insurgentes

TACOS, *TORTAS*, AND SNACKS
Mercado Roma $$

Opened in 2015, this stylish architect-designed market and food court is filled with lunch counters and food stands from some of the most well-known restaurants in the city, from classics like the 1935 vintage Churrería El Moro to newer sensations, like a petite spinoff of Ricardo Muñoz Zurita's Azul Histórico. It's often packed in the afternoons, but if you don't mind a crowd, it's a fun place to mill around, sip on a beet juice, and sample some Wagyu tacos or a *torta* stuffed with Spanish-style sausage and cheese.
MAP 5: Querétaro 225, 55/5564-1396, http://mercadoroma.com; Sun.-Wed. 9am-8pm, Thurs.-Sat. 9am-11pm, hours vary by restaurant; Metro: Insurgentes, Metrobús: Sonora

EATING IN THE OFF HOURS

New York has claimed the reputation as "the city that never sleeps," but Mexico's capital has its own round-the-clock culture. For many capital residents, late nights aren't an anomaly, but a way of life, and there's never an hour of the day when you won't find great eats and a good time here. Here's where to go...

IF YOUR 1-YEAR-OLD GOT YOU UP AT 5AM
Take advantage of the early rising to have breakfast at traditional **Fonda Margarita** (page 140), a super-casual and beloved breakfast-only restaurant where a line starts to form before the 5:30am opening.

IF YOUR FAMILY WANTS A TREAT AFTER THE SHOW AT BELLAS ARTES
Go out for a creamy hot chocolate and a sugar-topped churro at **Churrería El Moro** (page 114), a lovely old-fashioned sandwich and *churro* shop that, believe it or not, never closes.

IF YOU CAN'T DECIDE BETWEEN SLEEP AND TACOS
In the Condesa, you can eat some of the city's best *pastores* in bed: **El Califa** (page 130) delivers until 4am.

IF YOU'RE PARTYING IN THE ZONA ROSA
Go for a late-night (or early-morning) refuel at **La Casa de Toño** (Londres 144, 55/5386-1125, daily 24 hours), where you can get a steaming bowl of pozole or a plate of stick-to-your-ribs flautas at any hour of the day or night.

IF THE COCKTAIL BARS HAVE ALL CLOSED IN THE ROMA
Join other revelers for a late-night taco run at the corner of **Insurgentes and Álvaro Obregón**, where popular tacos stands are open all night long.

IF YOU REALLY DON'T WANT THE PARTY TO STOP
Head south to the favored post-party spot **El Gallito** (Insurgentes Sur 858, 55/5687-3722, daily 5pm-5am), which many say is so named because it's open until the *gallo* (rooster) crows. You'll find plenty of other late-night revelers there.

IF YOU'RE MASSIVELY JET LAGGED AND ALREADY MISS PARIS
Join other stylish jet setters for a 3am meal at **Au Pied de Cochon** (page 125), a fancy French restaurant in the InterContinental Presidente Mexico City. It is, remarkably, open 24 hours a day.

El Califa $

Many say that this *taquería* makes the best *pastores* in the city, though you can also come here for tacos stuffed with rib-eye, cheese and chile peppers, and *arrachera*, among other fillings, all served in freshly made tortillas. Accompany your plate with a beer and a bowl of *frijoles charros*, and you've got a filling and memorable meal, on a very low budget. A family-friendly spot by day, it's open till the wee hours, when it's a popular post-party stop. **MAP 5:** Altata 22, 55/5271-7666, www. elcalifa.com.mx; daily 1pm-4am; Metro: Chilpancingo

El Jarocho $

Near the Mercado de Medellín, El Jarocho is a two-story no-frills restaurant, opened in 1947, that serves breakfast, lunch, and dinner. Many Roma locals come here for the spread of *tacos de guisado*. A popular *almuerzo* in Mexico City, *tacos de guisado* are made with a range of traditional fillings prepared in clay pots, like shredded chicken in a pumpkin-seed sauce, *chile relleno*, or *rajas con crema* (green chiles in cream sauce). Note that the entrance is on the street Campeche.

MAP 5: Tapachula 94, 55/5574-5303, http://taqueriaeljarocho.com.mx; Mon.-Sat. 8am-10pm, Sun. 8am-7pm; Metro: Chilpancingo, Metrobús: Campeche

El Tizoncito $

With two locations two blocks away from one another—one a stool-and-bar, eat-and-run affair (at Campeche and Tamaulipas), and this more formal sit-down restaurant—El Tizoncito is a taco destination in Mexico City, now with branches across the city. At each you'll find tasty *tacos al pastor* and other *antojitos*, along with beer and soft drinks. Prices are a bit higher than most *taquerías*, but the food is reliably good and service is swift.

MAP 5: Tamaulipas 122, 55/5286-2117, www.eltizoncito.com.mx; daily noon-2:30am; Metro: Patriotismo

Tacos El Güero (Tacos Hola) $

This hole-in-the-wall spot is a neighborhood institution, known for its tasty *tacos de guisado*. You choose your fillings from the daily offerings—like potato with chorizo, shredded chicken, or spinach—which are stuffed into a double tortilla and topped with beans, rice, or guacamole on request. If you come during the lunch rush, don't be deterred—just join the crowd and be patient. The efficient *taqueros* will make sure everyone gets served.

MAP 5: Amsterdam 135; Mon.-Sat. 10:30am to around 4pm; Metro: Chilpancingo

Tacos Gus $

Something of an anomaly in the taco world, this low-key little shop sells a range of traditional *tacos de guisado* using natural, often organic ingredients, and offers plenty of delicious options for vegetarians. *Guisados*, or fillings, are lined up in clay pots, where you can choose between options like *chile relleno*, cauliflower, and *picadillo* (seasoned ground beef), then top it with your choice of beans, cheese, or a generous dollop of guacamole.

MAP 5: Ometusco 56, 55/5271-6090, www.grangus.com; Mon.-Fri. 9am-5am, Sat. 9am-4pm; Metro: Chilpancingo

Taquería El Farolito $

This famous taco shop first opened in 1962 in the Colonia Condesa, and the original location continues to be a popular place for a quick, delicious meal. The specialties here are charcoal-grilled meats like *arrachera*, chorizo, and rib eye, which you can order in tacos, in a *volcán* (a tostada covered with melted cheese), and atop *huaraches* (thicker, torpedo-shaped corn cakes), among other presentations.

MAP 5: Altata 19, 55/5277-3052, http://tacoselfarolito.com.mx; Sun.-Mon. noon-midnight, Tues.-Wed. noon-1am, Thurs. noon-2am, Fri.-Sat. noon-3am; Metro: Chilpancingo

Taquería El Greco $

The *taco árabe* with pita bread is a popular culinary fusion of Middle Eastern shawarma-style wraps and Mexican *tacos al pastor*. It's the specialty of the house at this small *taquería*, a mainstay in Condesa. Here, lean pork is cooked on a spit, then sliced off and crisped further on the grill before going into the various tacos and *tortas*, including the *árabe*. The same *taquero* has been slicing tacos here for decades, and the food is ace.

MAP 5: Michoacán 54, 55/5553-5742; Mon.-Sat. 2pm-10pm; Metro: Chilpancingo

SEAFOOD

Contramar $$

A popular lunch spot in the Roma Norte, Contramar is widely heralded as the city's top spot for seafood. The bright, airy dining room is always bustling with waiters rushing plates of iced oysters to loud, happy, well-heeled diners. Ceviches, *tacos de camarón,* fried fish, and the beloved *tostadas de atún* (tuna tostadas) are reliably well prepared, and go equally well with a glass of white wine or a cold *cerveza.* Reservations aren't accepted.

MAP 5: Durango 200, 55/5514-9217 or 55/5514-3169, www.contramar.com.mx; Sun.-Thurs. 1pm-6pm, Fri.-Sat. noon-8pm; Metro: Sevilla

La Docena $$

The original La Docena was a hit in its hometown of Guadalajara, and in 2015, the owners opened a second branch in the Roma, to much local enthusiasm. Oysters, the house specialty, are served on the half shell, but also grilled and in po' boys (and in beer with Clamato, if you're feeling adventurous). The atmosphere is festive, especially on the weekends, when the sidewalk tables and bar seats fill with diners.

MAP 5: Álvaro Obregón 31, 55/5208-0748; daily 1:30pm-1am; Metro: Niños Héroes or Insurgentes, Metrobús: Jardín Pushkin

El Pescadito $

At lunchtime, there's often a long line running out the door of this friendly *taquería,* which serves delicious Sonora-style fish tacos at bargain prices. The classic taco is stuffed with deep-fried fish and served in a double tortilla, but the gooey *chile relleno* taco, topped with fried shrimp, is just as good. Order directly from the guys cooking the fish, then dress up your tacos with coleslaw, cabbage, tomatoes, and a spoonful of green or red salsa at the communal bar.

MAP 5: Atlixco 38, 55/6268-3045, www.elpescadito.com.mx; daily 11am-6pm; Metro: Patriotismo or Juanacatlán

ORGANIC AND VEGETARIAN
The Green Corner $$

An all-natural sidewalk café with adjoining organic grocery store, the Green Corner is a relaxing place for a meal, especially good if you're in the mood for something fresh and lighter. In addition to the à la carte options, like stir-fries, sandwiches, and salads, there are three multicourse lunch specials served each day—one with meat, one vegetarian, and one macrobiotic. Well priced and tasty, the daily menu often sells out by midafternoon.

MAP 5: Mazatlán 81, 55/1054-7699, www.thegreencorner.org; daily 8am-10pm; Metro: Patriotismo

ASIAN
Mog $$

This hugely popular pan-Asian restaurant has excellent, inexpensive food and a cool hipster atmosphere, with eclectic vintage and custom-made furniture cluttering up the dimly lit main dining room. For chilly nights, the menu offers a wide selection of steaming ramen bowls and other Asian soups, like *pho,* as well as rice and curry dishes, grilled meats, teriyaki, and sushi. Everything is surprisingly generous and tasty, handily satisfying your yen for salt and umami.

MAP 5: Álvaro Obregón 40, 55/5264-0016; daily 1pm-11pm; Metro: Insurgentes

Galanga $$

A small, unassuming dining room on busy Guanajuato street is home to some of the best Asian food in the city. Here, Southeast Asian staples, from spring rolls to fried rice and curries, are not just flavorful and authentic, but beautifully presented. Combine this restaurant's quality with its economical price tag, and it's no surprise there is often a wait for a table on the weekends.

MAP 5: Guanajuato 202, 55/6550-4492, www.galangathaikitchen.com; Tues.-Sat. 1pm-10:30pm, Sun. 1pm-6pm; Metro: Insurgentes, Metrobús: Álvaro Obregón

ITALIAN
Rosetta $$$

At this Roma hot spot, chef Elena Reygadas serves consistently creative, fresh, and lovingly prepared Italian food to an always-packed dining room located in an elegantly restored mansion on Colima. Start the meal with an appetizer, like roasted bone marrow, then follow up with one of the delicious pastas or entrées, which always include interesting options, like beet risotto or housemade pappardelle with wild mushrooms. Reservations are generally necessary.

MAP 5: Colima 166, 55/5533-7804, www. rosetta.com.mx; Mon.-Sat. 1pm-11:30pm; Metro: Insurgentes, Metrobús: Álvaro Obregón

INTERNATIONAL
✪ Máximo Bistrot Local $$$

The market-to-table ethos is fundamental to the menu at Máximo Bistrot Local, where chef Eduardo Garcia brings his kitchen experience and culinary creativity to the restaurant's constantly changing menu. Depending on what's in season, lunch offerings could include anything from mussels in coconut broth to organic rib eye to chocolate crème brûlée. If you didn't get a reservation, try the chef's more casual breakfast and lunch spot, Lalo (Zacatecas 173, 55/5564-3388), just across the street.

MAP 5: Tonalá 133, 55/5264-4291, http://maximobistrot.com.mx; Tues.-Sat. 1pm-11pm, Sun. 11am-7pm; Metro: Insurgentes, Metrobús: Álvaro Obregón

Café La Gloria $$

One of the first cool restaurants to open in the Condesa neighborhood more than a decade ago, Café La Gloria has now become an old standby: a relaxed, unpretentious place for a good meal and friendly service. The comfortable dining room is decorated with changing artwork, there are cozy booths along the back wall, and tables are draped with red-and-white-checked tablecloths. The menu changes but tends toward European-style comfort staples, with salads, fish, and pasta.

MAP 5: Vicente Suárez 41-D, 55/5211-4185; Mon.-Wed. 1pm-midnight, Thurs.-Fri. 1pm-1am, Sat. 10am-1am, Sun. 10am-midnight; Metro: Patriotismo

Huset $$

Set in the pretty shaded patio of a Colonia Roma mansion, this country-inspired restaurant opened in late 2015 and quickly became a city favorite. Focusing on farm-fresh ingredients, the menu changes frequently but tends to favor simple but sophisticated plates, like roast chicken (made in the in-house wood-fired oven), grilled snapper, or lemon gnocchi with mushrooms.

MAP 5: Colima 256, 55/5511-6767, http:// husetroma.com; Tues.-Wed. 2pm-midnight, Thurs.-Fri. 2pm-2am, Sat. 10am-2am, Sun. 10am-6pm; Metro: Insurgentes, Metrobús: Álvaro Obregón

Romita Comedor $$

This stylish restaurant and cocktail bar occupies the roof deck of an old mansion on Álvaro Obregón, with huge windows and a retractable roof creating an airy feeling and providing nice views from the tables—that is, if you can take your eyes off the beautiful people around you, nibbling on seafood cocktails and ceviches as they tip back frosty drinks. With such a beautiful setting, Romita might be forgiven a more lackadaisical kitchen, but the food is surprisingly delicious.

MAP 5: Álvaro Obregón 49, 52/5525-8975, www.romitacomedor.com; Tues.-Sat. 1pm-2am, Sun. 10am-6pm; Metro: Insurgentes or Niños Héroes, Metrobús: Álvaro Obregón

COFFEE AND SWEETS
Cardinal $

It's easy to develop a caffeine habit at this stellar coffee shop: Inside the small space, there are comfortable tables and chairs, atmospheric Edison bulbs hanging over the bar, free Wi-Fi, glass water bottles on every table, and, most important, ridiculously good coffee. Here, beans (all grown and roasted in Mexico) are carefully selected then matched with one of the café's many brewing methods, among them Aeropress, siphon, drip, Chemex, and, of course, espresso.

MAP 5: Córdoba 132, 55/6721-8874; Mon.-Fri. 8am-9pm, Sat. 9am-9pm, Sun. 10am-8pm; Metro: Niños Héroes or Insurgentes

Fournier Rousseau $

Satisfy your sweet tooth at this small but mighty bakery and cake shop, which creates a daily selection of delicious French-style croissants and baguettes, fruit-filled cheesecake with mascarpone, dense and delicious carrot cake, and rich, eggy flan, among other picture-perfect desserts. Order a slice of cake to share (they're sizable)

and take it to one of the two turquoise tables outside.

MAP 5: Córdoba 108, 55/6269-9486; daily 8am-9pm; Metro: Niños Héroes or Insurgentes

Neveria Roxy

Neveria Roxy $

This authentically vintage ice-cream parlor has been in business since the 1940s, serving generations of Condesa families who keep the place in business with their enthusiastic patronage. Order a cone with two scoops of traditional Mexican *nieve* (similar to sorbet or sherbet, generally using no dairy, or a lower dairy content than most ice creams). Everything is made in house, with flavors ranging from refreshing and familiar, like mandarin and lemon, to exotic, like passion fruit and tamarind.

MAP 5: Tamaulipas 161, 55/5256-1854, http://neveriaroxy.com.mx; daily 11am-8pm; Metro: Patriotismo

Panadería Pancracia $

One of the best artisan bakeries in town is tucked into a teensy hole-in-the-wall spot in the Roma, where they make dark and crusty baguettes, croissants, brioche, and mini-loaves of specialty bread, for which the selection changes daily, as well as what may be the best *conchas* (a type of traditional sweet roll) in Mexico City. Pancracia sends the majority of these yeasty treasures to restaurants around the city, but lucky locals pick up a bag of whatever's coming out of the oven.

MAP 5: Chihuahua 181-A, 55/6284-1497; Tues.-Sat. 9am-6pm, Sun. 9am-4pm; Metro: Insurgentes

Coyoacán   Map 6

MEXICAN
Los Danzantes $$$
An elegant yet earthy restaurant, Los Danzantes serves contemporary Mexican dishes with a strong emphasis on local Mexican ingredients and a notable influence from the culinary traditions of the state of Oaxaca. You'll find classics like chicken breast in *mole negro*, as well as more experimental concepts, like ravioli stuffed with *huitlacoche* (the mushroom that grows on corn). Los Danzantes is famous for its excellent line of Oaxacan mezcal, which, naturally, is served in-house.

MAP 6: Jardín Centenario 12, 55/5658-6451 or 55/5554-1213, http:// losdanzantes.com; Mon.-Wed. 12:30-11pm, Thurs. 12:30-midnight, Fri.-Sat. 9am-1am, Sun. 9am-11pm; Metro: Viveros

Los Danzantes

Casa del Pan Papalotl $$
This long-running all-natural café (which also has a branch in San Cristóbal de las Casas, Chiapas) serves house-baked breads and breakfast foods, baguette sandwiches, and other tasty fare, with an emphasis on local, organic ingredients. The small dining room opens onto the street, where sidewalk tables are filled with hippie-esque diners. The perfect spot to pass a Sunday morning with a cup of tea and the paper, it often has a wait for weekend brunch.

MAP 6: Av. México 25, 55/3095-1767, www.casadelpan.com; Mon.-Fri. 8am-10pm, Sun. 9am-10pm; Metro: Viveros

☺ Corazón de Maguey $$
This *mezcalería* and restaurant has a modern Mexican atmosphere and an ultra-fun menu of traditional food from across the republic, with a particularly strong emphasis on Oaxacan cuisine. On a leisurely afternoon in Coyoacán, this is a perfect place to order a flight of mezcal and a bunch of unusual bar snacks, like hibiscus-filled crispy tacos, guacamole with fried grasshoppers, or a *tlayuda* (a giant crispy tortilla filled with beans, meat, and cheese).

Plaza Jardín Centenario 9A, 55/5554-7555, http://corazondemaguey. com; Sun.-Wed. 1pm-1am, Thurs.-Fri. 12:30pm-1:30am, Sat.-Sun. 9am-2am, kitchen closes about an hour before closing times; Metro: Viveros

Fonda El Morral $$

This traditional Mexican restaurant is well suited to the old-fashioned feeling in Coyoacán, decorated with painted Talavera tiles and wood furnishings, and attended by a cadre of waiters in vests and bow ties. It's a good choice in the morning, when the menu covers many of the most beloved Mexican breakfast dishes, from *chilaquiles* to *huevos rancheros.* For lunch and dinner, traditional plates like carne asada and chicken in mole are served with handmade tortillas.

MAP 6: Allende 2, 55/5554-0298; daily 7am-10pm; Metro: Viveros

Merendero Las Lupitas

Merendero Las Lupitas $

A *merendero* is a traditional restaurant serving light suppers, and though Merendero Las Lupitas is technically open in the daytime, it's best to go in the evening, when the pleasant atmosphere, on the tranquil Plaza Santa Catarina, is the perfect place to wrap up the day. The menu is a notable selection of dishes from northern Mexico, a surprising rarity in the capital. Try the *enchiladas potosinas* (fried-cheese enchiladas) or the burritos stuffed with *chilorio* (slow-cooked pork in chile sauce).

MAP 6: Plaza Santa Catarina 4, 55/5554-3353; Mon.-Sat. 8:30am-midnight, Sun. 8:30am-11pm; Metro: Viveros

TACOS, *TORTAS,* AND SNACKS

Pepe Coyotes $

With its massive spit of red-hued *pastor* spinning temptingly in the doorway, it's hard to miss Pepe Coyotes when walking up Avenida Hidalgo from the main plaza in Coyoacán. At this simple little eatery, you'll get filling tacos, *alambres* (stir-fried meat and vegetables), and savory pozole (a hominy soup) for very reasonable prices, and there's a full bar, if you'd like to accompany your food with a beer or a cocktail.

MAP 6: Av. Hidalgo 295, 55/5659-8902, http://pepecoyotes.com.mx; daily 8am-1:30am; Metro: Viveros

Super Tacos Chupacabra $

One of the most famous food stands in the city, this impressive street-side operation is a meat-lover's dream, with busy *taqueros* rapidly plating orders for tacos filled with chorizo, *bistec* (beef), and *cecina* (salt-cured beef) for a swarm of customers. One thing that distinguishes Chupacabra from so many other taco stands is the variety of toppings—like potatoes, grilled onions, and prickly pear—lined up at the bar, which customers can pile onto their tacos.

FIVE REGIONAL BITES: ICONIC MEXICAN DISHES

As the capital city, as well as the country's biggest economy, Mexico City receives a great deal of immigration from the greater republic, and, naturally, many of these newer residents yearn for the flavors of home. Restaurants serving regional food are not uncommon. In fact, some of these regional bites have become so popular, they are now a mainstay in the city's cuisine. Here are five regional dishes you're likely to see all over the capital.

CHILES EN NOGADA
Dressed in the colors of the Mexican flag, a *chile en nogada* is a large poblano pepper stuffed with ground meat, almonds, dried fruit, and spices, then topped with a creamy walnut sauce and dotted with fresh pomegranate seeds. It is generally served at room temperature. Mexico's national dish, *chiles en nogada* are typically made in celebration of the September Independence Day holidays, in part because pomegranate comes into season in that month. This unusual take on the chile relleno is so popular that you can find it in restaurants throughout the city, but they are native to Puebla, the Mexican state just south of the capital.

HUACHINANGO A LA VERACRUZANA
Huachinango, or snapper, caught in the Gulf of Mexico, is one of the most popular fish along the Atlantic coast, where it is often served in the "Veracruz style," or *a la Veracruzana*, baked or fried in a tomato-based sauce with olives, capers, onions, garlic, and chile pepper, along with a mix of spices.

COCHINITA PIBIL
In the Yucatán, pulled pork is slow-cooked with citrus and ground seeds from the achiote tree. The bright-red and very fragrant seeds give this dish its keynote flavor, popular throughout Mexico City. You'll see *cochinita* on restaurant menus, served in *tortas*, or rolled into tacos.

POLLO CON MOLE NEGRO
Moles are elaborate sauces ground from seeds, nuts, chile peppers, and spices. *Mole negro* is one of the signature dishes in the state of Oaxaca, a rich, chocolate-based sauce that is traditionally served with chicken or turkey.

CHILORIO
A specialty of the northern Mexican state of Sinaloa, *chilorio* is cubed pork slowly simmered with a mix of dried ancho chile peppers, oregano, cilantro seed, cumin, vinegar, and garlic. It is generally served in flour tortillas, also a specialty of the north and surprisingly uncommon in most of Mexico City.

MAP 6: Lateral de Churubusco; Tues.-Sat. 7am-3am, Sun. 7am-midnight; Metro: Coyoacán

COFFEE AND SWEETS
Café Avellaneda $
Serious coffee drinkers frequently point out the excellence of this hole-in-the-wall café, just a block from the Plaza Hidalgo. It offers not just a selection of house-roasted beans from distinct Mexican regions, but a number of brewing methods too, including Aeropress, French press, and espresso.

There are two small tables inside the space and some stools at the bar, but it's just as nice to take your drink to the Plaza de la Conchita, a block away.
MAP 6: Higuera 40, 55/6553-3441; Mon.-Fri. 8am-10pm, Sat.-Sun. 10am-10pm; Metro: Coyoacán

Café El Jarocho $
A neighborhood institution, the aromatic corner coffee stand Café El Jarocho is always jammed with neighborhood locals sipping inexpensive mochas and nibbling

137

donuts. The only seating is the occasional milk crate outside or the iron benches along the sidewalk, where people gather for casual conversation throughout the week. There are several branches of Café El Jarocho in Coyoacán, including one not far from the Museo Frida Kahlo (Av. México 25-C, Sun.-Thurs. 6:30am-10pm, Fri.-Sat. 6:30am-11pm).

MAP 6: Calle Cuauhtémoc 134, 55/5554-5418, www.cafeeljarocho. mx; Sun.-Thurs. 6:30am-1am, Fri.-Sat. 6:30am-2am; Metro: Viveros

El Beneficio $

After touring the Museo Frida Kahlo, it's a short stroll to this sweet café, where you can order a full meal from the menu of breakfasts, breads, and sandwiches, or just get a brownie and a cappuccino to enjoy on one of the sidewalk tables, where locals and their dogs often linger. The pretty country-style ambience feels nicely suited to a day in Coyoacán.

MAP 6: Valentín Gómez Farías 85, 55/6724-9536; Sun.-Wed. 8am-8pm, Thurs.-Sat. 8am-9:30pm; Metro: Viveros

MARKETS

Mercado Coyoacán $

A few blocks from Coyoacán's central plaza, this pretty covered market stocks fresh fruits, vegetables, and other kitchen staples, as well as flowers and handicrafts. It is particularly well-known for its *marisquerías*, seafood stands serving shrimp cocktails, ceviches, and fried fish. The most famous of these is Jardín del Pulpo, at the corner of Allende and Malintzin. Inside the market, there are also popular tostada stands, each offering *cazuelas* (clay pots) filled with an array of savory toppings.

MAP 6: Malintzin and Ignacio Allende; daily 7am-5pm; Metro: Viveros

San Ángel   Map 6

MEXICAN

San Ángel Inn $$$

Built in the 17th century as a Carmelite monastery, later home to Spanish viceroys and, briefly, Emperor Maximilian and his wife, Carlota, the famed San Ángel Inn has seen a variety of guests over its three centuries. Today, the historic building is called San Ángel Inn, but it's a restaurant only, serving traditional Mexican food. The most famous items on the menu are undoubtedly the margaritas, served in little pitchers kept chilled in individual ice buckets.

MAP 6: Diego Rivera 50, 55/5616-1402 or 55/5616-2222, www.sanangelinn.com; Mon.-Sat. 1pm-1am, Sun. 1pm-10pm; Metro: Barranca del Muerto, Metrobús: La Bombilla

Azul y Oro $$$

Located in the heart of the UNAM's cultural center, this contemporary Mexican restaurant opened in a former student cafeteria. It's an unlikely setting for the restaurant's inventive Mexican menu, which draws much of its inspiration from the flavors of Yucatán, Oaxaca, and Veracruz, noted in dishes like duck-stuff *buñuelos* in mole sauce or shrimp in *pipián* (a pumpkin-seed sauce). Because of its location on the university campus, no alcohol is served.

MAP 6: Centro Cultural Universitaria, Insurgentes Sur 3000, 55/5622-7135, www.azul.rest; Mon.-Tues. 1pm-6pm, Wed.-Sat. 10am-8pm, Sun. 9am-7pm; Metro: Universidad, Metrobús: CCU

La Camelia

Fonda San Ángel $$

Right on Plaza San Jacinto in a two-story colonial building, the Fonda San Ángel is located exactly where you'd like to rest your legs and enjoy the scenery after touring the Bazaar Sábado. Come here to sip tequila and enjoy the afternoon at a patio table. *Sopa azteca* (tomato soup with fried tortillas, chiles, and cheese) followed by an *arrachera* (flank steak) with refried beans is a nice, traditional choice.

MAP 6: San Jacinto 3, 55/5550-1641, www.fondasanangel.com; Mon.-Thurs. 8am-midnight, Fri.-Sat. 8am-1am, Sun. 10am-7pm; Metro: Miguel Ángel de Quevedo, Metrobús: La Bombilla

L'Encanto de Lola $

This colorful, family-friendly sandwich shop is a nice place for a casual, inexpensive, yet memorable meal in downtown San Ángel. The menu is mostly dedicated to *tortas*, Mexican-style sandwiches served on a white roll called a *telera*. Here, your options range from traditional combos like cheese and chorizo to contemporary choices, like a vegetarian *torta* with artichoke hearts and black olives. With big windows and bright, whimsical decor, it's popular with local families on the weekends.

MAP 6: Amargura 14, 55/5550-8429, http://encantodelola.tumblr.com; daily noon-7pm; Metro: Miguel Ángel de Quevedo, Metrobús: La Bombilla

SEAFOOD
La Camelia $$

A casual cantina right off the main plaza in San Ángel, this is a low-key, inexpensive place for a cold beer and fresh seafood. Try the red snapper with a green sauce made with *hoja santa* herbs and cilantro or *tostada camellia*, with either shrimp, octopus, or fish ceviche. There is sidewalk seating out front, and on a nice day, it's a great place to linger.

MAP 6: Madero 3, 55/5550-4680; Mon.-Thurs. 2pm-8:30pm, Fri.-Sat. 2pm-2:30am, Sun. 2pm-8pm; Metro: Miguel Ángel de Quevedo

FRENCH
Cluny $$

This attractive French bistro has a charming belle époque atmosphere and an appealing menu of bistro staples like quiche, salads, crepes, and steak frites. They've been in business in San Ángel since the 1970s, maintaining a dedicated clientele for fair prices and nicely prepared food. It's a cozy spot for a quiet evening out.

MAP 6: Av. La Paz 57, 55/5550-7350, www.cluny.com.mx; Mon.-Sat. 12:30pm-midnight, Sun. 12:30pm-11pm; Metro: Miguel Ángel de Quevedo, Metrobús: La Bombilla

MARKETS
Mercado Melchor Múzquiz de San Ángel $

Along Avenida Revolución, this lovely neighborhood market is immediately recognizable for the colorful murals painted above the main arcades by artist Ariosto Otero. In 1958, the covered market was built on the site of what was once an open-air market, where it is rumored that Diego Rivera and Frida Kahlo did their shopping. It's a very nice, inexpensive spot for a traditional snack, like *tacos de guisado* or a seafood cocktail, as well as for shopping.

MAP 6: Av. Revolución and Melchor Múzquiz; daily 8am-5pm; Metro: Miguel Ángel de Quevedo, Metrobús: La Bombilla

Greater Mexico City   Map 7

MEXICAN
✪ Fonda Margarita $$

Even if you get there as dawn is breaking, you might still have to wait for a seat at this super-popular, ultra-casual breakfast spot, touted by many as the best traditional *fonda* in the city. As soon as you walk in, you'll see a row of clay pots filled with different Mexican dishes, gentling bubbling over an open charcoal fire. They sometimes run out of certain *guisos* (dishes) by mid-morning, but you can't go wrong with anything on the menu. The famous *tortas de carne* (meat sandwiches) are a guaranteed way to fill your stomach till midday.

MAP 7: Adolfo Prieto 1354, 55/5559-6358, http://fondamargarita.com; Tues.-Sun. 5:30am-11:30am; Metro: Insurgentes Sur, Metrobús: Parque Hundido

Arroyo $$

Though a bit off the beaten path, this massive family-style restaurant in Tlalpan is hugely entertaining. Opened in the 1940s, the restaurant has an extensive menu of Mexican classics, from enchiladas to mole, though the best item is the flavorful *barbacoa* (lamb), slow-cooked in a brick pit on-site. There is a small playground for kids adjoining the two massive dining rooms, fluttering with paper flags, and, best of all, live music and dance shows take place throughout the afternoon on Saturday and Sunday.

MAP 7: Insurgentes Sur 4003, Tlalpan Centro, 55/5573-4344 or 55/9117-1350, www.arroyorestaurante.com.mx; daily 8am-8pm; Metrobús: Fuentes Brotantes

NIGHTLIFE

Long after sunset, Mexico City remains alight. From old cantinas to chic nightclubs, traditional dance halls to cool mezcal-centric hideaways, there is something for everyone in this buzzing city.

Going out big is a way of life for many *chilangos,* and serious partying isn't limited to teenagers and twenty-somethings; at the humblest cantina and the slickest club, you'll find a mixed-age crowd. The common denominator is the desire to have a good time, and once a party gets going, even daylight won't stop it. Cantinas, traditional Mexican bars that often serve food, are full from the early afternoon to the closing bell, and nightclubs stay packed until dawn. A multitude of "after" bars open when other night spots close, at 4 or 5am, and many taco joints operate in the wee hours.

Each neighborhood's unique flavor is duly expressed in its nightlife. Hip bars and clubs are concentrated in the Roma and Condesa, while the Centro is known for cantinas, pulque bars, and other old-fashioned establishments. Hotel bars are a good choice in tony Polanco, and the Zona Rosa (especially Amberes street) is the center of the gay after-hours scene.

preparing a fresh cocktail

Mexico City's bars, cantinas, and clubs tend to be friendly places, where you're likely to find yourself chatting with strangers or stirring up some fun on the dance floor. Going out is a good way to meet people, practice your Spanish, and get a feel for the local lifestyle.

HIGHLIGHTS

✪ **MOST IMPRESSIVE VIEW:** Many rooftop bars and restaurants in Mexico City boast great views, but none compare to the sweeping vistas from the 41st-floor **Miralto** in the Torre Latinoamericana (page 143).

✪ **HAPPIEST CROWD:** Come to party with the upbeat crowd at **El Marrakech Salón,** a friendly gay bar on nightlife-centric República de Cuba, one of the most popular spots in the Centro (page 145).

✪ **BEST CLASSIC CANTINA:** You'll find a traditional cantina atmosphere at **Tío Pepe,** complete with swinging doors, Formica tables, a rundown art nouveau bar, and roving musical trios (page 145).

✪ **TASTIEST PULQUE:** There's always a youthful crowd at **Pulquería Las Duelistas,** but patrons of any age will appreciate the top-quality pulques at this long-running spot (page 147).

✪ **HUSH-HUSH HOT SPOT:** A speakeasy-style bar with a beautiful clientele, **Jules Basement** hasn't remained clandestine, but it has remained incredibly cool (page 149).

✪ **EVERYONE'S FAVORITE NEIGHBORHOOD BAR:** A reliably fun place for a drink or two, **Pata Negra** has maintained its popularity in the Condesa neighborhood with nightly live music, a relaxed atmosphere, and low prices (page 152).

✪ **TOP STOP FOR MEZCAL LOVERS:** Sample some excellent small-batch mezcal in the low-lit, intimate atmosphere at **La Clandestina,** a small "clandestine" bar in the Roma (page 152).

✪ **MOST EXCLUSIVE NIGHTCLUB:** If you can get past the doorman and into the club at **M. N. Roy,** you'll be rewarded with beats from famous DJs and a dazzling atmosphere (page 153).

✪ **BEST SPOT FOR ROCKERS:** For ear-splitting alternative punk, ska, or indie bands from Mexico City and beyond, squeeze into **Multiforo Alicia,** a rock institution in the western Roma neighborhood (page 154).

✪ **BEST BILLIARDS:** A mainstay in the Condesa, **Salón Malafama** is a casual, fun pool hall, with a hip crowd, gourmet bar snacks, and live music on the weekends (page 155).

Centro Histórico Map 1

BARS AND LOUNGES
Hostería La Bota

A student-friendly watering hole, Hostería La Bota is a mainstay among the small crop of bars and *mezcalerías* on the pedestrian street San Jerónimo, just behind the Universidad del Claustro de Sor Juana. Come here for poetry readings, live music, and book presentations, or just to enjoy a very cold beer in a low-key environment. With its worn wooden tables covered in notes and scribbles and a barroom filled floor-to-ceiling with posters, the atmosphere is college-town cool.

MAP 1: San Jerónimo 40, 55/5709-9016; Sun.-Wed. 1:30pm-midnight, Thurs.-Sat. 1:30pm-2am; no cover; Metro: Isabel la Católica

✪ Miralto

The famous observation deck at the top of the Torre Latinoamericana is on the building's 44th floor, but you can linger over the same view (and a martini) at Miralto, a restaurant and bar on the 41st floor of the tower. Though the setting couldn't feel more million-dollar, Miralto is no more expensive than any other bar in the area, and there's no time of day when the view is anything short of breathtaking. If you are going to the restaurant, reservations are necessary; the bar is first-come, first-serve.

MAP 1: Eje Central 2, 41st fl., 55/5518-1710, www.miralto.com.mx; Mon. 8am-8pm, Tues.-Wed. 8am-11pm, Thurs.-Sat. 8am-2am, Sun. 9am-8pm; no cover; Metro: Bellas Artes

CANTINAS
La Faena

Set in a lovely, crumbling colonial-era building, this rather unusual bar pays homage to bullfighting: Here, ornate old matador costumes fill glass display cases around the barroom, while the old tile floors and dusty chandeliers make an oddly elegant contrast to the decidedly unpretentious plastic chairs and cantina tables that fill the space. Clientele is a varied local crowd, but don't be surprised to see a hipster or two in the mix. Cash only.

MAP 1: Venustiano Carranza 49B, 55/5510-4417; Mon., Thurs. 11am-11:30pm, Fri.-Sat. 11am-2:30am, Sun. 11am-9pm; no cover; Metro: San Juan Letrán

Mancera

Mancera

Just next door to La Faena, Mancera is an old-fashioned cantina, with a sedate, turn-of-the-20th-century

NIGHTLIFE LISTINGS

It's hard to keep up with everything there is to see and do in Mexico City, but a few periodicals can help you navigate the onslaught of movies, art openings, museum shows, concerts, and sporting events taking place across the city. For up-to-date listings on what's happening when you're in town, check out the following Spanish-language publications.

TIME OUT MEXICO

The international magazine *Time Out* (www.timeoutmexico.mx) brings its signature service journalism to the capital, covering nightlife, dining, film, art and culture, and shopping throughout the metropolis. Witty and perceptive, the print version of *Time Out* is free to readers (pick it up wherever you see a copy), though you can also download the entire edition on the website.

TIEMPO LIBRE

With more than 30 years in print, *Tiempo Libre* (www.tiempolibre.com.mx) was, for many years, the only periodical covering entertainment and cultural events in the capital. It's been joined by some newcomers but remains an excellent source of listings for upcoming concerts and events in the city. It's for sale in most newspaper stands in the capital.

CHILANGO

This online magazine (www.chilango.com) covers upcoming events in the city, in addition to maintaining extensive listings for restaurants, bars, shops, museums, and more, in every neighborhood in the city.

---

atmosphere. Opened in 1912, the cantina retains many original details, like wood-paneled walls, oversize oil paintings, and an old-fashioned bar with a glass hood and mirrors. Rarely too crowded, it's ideal for sipping a glass of quality tequila while decompressing from the chaos of the Centro. **MAP 1:** Venustiano Carranza 49, 55/5521-9755; Mon.-Wed. 2pm-10pm, Thurs.-Sat. 2pm-2am; no cover; Metro: San Juan Letrán

Salón España

This small, no-nonsense cantina is a good place to explore the many flavors of Mexico's national drink, with a list of more than 200 tequilas available, from well known to rare, ranging in price US$3-20 per glass. Don't be deterred by the less-than-impressive entryway; the interior is clean, orderly, and efficient. *Botanas* (small plates) are served free with drinks every day.

MAP 1: Luis González Obregón 25, 55/5702-1719; Mon.-Sat. 11:30am-midnight, Sun. noon-7pm; no cover; Metro: Zócalo

LIVE MUSIC AND DANCING

Pasagüero

The perennially popular Pasagüero reopened with a new concept in the summer of 2013. Now partnered with the modern Coyoacán cantina La Bipo, this concert hall and art space

Pasagüero

is open all day, selling drinks and bar snacks, from ceviche to tacos, in addition to daily specials, popular with local lunchers. At night, rock and blues shows still play in the big, no-frills performance space in back.

MAP 1: Motolinia 33, 55/5512-6624, www.pasaguero.mx; Mon.-Tues. 1pm-midnight, Wed.-Thurs. 1pm-2am, Fri.-Sat. 1pm-3am, Sun. 1pm-10pm, showtimes vary; US$0-20; Metro: Allende

Zinco Jazz Club

This cosmopolitan jazz club is known for bringing some of the best performers to the capital, from international jazz trios to homegrown brass bands. The cozy venue has a classic cabaret atmosphere, with black walls, flickering candles, and a red curtain swaying behind the stage. If you're headed to Zinco, look for the basement door in the art deco Edificio Banco de México, on the corner of Motolinia and Cinco de Mayo.

MAP 1: Motolinia 20, 55/5512-3369, http://zincojazz.com; Wed.-Sat. 8pm-2:30am, showtimes vary; generally US$10-30; Metro: Bellas Artes

GAY AND LESBIAN

✪ El Marrakech Salón

This upbeat, ultra-fun, straight-friendly bar is hopping in the evenings, when an eclectic crowd convenes for DJs, people-watching, and kitschy entertainment. Things heat up here on the weekends, when strippers and drag shows get started around 11pm and the dance floor rocks till closing. The friendly attitude and youthful crowd have made this gay bar one of the most popular spots on the lively strip of dance halls and cantinas on República de Cuba.

MAP 1: República de Cuba 18; Thurs.-Sat. 8:15pm-2am; no cover; Metro: Bellas Artes

La Purísima

If you're having a ball at Marrakech and want to take the party up a notch, cross the street to La Purísima, a clubbier spot that nonetheless retains the same friendly atmosphere as its neighbor. Disco balls and strip shows lean a bit kitschy, but the upbeat crowd makes for a great night out.

MAP 1: República de Cuba 17, 55/5704-1995; Thurs.-Sat. 7pm-3am; no cover; Metro: Bellas Artes

Alameda Central   Map 2

CANTINAS

Salón Tenampa

Salón Tenampa, the legendary mariachi bar where it all started in Garibaldi, in 1925, is still going strong, and it remains a great place to spend a lively evening with a group of friends. With its paper flags hanging from the ceilings, murals on the wall, and ever-ebullient crowd, it's almost a guaranteed good time. It's fun to commission a few songs from the many mariachi groups that walk by, though confirm the price before they start playing.

MAP 2: Plaza Garibaldi 12, 55/5526-6176, www.salontenampa.com; Sun.-Thurs. 1pm-2am, Fri.-Sat. 1pm-4am; no cover; Metro: Garibaldi

✪ Tío Pepe

Located in the Centro's small and quirky Barrio Chino (Chinatown),

PULQUE

Though the Spanish brought beer-brewing techniques to the New World shortly after the conquest, local people had been producing a fermented beverage for centuries: A fizzy and highly nutritious drink called pulque, made from the sap of the maguey cactus, was consumed throughout central Mexico in the pre-Columbian era. Considered sacred by the Mexica, who rarely drank alcoholic beverages outside of special festival events, it was even then generally reserved as the drink for priests, nobles, and the elderly.

After the conquest, pulque was available to the masses and was very popular across Mexico. In Mexico City, there were *pulquerías* in every neighborhood; however, as beer producers attempted to make inroads with the population during the 19th century, they helped spread the misconception that pulque was less hygienic than bottled brews. The drink fell out of favor, and only a few of the old spots remained in business, catering to an ever-diminishing crowd.

pulque

Fortunately, this wonderful frothy drink is experiencing a much-deserved renaissance in Mexico. Some of the surviving old-time *pulquerías* have begun to attract a new, larger clientele, as young people develop an interest in the beverage, while nouveau *pulquerías* have opened in the Roma and Condesa neighborhoods, serving the drink in a more contemporary setting. (Note that traditional *pulquerías* serve pulque and only pulque. Newer places will often have a selection of beer or mezcal on the menu as well.)

With its slightly viscous texture and notably fermented flavor, pulque is an acquired taste for some, though others love it right away. It can be drunk in its natural state, though it is more popular in *curados*, flavored with fresh fruit pulp or nuts and sweetened with honey or cane sugar.

Tío Pepe is a wonderful old cantina that maintains a worn but grand early-20th-century atmosphere with its polished dark-wood bar, turquoise walls, and gold molding along the ceilings. Come early in the evening to sip tequila at one of the cozy booths with red-Formica-topped tables, as a friendly, relaxed crowd fills up the space. Sometimes roving musicians will arrive, enlivening the atmosphere further.

MAP 2: Independencia 26, 55/5521-9136; Mon.-Fri. noon-10pm, Sat. noon-11pm; no cover; Metro: Bellas Artes

TEQUILA AND MEZCAL
Bósforo

An unmarked bar a few blocks south of the Alameda Central, Bósforo's specialty is small-batch mezcal from Oaxaca and the greater republic. Bartenders can recommend a drink from the often-changing list, and shots are served with orange wedges and salt, as is traditional. Hidden behind metal doors but often crowded on the weekends, the bar has a pleasingly clandestine, locals-in-the-know atmosphere.

MAP 2: Luis Moya 31, 55/5512-1991; Wed. 4pm-1:30am, Thurs.-Sat. 4pm-2:30am; no cover; Metro: Bellas Artes

PULQUERÍAS

Pulquería La Hermosa Hortensia

A little bar on the Plaza Garibaldi, the Hermosa Hortensia was, for many years, one of the few traditional *pulquerías* visited by tourists. Founded in 1936, as the sign on the wall proudly proclaims, it's a historic establishment, serving mugs of good flavored pulque and wasting few resources on decor. As pulque gains popularity, the bar has become more mainstream, attracting students and other young people, but it remains a classic old-school spot.

MAP 2: Callejón de la Amargura 4, Plaza Garibaldi; daily noon-midnight; no cover; Metro: Garibaldi

☻ Pulquería Las Duelistas

Las Duelistas is one of the oldest traditional *pulquerías* in Mexico City, but you'd never guess it from the predominantly young clientele, who bring a bit of punk-rock vibe to the joint. It's a friendly, convivial place, and the *curados* are delicious, made fresh daily and served cold. Try fresh fruit and vegetable flavors like celery or guava. Like most traditional *pulquerías*, it closes early—and they sometimes run out of certain drinks before the 9pm closing.

Pulquería Las Duelistas

MAP 2: Aranda 28, 55/1394-0958; Mon.-Sat. 10am-9pm; no cover; Metro: San Juan Letrán

LIVE MUSIC AND DANCING

Salón Los Angeles

This atmospheric Latin dance hall's proud motto is *"Quién no conoce Los Angeles, no conoce México"* (Who doesn't know Los Angeles, doesn't know Mexico), a tribute to this ballroom's 75 years as a mainstay in the capital's dance scene. Here, top-quality live bands play *son cubano, danzón,* rumba, swing, and *cumbia,* among other tropical sounds, while well-dressed couples dance with purpose. The neighborhood is rough, so come and go in taxi or Uber.

MAP 2: Lerdo 206, Col. Guerrero, 55/5597-5181 or 55/5597-8847, http://salonlosangeles.mx; Tues. 5pm-10pm, Sat. 5pm-11pm; cost usually US$5-10; Metro: Garibaldi

BARS AND LOUNGES
Bar Milan

Long before the city was flooded with *mezcalerías* and concept shops, Bar Milan was playing indie music and serving pretty cocktails to a hipster crowd in the Juárez. Today, it's more a reliable classic than a cutting-edge destination, but it remains a very entertaining place for a night out, often filled with a slightly older crowd enjoying a bit of 1990s cool.

MAP 3: Milan 18, 55/5592-0031, www.barmilan.com.mx; Tues.-Sun. 8pm-2am; no cover; Metro: Cuauhtémoc, Metrobús: Reforma

CANTINAS
Bohemio's

It's hard to believe this low-key neighborhood cantina survives, right in the middle of the thumping nightclubs and cabarets of the Zona Rosa. But Bohemio's, a comfortable bar that serves draft beer and traditional Mexican snacks, manages to feel relaxed without feeling out of place. Wooden café tables, yellow wall lamps, and tiled walls give the barroom a warm Mexican atmosphere, and on the weeknights, there's a pleasant after-work crowd enjoying some drinks.

MAP 3: Londres 142, 55/5514-0790; Mon.-Sat. 1pm-1am; no cover; Metro: Insurgentes

TEQUILA AND MEZCAL
La Botica Mezcalería

La Botica was one of the first bars in Mexico City devoted to craft mezcal. In the years since its first, pleasingly no-frills location opened in the Colonia Condesa, the formula has proved a winner: Not only has La Botica opened several branches throughout the city (Campeche 396, Condesa, 55/5211-6045; Alfonso Reyes 120, Condesa, 55/5212-1167; Orizaba 161, Roma, 55/5574-6638; Isabel la Católica 30, Centro, 55/5574-6638; Arturo Ibáñez 2, Coyoacán, 55/5484-8255), but the spirit has become a mainstay in the chicest night spots in the city.

MAP 3: Amberes 1, 55/5511-1384, http://labotica.com.mx; Mon.-Sat. 6pm-2am, Sun. 6pm-midnight; no cover; Metro: Insurgentes

LIVE MUSIC
Parker & Lenox

"Hidden" behind Parker—a stylish American-diner-style restaurant serving burgers and fries, among other classics—Lenox is a speakeasy jazz club with cool old-timey design inspired by 1930s aesthetics. The period feel is furthered by nightly jazz performances, usually by high-quality local acts—and it all goes splendidly with a Negroni or an old-fashioned from the bar menu. If you're going on the weekend, it's best to reserve a table in advance.

MAP 3: Milan 14, 55/5546-6979; Tues.-Wed. 1pm-midnight, Thurs.-Sat. 1pm-2am; $0-10; Metro: Cuauhtémoc, Metrobús: Reforma

GAY AND LESBIAN
Kinky

The reincarnation of old-time favorite Lipstick, Kinky is a place you go for a straight-up good time, with numerous DJ-directed dance floors, a karaoke stage, and an open terrace

CANTINA CULTURE

Without a doubt, spending a few hours in a popular cantina is a quintessential Mexico City pastime. Sometimes historic, and invariably low-key, and usually inexpensive, cantinas are typically casual, no-nonsense places to eat and drink, filled with Formica-topped game tables for playing dominoes and brightly lit with neon lights. Many are distinguished by their friendly atmosphere and attentive table service—as well as for their excellent kitchens. Almost all cantinas offer free snacks, called *botanas*, with your drinks, which can range from a plate of peanuts to a full three-course meal (a course served with each drink you order). In fact, some cantinas function more like restaurants than bars, and have food that rivals the best eateries in the city.

La Bipo

with striking views of the Paseo de la Reforma. The low cover (which may include entry to Lollipop) and accessible drink prices—including beer sold by the liter—ensure a nightly crowd.

MAP 3: Amberes 1, 55/5514-4920, www.kinkybar.com.mx; Thurs.-Sat. 9:30pm-4am; US$3-4; Metro: Insurgentes

Lollipop

This friendly three-floor gay bar in the heart of the Zona Rosa's clubbiest block is a mainstay in the neighborhood. The sheer size attracts a mixed crowd, although, like many night spots along Amberes, it skews younger and male. There's a popular karaoke bar on the first floor and high-energy electronic-music dance floors on the second and third, packed till the early-morning hours. Cash only.

MAP 3: Amberes 14, 55/5207-5591; Thurs.-Sat. 9pm-4am; cover US$2-5; Metro: Insurgentes

Chapultepec and Polanco Map 4

BARS AND LOUNGES

✪ Jules Basement

This super-stylish speakeasy-style cocktail bar is hidden in the basement of restaurant La Surtidora, in Polanco, where the entryway is disguised behind what appears to be a refrigerator door. Once you're in, this basement bar is a comfortable place with a pretty crowd and pro cocktails—like the Oscar Wilde, made with Jameson, apple juice, and passion fruit. The atmosphere is complemented by frequent live DJs and weekly jazz performances. Reservations are generally required and essential on a weekend.

MAP 4: Julio Verne 93, 55/5280-1278, www.julesbasement.com; Tues.-Sun. 8pm-2am; no cover; Metro: Polanco

Terraza at the Hotel Hábita

The rooftop lounge at the Hotel Hábita has been a happening night spot since it opened in 2000. It's generally quiet during the daytime, but in the evening it draws a fashionable crowd for its mix of great cocktails and chic atmosphere. With no cover charge, it's a perfect place to sip a cocktail with the beautiful people of Polanco, and in often rowdy Mexico City it's a good choice for a slightly older, thirty-something crowd.

MAP 4: Hotel Hábita, Av. Mazaryk 201, 55/5282-3100; daily 7pm-2am; no cover; Metro: Polanco

DANCE CLUBS
Joy Room

It's easy to forget this upscale lounge is located in a mall once you've stepped inside the ultra-posh space, decked out with couches, lamps, purple mood lights, and a big illuminated bar. Here, a dressy crowd goes to drink, mingle, look good, and then, if the mood strikes, dance till late in the adjoining nightclub, Ragga (www.raggaantara. com, US$20 cover for men, open till 5am).

MAP 4: Plaza Antara, Ejercito Nacional 843, 55/5281-3181; Wed.-Sat. 10:30pm-6am; no cover; Metro: Polanco

Roma and Condesa   Map 5

BARS AND LOUNGES
Biergarten

On the top floor of Mercado Roma, this pretty rooftop bar is a nice place to relax away the afternoon or evening with a glass (or two) of draft beer. There is a new featured brew each month and a focus on national microbrews, though you'll also find some German and U.S. brands on the list, as well as creative cocktails. It can get intolerably crowded on the weekends, but the atmosphere and drinks are ace on a mellow afternoon.

MAP 5: Querétaro 225, 55/5264-3478, www.biergartenroma.com; Sun.-Wed. 1pm-11pm, Thurs.-Sat. 11am-1:30am; no cover; Metro: Sevilla, Metrobús: Sonora

Felina Bar

On the border of the Condesa and Escandón neighborhoods, this stylish neighborhood bar is a nice place to sip an expertly made Manhattan amid a crowd of locals and visitors. Remodeled in 2015, the bar is low-lit and attractive, with art deco details and long banquettes, but the new look hasn't changed Felina's fundamental character: It remains a relaxed place with a nice crowd and good music, conducive to a low-key evening with friends.

MAP 5: Ometusco 87, 55/5277-1917; Tues.-Sat. 6pm-2am; no cover; Metro: Patriotismo

PARA TODO MAL, MEZCAL. PARA TODO BIEN, TAMBIÉN.

A smooth yet potent drink, mezcal is a distilled liquor made from the heart of the maguey plant. Mezcal of different types and flavor profiles is produced throughout Mexico, usually in small batches at family ranches. Varieties of mezcal from the state of Oaxaca are particularly well known, and many present a distinct smoky flavor that comes from roasting the maguey leaves before distillation. In recent years, more producers in Oaxaca and around the country have begun to bottle and export the spirit. However, it is still largely a cottage industry, with mezcal produced in small batches—even bottled in recycled tequila bottles in many rural distilleries.

Tequila, made from the blue agave (a type of maguey) and produced by law in the state of Jalisco, is technically a very specialized type of mezcal. Like tequila, mezcal can be produced *blanco* (white) or *joven* (young), which means it hasn't been aged, as well as *reposado* (usually aged under a year) and *añejo* (aged for a year or more). Also like tequila, any high-quality mezcal is usually served straight and sipped slowly, with shots traditionally accompanied by orange slices and *sal de gusano* (salt with ground worm). Speaking of worms, mezcal is well known for the inclusion of a worm from the maguey cactus in bottles of the spirit, a practice still common in some parts of Oaxaca.

Until recently, mezcal production was rather limited, and it was rarely served in restaurants or bars outside the state of Oaxaca. Today, it has become a trendy drink of choice in the capital, even making its way onto the menus of fine-dining restaurants. Some small-batch brands of very good quality include Milagrito de Corazón, Enmascarado, Los Danzantes, Benevá, Cha Cha Cha, Alipus, and Fidencio, all produced in Oaxaca. And the old saying is more true than ever: *Para todo mal, mezcal. Para todo bien, también* (For everything bad, mezcal. For everything good, too).

Try mezcal at:

- **Bósforo** (page 146)

- **La Clandestina** (page 152)

- **La Botica Mezcalería** (page 148)

- **Los Danzantes** (page 135)

- **Mezcalero** (page 156)

Félix

This tiny, low-lit Roma bar gets so packed in the evenings that patrons overtake the sidewalk along Álvaro Obregón. Though most come for reasonably priced, beautifully prepared cocktails (as well as the nice selection of mezcal), there is also an open kitchen that prepares Mediterranean-inspired bar snacks (as well as non-Medi mini-burgers and tasty fries). Get there early if you want to snag a stool at the marble-topped bar.

MAP 5: Álvaro Obregón 64, 55/5264-0318; Tues.-Sat. 6pm-2am; no cover; Metro: Insurgentes

Jardín Chapultepec

Set in a plant-filled patio with gravel floors and picnic tables, this casual beer garden often feels like a friend's cool backyard party—but with Mexican craft beer on tap. If you want to make the afternoon of it, there's a menu of pizza and other bar snacks, and for major sporting events, they set up a big screen outside. On a warm afternoon, it's often crowded with locals and their dogs (it's pet-friendly).

MAP 5: Avenida Chapultepec 398, 55/7097-1302; daily 1pm-midnight; no cover; Metro: Insurgentes, Metrobús: Insurgentes

Licorería Limantour

Right on the main drag of Álvaro Obregón, this low-lit two-story bar takes its drinks seriously, with a menu full of unusual, creative cocktails made with good liquor and local herbs. Grab a seat at the bar before it fills up—which it always does on the weekends—to chat with the bartenders. After its success in the Roma, Limantour opened a snazzier second branch in Polanco (Oscar Wilde 9, 55/5280-1299).

MAP 5: Álvaro Obregón 106, 55/5264-4122, www.limantour.tv; Mon.-Tues. 6pm-midnight, Wed. 6pm-1am, Thurs.-Sat. 6pm-2am, Sun. 6pm-11pm; no cover, Metro: Insurgentes, Metrobús: Álvaro Obregón

✪ Pata Negra

With its long wood bar, consistently good music, and attractive clientele, this popular neighborhood spot is a nice place to chat and mingle. It's popular with expatriates and Condesa locals, there's almost always live music, and it can get very crowded on the weekends. In addition to the main bar, check out Salón Pata Negra (Tues.-Sat. 9pm-2am), a cool bar and concert space upstairs that often features Mexico City-based groups, as well as international talent, from jazz to flamenco to rock.

MAP 5: Tamaulipas 30, 55/5211-5563, www.patanegra.com.mx; daily 1:30pm-2am; no cover; Metro: Sevilla

CANTINAS
Centenario

Tucked between the stylish bars and restaurants of the Condesa neighborhood, this thoroughly unpretentious neighborhood cantina maintains a loyal clientele with its comfortable atmosphere, cheap drinks, and generally low-key patrons. The crowd is certainly a bit more gentrified than it was in the old days, but there's still a contingent of regulars chatting, playing dominos, or watching a soccer match in the barroom.

MAP 5: Vicente Suárez 42, 55/5553-5451; Mon.-Sat. noon-1am; no cover; Metro: Patriotismo

Covadonga

This spacious cantina near the Plaza Río de Janeiro was once a quiet place where men gathered to play dominos and sip tequila served from the fine old bar. In the past decade, however, it has also become popular with a hip Roma crew. Now, the seniors are joined by a bevy of artists and scenesters converging for drinks and Spanish food. It's a fun place for an evening out, uniting the old and new Roma.

MAP 5: Puebla 121, 55/5533-2922, http://banquetescovadonga.com.mx; Mon.-Sat. 1pm-2:30am; no cover; Metro: Insurgentes

TEQUILA AND MEZCAL
✪ La Clandestina

As the name suggests, this tucked-away mezcal bar feels rather clandestine, though its dim, hole-in-the-wall appearance is stylishly by design. Here, small-batch mezcal is served from big glass jugs lined up behind the bar; it's a good place to increase your knowledge of the spirit, as the menu details each mezcal's producer, region, proof, flavor profile, and price. After a taste, you may want to pick up a bottle of their Enmascarado mezcal to take home.

MAP 5: Av. Álvaro Obregón 298, 55/5525-1100, www.milagrito.com; Tues.-Sat. 5:30pm-2am; no cover; Metro: Sevilla, Metrobús: Álvaro Obregón

PULQUERÍAS

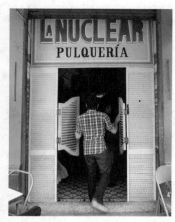

La Nuclear Pulquería

La Nuclear Pulquería

This enchanting little bar maintains the mellow, neighborhood atmosphere typical to classic *pulquerías* while introducing a dose of Roma cool to the mix. Here, fresh flavored pulques are ladled into clay tumblers, which you can sip at one of the folding tin tables on the sidewalk or in the row of cozy wooden booths in the narrow back room, which is decorated with sepia-toned murals and paper garlands.

MAP 5: Orizaba 161, 55/5574-5367; Mon.-Wed. 4pm-11pm, Thurs.-Sat. 4pm-2am; no cover; Metro: Insurgentes

Pulquería Los Insurgentes

The specialty at this big, popular bar, located in a four-story mansion on the busy Avenida Insurgentes, is pulque, brought fresh to the city from the nearby state of Tlaxcala and served natural or in flavored *curados* made with unrefined sugar and fruits. The changing daily selection might include flavors like pear, rice, oatmeal,

coconut, and strawberry, and there is a full bar, with beer on tap.

MAP 5: Insurgentes Sur 226, 55/4751-9326, www.pulquerialosinsurgentes.tv; Mon.-Wed. 2pm-1am, Thurs.-Sat. 1pm-3am; no cover; Metro: Insurgentes, Metrobús: Durango

DANCE CLUBS
Mama Rumba

After more than 20 years in business, Mama Rumba's popularity continues. This fun Cuban bar packs in crowds every night, with live bands playing to a lively, overcrowded dance floor fueled by generously served mojitos. It can be next to impossible to get a table here, but the scene is supercharged. Those who really want to shake it may find a little more space for dancing at the second branch in San Ángel (Altmirano 46, 55/5550-2959).

MAP 5: Querétaro 230, 55/5564-6920, www.mamarumba.com.mx; Wed.-Sat. 9pm-3am; generally no cover on weekdays, US$10 Fri.-Sat.; Metro: Insurgentes

✪ M. N. Roy

A private nightclub hidden behind the facade of an old-fashioned ice-cream shop, M. N. Roy is an ultra-exclusive destination that will appeal to veteran clubbers looking for an impressive night out. Once you get past the bouncer, the gorgeous architect-designed space is filled with towering ceilings, beautiful timber-lined walls, and able bartenders serving pricey cocktails. If you want to get in, look your best and cross your fingers: This velvet-rope club has a picky entry policy for those who aren't "members."

MAP 5: Merida 186, www.mnroyclub. com; Wed.-Sat. 11pm-6am; US$40, varies; Metro: Hospital General, Metrobús: Álvaro Obregón

Patrick Miller

Operated by famed DJ Patrick Miller, this Friday-night-only hot spot is for people who love to dance and, most especially, show off their moves. A mixed crowd gathers to shake it to Miller's well-known brand of Hi-NRG dance music, a style of '70s and early-'80s up-tempo electronica that has maintained a loyal following in Mexico City. Dance circles often form to let exhibitionists strut their stuff, as they've been doing at Miller's dance party for three decades and counting.

MAP 5: Mérida 17, 55/5511-5406, http:// patrickmiller.com.mx; Fri. 9pm-4am; US$5-10; Metro: Insurgentes, Metrobús: Álvaro Obregón

Rhodesia Club Social

At this youth-centric nightclub, three dimly lit floors are filled with pumping music, cheap shots, and a youthful crowd. Located in a "rundown" mansion off the Glorieta de las Cibeles, this clubby spot has some African touches (hence the name), but otherwise the vibe is straightforward disco. There's little attitude and no dress code—you'll find piercings and hoodies alongside heels and cocktail dresses amid this upbeat crowd. Here, the point is to drink, dance, and have fun.

MAP 5: Durango 181, 55/5533-8208, http://clubsocialrhodesia.tv; Wed.-Sat. 11pm-5am; US$10-20; Metro: Insurgentes

LIVE MUSIC

El Bataclán

This small cabaret, on the second floor of an old neighborhood mansion, hosts a mix of live music, theater, comedy, and vaudeville-type shows. Many come specifically to see Astrid Hadad (www.astridhadad. com), a superlative performer known for her elaborate costume changes and for combining biting social and political commentary with respectful take-offs of Mexico's *rancheras* and boleros. When she's not on tour, she frequently plays at El Bataclán.

MAP 5: Popocatépetl 25, 55/5511-7390, www.labodega.rest; most shows Fri. and Sat. at 9 or 10pm; US$20; Metro: Insurgentes

La Bodeguita en Medio

A nod to the famous Havana bar of the same name, this Cuban spot has an upbeat atmosphere every night of the week, with party-happy patrons sipping the Bodeguita's signature mojitos, nibbling on rice, beans, and fried plantains, and shouting over the live band. Inside the multilevel, dimly lit space, the walls are scribbled with notes and photographs. For those who want to practice their groove, there are salsa classes at least once a week.

MAP 5: Cozumel 37, 55/5553-0246, http:// labodeguitadelmedio.com.mx; daily 1pm-2am; no cover; Metro: Sevilla

✪ Multiforo Alicia

A bastion of punk culture and progressive politics, the famous Multiforo Alicia packs a few hundred enthusiastic young patrons into its barebones, second-floor concert space on the weekends. It really heats up, both literally and figuratively, as the show gets under way. The venue usually hosts Mexican bands—though not exclusively—often from Mexico City, with a focus on punk and garage rock. There will often be two or three acts each night.

MAP 5: Cuauhtémoc 91, 55/5511-2100, http://multiforoalicia.blogspot.com; Thurs.-Sat. 9pm-close; US$5-7; Metro: Cuauhtémoc

MEXICO'S MIGHTY MICROS

The vast majority of Mexico's beer production is dominated by two major conglomerates: Grupo Modelo (makers of Corona, Negra Modelo, Modelo Especial, León, Pacífico, and Victoria, among others) and Cervecería Cuauhtémoc Moctezuma (makers of Sol, Dos Equis, Bohemia, Carta Blanca, Indio, Tecate, and Superior).

The beers they produce have become symbols of Mexico; however, they aren't fully Mexican companies either. Grupo Modelo merged with Anheuser Busch InBev in 2013, while Cuauhtémoc Moctezuma is a subsidiary of Heineken International. As these brands become more multinational, craft beer producers have begun to pop up around the country, introducing new flavors to the range of traditionally light and milder Mexican beer. In 2013, microbrewers were massively benefitted when the government ruled that the two major breweries had to limit their exclusivity contracts to a quarter of their clients.

You'll notice a lot of craft beer in Mexico City today. Independent liquor stores and groceries usually carry a selection, and artisanal beer is practically a requirement in trendy restaurants.

WHERE TO GET IT
If you'd like to buy craft beer with enthusiastic and knowledgeable folks, try the small but impressively stocked **La Belga** (Orizaba 161, 55/3547-9558, www.labelga.com.mx) in the Roma, where they carry a large selection of both imported and national specialty beer. A few bars also specialize in craft brews. Owned by the folks behind Cervecería Primus, **La Graciela** (Orizaba 161, 55/5584-2728) makes its own beer in-house, with specials ranging from pilsner to brown ales. They also have beer on tap from several other producers; get a sampler if you want to try a bunch. A popular mini-chain of craft-beer bars, **El Depósito World Beer Store** has a branch in the Condesa (Av. Baja California 375, 55/5227-0716). Though not the most atmospheric option (grab a sidewalk table, if one is available), **Fiebre de Malta** (Río Lerma 156, 55/5207-0491) in the Cuauhtémoc is another craft mecca, with beers in bottles and on tap from Minerva, Cosaco, and more.

WHAT TO TRY
Among the best-known microbreweries in Mexico are Guadalajara-based **Minerva** (www.cervezaminerva.mx) and **Cervecería Primus** (www.primus.com.mx), from San Juan del Río, which produces beer under the names Tempus and Jabalí. Together with Minerva, Primus was active in denouncing the "duopoly" of Grupo Modelo and Cuauhtémoc Moctezuma and promoting new craft producers. Other well-known labels include **Cucapá**, a Mexicali-based brewery that produces blonde ale, amber ale, American pale ale, and IPA, among other signature brews. Made in Mexico City, **Cosaco** is a small-batch beer that isn't bottled; you can find it on tap in some specialty beer bars, including **Lucille** (page 155) and **Fiebre de Malta** (Río Lerma 156, 55/5207-0491). A Baja California-based brewery, **Tijuana** (www.tjbeer.com), makes European-style beers, including light and dark lagers, pilsner, and bock. Other small producers include Escollo, Baja Brewing Company, Cerveza Azteca, Calavera, and Alebrije, with new names rapidly joining the list.

BILLIARDS
Lucille

For years, this well-located corner spot was a rather barebones pool hall. After a nice renovation, it's less a pool hall and more a neighborhood bar with a few pool tables. The decor is still low-key, but there are homey touches like chandeliers and framed posters. If you come to play, the tables are inexpensive (around US$6 an hour), though many patrons are there to drink craft beer, eat pizza, and maybe cue up a game later in the evening.

MAP 5: Orizaba 99, 55/5207-8441; Mon.-Wed. noon-midnight, Thurs.-Sat. 11am-2am, Sun. noon-10pm; billiards US$6/ hour; Metro: Insurgentes, Metrobús: Álvaro Obregón

✪ Salón Malafama

This attractive billiard hall is filled front to back with red-felt-topped pool tables, and it is always packed with a young crowd drinking and racking up games. It's a great, mellow place to pass several pleasant hours on a weekend night before going out, though it's lively enough to be a destination in its own right. If you want to beat the crowds, go in the early afternoon, when there are usually free tables.

MAP 5: Michoacán 78, 55/5553-5138, http://salonmalafama.com.mx; Sun.-Thurs. noon-1am, Fri.-Sat. 1pm-2am; no cover, billiards US$9/hour; Metro: Patriotismo, Metrobús: Sonora

GAY AND LESBIAN
Elektrosundays by Híbrido
In pointed defiance of Monday morning, Elektrosundays by Híbrido is an ultra-popular Sunday-night-only

Salón Malafama

affair. It is always packed with an attractive, slightly upscale crowd, with live DJs and dancers keeping the party going strong until the early-morning hours. Not surprisingly, it can be particularly busy on a long weekend.

MAP 5: Coahuila 92, 55/5574-5367; Sun. 10pm- 6am; $5-15; Metro: Insurgentes

Coyoacán   Map 6

BARS AND LOUNGES
Mezcalero
A relaxing bar just behind the Parroquia de San Juan Bautista, Mezcalero is a nice place to have a drink on the sidewalk tables in the late afternoon—or, alternatively, to stay up late partying, buoyed by the exuberance of Coyoacán's youthful night scene. As the name hints, there is a nice selection of mezcal, as well as beer and cocktails. If all the nice tables are full, grab a seat at La Celestina, another youthful cocktail bar, next door.

MAP 6: Caballo Calco 14, 55/5554-7027; Mon.-Thurs. 1:30pm-2am, Fri.-Sat. 9am-2am, Sun. 9am-11pm; no cover; Metro: Viveros

CANTINAS
La Bipo
With a convivial local crowd and an atmosphere that blends new-school hip with quirky old-school kitsch, this casual nouveau cantina serves a menu of tempting bar snacks, like fish tacos and hibiscus-filled quesadillas. Upstairs, there is an open-roof terrace where smokers converge, though the funky downstairs bar has more style. It's a great place to spend a few hours discussing parties or politics over a plate of food and a shot of mezcal, as many Coyoacán locals do.

MAP 6: Malintzin 155, 55/5484-8230; Sun.-Tues. 1pm-11pm, Wed.-Thurs. 1pm-1am, Fri.-Sat. 1pm-2am; no cover; Metro: Viveros

CURE THE *CRUDA*

If going out big is a way of life in Mexico City, it's no surprise that there are ample **hangover remedies** reputed to alleviate the post-party blues. If you've got a *cruda* (hangover) after a night out, here are some local solutions:

VUELVE A LA VIDA
One of the most popular hangover remedies is the famous *vuelve a la vida* (literally a "return to life"), a cold mixed-seafood cocktail, tossed with tomato, lime juice, cilantro, and lots of chile—the worse the hangover, the spicier you go to "sweat it out." Across Mexico, it's not uncommon to see bleary-eyed breakfasters lining up at seafood stalls in the early morning hours. Try it for yourself at **Jardín del Pulpo** in **Mercado Coyoacán** (page 138), the neighborhood's central food market.

POLLA
On the stranger end of the spectrum, a *polla* is a blended smoothie made from orange juice, *jerez* (sherry), a raw quail egg, and a touch of vanilla. It's sold at **street-side juice stands** throughout the city. The idea is to down your *polla* rapidly to alleviate your hangover lickety-split.

BIRRIA
Birria, a goat-meat stew, is widely known as a hangover cure. Served boiling hot, then doused with chile and lime juice, it will certainly get you sweating. Try **La Polar** (page 120) in the San Rafael neighborhood for some of the city's best, and you'll find plenty of other diners, post-revelry, basking in the healing heat.

BARBACOA
Barbacoa, or slow-cooked lamb, is also a popular day-after remedy. Specifically, post-partiers seek out the pungent lamb broth served at most **barbacoa stands.** Spoon in some ultra-spicy salsa, top it off with white onions and cilantro, and sweat it all out.

La Coyoacana

Right in the heart of historic Coyoacán, this traditional cantina is a popular spot for visitors to rest their legs and have a few drinks on the pretty covered patio. On busy nights, musicians for hire mingle amid the revelers. With its low cost, central location, and merry atmosphere, there is often a wait for a table on the weekends.

MAP 6: Higuera 14, 55/5658-5337, www.lacoyoacana.com; Mon.-Wed. 1pm-midnight, Thurs.-Sat. 1pm-2am, Sun. 1pm-9pm; no cover; Metro: Viveros

LIVE MUSIC
El Vicio

A varied lineup can be found at this venue in Coyoacán, an incarnation of the long-running El Hábito, originally founded in 1954 by poet and essayist Salvador Novo. Often funny and irreverent shows include stand-up comedy, independent music, and monologues, and some performances benefit social organizations. As at many cabarets in Mexico City, you'll need proficient Spanish and some familiarity with Mexican politics and society to enjoy the show.

MAP 6: Madrid 13, 55/5659-1139, www.elvicio.com.mx; shows Wed.-Sat., hours vary; US$15-25; Metro: Viveros

ARTS AND CULTURE

Mexico City is the country's cultural heart, home to an inspiring diversity of museums, galleries, cinemas, photo archives, concert halls, and theaters.

You can count on finding top-quality exhibits at renowned spaces, like the contemporary-art-focused Museo Rufino Tamayo or the beloved decorative-arts space Museo Franz Mayer. However, lesser-known venues are often just as compelling, like the Laboratorio de Arte Alameda, which explores the intersection of art and technology.

Museo Nacional de Culturas Populares, Coyoacán

Most museums charge a small admission fee and function as truly public spaces, where tourists will find themselves surrounded by schoolchildren and families. Most museums and cultural centers also host frequent (and usually free) special events like concerts and movie screenings.

Across institutions, a pervasive interest in avant-garde work manifests itself alongside centuries-old artistic traditions. In some cases, historic buildings have been taken over by contemporary projects, like the Ex-Teresa Arte Actual, where the nave of a 17th-century baroque church is now an experimental gallery space.

Music, theater, and dance are traditional disciplines in Mexico, with a national character that expresses itself in everything from politically charged variety shows to folk dances. There's never a shortage of big-name rockers in the capital, but you can also see exuberant Cuban bands, flamenco vocalists, and other international stars in the city's myriad concert venues.

HIGHLIGHTS

✪ **BEST REINVENTION:** After a three-plus-year renovation, the long-running **Centro de la Imagen** reopened in 2015 with renewed energy and expansive, contemporary gallery spaces dedicated to photography, past and present (page 163).

✪ **BEST CELEBRATION OF LOCAL CRAFTS:** Beautifully curated and highly entertaining, the **Museo de Arte Popular** celebrates Mexico's traditions in popular art and handicrafts through an excellent permanent collection, as well as rotating exhibitions (page 163).

✪ **TOP DESIGN SCHOOL:** Explore three centuries of New World design at **Museo Franz Mayer,** a long-running decorative-arts museum on the Alameda Central (page 165).

✪ **MOST MEMORABLE EVENING OUT:** Modern aesthetics and traditional dance come together in the celebrated ensemble **Ballet Folklórico de México de Amalia Hernández,** which performs twice weekly at the **Palacio de Bellas Artes** (page 166).

✪ **BEST ALT MUSEUM:** From its early ties to the local punk-rock scene to its excellent avant-garde art shows today, the **Museo Universitario del Chopo** is worth a special trip to the urban Santa María la Ribera neighborhood (page 168).

✪ **ARTSIEST HOT SPOT:** Helmed by one of the most important art collectors in the world, **Museo Jumex** is a top-notch contemporary art space that collaborates frequently with some of the world's most famous museums (page 171).

✪ **FINEST MOVIE MECCA:** Since its founding in the 1970s, the **Cineteca Nacional** has maintained a reputation as the city's finest independent *cineclub*, showing everything from Cannes-awarded documentaries to retrospective series (page 174).

✪ **BEST CONTEMPORARY ART MUSEUM:** Located on UNAM's main campus, the **Museo Universitario Arte Contemporáneo** (MUAC) is one of the city's most exciting places to see contemporary art (page 177).

✪ **MOST STRIKING ARCHITECTURE:** Diego Rivera's remarkable collection of pre-Columbian art and artifacts is on display at the wholly original **Museo Anahuacalli** (page 179).

✪ **BEST DIEGO-AND-FRIDA MUSEUM:** Housed in a stunning 16th-century hacienda surrounded by lush gardens, the **Museo Dolores Olmedo** showcases Olmedo's personal art and archaeology collection, which includes many works by Rivera and Kahlo (page 180).

CULTURAL CENTERS

Casa Vecina

Bringing new proposals in art and design to the greater community is part of the mission at Casa Vecina, an art and cultural center located on the corner of the Callejón de Mesones and the pedestrian street Regina. As one of its main activities, the center operates ongoing three-month-long artist residencies; working in downstairs studios where they are visible to passersby, resident artists use the space to create original works of art that are later on display in the charming galleries upstairs.

MAP 1: Primer Callejón de Mesones 7, 55/5709-1540, http://casavecina. com; Tues.-Thurs. 10am-7pm, Wed.-Sat. 10am-5pm; free; Metro: Isabel la Católica

GALLERIES

Galería de Arte de la SHCP

The Mexican government allows working visual artists to pay a portion of their annual taxes with art. As a result of this program, the Minister of Finance and Public Credit has amassed a rather diverse collection of work from across the republic. You can see a selection of that massive reserve at the free SHCP gallery, which is on the ground floor of a neoclassical 19th-century mansion, just behind the cathedral. Exhibits change frequently and include varied but generally high-quality painting and sculpture.

MAP 1: Guatemala 8, 55/9688-1245; daily 10am-7pm; free; Metro: Zócalo

MUSEUMS

Casa de la Primera Imprenta de América

Nestled amid the grand palaces of Moneda, this little building was likely constructed in the early 16th century, though it gained national importance about 10 years later when it became the home of New Spain's first printing press. Today, it is a cultural center, operated by the Universidad Autónoma Metropolitana, showcasing ongoing exhibits related to books, typography, and art. It also holds a replica of the original printing press, which was brought to Mexico from Italy in 1539.

MAP 1: Licenciado Primo de Verdad 10, 55/5522-1535; Mon.-Fri. 10am-5pm, Sat. 10am-3pm; free; Metro: Zócalo

Ex-Teresa Arte Actual

On the small side street Licenciado Verdad, a towering 17th-century baroque church has been transformed into a wholly unique gallery space dedicated to contemporary performance, installation, and sound art. Shows often have a very experimental focus, which contrasts sharply with the atmosphere in the old church; what was once the main nave—with its wobbly, sinking floors—has been cleared to create the exhibition space. The gallery sometimes doubles as a cinema in the evening.

MAP 1: Licenciado Verdad 8, 55/4122-8020, www.exteresa.bellasartes.gob.mx; daily 10am-6pm; free; Metro: Zócalo

NOCHE DE MUSEOS

The last Wednesday of every month, museums throughout the city stay open until 10pm, generally providing free (in a few cases, reduced-price) admission to visitors after official closing time. Many museums go far beyond simply opening their doors to the public, however, planning concerts, speakers, or guided tours of the galleries after hours. In 2015-2016, for example, there was a baroque music concert in the Museo Mural Diego Rivera, a screening of *Nosferatu* with live music in the Museo Franz Mayer, free guided tours in the Museo Nacional de Historia in the Castillo de Chapultepec, a piano concert in the Palacio Nacional, and a Middle Eastern dance performance at the Antiguo Colegio de San Ildefonso.

Some wonderful institutions participate in the event throughout the city, but you'll cover the most ground in the Centro Histórico, where the vast majority of museums participate, and many are within close walking distance of each other. If you're in town, it's a great opportunity to visit several different spaces in a single evening.

Museo Archivo de la Fotografía

A fascinating stop for photography and history buffs, this small museum features rotating exhibits from its massive permanent collection of photographs of 19th- and 20th-century Mexico City. These images showcase the rapid and often miraculous transformations that took place in the capital during the previous decades. The galleries are located in the 16th-century Casa de las Ajaracas, the final structure on the street República de Guatemala. The buildings next door were demolished in 1994 to continue excavation of the Templo Mayor archaeological site.

Museo Archivo de la Fotografía

MAP 1: República de Guatemala 34, 55/2616-7057, www.cultura.df.gob.mx; Tues.-Sun. 10am-6pm; free; Metro: Zócalo

Museo del Estanquillo

This entertaining museum was established by Carlos Monsiváis, a political activist, journalist, and prolific chronicler of life in Mexico City, who remains influential even after his 2010 death (among other works, Monsiváis's collection of essays *Los Rituales del Caos* is a classic portrayal of the capital). The museum organizes rotating thematic shows dedicated to Mexican art and culture, as well as exhibits showcasing the writer's personal collection of sketches, photos, advertisements, comics, and more.

MAP 1: Isabel la Católica 26 at Madero, 55/5521-3052, ext. 101, www. museodelestanquillo.com; Wed.-Mon. 10am-6pm; free; Metro: Allende

Museo Mexicano de Diseño (MUMEDI)

In an 18th-century palace just a few steps from the Zócalo, this multipurpose cultural center is dedicated to contemporary Mexican art and design. Most visitors come to drink a coffee in the cute café or browse the charming gift shop, but there is also a gallery that hosts rotating themed exhibitions, which change every few months. The gallery is accessible only by guided tours, given on the hour (buy tickets in the gift shop).

MAP 1: Madero 74, 55/5510-8609, www.mumedi.org; Mon. 11:30am-8pm, Tues.-Sun. 10am-8pm; US$2; Metro: Zócalo

THEATER, CLASSICAL MUSIC, AND DANCE

Teatro de la Ciudad de México, Esperanza Iris

Designed to resemble La Scala, in Milan, the Teatro de la Ciudad was constructed in the early 20th century by actress Esperanza Iris. After its inauguration, it was the top performance venue in the city, though its audience declined after the opening of the Palacio de Bellas Artes in the 1930s. Later sold to the city, only the theater's neoclassical exterior remains intact. Today, it hosts performances from a range of disciplines, from flamenco to circus acts.

MAP 1: Donceles 36, 55/5510-2197; US$10-50, depending on seats; Metro: Allende

Museo del Estanquillo

CONCERT VENUES

Teatro Metropólitan

Originally built as a cinema in the 1940s, this famous old theater was revamped as a concert venue in the 1980s. Despite its cool art deco facade, its interior is neoclassical, including giant classical sculptures in the orchestra pit. Located just a few blocks from the Alameda, it puts on rock en español and Latin music shows. You can purchase tickets through Ticketmaster.

MAP 2: Av. Independencia 90, 55/5510-1035; showtimes generally between 6pm and 9pm; US$5-15 depending on performer and seats; Metro: Hidalgo

Laboratorio de Arte Alameda

MUSEUMS

✪ Centro de la Imagen

After a three-year-long renovation, this breathtaking public photography gallery reopened in October 2015 with expanded exhibition spaces, projection rooms, and a changing outdoor "photo mural." The center offers frequent workshops and special events, while ongoing exhibits focus on both contemporary work and the history of photography. It's worth visiting the space just to see the architectural creativity of the new galleries, which were built inside an 18th-century cigarette factory.

MAP 2: Plaza de la Ciudadela 2, 55/4155-0850, http://centrodelaimagen. conaculta.gob.mx; Wed.-Fri. noon-9pm; free; Metro: Balderas

Laboratorio de Arte Alameda

Mexico City's penchant for combining avant-garde ideas and old-fashioned spaces is beautifully manifested in the Laboratorio de Arte Alameda. Located in the former convent of San Diego, right on the Alameda Central, this highly regarded contemporary-art museum was opened in 2000, with usually excellent ongoing exhibitions exploring the relationship between art and technology. As such, there is often a heavy emphasis on video and electronic art, with many works conceived specifically for the space.

MAP 2: Dr. Mora 7, 55/8647-5660, www. artealameda.bellasartes.gob.mx; Tues.-Sun. 9am-5pm; US$1.50; students, teachers, and seniors free; general admission free Sun.; Metro: Hidalgo

✪ Museo de Arte Popular

The Museo de Arte Popular (MAP), in a five-story art deco building, is dedicated to the preservation and exhibition of Mexican folk art and craft. Unlike most craft museums, MAP isn't organized by region or chronology, but by theme, like "religion," "parties," and "daily life," with antique and contemporary pieces from a range of traditions exhibited together. Many of the pieces on

EVENTS IN THE ARTS

In addition to the multitude of museums, galleries, movie houses, cultural centers, theaters, forums, and other places to see art, performances, and design in Mexico City, there are several high-profile annual events worth noting.

ZSONA MACO
When: Held over five days in February.
What: Established in 2004, Mexico City's largest and most prestigious contemporary-art fair, Zsona MACO (http://zsonamaco.com), includes booths by the most prestigious names in Mexico City, as well as some very well-known galleries from the United States, Europe, and Latin America. Come to browse the stands, see some interesting art (with much produced locally), and enjoy the pretty people watching at the Centro Banamex, in the Lomas de Sotelo neighborhood.

MATERIAL ART FAIR
When: February, at the same time as Zsona MACO.
What: Running at the same time as Zsona MACO, this smaller, more alternative art fair represents emerging artists and galleries from both Mexico and abroad. Founded in 2014, this fair, like MACO before it, is certain to become more prestigious as it grows. In 2016, it was held in the Expo Reforma in the Juárez neighborhood, but location may vary from year to year.

FESTIVAL DEL CENTRO HISTÓRICO DE LA CIUDAD DE MÉXICO
When: Held over several weeks in March and April
What: Take a tour of the city's many impressive theaters, performance spaces, cultural centers, and public plazas during the Festival del Centro Histórico (http://festival.org.mx), one of the country's largest arts festival, which includes music, dance, theater, and visual arts exhibits. The agenda in 2016 included performances by Québécois dance troupe Le Carré des Lombes in the Teatro de la Ciudad and a concert by French pianist Lucas Debargue in the Palacio de Bellas Artes, among many other events.

FOTOSEPTIEMBRE
When: Held biannually, over a month in September.
What: This festival celebrates the art of photography, with a month-long series of talks, workshops, and exhibitions dedicated to the medium. Though largely spearheaded by the Centro de la Imagen in the Centro Histórico, many other important venues participate in the event.

DESIGN WEEK MEXICO
When: Held over a week in October.
What: Mexico City's contemporary achievements in industrial and graphic design, architecture, and other applied arts are showcased throughout the city during this autumn festival and educational event. The impressive program includes installations, professional talks, and design exhibitions at major city venues, like the Museo Tamayo, with a specially recognized country and Mexican state given a place of honor during the events (in 2015, it was Italy and Chiapas, respectively). See past and future agendas at www.designweekmexico.com.

display are highly original and rare, though the museum also makes space for beautiful everyday objects and more simple handicrafts. In the fifth-floor galleries, there is a wonderful 1947 mural by Mexican artist Miguel Covarrubias that was rescued from a nearby building and installed at the museum. On the second floor, the museum hosts temporary exhibitions. **MAP 2:** Revillagigedo at Independencia, 55/5510-2201, www.map.cdmx.gob.mx; Tues.-Sun. 10am-5pm, Wed. until 9pm; US$4; Metro: Juárez

Museo del Tequila y El Mezcal

This small museum chronicling the history and culture of agave distillation in Mexico opened as a part of the Plaza Garibaldi's 2010 renovation. In addition to the permanent exhibit, which includes a site-appropriate display dedicated to mariachi music, the museum hosts special events and rotating exhibits related to spirits. Your tour of the museum ends on the roof deck, where guests can enjoy a view of Plaza Garibaldi over a small complimentary shot of tequila and mezcal.

MAP 2: Plaza Garibaldi, 55/5529-1238, www.mutemgaribaldi.mx; museum Sun.-Wed. 11am-10pm, Thurs.-Sat. 11am-midnight; terrace and cantina Sun.-Wed. 1pm-10pm, Thurs.-Sat. 1pm-2am; US$4; Metro: Garibaldi

✪ Museo Franz Mayer

Explore the roots of Mexican artisan and aesthetic traditions at this interesting design museum, which displays the impressive collection of German-born financier Franz Mayer, including furniture, religious artifacts, tapestries, and books dating from the 16th through the 19th centuries. In addition to Mayer's collection, the museum continues to make new acquisitions and hold ongoing shows dedicated to contemporary decorative arts. Located

Museo Franz Mayer

in the former San Juan de Dios monastery, the space itself is both historic and beautiful.

MAP 2: Av. Hidalgo 45, 55/5518-2266, www.franzmayer.org.mx; Tues.-Sun. 10am-5pm; US$4, US$2 students and teachers, free for those over 60 and under 12 years old, general admission free on Tues.; Metro: Hidalgo

Museo Memoria y Tolerancia

This striking modern museum, designed to promote tolerance, nonviolence, and human rights, has a permanent exhibition divided into two parts: Memory, which explores 20th-century genocides, and Tolerance, which explores diversity, dialogue, human rights, and other related themes, both in Mexico and internationally. There is also a kid-centric exhibit, designed to teach the values of unity and tolerance to schoolchildren. Most notably, the museum hosts interesting temporary exhibits, like the 2016 Yoko Ono show "Land of Hope."

MAP 2: Plaza Juárez s/n, 55/5130-5555, www.myt.org.mx; Tues.-Fri. 9am-6pm, Sat.-Sun. 10am-7pm; US$4, US$3.25 students, teachers, and seniors; Metro: Bellas Artes or Hidalgo, Metrobús: Bellas Artes or Hidalgo

Museo Mural Diego Rivera

On a corner of the Alameda Central, this petite museum is dedicated to Diego Rivera's mural *Sueño de una Tarde Dominical en la Alameda Central* (Dream of a Sunday Afternoon in the Alameda Central), which he originally created for the Hotel del Prado in 1947-1948. The marvelously composed park scene portrays many famous Mexican personalities, including Hernán Cortés, former presidents Porfirio Díaz and Antonio López de Santa Anna, printmaker José

165

Guadalupe Posada, and artist Frida Kahlo.

MAP 2: Corner of Balderas and Colón, 55/1555-1900, www.museomuraldiegorivera.bellasartes.gob.mx; Tues.-Sun. 10am-6pm; US$1.50; Metro: Hidalgo

Museo Nacional de la Estampa

Printmaking has an important place in Mexican art and popular culture, and the Museo Nacional de la Estampa, or MUNAE, celebrates that tradition with ongoing exhibitions of woodcut, lithography, engraving, and other printed works by well-known Mexican (and sometimes international) artists. The museum's collection of more than 12,000 prints includes works by David Alfaro Siqueiros and Rufino Tamayo, as well as an extensive collection of work by celebrated Mexican satirist and printmaker José Guadalupe Posada.

MAP 2: Hidalgo 39, 55/8647-5220, www.museonacionaldelaestampa.bellasartes.gob.mx; Tues.-Sun. 10am-6pm; US$1, free on Sun., students and teachers free daily; Metro: Bellas Artes

THEATER, CLASSICAL MUSIC, AND DANCE
✪ Palacio de Bellas Artes

The theater inside the Palacio de Bellas Artes is the building's opulent

Palacio de Bellas Artes

keystone, with box seats rising along the stage, murals on the walls, and a Tiffany glass curtain onstage. The performance schedule features international music and dance, but particularly noteworthy is the Ballet Folklórico de México de Amalia Hernández, which performs in the theater every Sunday. Originally founded by Hernández and her daughter, the Ballet Folklórico showcases traditional dances and music from across Mexico, performed in colorful costume.

MAP 2: Eje Central and Av. Juárez, 55/5512-2593, www.palacio.bellasartes.gob.mx; showtimes vary; US$15-100, depending on seats and event; Metro: Bellas Artes

CULTURAL CENTERS
Centro Cultural Digital

Just outside the main gates to the Bosque de Chapultepec, the Centro Cultural Digital is a two-story sub-terranean cultural center dedicated to the intersection of technology, art, Internet, video games, and new-media disciplines. Stop in and you might find a massive sound-and-light installation in the downstairs gallery, or dozens of local teenagers participating in a weekend-long videogame-programming competition. There's an active cinema program on-site, as well as frequent workshops related to digital culture.

MAP 3: Paseo de la Reforma s/n, esq. Lieja, 55/1000-2637, www.centroculturadigital. mx; Tues.-Sun. 11am-7pm; free; Metro: Chapultepec

Galería Marso

GALLERIES
Galería Hilario Galguera

This contemporary gallery in a restored mansion on a quiet street in the San Rafael neighborhood garnered international press after hosting a major show by world-famous British artist Damien Hirst in 2006. In addition to this splashy exhibition, the gallery's streak of excellence continues, with ongoing exhibitions of both Mexican and international artists, including Jannis Kounellis, James HD Brown, and Daniel Lezama. The gallery's front door is always closed; ring the doorbell to enter.

MAP 3: Francisco Pimentel 3, 55/5546-6703, www.galeriahilariogalguera. com; Mon.-Thurs. 10:30am-5:30pm, Fri. 10am-2pm, Sat. by appointment; free; Metro: San Cosme

Galería Marso

Opened in 2012, this interesting contemporary gallery has ongoing exhibitions by emerging and mid-career artists, with a focus on Latin American and Mexican artists. The unique galleries in a massive Colonia Juárez mansion have soaring ceilings, parquet floors, and French doors. Stop by on a weekday and you'll likely have the place all to yourself.

MAP 3: Berlin 37, 55/6276-2275, www. marso.com.mx; Tues.-Fri. 10am-6pm, free; Metro: Insurgentes

MUSEUMS
Museo Experimental El Eco

Another of the many valuable cultural institutions overseen by the Universidad Nacional Autónoma de México, this small avant-garde museum was originally founded by German-born Mexican artist Mathias Goeritz in the mid-20th century. The space aims to be both experimental and interdisciplinary, with several large galleries with towering ceilings, a "bar area" (which doesn't function as a bar, though it looks like one), and a patio,

which includes a sculptural installation by Goeritz. The ongoing temporary exhibitions include installation, video, and sound art, many of which are specifically commissioned for the space.
MAP 3: Sullivan 43, 55/5535-5186, www.eleco.unam.mx; Tues.-Sun. 11am-6pm; free; Metro: Revolución, Metrobús: Reforma

Museo Nacional de San Carlos

Located in the opulent former palace of the Marqués de Buenavista, the Museo Nacional de San Carlos holds an impressive collection of European artwork, ranging from the 14th to the early 20th century. The collection was originally established in the 18th century at the Academia San Carlos art school and later augmented with a sizable donation from the Mexican government. The design of the palace is attributed to celebrated 18th-century Valencian architect Manuel Tolsá.
MAP 3: Av. Puente de Alvarado 50, 55/8647-5800, www.mnsancarlos.com; Wed.-Mon. 10am-6pm; US$2.50; Metro: Revolución or Hidalgo, Metrobús: Plaza de la República

✪ Museo Universitario del Chopo

The Museo Universitario del Chopo is housed in an impressive art nouveau structure, built in Dusseldorf and shipped to Mexico in the early 20th century. Later abandoned, the building was eventually declared a landmark, reopening as the Museo Universitario del Chopo in 1975. Featuring work by avant-garde artists, with themes addressing technology, gender identity, and other contemporary topics, the museum has a long connection to music and alternative subcultures. It helped to start the weekly album exchange that is today famous Saturday punk market Tianguis Cultural del Chopo.
MAP 3: Dr. Enrique González 10, Col. Santa María la Ribera, 55/5546-3471, www.chopo.unam.mx; Tues.-Sun. 10am-8pm; US$2.50, US$1 students, free on Wed.; Metro: San Cosme

Chapultepec and Polanco Map 4

CONCERT VENUES

Auditorio Nacional

One of the city's preeminent concert halls, with a capacity of 10,000, the Auditorio Nacional has a varied lineup that runs from internationally famous singers like Marc Anthony and Elton John, to popular *cumbia* groups and Mexican *banda*, to classical music concerts by international orchestras. Next door, the smaller Lunario (55/9138-1350, www.lunario.com.mx) is a 1,000-seat venue operated by the

Auditorio that hosts ongoing shows by lesser-known performers, with its equally varied programming running from jazz groups to funk.
MAP 4: Paseo de la Reforma 50, 55/9138-1350, www.auditorio.com.mx; daily 10am-6pm; US$25-200, depending on seats and event; Metro: Auditorio

CULTURAL CENTERS

Casa del Lago Juan José Arreola

Overseen by the Universidad Nacional Autónoma de México, this multimedia cultural and educational center operates an ongoing program of cinema, visual-arts exhibitions, concerts, theater, and poetry readings, in addition to offering workshops in disciplines as diverse as yoga, classical guitar, and chess. Housed in several turn-of-the-20th-century buildings next to the Lago de Chapultepec, the center was opened by writer Juan José Arreola in 1959, with a focus on promoting experimental artwork in a high-profile setting.

MAP 4: Bosque de Chapultepec, Primera Sección s/n, 55/5211-6086, www.casadellago.unam.mx; Wed.-Sun. 11am-5:30pm; free; Metro: Auditorio

GALLERIES

Galería de Arte Mexicano

Founded in 1935, the Galería de Arte Mexicano has a great legacy, having once hosted shows by the 20th century's most famous names, including Rivera, Kahlo, Orozco, Covarrubias, and Tamayo. In the residential San Miguel Chapultepec neighborhood, the gallery continues to focus on Mexico-based artists, representing well-known contemporary names, including Francisco Castro Leñero, Jan Hendrix, and Francisco Toledo. It's a beautiful space, and the exhibitions are high quality.

MAP 4: Gob. Rafael Rebollar 43, Col. San Miguel Chapultepec, 52/5272-5696, www. galeriadeartemexicano.com; Mon.-Fri. 10am-6pm; free; Metro: Juanacatlán or Constituyentes

Kurimanzutto

Partners José Kuri, Mónica Manzutto, and Gabriel Orozco opened this spacious contemporary gallery in 2008. Orozco shows his work here, as have numerous other high-profile international artists, including Allora y Calzadilla, Rirkrit Tiravanija, and Akram Zaatari. Opening parties are well-attended by a chic crowd, but the true attraction here is the excellent art. Drop by during the week and you're likely to have the gallery all to yourself.

MAP 4: Gob. Rafael Rebollar 94, 55/5256-2408, www.kurimanzutto.com; Tues.-Thurs. 11am-6pm, Fri.-Sat. 11am-4pm; free; Metro: Constituyentes or Juanacatlán

Labor

Located in an unmarked turquoise home, just across the street from the Casa Luis Barragán, this tucked-away contemporary gallery represents an interesting roster of international artists, including notable Mexican artist Pedro Reyes. Originally opened in 2010, it relocated to this quiet home in 2012, where a shaded garden adjoins the clean, white gallery space. Ring the doorbell during business hours and you'll be buzzed in.

MAP 4: Francisco Ramírez 5 , Col. Daniel Garza, 55/6304-8755, www.labor.org.mx; Mon.-Thurs. 11am-6pm, Fri. 11am-4pm, Sat. 11am-5pm and by appointment; free; Metro: Constituyentes

Luis Adelantado Mexico

In 2009, Valencia, Spain-based gallerist Luis Adelantado's Mexico City gallery opened in a giant warehouse north of Polanco. With its concrete floors and towering white walls, the space is minimal and urban-chic, well suited to the avant-garde exhibitions of large-scale work that the gallery often hosts. Check out the smaller galleries in the back of the space (and don't miss the off-the-wall bathrooms).

MAP 4: Laguna de Términos 260, Col. Anahuac, 55/5545-6645, www. luisadelantado.com; Mon.-Fri. 10am-6pm; free; Metro: San Joaquín

MUSEUMS

Archivo Diseño y Arquitectura

Right next door to the Casa Luis Barragán, the Archivo Diseño y Arquitectura is a gallery space and archive dedicated to industrial and decorative design, with more than 2,800 objects in its permanent collection. The main gallery, located on the first floor of a lovely midcentury home, overlooks the lushly landscaped back garden and reflecting pool. There, you'll see a changing lineup of thematic shows, with pieces drawn from the archive by guest curators.

MAP 4: General Francisco Ramírez 4, 55/2614-1063, http://archivonline. org; Mon.-Fri. 10am-6pm; free; Metro: Constituyentes or Tacubaya

Museo de Arte Moderno

Inaugurated in 1964, Mexico City's largest modern-art museum is housed in an industrial concrete building, with a central atrium surrounded by the four main exhibition halls, three of which are dedicated to changing exhibits, while the fourth displays work from the permanent collection. The quality of the exhibits varies; however, the museum's permanent collection contains work by Diego Rivera, Leonora Carrington, and Remedios Varo, as well as Frida Kahlo's largest work, *Las Dos Fridas*, a twin self-portrait by the artist.

MAP 4: Paseo de la Reforma and Gandhi, 55/8647-5530, www.museoartemoderno. com; Tues.-Sun. 10:15am-5:30pm; US$2, free on Sun.; Metro: Chapultepec

Museo de Historia Natural and Museo Jardín del Agua

Mexico City's old-timey natural-history museum first opened in 1790, though it changed locations several times before moving to its current space, in Chapultepec, in 1964. Today,

Archivo Diseño y Arquitectura

CONTEMPORARY ART

The contemporary art scene in Mexico City, which was still rather small a decade ago, has been growing rapidly in recent years, with the opening (and reopening) of some flagship institutions. Today there is a perceptible energy within the city's flourishing art scene.

Tapping into local talent, many galleries in Mexico City represent emerging and mid-career artists who haven't yet reached a wide audience, though you'll also find well-established and long-running art spaces, some representing important names in Mexican art.

Museo Universitario del Chopo

it's filled with vintage wildlife dioramas, taxidermy animals, and fossils. In 2012, the museum inaugurated a new ecological and art project, Museo Jardín del Agua, through which it restored 16 hectares in surrounding Chapultepec park, including the Diego Rivera fountain-mural *El Agua, Origen de la Vida en la Tierra* (*Water, the Origin of Life on Earth*).

MAP 4: Segunda Sección, Bosque de Chapultepec, 55/5515-0739, ext. 112 and 113, www.sedema.df.gob.mx/ museodehistorianatural; Tues.-Sun. 9am-5pm; US$2 includes admission to Rivera mural, children and seniors free, general admission free on Tues.; Metro: Chapultepec

✪ Museo Jumex

Over the past two decades, the Fundación Jumex, owned by juice-company heir Eugenio López Alonso, has assembled what is largely regarded as the most important collection of art in Latin America. In 2013, the foundation inaugurated a contemporary-art museum, designed by David Chipperfield, next to Carlos Slim's eye-catching Museo Soumaya. Small but beautifully designed, the museum has quickly become one of the most interesting contemporary-art venues in the city.

MAP 4: Miguel de Cervantes Saavedra 303, Col. Ampliación Granada, 55/5395-2615, http://fundacionjumex. org; Tues.-Sun. 11am-8pm; US$2 Mexican nationals, US$3 foreign nationals

Museo Rufino Tamayo

Founded by Oaxacan artist Rufino Tamayo, this excellent contemporary-art museum opened in 1981 and continues to host high-quality temporary exhibitions by both Mexican and international artists. (Contrary to what some visitors expect, Tamayo's work is shown only infrequently, as part of special exhibitions.) After an extensive 2012 remodel, there are now expanded gallery spaces in the eastern wing, as well as a very attractive (and delicious) café and a design-centric gift shop.

MAP 4: Paseo de la Reforma 51, 55/4122-8200, www.museotamayo.org; Tues.-Sun. 10am-6pm; US$3.50, children under 12, students, and teachers free, general admission free on Sun.; Metro: Chapultepec

Museo Sala de Arte Público David Alfaro Siqueiros

Celebrated 20th-century muralist David Alfaro Siqueiros dedicated his life to creating public art, and this small but wonderful museum honors his legacy by displaying works by Siqueiros himself, in addition to hosting fine exhibitions of contemporary art. In keeping with the theme, the museum's facade is constantly repainted via the museum's *Proyecto Fachada* (Facade Project), exploring themes in politics and social justice that were close to Siqueiros's heart.

MAP 4: Tres Picos 29, Polanco, 55/8647-5340, www.saps-latallera.org; Tues.-Sun. 10am-6pm; US$1, free for students, teachers, seniors, and children under 12; Metro: Auditorio

Museo Soumaya

In the 1990s, Mexican multibillionaire Carlos Slim opened the Museo Soumaya as a place to house and exhibit his extensive art collection. Originally located in the south of the city, the collection moved to a new US$70 million space in 2011, designed by Slim's son-in-law Fernando Romero. The building's striking exterior, a glittery swoosh of asymmetrical metal, covers five stories of galleries exhibiting European and Mexican art from the Renaissance to the present day.

MAP 4: Plaza Carso, Blvd. Miguel de Cervantes Saavedra 303, Col. Ampliación Granada, 55/1103-9800, www.soumaya. com.mx; daily 10:30am-6:30pm; free; Metro: Polanco or San Joaquín

Papalote Museo del Niño

Mexico City's wonderful children's museum fills a massive blue-tiled building just south of the amusement park in Bosque de Chapultepec. The "touch, play, and learn" exhibits cover themes like science, the human body, and communications, engaging children with hands-on activities. Note that audiovisual materials throughout the museum, including movies, are in Spanish. The museum has limited capacity (there can be a wait to get in), though it is still rather crowded on the weekends.

MAP 4: Av. Constituyentes 268, Segunda Sección, Bosque de Chapultepec, 55/5237-1773, www.papalote.org.mx; Mon.-Wed. and Fri. 9am-6pm, Thurs. 7pm-11pm, Sat.-Sun. and holidays 10am-7pm; US$10, free for children under 2; Metro: Constituyentes

Museo Soumaya

CULTURAL CENTERS
Casa Lamm
An opulent Colonia Roma mansion, Casa Lamm was originally built by architect Lewis Lamm in 1911. Today, it's home to a small art school (which offers workshops, as well as undergraduate and graduate programs), a light-filled contemporary-art gallery, and chic fusion restaurant **Nueve Nueve** (55/5525-9795, Mon.-Wed. 1:30pm-11pm, Thurs.-Sat. 1:30pm-midnight, Sun. 1:30pm-6pm). In the basement, the well-stocked **Biblioteca de Arte** (Mon.-Fri. 9am-7pm) has a large selection of contemporary- and modern-art books.

MAP 5: Álvaro Obregón 99, 55/5525-3938, www.casalamm.com.mx, www.galeriacasalamm.com.mx, www.nuevenueve.com.mx; cultural center Mon.-Wed. 10am-11pm, Thurs.-Sat. 10am-midnight, Sun. 10am-7pm; gallery Mon.-Sat. 10am-7pm, Sun. 10am-5pm; free; Metro: Insurgentes

GALLERIES
Galería OMR
OMR has maintained a strong reputation for contemporary art in Mexico City since its founding in 1983. Preceding many of the popular galleries in the Roma, OMR has in many ways set the tone for the neighborhood, supporting emerging artists and avant-garde propositions. In 2016, it moved from its longtime space beside the Plaza Río de Janeiro to the Sala Margolin, which was, for 60 years, a wonderful bookstore and record shop that specialized in classical music.

MAP 5: Córdoba 100, 55/5511-1179 or 55/5207-1080, www.galeriaomr.com; Tues.-Fri. 10am-2:30pm and 4pm-7pm, Sat. noon-6pm; free; Metro: Insurgentes

Proyectos Monclova
A young gallery that has already garnered a stellar reputation in the city for contemporary art, Proyectos Monclova is in a white-walled warehouselike space in the Colonia Roma, reminiscent of New York's Chelsea gallery district. Showing both Mexican and international artists, the gallery offers a rotating mix of photography, sculpture, installation, and mixed-media pieces. In addition, it hosts occasional performance events.

MAP 5: Colima 55, 55/4754-3546, http://proyectosmonclova.com; Tues.-Fri. 11am-6pm, Sat. 11am-4pm; free; Metro: Insurgentes

MUSEUMS
Museo del Objeto del Objeto
This small museum, housed in a lovely Beaux Artes mansion, focuses on the history of design and communications in Mexico City. Every few months, the museum inaugurates a new exhibit, dedicated to a theme like *lucha libre* or the history of the Roma neighborhood. Stories are often told via everyday objects, like matchbooks, enameled tin boxes, toys, watches, and posters, many of which are part of the museum's collection of over 100,000 design pieces.

MAP 5: Colima 145, 55/5533-9637, www.elmodo.mx; Tues.-Sun. 10am-6pm; US$3, US$1.50 students, teachers, and Roma neighborhood residents (with ID), children under 12 free; Metro: Insurgentes

Museo Universitario de Ciencias y Artes Roma (MUCA Roma)

The youthful Roma neighborhood is an ideal location for this high-quality contemporary art space, one of the many projects overseen by the Universidad Nacional Autónoma de México. In a fine old Porfiriato-era mansion, there are several exhibition spaces with polished concrete floors and white walls, which show interesting and often experimental work by emerging and mid-career artists. There's no admission charge, so it's worth peeking in while touring the neighborhood.

MAP 5: Tonalá 51, Roma Norte, 55/5511-0925; Mon.-Fri. 10am-6pm, Sat.-Sun. 10am-8pm; free; Metro: Insurgentes

THEATER, CLASSICAL MUSIC, AND DANCE

Foro Shakespeare

Originally founded as a bookshop specializing in theater, the Foro Shakespeare eventually grew to include several performance spaces.

Foro Shakespeare

Today, it's a nonprofit arts organization with a reputation for launching the careers of playwrights and actors. The 200-seat main venue puts on a range of musicals, comedies, and dramas (in Spanish), while you might find monologues or stand-up comedy in the smaller performance spaces.

MAP 5: Zamora 7, 55/5256-0014, www.foroshakespeare.com; showtimes vary, but generally matinees 1pm, evening performance 7pm-10:30pm; $12-20, Metro: Chapultepec

Coyoacán

Map 6

CINEMA

✪ Cineteca Nacional

Founded in 1974, the Cineteca Nacional is a movie lover's paradise, with a lineup of international, independent, and art-house films, shown by the dozens each week. Here you can see everything from experimental Mexican short films to an Akira Kurosawa retrospective to new blockbuster releases. The Cineteca maintains a huge film archive and publishes its own line of books on film. In 2012, the Cineteca buildings were renovated and expanded, including the addition of a new outdoor cinema that shows movies alfresco.

MAP 6: Av. México Coyoacán 389, 55/4155-1200 or 55/4155-1190, www.cinetecanacional.net; screenings daily 11am-9pm; US$3.50, US$2 students; Metro: Coyoacán

MUSEUMS

Fonoteca Nacional

The Fonoteca Nacional is a rather unusual project: Through a mix of recordings and audiovisual material, this archive seeks to preserve the unique sounds of Mexico, from the brassy tones of a band playing outside a Metro station to the sizzle of meat frying at a taco stand. Housed in Casa Alvarado, an 18th-century hacienda, the Fonoteca exhibits work by artists and historians documenting sound and hosts ongoing musical performances—all gratis—as well as guided listening tours of the archive.

MAP 6: Francisco Sosa 383, 55/4155-1007, www.fonotecanacional.gob.mx; Mon.-Fri. 9am-7pm, Sat. 9am-6pm; free; Metro: Viveros

Museo Nacional de Culturas Populares

Promoting the study and understanding of Mexico's diverse popular-art and craft traditions, this museum is interesting from both an anthropological and aesthetic perspective. Overseen by the National Council for Culture and Arts, or Conaculta, the museum doesn't maintain a permanent collection, instead organizing temporary exhibitions featuring work from specific regions or cultures, or around certain themes, like lunar metaphors; it also occasionally exhibits work by indigenous cultures from other parts of the world.

MAP 6: Av. Hidalgo 289, 55/4155-0920, http://museoculturaspopulares.gob. mx; Tues.-Thurs. 10am-6pm, Fri.-Sun. 10am-8pm; donation requested; Metro: Viveros

Fonoteca Nacional

CINEMA
Filmoteca UNAM

UNAM, the national university, has a major film program, which includes film studies, restoration, and a huge film library. The Sala Julio Bracho, Sala José Revueltas, and Sala Carlos Monsiváis, the university's three main screening rooms, are located on the university campus, in the south of the city. In addition, UNAM runs screening rooms at the **Museo Universitario del Chopo.**

MAP 6: Av. Insurgentes Sur 3000, Ciudad Universitaria in UNAM, 55/5622-9374, www. filmoteca.unam.mx; hours vary; US$2, US$1 students; Metro: Universidad

MUSEUMS
Espacio Escultórico de la UNAM

A 1970s collaboration between artists including Federico Silva, Mathias Goeritz, Helen Escobedo, and Manuel Felguérez resulted in the national university's unique Espacio Escultórico (Sculpture Space), a monumental sculpture garden built within an open expanse of volcanic rock and scrubby brush. It is an iconic destination on the UNAM campus, drawing art and ecology into a unique dialogue. The keynote piece is a massive, circular concrete sculpture, which is often used for performances or student meetings.

MAP 6: Circuito Mario de la Cueva and Insurgentes Sur, Ciudad Universitaria, 55/5622-7003, www.cultura.unam.mx; daily 24 hours; free; Metro: Universidad, Metrobús: CCU

Museo Casa Estudio Diego Rivera

In 1931, artist Juan O'Gorman designed two small functionalist homes, joined by a footbridge, for Frida Kahlo and Diego Rivera. Kahlo lived there until 1941 and Rivera until his death, in 1954. The homes were opened to the public as a museum in 1986. Rivera's studio has been preserved as it was during his lifetime, providing a touching look into the artist's personal aesthetics; some of his pre-Columbian artifacts and Mexican handicrafts are also on display.

MAP 6: Av. Diego Rivera at Altavista, 55/8647-5470, www.estudiodiegorivera. bellasartes.gob.mx; Tues.-Sun. 10am-6pm; US$1; Metro: Barranca del Muerto

Museo de Arte Carrillo Gil

One of the nicest art museums in the city, the Carrillo Gil is housed in a modern, multistory stone building in San Ángel. The museum's permanent collection, originally donated by its namesake, includes work from modernist masters like Pablo Picasso and contemporary art stars like Gabriel Orozco. Even more interesting, the museum mounts ongoing large-scale exhibitions of artwork by current Mexican and international artists, for which opening parties are usually packed to the brim.

MAP 6: Av. Revolución 1608, 55/8647-5450, www.museodeartecarrillogil. com; Tues.-Sun. 10am-6pm; US$1.50, US$0.90 students, free for children under 12 and on Sun.; Metro: Barranca del Muerto

✪ Museo Universitario Arte Contemporáneo

In the heart of the UNAM campus, this excellent museum has consistently been one of the best places to see contemporary art in Mexico City since it opened in 2008. Designed by Teodoro González de León, the building is architecturally stunning and well-designed for viewing art, with large glass walls flooding gallery spaces with natural light. Frequently rotating exhibitions from both Mexican and international artists range from photography to thematic retrospectives to major installation works.

MAP 6: Insurgentes Sur 3000, 55/5622-6972, www.muac.unam.mx; Wed., Fri., and Sun. 10am-6pm, Thurs. and Sat. 10am-8pm; Wed. and Sun. US$1.50, Thurs.-Sat. US$3.50, children under 12 free; Metro: Universidad, Metrobús: CCU

THEATER, CLASSICAL MUSIC, AND DANCE

Sala Nezahualcóyotl

In the heart of the university's cultural center, this picturesque and highly respected concert hall is the home of UNAM's philharmonic orchestra, though it also hosts national and international performers in jazz, chamber music, and other genres. Built in the mid-1970s, the theater was designed to resemble Amsterdam's Royal Concertgebouw theater, and there are excellent acoustics throughout the space. Balcony seats are often a bargain.

MAP 6: Insurgentes Sur 3000, 55/5622-7125, www.musica.unam.mx; box office Tues.-Sat. 10am-2pm, Wed.-Sat. 4:30pm-8:30pm, Sun. 10am-1:30pm; US$5-15 depending on seats, half price for students and teachers; Metro: Universidad, Metrobús: Ciudad Universitaria

Museo Casa Estudio Diego Rivera

A FILM LOVER'S GUIDE TO MEXICO CITY

INDEPENDENT MOVIE HOUSES
- In the Roma Sur, **Cine Tonalá** (Tonalá 261, 55/5264-4101, www.cinetonala.com) is an art-house cinema, multidisciplinary performance space, and underground night spot with an admirable focus on independent, director-driven film. The lineup changes weekly but usually includes four movies every day, with titles from across the world.

- The **Cineteca Nacional** (page 174) is the movie house par excellence in Mexico City. In addition to its own extensive programming, the Cineteca oversees programming at the Cine Lido in the Centro Cultural Bella Época, in the heart of the Condesa (Tamaulipas 202, 55/5276-7110).

- A funky alternative cinema, **La Casa del Cine** (República de Uruguay 52, 55/5512-4243, http://lacasadelcine.mx) was founded with the mission to promote young Mexican filmmakers. It shows works from international film festivals, independent Mexican film, and bigger budget movies that are a few years old, in addition to participating in film festivals in the city.

CINECLUBS
- Located in the **Museo de Arte Carrillo Gil** (page 176), a wonderful contemporary-art space in San Ángel, **Cineclub Revolución** (Av. Revolución 1608, San Ángel, 55/5550-6260, www.museodeartecarrillogil.com) shows artsy and avant-garde films every Tuesday evening at 8pm, with free admission. It also participates in film festivals.

- On Monday night, the chic **Condesa DF** boutique hotel (page 227) shows independent and alternative movies as a part of larger film series designed by guest curators or through film festivals; screenings are free and include popcorn.

- The free movie house in the **Centro Cultural Digital** (page 167) frequently participates in citywide film festivals.

BEST FILM FESTIVALS
- The **Festival Internacional de Cine UNAM** (www.ficunam.unam.mx) is a juried film competition overseen by the national university. It screens dozens of contemporary independent films during the second half of February and includes a prize category for feature-length Mexican films. Venues range from the university's cinemas to Cine Tonalá to outdoor plazas.

- An excellent annual documentary film festival, founded by Gael García Bernal, Diego Luna, and Pablo Cruz in 2006, **Ambulante** (55/5511-5073, http://ambulante.com.mx) shows over 100 international and national nonfiction films in movie theaters and *cineclubs* across the capital, with many free events during its springtime run.

- Held in January and February, **Distrital** (http://distrital.mx) is a 150-plus-title film festival dedicated to experimental and multidisciplinary projects, with a roster of international movies shown at venues throughout the city, including at the Cineteca. The festival also allows audiences to watch selections online.

MOST UNUSUAL VENUE
- Float in a paddleboat while watching movies projected over the Lago Menor in the Bosque de Chapultepec as part of **LanchaCinema.** Tickets are free, but come early if you want to snag a boat (there are chairs for those who are late). The series is run by Cinema Coyote (www.cinemacoyote.com).

Teatro de los Insurgentes

This prestigious theater on southern stretch of Avenida Insurgentes, built in 1953, has a striking round facade decorated with a colorful mural by Diego Rivera entitled *La Historia del Teatro* (*The History of the Theater*). This theater generally puts on major dramatic productions by Mexican playwrights, many starring big-name actors. In 2008, for example, John Malkovich directed *El Buen Canario* (*The Good Canary*) at the theater, with movie stars Diego Luna and Daniel Giménez Cacho.

MAP 6: Av. Insurgentes Sur 1587, 55/5598-6894 or 55/5611-4253, http://teatroinsurgentes.com.mx; shows usually Thurs.-Sun.; US$20-60 depending on seats; Metro: Barranca del Muerto

Teatro Helénico

One of the most active theaters Mexico City today is this 450-seat space in southern Mexico City, in the former Hellenic Cultural Center, which was taken over by the government cultural institute in 1990. Apart from the main theater, which shows a wide variety of shows throughout the year, there is also a small space known as **La Gruta** (The Cave), where more experimental shows are put on for a smaller audience.

MAP 6: Av. Revolución 1500, 55/4155-0919, www.helenico.gob.mx; box office daily 12:30pm -8:30pm, shows most days at 8:30pm; US$10-15 for most shows; Metro: Barranca del Muerto or Coyoacán

Greater Mexico City   Map 7

CONCERT VENUES

Palacio de los Deportes

Larger *rockero* shows, particularly by major international groups touring in Mexico, like White Stripes, Bon Jovi, Lenny Kravitz, and others, are often held at the "Sports Palace." The indoor arena was originally built for the 1968 Olympics and has a capacity of 20,000. Major concerts are also sometimes held at the outdoor **Foro Sol** in the adjacent Autódromo Hermanos Rodríguez car racetrack.

MAP 7: Av. Río Churubusco at Viaducto, 55/5237-9999, www.ticketmaster.com.mx; hours and cost vary according to event; Metro: Velódromo

MUSEUMS

✪ Museo Anahuacalli

Diego Rivera was a prodigious collector of pre-Columbian art, and he constructed this pyramid-shaped museum to house his marvelous acquisitions. In addition to showcasing Rivera's varied art, artifacts, and sculpture from Mixteca, Mexica, Teotihuacán, and Veracruz cultures, among others, there are often contemporary exhibits in the space, as well as

Museo Anahuacalli

...l altars assembled in
...r Día de los Muertos.
...he Museo Frida Kahlo
...y to the Anahuacalli, and
...s provides transport be-
... two for about US$8.

MAP 7: Calle de Museo 150, Col. San Pablo Tepetlapa, 55/5617-4310, www. museoanahuacalli.org.mx; Wed.-Sun. 10am-6pm; US$3, US$1 students under 16 and seniors, free for children under 6; Tren Ligero: Xotepingo

Museo del Juguete Antiguo México

Avid toy collector Roberto Shimizu has united his huge collection of over 40,000 dolls, model cars and trucks, stuffed animals, wrestling figurines, and other curiosities in this jam-packed and delightful museum, which claims to have the largest toy collection in the world. It's off the beaten track in the rougher Colonia Doctores, but just a block from Metro Obrera (and a quick Uber from the Roma).

MAP 7: Dr. Olvera 15, Col. Doctores, 55/5588-2100, www.museodeljuguete.mx; Mon.-Fri. 9am-6pm, Sat. 9am-4pm, Sun. 10am-6pm; US$3, Metro: Obrera

✪ Museo Dolores Olmedo

Dolores Olmedo Patiño was an art collector, philanthropist, and lifelong friend of Diego Rivera's. In the 1960s, Olmedo bought the marvelous 16th-century Hacienda La Noria in Xochimilco, which she later donated to the public to establish her namesake museum. Olmedo's collection of Riveras ranges from his earliest paintings to large-scale murals. With 25 pieces, the museum also holds the largest private collection of Frida Kahlo's work in the world, including *La Columna Rota* (*The Broken Column*).

MAP 7: Av. México 5843, Col. La Noria, 55/5555-1221 or 55/5555-0891, www. museodoloresolmedo.org.mx; Tues.-Sun. 10am-6pm; US$5; Tren Ligero: La Noria

SPORTS AND ACTIVITIES

Not all urban culture takes place in museums and concert halls. Mexico City's varied sports and recreational activities are likewise memorable, one-of-a-kind experiences. With a stadium full of devoted fans and a generally jovial atmosphere, soccer matches are a reliably good time. There are three major-league teams based in Mexico City, each with its own home stadium, and the generations of rivalry between hometown soccer clubs (particularly América and the Pumas) make for a lively crowd.

Another thoroughly Mexican experience is the *charreada,* an old-fashioned show of horseman-ship (similar to rodeo in the United States) wherein traditionally dressed *charros* (cowboys) work as a team to perform a series of typical ranch duties, such as roping steer, bull-riding, and horse-trip-ping. Though its camp and humor contrasts to the elegance of the *charreada,* viewers may be sur-prised by the athleticism and artistry at Mexico's famously spirited *lucha libre* (professional wres-tling) competitions. For car-racing fans, Mexico City hosted its first Formula One Grand Prix in 2015, after a decade-long hiatus.

Ecobici public bicycle station

If you want to get some exercise, there are plenty of nice parks in and around the city, most notably, the beautiful and vast Bosque de Chapultepec, which blankets almost 1700 acres of central Mexico City, and is the home to countless fountains and monuments, shady groves, and the Mexican presidential palace.

✪ **CAMPIEST GOOD TIME:** To see Mexico's famous *lucha libre* at its best, get tickets to a fight at the **Arena México.** Outlandishly costumed wrestlers perform perfectly choreographed, acrobatic stunts to the cheers of an enthusiastic crowd (page 183).

✪ **BIGGEST URBAN RIDE:** On the last Sunday of every month, join tens of thousands of cyclists for the **Ciclatón,** a 32-kilometer bike course through the city's major thoroughfares (page 185).

✪ **BEST GREEN RESPITE:** A huge urban park, right in the center of Mexico City, **Bosque de Chapultepec** is a beloved weekend destination and a great place to breathe some fresh air, have a picnic, or stroll (page 185).

✪ **BEST STROLLING PARK:** A plant nursery and urban park, the historic and beautiful **Viveros de Coyoacán** was established in the early 20th century by vanguard conservationist Miguel Ángel de Quevedo (page 188).

✪ **BEST *FÚTBOL* STADIUMS:** For most regular league games, the intimate **Estadio Olímpico** at UNAM is the best place to watch the game, rather than the crowd. But the 100,000-seat **Estadio Azteca** is quite a spectacle if you can grab a seat for a national team match (pages 188 and 191).

✪ **NICEST SATURDAY AFTERNOON:** A great place for a low-key afternoon sipping drinks and betting on horses, the attractive **Hipódromo de las Américas** is the only racetrack in the capital and home of the annual Mexican Derby (page 190).

Centro Histórico

Map 1

ACTIVITIES

ALAMEDA CENTRAL

ICE SKATING
Ice Skating in the Zócalo
In what has now become a holiday tradition, the municipal government installs a giant ice-skating rink (over 600 square meters!) and a sledding hill in the Zócalo every December. Skate rentals (over 2,500 pairs were available in 2015-2016!) and skating are free with a valid identification. Not surprisingly, there can be a wait of several hours on busy days. If you do get out on the ice, you'll glide below the famous facades of the Palacio Nacional and the Metropolitan Cathedral. Whether you brave the lines or not, it's a quirky celebratory event right in the heart of the city.

MAP 1: The Zócalo, Plaza de la Constitución, bordered by Madero, Moneda, 16 de Septiembre, Corregidora, 5 de Febrero, República de Brasil, and Pino Suárez; 10am-10pm daily early Dec.-mid Jan; free; Metro: Metro: Zócalo

SPECTATOR SPORTS
LUCHA LIBRE
Arena Coliseo
This popular wrestling arena is rough and tumble, and a trip here is definitely an adventure. The audience is a bit rowdy, but foreign visitors will feel safe among the crowd, as long as they sit well back from the ring to avoid flying bodies and chairs. Use precaution coming and going from the stadium, especially after dark.

MAP 1: República de Perú 77, 55/5588-0266, www.cmll.com; matches usually Tues. and Fri. 7:30pm; US$3-11; Metro: Garibaldi

ice skating in the Zócalo

Alameda Central

Map 2

SPECTATOR SPORTS
LUCHA LIBRE
✪ Arena México
The best place in Mexico City to see a *lucha libre* match is at the Arena México on Friday night. This "Catedral de la Lucha" has been in business for more than 50 years and is still going strong. It draws a mixed crowd and is a generally convivial environment; you'll see plenty of younger kids with their parents, enjoying the spectacle.

MAP 2: Dr. La Vista 189, Col. Doctores, 55/5588-0508, www.cmll.com; matches usually Tues. 7:30, Fri. 8:30pm, Sun. 5pm; US$6-20; Metro: Cuauhtémoc

EL SANTO, SUPERBARRIO, AND *LUCHA LIBRE*

Lucha libre, a spectacularly campy, ultra-upbeat, and surprisingly athletic style of freestyle wrestling, has been one of Mexico's most popular spectator sports since the early 20th century. In a number of ways, *lucha libre* resembles the massive arena shows put on by professional wrestling organizations in the United States, with dramatic choreographed performances, long-standing and contentious rivalries between wrestlers, and story lines driven by the divide between the "good guys" and the "bad guys" (in Mexico, these two camps are the clean-cut, colorfully dressed *técnicos* and the villainous black-clad *rudos*). At the same time, *lucha libre* matches are very different in style than what you'd find in the WWE ring, incorporating more fighters from lighter weight classes as well as a strong emphasis on impressive acrobatics and aerial moves. The best wrestlers are excellent athletes and

masks worn by wrestlers in the *lucha libre* matches

charismatic showmen, drawing diverse fans of every age and riling up the crowd with their genuinely exciting performances.

In the ring, Mexican wrestlers all have flamboyant alter egos, and they typically dress in flashy, colorful tights and capes. Most notably, all don a signature face-covering mask, which conceals their true identity from the public (masks are a popular Mexican souvenir found in knickknack shops and artisan markets). In important matches, opponents will often bet their masks in the duel; the loser must remove his mask and turn it over to the victor at the end, the ultimate sacrifice for a *luchador* (wrestler).

Though the sport first gained a foothold in Mexico at the beginning of the 20th century, *lucha libre*'s popularity reached an apex during the 1950s, when *luchadores* became tremendously famous outside the ring. Notably, the silver-masked avenger El Santo (the Saint) remains the most well-known name in Mexican wrestling to this day. Following a five-decade career in the ring, he was buried in his wrestling mask after his death in 1984. El Santo and other big stars—like Blue Demon, Mil Máscaras, and, later, El Santo's son (appropriately known as El Hijo de Santo)—are beloved for their starring roles in a slew of hammy, borderline surrealist films from the 1950s and '60s, wherein famous wrestlers duke it out with mummies, vampires, and other campy villains.

With its populist appeal and memorable characters, *lucha libre* has even been the inspiration for a real-life activist, known as Superbarrio, who organizes protests in support of labor unions and the poor. In the capital, you can see Superbarrio's signature "SB" symbol painted onto the walls of buildings that are inhabited by squatters, indicating that Superbarrio and his allies are protecting the inhabitants from eviction. In 1996, Superbarrio declared himself a candidate for president in the United States, holding mock campaign events in both the United States and Mexico, dressed in cherry-red tights, mask, and cape.

Like many of Mexico's inimitable traditions, *lucha libre* is experiencing a surge in popularity today, as new, younger stars like the wrestler Místico draw huge crowds, and a growing range of people and classes attend arena matches. The sport's appeal is also creeping northward: In the United States, a popular children's cartoon, *Mucha Lucha*, stars Mexican wrestlers as protagonists; some well-known Mexican wrestlers have signed with WWE; and *lucha libre* promoters are organizing events and expanding their reach within the American audience. Mexican-style *lucha libre* is also very popular in Japan, and several Japanese *luchadores* have gained widespread popularity in Mexico.

Paseo de la Reforma   Map 3

CYCLING
✪ Ciclatón
The final Sunday of every month, the city closes several of its major thoroughfares to automobile traffic 8am-2pm, allowing tens of thousands of cyclists to pedal uninhibited through the city's central districts. Hydration, medical-attention, and bike-repair stations are set up throughout 32-kilometer route, which runs from the Roma through the Centro Histórico, south along Río Churubusco, and finally north via Patriotismo. Check the Ciclatón's official website for the most recent news and route updates.

MAP 3: Reforma Glorieta de la Palma (Station 1), http://indeporte.mx/cicloton; final Sunday of each month, 8am-2pm; Metro: Insurgentes

Chapultepec and Polanco   Map 4

AMUSEMENT PARKS
La Feria de Chapultepec
Mexico City's adrenaline-seeking youth prefer the extreme rides at Six Flags in Tlalpan, but this smaller, more old-fashioned amusement park is a nice family-oriented option, with a carousel, a haunted house, and bumper cars—as well as a few newfangled terror rides, like the 50-meter free fall. The signature attraction is the towering wooden roller coaster, or *montaña rusa*, built in 1964. If you want to experience it, no need to buy a day pass; a single ride costs US$1.50.

MAP 4: Segunda Sección, Bosque de Chapultepec, 55/5230-2121, www. feriachapultepec.com.mx; generally Tues.-Fri. 11am-6pm, Sat.-Sun. 10am-8pm; US$5 for 30 rides, US$9 for 46; Metro: Constituyentes

CYCLING
Noches de Bici
The multidisciplinary cultural and art center Casa del Lago runs guided Wednesday-night bicycle tours of the Bosque de Chapultepec, stopping at various points of interest while relaying legends and history of the park (in Spanish) via loudspeaker. There is space for up to 60 cyclists, though check the Casa de Lago's website to be sure the tours are in season.

MAP 4: Bosque de Chapultepec, Primera Sección s/n, 55/5211-6086, www. casadellago.unam.mx; in season, Wed. 6:30pm; US$3; Metro: Chapultepec

PARKS
✪ Bosque de Chapultepec
Covering nearly 700 hectares of forested land, the Bosque de Chapultepec not only provides respite for weekenders but also helps control the climate and air quality in the water-starved, pavement-covered Valley of Mexico. With its natural springs and verdant vegetation, the area around the Cerro de Chapultepec was once a retreat for Mexica emperors and, later, colonial-era aristocrats; there are ruins of

numerous pre-Columbian baths in the park. Today, the tree-lined pathways of the Primera Sección (First Section) of Chapultepec are popular for jogging, dog-walking, and in-line skating, and they're thronged with strolling families (and food vendors and toy sellers) on Sundays. If time allows, it's interesting to explore the Segunda Sección (Second Section), a bit more remote from major thoroughfares but filled with shaded forests, unusual fountains, and quiet plazas.

MAP 4: Between Paseo de la Reforma and Av. Constituyentes, 55/5212-2171, www.sma.df.gob.mx/bosquedechapultepec; Primera Sección Tues.-Sun. 5am-4:30pm, other sections daily 24 hours; free; Metro: Chapultepec, Auditorio, Constituyentes

SPECTATOR SPORTS
CHARREADA
Rancho del Charro
Javier Rojo Gómez

The *charreada* is a traditional show of horsemanship and ranching skills, similar to rodeo in the southern United States, but with a more gentlemanly air. *Charreadas* are staged in skillet-shaped *lienzos charros* (*charro* rings), which are managed by private associations. Though open to everyone, *charrería* is a rather expensive pastime, requiring the maintenance of trained horses and elaborate clothing, so most *charros,* especially in the capital, come from upper-class families. *Charreadas* between the Asociación Nacional de Charros and competing associations are held in this *lienzo charro* throughout the year, often on Sunday (though not every weekend, so plan ahead). Events often play to a full house. Located in the third section of Chapultepec park, it is the most central spot to see *charreadas* in the city.

MAP 4: Av. Constituyentes 500, 55/5277-8706; hours vary, usually Sun. around midday; cost varies; Metro: Observatorio

motorized train in the Bosque de Chapultepec

BIKE MEXICO CITY

Not long ago, riding a bicycle in central Mexico City was a death-defying proposition, braved by only by a few die-hard cyclists and those who had no more efficient means of getting around. Today, the city has cordoned off a network of new bike lanes throughout the central neighborhoods and, most impressive, rolled out a massive (and still growing) urban bike-share program called **Ecobici.** Now it's common to see riders of every stripe pedaling bright-red Ecobici five-speeds along the Paseo de la Reforma or through Roma on their way to work, to restaurants, or to the movies.

Ecobici public bicycle

Annual subscriptions to Ecobici cost less than US$35 per year, and there are bike stations throughout the Roma, Condesa, Centro Histórico, Juárez, Polanco, San Rafael, Del Valle, Napoles, and Mixcoac neighborhoods, as well as along the Paseo de la Reforma. Visitors can register for a temporary membership with a valid ID (passport or resident visa) and a credit card, for about US$16 for a week or US$10 for three days. Several kiosks and offices in the center of the city accept paperwork and issue Ecobici cards, including an office in the Roma (Campeche 175, Mon.-Fri. 9am-6pm, Sat. 10am-2pm) and a kiosk in front of the shopping center Reforma 222 (Paseo de la Reforma between Havre and Napoles, Mon.-Fri. 10am-noon and 1pm-6pm, Sat.-Sun. 10am-4pm), among others.

You can find a full list of registration offices, a map of current Ecobici stations, and a map of municipal bike lanes at the official website (www.ecobici.df.gob.mx).

Roma and Condesa Map 5

CYCLING
People for Bikes

This cool Roma shop has plenty of merchandise for the urban and off-road cyclist, from specialty bicycles to shoes, helmets, and accessories. They also run weekly Thursday night rides (minus the last Thursday of the month) through the city, as well as weekend bike trips to nearby parkland, like the Desierto de los Leones.
MAP 5: Zacatecas 55, 55/5264-1457, www.pfb.com.mx; Mon.-Sat. 10am-8pm, Sun. 10am-5pm; Metro: Niños Heroes

Coyoacán Map 6

CYCLING
Equal Bicigratis

Nonprofit Equal Bicigratis offers free bike loans for those who'd like to pedal around the city. All you need is a valid ID (passport and driver's license are both accepted) and the bike is yours for three hours. There are several Bicigratis kiosks in the city, including one in Plaza Hidalgo in central Coyoacán and another in the Roma (Durango and Glorieta de las Cibeles).

Check their Twitter account (@bicigratis) to make sure the stations are open.
MAP 6: Plaza Hidalgo, at Ignacio Allende and Av. Miguel Hidalgo, 55/5574-6798; Tues.-Sun. 10:30am-1pm and 1:30pm-4:45pm; Sun. 8:30am-3:30pm; free; Metro: Sevilla

PARKS

✪ Viveros de Coyoacán

In 1901, architect and early environmentalist Miguel Ángel de Quevedo donated a hectare of land to the city to create a public nursery. Officially opened in 1907, it was the first open space dedicated to growing trees and plants for public use in the city. Today, it's a popular place for neighborhood locals out for a stroll, especially during the early morning and late afternoon. Open yoga and tai chi classes are often held in the park.
MAP 6: Between Universidad, Madrid, Melchor Ocampo, and Pérez Valenzuela, www.viveroscoyoacan.gob.mx; daily 6am-6pm; free; Metro: Viveros

San Ángel   Map 6

PARKS

Jardín Botánico del Instituto de Biología

Operated by UNAM's biological sciences department, this expansive botanical garden, located in the southern stretches of the university campus, cultivates more than 1,600 plant species from Mexico's deserts, forests, and jungles as a part of its mission to promote the conservation of endangered and endemic species. There are frequent plant-related workshops, themed tours of the garden, and family-oriented activities on Saturday.
MAP 6: Tercer Circuito exterior, s/n, Ciudad Universitaria Coyoacán, 55/5622-9047 or 55/56 22-9063; winter hours Mon.-Fri. 9am-4:30pm, Sat. 9am-4pm, summer hours Mon.-Fri. 9am-5:30pm; $3; Metrobús: Centro Cultural Universitario

SPECTATOR SPORTS

SOCCER

✪ Estadio Olímpico

This unusually intimate soccer stadium is home to the UNAM Pumas. There is a Diego Rivera fresco over the entrance. The UNAM Pumas are frequently one of the better teams in Mexico, known for fielding relatively young players (although not from the UNAM—students do not play on the team). Going to see a Pumas game at Estadio Olímpico is always good fun, as the *porras* (fan clubs) of the Pumas are well known for their elaborate and often hilarious (and profane) chants.
MAP 6: Insurgentes Sur just south of Eje 10 Sur at Ciudad Universitaria, http://clubpumasunam.com; hours vary; most games US$5-15; Metro: Universidad, Metrobús: Ciudad Universitaria

PARKS

Desierto de los Leones

Desierto de los Leones is a natural preserve covering 5,000 square kilometers of wooded forest in southern Mexico City, centered around the remains of an a 17th-century convent. Picnickers frequent the groves and gardens around the monastery, while hikers and mountain bikers roam the dirt roads and trails in the hills above.

Desiertos were Spanish Carmelite monasteries, built with the intention of isolating monks from modern life. Visitors can explore the subterranean tunnels of the old monastery with a guide. The woods around Desierto de los Leones are well patrolled, particularly on weekends, making it safe for hiking and biking. Most people simply wander the areas around the monastery, but there are longer, more rigorous hiking trails in the woods, too.

From the south, take the Camino al Desierto from its junction with the Periférico Sur, at Calle Altavista in San Ángel. Alternatively, a bus runs from the Barranca del Muerto Metro station up to the monastery on Saturday and Sunday 6am-5pm.

MAP 7: Carretera México-Toluca, Col. La Venta, 55/5814-1171, http://desiertodelosleones.mx; park daily 7am-6pm; monastery Tues.-Sun. 10am-7pm; US$1 monastery; Metro: Barranca del Muerto, then by bus (Sat. and Sun. only)

Parque Ecológico de Xochimilco (PEX)

This recreational park was founded as part of the Ecological Rescue Plan for Xochimilco, an ambitious strategy to include water reclamation, agricultural reactivation, and historical and archaeological studies. The 189-hectare Parque Ecológico de Xochimilco, or PEX, consists of lakes, *ciénegas* (underground springs), and canals. Wide gravel and asphalt walking paths wind through the park, making this a great place to get some exercise and relatively fresh air. One path leads through the flower-lined Paseo de las Flores.

Parque Ecológico de Xochimilco

The best way to get to the park, which is a couple of kilometers from downtown Xochimilco (too far to walk), is to take a taxi. The entrance is found by taking Avenida División del Norte to the Glorieta de Vaqueritos traffic circle, then turning onto the side road (not the main highway) of the Periférico ring highway and looking for signs. The park entrance has a colorful painted arch similar to those decorating the canal boats.

MAP 7: Periférico Sur at Canal de Cuemanco, Xochimilco, 55/5673-7890, www.pex.org.mx; summer Tues.-Sun. 9am-6pm; winter Tues.-Sun. 10am-4pm; US$3 adults, US$1 over age 60, US$0.50 under age 12; Tren Ligero: Xochimilco station, then by taxi

Parque Hundido

Parque Hundido (Sunken Park) is a large leafy park along Insurgentes that is indeed several meters below street level. The gravel and dirt paths of the park, lined with about 50 reproductions of pre-Hispanic sculptures, are a good place for a jog, as many locals can attest. Across Insurgentes from Parque Hundido in the Colonia del Valle is the smaller Parque San Lorenzo (at the intersection of San Lorenzo and Fresas).

MAP 7: Av. Insurgentes between Eje 6 Sur and Eje 7 Sur; daily 24 hours; free; Metro: Mixcoac, Metrobús: Parque Hundido

SPECTATOR SPORTS
SPORTS ARENAS
Arena Ciudad de México

This 22,000-capacity stadium opened in Azcapotzalco in 2012. It holds major music and sports events; it has hosted concerts by Miley Cyrus and Aerosmith, along with exhibitions by the NBA and UFC mixed martial arts. It's a five-minute walk from the Metro Line 6.

MAP 7: Av. de las Granjas 800, Azcapotzalco, 55/1515-4100, www.arenaciudaddemexico.com; Metro: Ferreria/Arena Ciudad de México

BASEBALL
Foro Sol

Although it can't quite compare to soccer, béisbol is also very popular in Mexico. Mexico has two leagues, the Liga del Pacífico, which plays in the northwestern part of the country, and the Liga Mexicana de Béisbol, which fields teams pretty much everywhere else. The Liga Mexicana has 16 teams, including the Diablos Rojos of Mexico City.

The Diablos Rojos play at the Foro Sol, which seats 26,000 spectators and is within the Autódromo Hermanos Rodríguez. The baseball season runs between March and July, with the playoffs in August.

MAP 7: Av. Viaducto Río de la Piedad y Río Churubusco, Col. Granjas, 55/5639-8722, www.diablos.com.mx; games start from 4pm to 8pm, weekdays and weekends; US$1-7 depending on seats; Metro: Ciudad Deportiva

FORMULA ONE
Autódromo Hermanos Rodríguez

Ricardo and Pedro Rodríguez were stars of Formula One racing in Mexico during the 1960s, though both of their lives were cut short in racing accidents. The brothers lend their name to this race course in eastern Mexico City, where 15 Grand Prix championships were held, 1963-1970 and 1986-1992. In 2015, the Formula One Grand Prix returned to Mexico for the first time in more than two decades, the first of a five-year deal for continuing championships, with other car racing events throughout the year.

MAP 7: Av. Viaducto Río de la Piedad s/n, Iztacalco, www.autodromohr.com; tickets available through Ticketmaster; Metro: Ciudad Deportiva

HORSE RACING
✪ Hipódromo de las Américas

Horse racing has a lengthy history in Mexico City, but currently there is only one racetrack within the city. This 1.5-kilometer oval course is a relaxing place to spend a warm afternoon,

Estadio Azteca

watching the races and placing a few bets with a beer in hand. The *hipódromo* is just west of the Periférico, beyond Polanco in Colonia Lomas de Sotelo. By public transport, get off at either Chapultepec or Auditorio Metro station and look for buses marked Hipódromo driving west on Paseo de la Reforma.

MAP 7: Av. Industria Militar, 55/5387-0600, www.hipodromo.com.mx; Thurs. 5:30pm-10pm and Fri.-Sun. 3pm-8pm; US$2 general admission, US$5 for box/mezzanine seating; Metro: Chapultepec or Auditorio, then by bus

SOCCER
✪ Estadio Azteca

Mexico's largest stadium, Estadio Azteca, is a major concert and event venue in addition to being home to popular soccer clubs Las Águilas del América and Los Rayos de Necaxa. The national team also plays most of its important matches here. Opened in 1966, it was designed by architects Pedro Ramírez Vázquez and Rafael Mijares Alcérreca, with a capacity to seat almost 100,000. With such dimensions, the roar of the crowd can be exhilarating.

MAP 7: Calzada de Tlalpan 3465, Col. Santa Úrsula, www.esmas.com; hours vary; most games US$5-15; Tren Ligero: Estadio Azteca

Estadio Azul

The closest stadium to downtown Mexico City is this semi-sunken mid-sized stadium right next to the Plaza México bullfighting ring. This is home to the Cementeros de Cruz Azul, one of Mexico City's super-popular hometown soccer clubs. The small size and central location make this a good choice for someone looking to get a flavor of Mexican *fútbol*.

MAP 7: Just off Insurgentes Sur at Holbein, Col. Ciudad de los Deportes, www.cruzazulfc.com; hours vary; most games US$5-15; Metro: San Antonio, Metrobús: Insurgentes

SHOPS

A powerful trading hub since the pre-Columbian era, Mexico City has commerce hardwired into its history. In this massive metropolis, trade is going on in every neighborhood and on every level, from the high-fashion designer boutiques of Polanco to the industrious independent street vendors who weave through traffic jams to sell bottled water, cigarettes, and candy to idling drivers.

beaded necklaces

Mexico City's urban markets are among the most interesting places to shop or simply wander. Though they face aggressive competition from big-box stores, traditional markets remain an invaluable part of local culture and are the best places to stock up on fruit, tortillas, and other kitchen staples.

From lacquered wood trays from the state of Michoacán to delicately crafted pottery from Oaxaca, Mexico's wonderful folk art and craft traditions are represented at various shops and markets. You can also find vintage craft pieces, collectibles, and other knickknacks in the city's flea markets.

As evidenced by its rich artistic heritage, Mexico City has always been a place both sui generis in its creativity and heavily influenced by global trends in art and design. Mexico City's design scene continues to flourish, and many homegrown designers are making an international name for themselves in interiors, furniture, clothing, and accessories, with a number incorporating traditional Mexican aesthetics into their creations.

HIGHLIGHTS

✪ **BEST TEXTILES:** The tunics, shawls, embroidered blouses, and other gorgeous fabrics at **Remigio,** owned by Oaxacan textile expert Remigio Mestas, are not just clothing and home goods but keepsakes (page 195).

✪ **BEST TRADITIONAL SWEETS:** A charming old-fashioned sweet shop in the Centro Histórico, the **Dulcería de Celaya** has been selling delicious candies, dried fruits, and other confections for over 100 years (page 196).

✪ **MOST ATMOSPHERIC MARKET:** Peddling everything from children's toys to herbal remedies to intriguing black-magic potions, the **Mercado Sonora** is one of the city's most unusual markets (page 197).

✪ **MOST VARIED VINTAGE MARKET:** Every Sunday morning, the bustling **La Lagunilla** open-air market, north of the Centro, is filled with a wonderful assortment of old books, furniture, toys, jewelry, and other collectibles from years past (page 198).

✪ **BEST TRADITIONAL CRAFTS:** The government-run **FONART** promotes popular art and craft traditions throughout Mexican communities, selling a wonderful, ever-changing selection of *artesanías* in its well-priced shops (page 198).

✪ **BEST GOURMET MARKET:** Sip a tiny glass of wine while nibbling on Spanish cheese and honey, or pick up some *huitlacoche* (corn fungus), starfruit, and iguana meat at the small but amazingly well-stocked **Mercado San Juan** (page 199).

✪ **BEST BOOKSHOP FOR BROWSING:** The light-filled, amply stocked **Librería Rosario Castellanos** is a nice place to explore the stacks or sip a coffee. The building is in a beautifully remodeled former art-deco cinema (page 204).

✪ **COOLEST BOUTIQUE:** The tiny but surprisingly wonderful little shop **Goodbye Folk** in the Colonia Roma sells a line of ultra-cool, handmade shoes for men and women, as well as vintage clothing (page 206).

✪ **BEST HIGH-END *ARTESANÍAS*:** Visit San Ángel on Saturday for the wonderful craft market **Bazaar Sábado,** and don't miss the opportunity to browse the gorgeous and diverse handicrafts for sale in the **Casa del Obispo** (pages 210 and 212).

shopping in the Polanco

SHOPPING DISTRICTS

Polanco

Polanco's tony main avenue, **Presidente Masaryk,** is lined with upscale European and American fashion houses like Fendi, Louis Vuitton, and DKNY; newer design and jewelry shops; and posh sidewalk cafés and restaurants. Come here to pick up pricey luxury items with a monied set or to enjoy a bit of high-end window-shopping.

MAP 4: Presidente Masaryk between Newton and Moliere; Metro: Polanco

Roma

Álvaro Obregón has long been the heart of the Roma, and as the neighborhood becomes more trendy, cute boutiques and galleries have cropped up alongside the avenue's old bookshops and ice-cream parlors. More recently, the parallel street **Colima** has become a hub of trendy fashion design and concept shops, where you'll find everything from super-funky vintage-clothing stores to a branch of international clothier American Apparel.

MAP 5: Colima between Insurgentes and Av. Cuauhtémoc, and Álvaro Obregón between Insurgentes and Av. Cuauhtémoc; Metro: Insurgentes

ANTIQUES AND COLLECTIBLES
Nacional Monte de Piedad
Housed in a colonial-era building on what was once the estate of Hernán Cortés, this massive nonprofit pawn shop offers fixed low-interest loans to the needy in exchange for pawned household items. In times of economic crisis, people line the surrounding blocks waiting to put their personal possessions, from watches to blenders, in hock for a loan. You'll mostly find jewelry, gemstones, TVs, smartphones, and tools on sale, but the second floor is dedicated to art and antiques.
MAP 1: Monte de Piedad 7, 55/5278-1700 or 55/5278-1800, www.montepiedad.com.mx; Mon.-Fri. 8:30am-6pm, Sat. 8:30am-1pm; Metro: Zócalo

ARTS AND CRAFTS
Tienda-Librería del Palacio de Cultura Banamex
If you are inspired by the popular art and handicrafts showcased in the galleries at the Palacio de Cultura Banamex, take a turn around its small but exquisite gift shop, where expertly selected pieces of *artesanía*—from hand-painted hollowed gourds to elaborate ceramic *arboles de la vida* (trees of life), are on sale. It also stocks the Banamex Foundation's collection of Mexican art and culture books, which are wonderful reference materials for anyone interested in Mexico's artisan traditions.
MAP 1: Madero 17, 55/1226-0166, http://fomentoculturalbanamex.org; daily 10am-7pm; Metro: Bellas Artes

CLOTHING, SHOES, AND ACCESSORIES
Fábrica Social
The brightly colored clothing that swings on the racks at this small boutique unites social conscience and creativity. To create their unique apparel, this nonprofit group brings together contemporary designers and indigenous artisans, who work together on the design and development of seasonal lines of womenswear that pair traditional techniques with a modern aesthetic. Though pricier than most traditional Mexican clothing, the styles are contemporary enough to suit more urban clients.
MAP 1: Isabel la Católica 30, 55/5512-0730, www.fabricasocial.org; Mon.-Sat. 10am-8pm, Sun. 10am-6pm; Metro: Zócalo

La Hacienda
Along the Eje Central, just south of Plaza Garibaldi, there is a row of shops selling Mexican-made Western gear. Among the largest is La Hacienda, where you can find everything a rancher needs, from silver-plated belt buckles to collared shirts—even handmade harnesses and saddles. The aesthetic is more typical to northern Mexico than it is to the capital; if you want a pair of snakeskin boots, though, this is a good place to get them.
MAP 1: Belisario Domínguez 3, Local 8, 55/5512-3161; Mon.-Sat. 10am-9pm, Sun. 11am-8pm; Metro: Bellas Artes

✪ Remigio
Owned by one of Mexico's most well-known textile merchants, this wonderful shop sells fine handmade clothing

and fabrics from the southern state of Oaxaca. Here, old painted chests and wooden shelves are piled with gorgeous hand-loomed textiles, meticulously embroidered blouses, colorful cotton *huipiles* (a traditional tunic from Oaxaca), and elegantly simple plant-dyed fabrics. The work here is high quality and absolutely original, with upscale prices to match.

MAP 1: Isabel la Católica 30-7, 2nd fl., 55/4552-9471; Mon.-Sat. 11am-8pm, Sun. 10am-6pm; Metro: Zócalo

Sombreros Tardan

This quality hat shop has been in business, right on the Zócalo, since 1847. Though the business originally began as an import shop, it was later bought by the Tardan family, who developed their own line of felt and wool hats during the early 20th century. Tardan remains among the best hat makers in Mexico. Come here to browse the nice selection of men's sombreros, which run from beanies to cotton caps to Panama hats.

MAP 1: Plaza de la Constitution 7, 55/5512-3902, www.tardan.com.mx; Mon.-Sat. 10am-7pm; Metro: Zócalo

DESIGN AND GIFT SHOPS
MUMEDI Shop

The shop inside the Museo Mexicano de Diseño (Mexican Museum of Design) was not added as an afterthought; rather it is a principal element in the museum's mission to promote Mexican design, and it contains just as much interesting work as the adjoining gallery space (if not more). A great place to pick up a unique gift or souvenir, MUMEDI stocks graphic tees, jewelry, toys, ceramics, wallets, handbags, and other curiosities, of which

about 80 percent were designed by Mexicans.

MAP 1: Madero 74, 55/5510-8609, www. mumedi.mx; Mon. 11:30am-9pm, Tues.-Sun. 8am-9pm; Metro: Zócalo

GOURMET FOOD AND IMPORTS
✪ Dulcería de Celaya

This old-fashioned sweet shop is a feast for the eyes as well as the taste buds: Its 19th-century interior is filled with gilded moldings, mirrored walls, and glimmering display cases filled with handmade candies. If you aren't familiar with Mexican sweets, this old shop is a great place to start, though it sets the bar high—it's been in business since 1874, so the recipes have been perfected. Try the excellent coconut-stuffed limes; crystallized fruit, like figs, sweet potatoes, and *acitrón* (cactus); or lightly sweetened, fluffy meringues.

MAP 1: Cinco de Mayo 39, 55/5521-1787, www.dulceriadecelaya.com; daily 10:30am-7:30pm; Metro: Allende

Dulcería de Celaya

TRADITIONAL MARKETS

Mesoamerican civilizations as far back as the early Olmecs on the Gulf Coast established open-air marketplaces for trade and commerce, and after the Spanish conquest, many important pre-Columbian markets continued to operate throughout the New World, including the giant market square in what is today the Zócalo. Often atmospheric and interesting, neighborhood markets are hands down the best places to shop for fruits and vegetables, dairy, meat, and tortillas, and many have a "claim to fame," like specializing in a particular cuisine or boasting a large selection of flowers and piñatas. In addition, weekly markets sell crafts, antiques, specialty food, and more.

Mercado San Juan

If you only have time to visit one market, there is none more emblematic of the city than the immense and atmospheric **Mercado de la Merced** on the edge of the Centro Histórico. Right next to the Merced, the **Mercado Sonora** is best known for its off-beat, esoteric offerings, like medicinal herbs, healing candles, witchcraft products, and live animals. The **Mercado San Juan** in the old San Juan neighborhood is known throughout the city for its unusual selection of meats and produce, like quail eggs, tropical fruits, alligator steaks, toasted grasshoppers, and other delicacies. **Bazaar Sábado,** held every Saturday in San Ángel, is a well-known place to shop for traditional Mexican crafts as well as handmade leather goods, shoes, candles, and other souvenirs. **Tianguis Cultural del Chopo,** held every Saturday, is an open-air market selling records, rock posters, band T-shirts, and every other manner of music memorabilia. Finally, for an on-the-ground perspective on Mexico City's food economy, head to the **Central de Abasto,** a wholesale market that supplies 80 percent of the capital's edibles. There is nothing you won't find here, from potatoes to crab meat, and the sheer size is astonishing.

PUBLIC MARKETS

✪ Mercado Sonora

Just south of the Mercado de la Merced, the interesting Mercado Sonora sells traditional goods for home and kitchen and, most famously, supplies for healing and witchcraft. Some stands are dedicated to herbs and traditional remedies, while others sell esoteric items, like amulets, candles, and colored stones. As is common in many markets in Mexico, animals are on sale in back, including dogs, cats, hamsters, snakes, and rabbits, as well as, unfortunately, exotic species, like rare birds and parrots.

MAP 1: Av. Fray Servando Teresa de Mier 419, 55/1931-1931, www.mercadosonora.com.mx, daily 8am-5pm; Metro: Merced

SHOPPING CENTERS

The Shops at Downtown

Located within the same colonial-era palace as the stylish Downtown Hotel, this small yet elegant shopping center is dedicated to Mexican-made products and Mexican-owned retail. With shops selling everything from chic clothing and specialty chocolate to ecological household supplies and high-end handicrafts, this shopping center is a great place to spend a few hours looking for a gift, and its historic breezeways are wonderful for wandering on a warm afternoon.

MAP 1: Isabel la Católica 30, 55/5521-2098, http://theshops.mx; daily 11am-9pm; Metro: Zócalo

Alameda Central   Map 2

ANTIQUES AND COLLECTIBLES

✪ La Lagunilla

The popular La Lagunilla flea market sets up along the Paseo de la Reforma every Sunday, just outside the La Lagunilla covered market, spilling onto a few side streets heading east into Tepito. It's an interesting place to wander for an hour or two, browsing the piles of old books, silverware, luggage, curios, movie posters, vinyls, antique furniture, art, tin toys, old photographs, vintage jewelry, and other unique items for sale. Get there early for the best selection.

MAP 2: Several blocks along and east of Paseo de la Reforma at the corner of Eje 1 Norte; Sun. 9am-5pm; Metro: Garibaldi

La Ciudadela Centro Artesanal

ARTS AND CRAFTS
La Ciudadela Centro Artesanal

A few blocks south of the Alameda Central, La Ciudadela is an open-air craft market, where over 300 vendors sell handmade products from across the country. Prices here are incredibly reasonable, and the selection is extensive, covering many of Mexico's major craft traditions, from ceramics from Tlaquepaque and Talavera from Puebla to wooden utensils, woven baskets, shawls, and musical instruments. Take your time browsing the selection, as quality varies tremendously by vendor.

MAP 2: Plaza de la Ciudadela 1 and 5, 55/5510-1828, www.laciudadela.com.mx; Mon.-Sat. 9am-7pm, Sun. 9am-6pm; Metro: Balderas

✪ FONART

The Fondo Nacional para el Fomento de las Artesanías (FONART) is a government trust dedicated to strengthening and promoting arts and crafts traditions throughout Mexico. As part of its mission, the organization operates several wonderful shops, where you can buy high-quality ceramics, textiles, and other unique items from native communities, knowing that artisans will directly benefit from your purchase. There is another branch nearby, in the Juárez neighborhood (Paseo de la Reforma 116,

55/5546-7163, Mon.-Fri. 10am-7pm, Sat.-Sun. 10am-4pm).

MAP 2: Av. Juárez 89, 55/5521-0171, www. fonart.gob.mx; Mon.-Fri. 10am-8pm, Sat. 10am-7pm, Sun. 11am-5pm; Metro: Hidalgo

Tienda MAP

In complement to the stunning variety of craft in the galleries upstairs, the pleasantly overstocked gift shop at the Museo Nacional de Artes Populares has an extensive collection of traditional Mexican *artesanías*, including elaborate *arboles de la vida*, metalwork and jewelry, lacquered wood trays and boxes, and an array of textiles. If you don't make it to the museum, there is another branch of the gift shop in Polanco (Emilio Castelar 22, 55/5281-3135, daily 9am-6pm).

MAP 2: Revillagigedo 11 (entrance on Independencia), 55/5518-1649, www. tiendamap.com; daily 10am-6pm; Metro: Juárez

Utilitario Mexicano

Stocking a well-curated collection of simple home goods and kitchen essentials, all of Mexican origin, Utilitario Mexicano may make you see a metal lime juicer, a simple aluminum cup, or a flouncy feather duster in a new light. Thanks to the low prices and undeniably useful products on display, it's hard to leave empty-handed.

MAP 2: Barrio Alameda, Dr. Mora 9, Local 3, 55/5512-9384, www.utilitariomexicano. com; Mon.-Sat. noon-8pm, Sun. noon-6pm; Metro: Juárez

BOOKS

Librería Educal

On the ground floor of the Palacio de Bellas Artes, this well-curated bookshop is operated by Conaculta, Mexico's National Council for the Arts. The glass-walled space, which looks out on Bellas Artes' marble atrium, is stocked with history, anthropology, and art books, mostly in Spanish. Conaculta operates similar bookstores, also named Educal, in the Museo Nacional de la Culturas Populares (Hidalgo 289, Coyoacán, 55/5658-9764), Biblioteca de México at the Ciudadela (Tolsá 4, 55/5709-6660), and the Biblioteca Vasconcelos (Eje Norte 1, 55/9157-2800, ext. 4044).

MAP 2: Av. Juárez and Eje Central, 55/5521-9760, www.educal.com.mx; Mon. 11am-7pm, Tues.-Sun. 10am-8pm; Metro: Bellas Artes

CLOTHING, SHOES, AND ACCESSORIES

Navaja

This skate shop in the Barrio Alameda building has a line of boards and accessories designed in-house (and made in the United States), in addition to Navaja hoodies and hats, imported skateboards, and tennis shoes. Take your goods right outside: Skateboarders often practice their moves around the lampposts and concrete planter boxes just outside Barrio Alameda.

MAP 2: Barrio Alameda, Dr. Mora 9, 55/5510-0312, www.navaja.tv; daily 11am-8pm; Metro: Juárez

PUBLIC MARKETS

✪ Mercado San Juan

The San Juan market is known for its exotic produce, unusual meats (from crocodile to iguana), fresh fish, and abundance of gourmet and imported products. It's a great place to shop for food to take home, like mole sauce and vanilla beans, or to pick up something unusual, like starfruit or razor clams. It's small but densely packed, so

Mercado San Juan

wander around to see what's on offer; many vendors will offer you a taste of what they're selling.

MAP 2: Ernesto Pugibet, between Luis Moya and Plaza de San Juan; daily 7am-5pm; Metro: San Juan Letrán

SHOPPING CENTERS

Barrio Alameda

A 1920 art deco building, right on the Alameda Central, has been beautifully restored and reopened as Barrio Alameda, a shopping and cultural center. You'll find restaurants, a café, design shops, a yoga studio, a barber shop, and several galleries on three separate floors surrounding a central atrium. Note that there is no elevator in the building.

MAP 2: Dr. Mora 9, 55/5512-3810, www. barrioalameda.com; daily 11am-1am, shop hours vary; Metro: Hidalgo

Paseo de la Reforma   Map 3

ANTIQUES AND COLLECTIBLES

Centro de Antigüedades Plaza del Ángel

This open-air plaza in the Zona Rosa is filled with atmospheric antiques shops. Here, you'll find furniture, paintings, art objects, silver, and decorative pieces from the 19th and mid-20th centuries, as well as a smattering of European and Asian pieces. On Saturday and Sunday, additional vendors sell jewelry, sculpture, old photographs, postcards, and other sundries, from nicely preserved vintage to high-end antiques, laid out on rugs or on folding tables in the plaza.

MAP 3: Londres 161 and Hamburgo 150, www.antiguedadesplazadelangel.com. mx; Mon.-Fri. 11am-7pm, Sat. 10am-5pm, Sun. noon-5pm; market Sat.-Sun. 9am-4pm; Metro: Insurgentes

CLOTHING, SHOES, AND ACCESSORIES

Manuel Sekkel

Argentine-born, Mexico City-based Daniel Sekkel's line of highly original shoes might be the ultimate in design fusion. Working with artisans in the Yucatán, he creates fabric "China flats" with hand-embroidered finishes and short leather boots elaborated with richly trimmed patches, as well as original flats, lace-ups, and leather shoes for both men and women. This is his permanent shop in Fusión Casa de Diseñadores, though you can find him at the Bazaar Sábado in San Ángel.

MAP 3: Londres 37, 55/5511-6328; Tues.-Sat. noon-8pm, Sun. 11am-7pm; Metro: Insurgentes, Metrobús: Hamburgo

Fusión Casa de Diseñadores

DESIGN SHOPS

Fusión Casa de Diseñadores

Bazaar Fusión, a traveling market of Mexico-based independent designers, has organized pop-ups throughout the city since 2003, but it finally established a permanent residence in a belle époque mansion in Colonia Juárez, just east of the Zona Rosa. Today, varied shops sells housewares, jewelry, handbags, clothing, and children's toys, among other design products. On Saturday, more designers join the crowd, setting up booths in the open-air courtyard.

MAP 3: Londres 37, 55/5511-6328, www.proyectofusion.com.mx; Tues.-Sat. noon-8pm, Sun. 11am-7pm; Metro: Insurgentes, Metrobús: Hamburgo

Taller LU'UM

Design collective Taller LU'UM works with traditional artisan communities to produce an original line of contemporary home goods and accessories. At this small showroom in the San Rafael neighborhood, you can see samples of their work, like hanging lamps, mobiles, bedspreads, and furnishings. In a unique twist on the traditional display, accessories are often suspended from the ceiling, rather than laid out on tables or shelves.

MAP 3: Gabino Barreda 104, 55/5535-8413, www.tallerluum.com. mx; Mon.-Fri. 10:30am-6pm, Sat.-Sun. by appointment; Metro: San Cosme

Taxonomía

This eye-catching shop in the lobby of design-centric Hotel Carlota is run by La Metropolitana, a design collective that also created custom furnishings for the hotel. Focused entirely on Mexican-designed merchandise, you'll find avant-garde clothing, leather wallets, ceramic vases, eyeglasses, jars of honey, and other sundries, at varying price points, all cleanly displayed in the modern-industrial space.

MAP 3: Hotel Carlota, Río Amazonas 73, 55/5511-6300, www.taxonomia.mx; daily 9am-8pm; Metro: Insurgentes or Cuauhtémoc, Metrobús: Reforma

MUSIC
Tianguis Cultural del Chopo
Just north of the Buena Vista train station, this open-air street market was initially founded as a site of exchange for rare-record collectors and music fans. Today, over 200 stands sell vinyl and CDs, band T-shirts, posters, and other punk- and music-related goods, with booths that specialize in thrash metal, rare or out-of-print titles, and bootlegs. Held on Saturday, it's always packed with a young crowd decked out in tattoos, piercings, and head-to-toe black.

MAP 3: Along Aldama, at Eje 1 Norte, in Col. Buena Vista; Sat. 10am-5pm; Metro: Buenavista

Chapultepec and Polanco Map 4

ARTS AND CRAFTS
Uriarte Talavera
In the early colonies, Spanish settlers introduced Talavera-style tin-enameled glazing to Mexico's skilled potters. The technique flourished in the New World, where artisans incorporated dazzling pigments and expressive painting styles to the process. Talavera became a hallmark of the state of Puebla, and Uriarte—established in 1824—is the country's oldest and most revered producer. Come to their Polanco store to see gorgeous, hand-painted designs on flatware, mugs, tea sets, vases, and more.

MAP 4: Galileo 67, 55/5280-0635, www.uriartetalavera.com.mx; Mon.-Fri. 11am-7pm, Sat. 11am-3pm; Metro: Polanco

BOOKS
El Péndulo
This high-quality bookstore opened its first branch in the Condesa (Nuevo León 115, 55/5286/9493; Mon.-Fri. 8am-11pm, Sat.-Sun. 9am-11pm), but it has since expanded across the city, with shops in Zona Rosa (Hamburgo 126, 55/5208-2327; Mon.-Fri. 8am-11pm, Sat.-Sun. 9am-11pm) and Roma (Álvaro Obregón 86, 55/5574-7034; Mon.-Wed. 8am-11pm, Thurs.-Fri. 8am-midnight, Sat. 9am-midnight, Sun. 9am-11pm) as well as this one in Polanco. Branches share a cozy decor with an earthy color scheme, as well as in-house coffee shop Cafebrería. Though predominantly stocking Spanish titles, the Polanco branch has a nice English fiction selection, mixing both classics and contemporary novels.

MAP 4: Alejandro Dumas, 55/5286-9493, www.pendulo.com; Mon.-Fri. 8am-11pm, Sat.-Sun. 9am-11pm; Metro: Chilpancingo

El Péndulo

CLOTHING, SHOES, AND ACCESSORIES
Common People
Occupying two stories of a 1940s mansion in front of the Parque Lincoln in Polanco, this upscale "concept store" feels more like a collective of designers, with numerous rooms dedicated to different styles and themes. Here, you'll find high-end international labels like Comme de Garçons and Prada, jewelry from Mexican designer Sangre de mi Sangre, and furnishings from the capital's designer Chic by Accident, as well as more tongue-in-cheek items like games and pet clothes.

MAP 4: Emilio Castelar 149, 55/5281-0800, www.commonpeople.com.mx; Tues.-Sun. 11am-9pm; Metro: Polanco

Pineda Covalín
Founded by two Mexican designers, Cristina Pineda and Ricardo Covalín, this high-end accessories company sells purses, ponchos, scarves, neckties, and other wearables, most of which are made of silk and are printed with colorful Mexican-inspired designs. For those who'd like a touch of something Mexican in their wardrobe but don't plan to buy traditional clothes, it's an elegant option. There are numerous branches, including in the Shops at Downtown (Isabela Católica 30, 55/5510-4421; Mon.-Sat. 10am-9pm, Sun. 9am-8pm) and inside the Sheraton (Paseo de la Reforma 325, 55/5533-5562; daily 9am-8pm).

MAP 4: Campos Eliseos 215, 55/5282-2720, www.pinedacovalin.com; daily 9am-8pm; Metro: Polanco

DESIGN AND INTERIORS
Pirwi
This environmentally friendly design collective makes clean-lined, elegantly casual modern furnishings and home accessories out of sustainable sources, often using birch plywood (in different color finishes) or salvaged wood for their line of dining tables, chairs, benches, bookshelves, coat racks, and loungers. You can see their latest designs in their showroom, located in a light-filled two-story mansion in Polanco.

MAP 4: Alejandro Dumas 124, 55/1579-6514, http://pirwi.com; Mon.-Thurs. 10am-8pm, Fri. 10am-3pm, Sat. 10am-6pm; Metro: Polanco

Studio Roca
Get a taste of Studio Roca's cool modern aesthetic at the company's spacious two-story showroom in Polanco, where they exhibit a proprietary line of home furnishings, lighting, rugs, and accessories, in addition to a smattering of pieces from international designers. In Mexico City, the studio has designed interiors for the Museo de Arte Moderno and the St. Regis's residential suites, among others. They have a smaller shop in the Condesa (Amsterdam 271, 55/5004-1971).

MAP 4: Horacio 907, 55/9149-0009, www.studioroca.com; Mon.-Sat. 10:30am-7:30pm; Metro: Polanco

JEWELRY
Talleres de los Ballesteros
This upscale silver shop was originally founded in Taxco, Guerrero, a city known for its silver mines as well as its important contribution to the development of a uniquely Mexican aesthetic in jewelry design, which combines pre-Columbian elements with modern sensibilities. At this high-end Polanco boutique, both sterling jewelry and tableware from Ballesteros's Taxco workshop are for sale in a wide variety of styles, with

some very nice traditionally Mexican work along with contemporary pieces.
MAP 4: Av. Presidente Masaryk 126, 55/5545-4109, www.ballesteros.net; Mon.-Sat. 10am-7pm; Metro: Polanco

Tane

Tane is one of the finest long-running silver shops in Mexico, producing both jewelry and silver accessories for the home. Designs are generally elegant and modern, though the collections also include some one-of-a-kind pieces and artist-designed series. Prices are high-end, especially for their home collection, but the workmanship is beautiful. There are additional locations in San Ángel (Altavista 147, #7, San Ángel Inn, 55/5550-5632, Mon.-Sat. 11am-8pm) and in the Four Seasons hotel (Paseo de la Reforma 500, 55/5203-2624, Mon.-Sat. 10am-7pm).
MAP 4: Presidente Mazaryk 430, 55/5282-6200, www.tane.com.mx; Mon.-Fri. 10am-7pm, Sat. 11am-7pm; Metro: Polanco

Roma and Condesa — Map 5

ANTIQUES AND COLLECTIBLES

Mercado de Cuauhtémoc

One of the most fun, funkiest, and lesser-known vintage markets in the city, the weekly Mercado de Cuauhtémoc, in the Jardín Dr. Ignacio Chávez, is worth a stop on a leisurely Saturday morning. Intrepid buyers with a good eye will stumble upon some real gems—like midcentury furniture, old radios, and vintage toys— amid a sea of plastic dolls, old pens, watches, and incense.
MAP 5: Jardín Dr. Ignacio Chávez, Cuauhtémoc y Dr. Liceaga, Roma; Sat. 9am-3pm; Metro: Niños Héroes

BOOKS

Librería Francisco Javier Clavijero

Run by the government's Instituto Nacional de Antropología e Historia (INAH), this bookstore specializes in books and magazines related to Mexican history, archaeology, and culture. The majority are published by the INAH itself, but they also carry works by other publishers related to these topics, almost entirely in Spanish. In addition, you'll find the latest bulletins on INAH's work and a selection of reproductions of jewelry, carvings, and other archaeological discoveries found in Mexico.
MAP 5: Córdoba 43, 55/4040-4300; Mon.-Fri. 9am-6pm, Sat. 9am-2pm; Metro: Insurgentes

✪ Librería Rosario Castellanos

Run by the Fonda de Cultura y Económica (FCE), this bookshop has one of the best selections of Spanish-language titles in the city, including literature, culture, history, and sociology books published by the FCE. Located in the art deco Cine Lido building in the Centro Cultural Bella Época, the light-filled space has high ceilings decorated with glass panels by artist Jan Hendrix. There are comfy chairs throughout the stacks, a carpeted kids' section, and an in-house coffee shop.

Librería Rosario Castellanos

MAP 5: Tamaulipas 202, 55/5276-7110, www.fondodeculturaeconomica.com; daily 9am-11pm; Metro: Patriotismo

Under the Volcano Books

Named for the Malcolm Lowry novel about a British attaché living in Cuernavaca, this cozy English-language bookstore is on the second floor of the American Legion building in the Condesa. There's a wide selection of well-priced second-hand books in English, with an emphasis on fiction, though it also stocks poetry, history, essays, and more.

MAP 5: Celaya 25, http://underthevolcanobooks.com; Mon.-Sat. 11am-6pm; Metro: Sevilla

CLOTHING, SHOES, AND ACCESSORIES
180° Shop

Among the most well-stocked and charming of the Roma's many boutiques, 180° Shop sells a fun collection of urbanwear and accessories, like graphic tees, tennis shoes, skateboards, handbags, and design books and city guides, in addition to their proprietary line of hoodies, miniskirts, T-shirts, and other hipster essentials. In 2015, the shop introduced a small line of children's clothes, including hand-embroidered shirts.

MAP 5: Colima 180, 55/5525-5626, www.180grados.mx; Mon.-Sat. 10:30am-8pm, Sun. 10:30am-6pm; Metro: Insurgentes

Anteojería Dr. York

If you're in the market for some cool new spectacles, this hip Colonia Roma optician's office has an ample collection to choose from, including unique sunglasses, designer brand eyeglasses, and vintage frames, all attractively displayed on wood shelves, as well as a selection of books by small and alternative presses, chosen by one of the literature-loving owners.

MAP 5: Álvaro Obregón 187, 55/5207-9359, www.dr-york.com; Mon.-Sat. 11am-8pm; Metro: Insurgentes

Carla Fernández

Carla Fernández's eponymous line of men's and women's clothing is largely inspired by Mexico's traditional aesthetics. Working with artisan communities, Fernández produces elegant, contemporary dresses, blouses, pants, ponchos, and shawls that incorporate traditional details, like elaborate embroidery and handmade textiles. In addition to her attractive modern boutique in the Roma, Fernández also has a branch in the Shops at Downtown (Isabel la Católica 30, 55/5510-9624; Mon.-Sat. 11am-9pm, Sun. 11am-7pm) and a booth at the Bazaar Sábado in San Ángel on Saturday.

MAP 5: Álvaro Obregón 200, 55/5264-2226, www.carlafernandez.com; Mon.-Sat. 11am-8pm, Sun. 11am-6pm; Metro: Insurgentes, Metrobús: Álvaro Obregón

Carmen Rion

This womenswear designer unites a high-fashion sensibility with distinctly Mexican colors and aesthetics. Draped dresses, shawls, and unusually cut skirts make up a large part of her collections, which often have bright woven collars or traditional Mexican-style embroidery and are rendered in intense, classically Mexican tones, like hot pinks, turquoise, and saturated yellow. Most clothing is for women, but men will find some updated versions of the Mexican *guayabera* shirt as well.

MAP 5: Av. México 135, 55/5564-1666, www.carmenrion.com; daily 10am-8pm; Metro: Chilpancingo

✪ Goodbye Folk

This narrow Roma storefront is home to a vintage shop, a hair salon, and an independent shoemaker. Come to browse unique, custom-tailored vintage dresses, blue jeans, button-downs, leather jackets, and more. The heart and soul of the shop is the shoes, which can be bought in the showroom or custom-created in your size. Mixing both contemporary and old-timey aesthetics, you might find polka-dot beetle boots, aquamarine oxfords, or vintage-inspired lace-up leather booties.

MAP 5: Colima 198, 55/5541-2509, http://goodbyefolk.com; Mon.-Fri. 9am-9pm, Sat.-Sun. 11am-8pm; Metro: Insurgentes

Panam

Made in Cuautitlán Izcalli since the 1960s, Panam sneakers were hugely popular through the 1980s, though their ubiquity dropped off thereafter. At a quarter of the price you'd pay for a pair of Pumas, they've made a bit of a resurgence with stylish *chilangos*. You can get a pair in their small shop in the Condesa, where you'll find the classic model and some unique design collaborations with Indio beer and Frida Kahlo, among others.

MAP 5: Vicente Suárez 38, 55/5511-7351, www.panam.com.mx; Sun.-Tues. 10am-7pm, Wed.-Thurs. 10am-8pm, Fri.-Sat. 10am-9pm; Metro: Chilpancingo

Panam

DESIGN AND GIFT SHOPS

Canasta Básica

Design collective La Metropolitana opened this clean and homey showroom in the basement of a Roma mansion in 2015, where visitors can browse a proprietary line of furniture and home accessories, including long wood tables, benches, wood-and-wicker chairs, and ceramic flatware and tea sets. The group also includes a few of their favorite kitchen staples—also for sale—amid the displays, including salsas, chile peppers, and tea samplers.

MAP 5: Córdoba 125, 55/6726-7343, www.lametropolitana.com.mx; Tues.-Sat. 11am-8pm, Sun. noon-5pm; Metro: Insurgentes, Metrobús: Álvaro Obregón

MARKETS ON WHEELS

In addition to covered neighborhood markets, most *colonias* also have one or two temporary outdoor markets that set up once a week on a closed street or sidewalk. Some are simple affairs, with 10-15 stands selling fruits and vegetables, meats, and cheese, as well as tacos and other street snacks. Others are massive 100-plus-vendor markets, where you can buy all your kitchen basics plus a range of tasty snacks. Often referred to as *mercados sobre ruedas* (markets on wheels), or *tianguis* (from the Nahuatl word for an open-air market), they can be wonderful places to shop, to munch, and to get a sense of a neighborhood.

Most *mercados sobre ruedas* run from about 9am or 10am to 6pm, though they tend to wind down after the *comida,* around 4pm. Here are a few of the best:

PACHUCA AND JUAN DE LA BARRERA, CONDESA
This bustling street market takes over Calle Pachuca in the northwest Condesa every Tuesday. Come to shop for handmade tortillas, fresh fruit, herbs, vegetables, and mushrooms—or simply come to chow down at the many delicious street stands. You'll find tacos, freshly fried *flautas,* handmade quesadillas, and *huaraches,* among other tasty bites. At lunchtime, popular food stands are thronged by locals; some even have tables and chairs for dining.

TIANGUIS DEL ORO, GLORIETA DE LAS CIBELES AND CALLE DE ORO, ROMA
There are street vendors every day along Calle de Oro in the Roma, but this open-air market is biggest and best on Wednesday, Saturday, and Sunday, when many additional stands open up. There is a wide assortment of great grub, but particularly notable is the Argentine grill, **Parrilladas Bariloche,** which serves thick South American steaks to hungry crowds for very low prices and in an anomalous market atmosphere.

TIANGUIS DE LOS JUEVES, CAROLINA AND HOLBEIN, NAPOLES
A massive open-air market sets up in the street between the Plaza de Toros and the Estadio Cruz Azul in the Noche Buena neighborhood every Thursday. With hundreds of vendors, it's a labyrinth of delicious aromas, tropical colors, and human traffic jams. Come for the *gorditas,* the tacos, the *nieves,* and the excellent food shopping.

NUEVO LEÓN AND OMETUSCO, CONDESA
This small but pleasant Friday market has fresh produce and dairy for sale, as well as a tempting array of snacks. Grab a seat to dig into a massive *huarache* with a fried egg on top, handmade quesadillas, and other sundries.

MERCADO EL 100, PLAZA DEL LANZADOR
This ecological market's mission is to promote products that come from within 100 miles (160 kilometers) of Mexico City. Part of the growing organic and eco movement in the capital, this Saturday market in the Roma gets a lot of foot traffic from progressive locals. (Note that this market closes earlier, around 2pm or 3pm.)

FILADELFIA AND PENNSYLVANIA, NAPOLES
Just beside the World Trade Center, this big Sunday market is a great place to stock up for the week with fruits, veggies, meats, cheeses, and other staples or, of course, have a *tlacoyo,* a taco, or other freshly made snack.

GOURMET FOOD AND IMPORTS
Delirio
This popular bistro sells a range of gourmet products, many with a Mexican heritage. You can pick up crusty bread, cheeses, charcuterie, olive oil from Baja California, freshly baked cookies and pastries, and bottles of Mexican wine, as well as interesting jams and salsas (like *tejocote* fruit with *morita* chiles) jarred under chef Monica Patiño's label. If browsing makes you hungry, order a fresh salad, a slice of

quiche, and a cup of coffee, then grab a seat at one of the sidewalk tables.

MAP 5: Monterrey 116, 55/5584-0870, www.delirio.mx; Mon.-Wed. 9am-10pm, Thurs.-Sat. 9am-midnight, Sun. 9am-7pm; Metro: Insurgentes, Metrobús: Álvaro Obregón

JEWELRY
Sangre de Mi Sangre

Located in the beautiful Edificio Balmori on the corner of Orizaba and Álvaro Obregón, this ground-floor jewelry shop sells handmade and custom-designed jewelry in silver and gold by Monterrey-born designer Mariana Villareal. The collections change periodically but often include dramatic and oversize pieces. Depending on what's in the store, you might find elaborate nature-inspired rings with stones or silver spiders, or very clean, urban-chic styles.

MAP 5: Orizaba 101, L-F, 55/5511-8599, http://sdemis.com; Mon.-Fri. 11am-8pm, Sat. 11am-7pm; Metro: Insurgentes

MUSIC
Retroactivo Records

This well-stocked record shop in the Roma caters to local vinyl collectors with rare and imported LPs among its tens of thousands of titles. The focus is on used records, though they also have new albums, and you'll find a wide selection of musical styles from the 1960s through the 1990s, in genres from disco to rock. They also sell audio equipment and accessories.

MAP 5: Jalapa 125, 55/5564-2565, www.retroactivorecords.com.mx; Mon.-Sat. 11am-8pm; Metro: Insurgentes, Metrobús: Álvaro Obregón

PUBLIC MARKETS
Mercado de Medellín

This neighborhood market in the Roma Sur is spacious and well-lit, with dozens of produce stands piled high with fresh fruits and vegetables, cheesemongers, and fresh tortillas on sale. Mercado de Medellín is known for its excellent seafood sold in bulk, as well as for the vendors selling goods from Yucatán peninsula, like habanero salsas and pickled onions.

MAP 5: Medellín 234; daily 8am-5pm; Metro: Chilpancingo, Metrobús: Campeche

WINE AND LIQUOR
La Naval

Opened in the early 20th century, La Naval is an old-fashioned import shop specializing in quality wine and liquor. There is a very nice selection of tequila and mezcal, as well as imported liquor, beer, and fancy soft drinks. With a heavy emphasis on European imports, the store also sells cheese, salt cod, charcuterie, olives, olive oils, and crackers. It's all packed together on super-stocked shelves, and during the holidays the scene can get quite hectic.

MAP 5: Av. Insurgentes Sur 373 at Michoacán, 55/5584-3500, www.lanaval.com.mx; Mon.-Sat. 8am-9pm; Metro: Chilpancingo

Sabrá Dios?

If you're looking for an unusual gift for an unusually discriminating friend, try this teensy shop in the Condesa, which specializes in small-batch spirits, including rare bottles of mezcal from Guerrero or Durango and sotol, a distilled spirit native to northern Mexico, made from the sotol plant. They also sell a small selection of gourmet goods, like dried meats and fruit, and specialty salts, meant to accompany a shot of mezcal.

MAP 5: Veracruz 15-A, 55/5211-7623, www.sabra-dios.com; Mon.-Sat. 9am-9pm; Metro: Chilpancingo

Coyoacán

Map 6

ARTS AND CRAFTS

Bazar Artesanal Mexicano de Coyoacán

There's a weekend craft market in central Coyoacán, in front of the Jardín Hidalgo. Though not as refined or famous as Bazaar Sábado in neighboring San Ángel, it is nonetheless a colorful place to look for affordable craft pieces. In addition to traditional *artesanías* like woven baskets, embroidered blouses, and *alebrijes* (hand-painted wood animal figurines from Oaxaca), a great number of vendors sell candles, incense, journals, handmade paper, beaded jewelry, and other more contemporary knickknacks.
MAP 6: Felipe Carrillo Puerto 25; Fri.-Sun. 11am-7pm; Metro: Viveros

Taller Experimental de Cerámica

Visit this long-running open-air ceramics studio in downtown Coyoacán to browse a tiny, jumbled showroom of glazed handmade ceramic pieces created by the workshop's owners, or find good bargains amid the dusty shelves of recently fired ceramic tableware, including mugs, plates, tea pots, bowls, vases, and more. In addition to retail, the workshop offers ongoing classes in wheel throwing, sculpture, and glazing. An eight-day course costs about US$125, and the schedule is flexible.
MAP 6: Centenario 63, 55/5554-6960, www.ceramicadiazdecossio.com.mx; Mon.-Fri. 10am-5pm; Metro: Juárez

BOOKS

Librería Gandhi

This beloved bookseller is one of the best in the city, with a broad selection of fiction, nonfiction, children's titles, and travel guides, mostly in Spanish, in its 15 branches in the capital. One of the largest branches is on Miguel Ángel de Quevedo in Coyoacán, just a few steps away from where the original Gandhi opened in 1971. There's a smaller branch across the street from Bellas Artes (Juárez 4, 55/5510-4231, Mon.-Fri. 10am-9pm, Sat.-Sun. 11am-8pm) in the Centro Histórico.
MAP 6: Miguel Ángel de Quevedo 121, 55/2625-0606, www.gandhi.com.mx ; Mon.-Fri. 9am-11pm, Sat.-Sun. 10am-11pm; Metro: Viveros

WINE AND LIQUOR

Barricas Don Tiburcio

This charming wine and specialty food shop is on a quiet street corner, just a few blocks east of Coyoacán's central plaza. With its old stone floors and exposed brick walls, the romantic atmosphere is naturally suited to a wine merchant. There are well-selected though generally upscale imported and domestic wines, a selection of cheeses, and jams, honey, and salsas made in Mexico.
MAP 6: Francisco Sosa 243, Santa Catarina Coyoacán, 55/5554-7359, www. barricasdontiburcio.com; Mon.-Sat. 11am-8pm, Sun. 11am-5pm; Metro: Viveros

ARTS AND CRAFTS

✪ Bazaar Sábado

Originally established in 1960, this is one of the nicest craft markets the city, located in the courtyard of a 17th-century stone building and spilling out into the Plaza San Jacinto. You'll find traditional artisan work, including blown glass, jewelry, ceramics, traditional masks, paper flowers, and clothing, as well as some contemporary designers selling their work. It's a popular Saturday destination for both residents and tourists, often bustling with browsers and filled with cheerful marimba music.

MAP 6: Plaza San Jacinto 11, 55/5616-0082, www.elbazaarsabado.com; Sat. 10am-6pm; Metro: Barranca del Muerto or Miguel Ángel de Quevedo

Caracol Púrpura

This small shop near the Plaza San Jacinto sells decorative crafts in a bright, gallery-like atmosphere. Some of the nicest pieces in the shop's collection include oversize beaded figurines made by the Huichol; delicately painted ceramics from Mata Ortiz, Chihuahua; and elaborate *arboles de la vida* (a ceramic sculptural tradition reaching back to the early colonial era) from Mexico state. There is another branch in the Shops at Downtown (Isabel la Católica 30, 55/5521-8000) in the Centro Histórico.

MAP 6: Juárez 2A, San Ángel, 55/5550-1450, www.caracolpurpura.com. mx; Wed.-Sun. 11am-6pm; Metro: Miguel Ángel de Quevedo

handcrafted crosses for sale at Bazaar Sábado

BEST SOUVENIRS: *ARTESANÍAS*

Mexico is known for its handicrafts, or *artesanías*, which often unite pre-Columbian artisan techniques with Spanish aesthetics. Like food and religious festivities, handicrafts are regionally specific.

CERAMICS

Long before the arrival of the Spanish, clay vessels were produced throughout Meso-america. Spaniards introduced kiln firing and ceramic glazes. The states of Puebla and Guanajuato are major producers of tin-glazed **majolica-style ceramics**, with the finest and most expensive ceramics produced in Puebla and referred to as **Talavera.** The town of Dolores Hidalgo, Guanajuato, is also known for its majolica-style ceramics, though Dolores's ceramics are considered "mass produced" compared to Puebla's, and are much cheaper.

In the state of Michoacán, potters produce shiny and elaborate **ceramic pineapples** without the use of a potter's wheel. Burnished clay pottery is also common in Michoacán, specifically from the town of Capula. Capula pottery is durable and recognizable because it is painted with hundreds of white dots. Also look for the shiny glazed platters and pots from Huancito, and the typical green and black pottery from Tzintzuntzan.

Arboles de la vida (trees of life) are sculptural pieces depicting trees with birds and figurines. You can find *arboles* from the state of Mexico and from Michoacán.

TEXTILES

Chales, rebozos, and *mantillas* are types of wraps or shawls that are produced throughout Mexico. The best (and priciest) shawls are made with natural fibers, usually silk or cotton. The famous silk *rebozos* of Santa María del Río are so finely woven that, despite their large size, they can pass through a woman's ring.

Manta, light cotton muslin, was mass-produced throughout Mexico and has long been the base for traditional Mexican clothing. Today, the majority of *manta* is imported from China, but clothing made from *manta* is produced throughout the country. Throughout town, you can find beautiful embroidered *manta* tunics and *huipiles* from Oaxaca, as well as the geometrically stitched *Magdalena huipiles* from Chiapas. In addition to *manta,* Oaxaca is a major producer of textiles and clothing that is often hand-loomed and colored with natural dye.

The country's most famous **rugs** come from Oaxaca. Woven with natural-dyed wool, they often depict pre-Hispanic designs or concepts. The best and most expensive rugs are made with natural fibers, though acrylic thread is common. To test for acrylic, take a rug into the sun. Unlike wool, acrylic will shine.

METALWORK

Stamped tin products **(hojalatería)** such as lamps, mirrors, and frames are a specialty of central Mexico. You'll also see shiny stamped copper pots, vases, and candlesticks from Michoacán. Metalwork traditions in Michoacán reach back to the pre-Columbian era, when locals were Mesoamerica's most advanced copper artisans, having developed new techniques in cold-hammering, soldering, and casting.

WOOD

Made from the wood of the copal tree, *alebrijes* are delicately carved and brightly painted animals and figurines, principally produced in San Antonio Arrazola, Oaxaca. Some of the more elaborate *alebrijes* can take weeks to create, and prices run the gamut.

Wooden **masks** are used in traditional ceremonies throughout Mexico, principally in the states of Oaxaca, Michoacán, and Guerrero. Designs include saints, devils, animals, and angels. Masks carry more significance if they have already been used in a ceremony.

GLASS

Hand-blown glass, or *vidrio soplado,* is produced in many parts of Mexico, particularly in Tonalá, Jalisco. Many shops in Mexico City sell these durable heavy glass pitchers, cups, and shot glasses (called *tequileros*) in a range of designs, often with a colored rim or dots.

✪ Casa del Obispo

Set in a colonial mansion with show-rooms surrounding a beautiful central courtyard, the Casa del Obispo is one of the most impressive and well-stocked craft shops in the city. If you are in the market for high-quality works of folk art and *artesanía*, you will find gorgeous pieces from all across Mexico at this well-curated store, from ceramics from Mata Ortiz, Chihuahua, to hammered-copper pans and lacquered gourds from Michoacán.

MAP 6: Juárez 1, San Ángel, 55/5616-8839; Wed.-Sun. 11am-6pm; Metro: Miguel Ángel de Quevedo

Casa del Obispo

GOURMET FOOD AND IMPORTS
Mundo Gourmet

This large shop in San Ángel caters to the wealthier residents of southern Mexico City with a superlative selection of wines from Mexico and around the world. Here, you'll find a good selection of national bottles from regions like Baja California and Coahuila, in varietals like Cabernet Sauvignon, Shiraz, and Chardonnay. The store also sells specialty cheeses, charcuterie, and other deli items, and also holds events and courses on wines.

MAP 6: Av. Revolución 1541, 55/5616-2162, http://mundogourmet.com.mx; Mon.-Sat. 9am-8pm, Sun. 11am-3pm; Metro: Barranca del Muerto

GREEN AND ECOLOGICAL SHOPS
Ecobutik

Specializing in ecologically responsible and organic products for the bath and home, this cute shop sells candles, green cosmetics and home cleaning products, handmade baby toys, reusable water bottles, and other smartly designed home goods. Run by organic-food brand Aires de Campo, the store also has a small selection of kitchen and baking supplies, like vanilla beans and coconut oil. There is a branch in the Shops at Downtown (Isabel la Católica 30, 55/5510-1336; Mon.-Sat. 10am-8pm, Sun. 10am-6pm) in the Centro.

MAP 6: Amargura 14, No. 1, 55/5550-9406, www.ecobutik.com; Mon.-Fri. 9:30am-7pm, Sat.-Sun. 11am-5pm; Metro: Miguel Ángel de Quevedo, Metrobús: Bombilla

PUBLIC MARKETS
Central de Abasto de la Ciudad de México

Covering three square kilometers in Iztapalapa, the Central de Abasto (Supply Center) is Mexico City's main wholesale market. It is the biggest food supplier in the country and the second biggest point of commerce in Mexico, after the Mexican Stock Exchange. Around 30,000 tons of food are sold here daily, from banana leaves and sugar cane to dried chiles and grains. The nine-hectare seafood section called La Nueva Viga displays a huge variety of fish from across the country. By its own estimates, the market receives 350,000 visitors annually and employs more than 70,000 people. Though it's not the most atmospheric shopping area in the city, the sheer quantity of products will interest curious travelers.

MAP 7: Canal Churubusco and Canal Apatlaco, Iztapalapa, www.ficeda.com.mx; daily 24 hours; Metro: Aculco

Mercado de Jamaica

Mexico City's largest flower market, the Mercado de Jamaica is a colorful, sweetly scented destination. Here, you'll find stalls selling thousands of varieties of flowers, as well as potted plants, fruit, and (naturally) food stalls for snacking. Fresh flowers are used abundantly in Mexico for decoration, altars, religious services, birthdays, and other special occasions. Visit in the days leading up to Día de Muertos to see tremendous shipments of *cempasúchil* (marigold), the flower of the dead.

MAP 7: Guillermo Prieto 45, Venustiano Carranza, 55/5741-1682; Mon.-Fri. 8am-6pm, Sat.-Sun. 7am-7pm, many flower vendors operate 24 hours; Metro: Jamaica

Mercado de Plantas y Flores Cuemanco

The area around Xochimilco has always been the valley's breadbasket, with farmers growing produce on the *chinampas*, or floating gardens, along the region's canals. In 1992, Mexico City's government started a project to rescue neglected *chinampas*, creating a new ecological park as well as the largest flower market in Latin America. The 13-hectare market, stocked with flowers as well as herbs, fruit trees, and medicinal plants, is not often visited by foreigners, but it is a colorful, interesting destination.

MAP 7: Periférico Sur, corner of Canal Nacional, Col. Cuemanco, 55/5676-8879; daily 10am-6pm; Tren Ligero: Xochimilco/ Bosque de Nativitas

GREATER MEXICO CITY

WHERE TO STAY

Guesthouses have existed in Mexico City since the early colonial era, when Catholic missionaries and other Spanish settlers would arrive in the New World and take up temporary residence in the palaces along the Alameda Central.

Hippodrome Hotel, the Condesa

Perhaps this heritage has contributed to making Mexico City such a hospitable place for travelers. Indeed, for a destination of its size and importance, Mexico City is filled with friendly, attractive, and surprisingly affordable hotels.

Mexico City offers a lot of variety when it comes to hotels, from creaky backpackers' favorites to luxury high-rise hotels that are destinations in themselves. There are charming bed-and-breakfasts in residential neighborhoods, boutique hotels with popular nightclubs, and design-centric hostels that cater to the Instagram-loving budget traveler.

The neighborhood you choose will be just as important in determining your experience as the place you stay. Many of the main attractions are located in the blocks surrounding the Zócalo, making the Centro Histórico and the area around the Alameda a good choice for first-time visitors. Given the capital's vast size, however, you're more likely to eat and go out in places near your hotel, which is one reason that travelers increasingly gravitate toward residential neighborhoods like the Roma and the Condesa. Polanco has always been a bastion of upscale, luxury hotels, and it remains so to this day.

All hotels charge a 15 percent IVA (value-added tax) and 2 percent city lodging tax. More expensive hotels may also tack on a 10 percent service charge, as

HIGHLIGHTS

✪ **MOST FASHIONABLE PALACE:** The gorgeous **Downtown Hotel** is in a colonial-era palace in the Centro. Modern guest rooms complement the historic architecture (page 218).

✪ **BEST MIDRANGE HOTEL:** For a comfortable, reasonably priced space in the Centro Histórico, **Hotel Catedral** is the perfect choice (page 220).

✪ **MOST CHARACTER ON A BUDGET:** Creaky and a bit offbeat, the **Hotel Isabel** is a favorite for travelers on a shoestring budget (page 221).

✪ **GREENEST SPOT:** Located in a renovated mansion, **El Patio 77** is an eco-friendly bed-and-breakfast with a ground-floor art gallery and a cool, off-the-beaten-track location (page 223).

✪ **BEST HOTEL FOR DESIGN LOVERS:** Delve into Mexican art and design at boutique **Hotel Carlota,** just steps from the Paseo de la Reforma (page 224).

✪ **MOST SOCIALLY MINDED SPACE:** More than an inexpensive crash pad, **Casa de los Amigos** is a social-justice organization, a house for refugees, and a gathering place for socially minded people (page 225).

✪ **MOST COMFORTABLE LANDMARK:** A jewel of midcentury modernist architecture, **Camino Real Mexico City** is one of the city's most interesting buildings. Consider a drink in the lobby bar, even if you're staying elsewhere (page 226).

✪ **BEST BOUTIQUE HOTEL:** A quiet luxury hotel in Polanco, **Las Alcobas** delivers personable service and plenty of amenities, with zero pretension (page 226).

✪ **HOMIEST ATMOSPHERE:** In the Condesa, the **Red Tree House** boasts a friendly staff and breeds a spirit of camaraderie among its guests, who gather in the gardens during happy hour (page 228).

PRICE KEY

$	Less than US$100 per night
$ $	US$100-200 per night
$ $ $	More than US$200 per night

WHERE TO STAY IF...

In such a large, sprawling city, what neighborhood you stay in is often as important as the accommodations you choose. Depending on how you plan to spend your time, some neighborhoods will be better suited to your trip than others.

YOU ONLY HAVE A WEEKEND...
...stay in the **Centro Histórico,** where the city's most important sights and cultural institutions are walking distance from your doorstep.

YOU WANT TO GET AWAY FROM IT ALL
(AND DON'T MIND PAYING FOR IT)...
...book a room along the park in **Polanco,** where fresh air and gorgeous views take the edge off city living.

YOU WANT TO PARTY...
...you won't be alone in the **Colonia Roma,** Mexico City's hippest neighborhood.

YOU'RE TRAVELING ON A BUDGET...
...stay in the **Centro Histórico,** a haven for budget travelers.

YOU WANT A LITTLE SOMETHING OF EVERYTHING
(AND DON'T MIND NOISE)...
...head straight to the **Zona Rosa.** It's perfectly located and safe at almost any hour of the day or night. But beware! It's a party capital and can be noisy at night.

YOU AREN'T REALLY A CITY PERSON...
...**head south.** There aren't many hotels south of the Viaducto, but those who want a less urban environment will be happiest in the clean and sunny south.

A MORNING JOG IS PART OF YOUR ROUTINE...
...stay in **Polanco** and enjoy the proximity to the many trails snaking through the forested Bosque de Chapultepec.

YOU ARE A SERIOUS FOODIE...
...you're in luck. There are great eats in every neighborhood in the capital.

---

well as additional costs for amenities, like Internet service. When booking, ask whether tax and service are included in quoted rates.

CHOOSING WHERE TO STAY

Centro Histórico

The Centro Histórico is the heart of it all: dense, noisy, and pulsing with energy. Staying in the Centro is an excellent choice for **first-time visitors.** Plus, some of the very best breakfast options—from Sanborns de los Azulejos to El Cardenal to Café El Popular—are downtown. There are many excellent accommodations in the Centro in every price category.

Though you'll find some new upscale options, the area remains a **backpacker's paradise,** with tons of super-cool hostels scattered throughout the district.

Alameda Central

The area around the Alameda Central is a good **jumping-off point for exploring the city.** It's an easy walk to all major sights in the Centro and better connected to the south of the city than the areas around the Zócalo, thanks to the proximity of the Paseo de la Reforma, several Metro lines, and two Metrobús lines.

There are several fancy spots around the Alameda, with budget ones a few blocks south. Here, you won't find the same worn charm as in many of the low-budget hotels a few blocks east, and after dark the area can feel a bit abandoned, though it is not particularly unsafe.

Paseo de la Reforma

Mexico City's grand central avenue is known for its luxury hotels, anchored by the venerable Four Seasons, just to the east of the Bosque de Chapultepec. Closer to the Centro, however, you'll find a few more inexpensive options along Reforma. The Tabacalera neighborhood, near the Monumento a la Revolución Mexicana, has long been a mecca of cheapie hotels. There are many more options for this area beyond those listed in this book, though some are rather shabby, so check your room before you check in.

Zona Rosa

Central, safe, and tourist-friendly, the Zona Rosa has always been a popular place to stay, even if it isn't the city's most enchanting neighborhood. Here, you'll find hotels at a range of price points, a major public-transportation hub at the Glorieta Insurgentes, and a late-night party scene that makes it safer to walk through the streets after dark (though nightclubs can also be a noisy nuisance for guests with street-view rooms). Just northwest of the Zona Rosa, the area around the U.S. embassy is also a safe and central destination, with accommodation options near main thoroughfares Insurgentes and the Paseo de la Reforma, as well as plenty of dining and nightlife options.

Polanco

Affluent Polanco has some of the most luxurious hotels in the city, including the string of famous high-rises overlooking Bosque de Chapultepec from the tony street Campos Eliseos. Many of these establishments are favored by international businesspeople, though tourists also book in Polanco, particularly at the architecturally notable Camino Real or the party-centric W.

Roma and Condesa

With the opening of several new hotels, the hippest neighborhoods in Mexico City have become increasingly popular places to stay. There are no high-rise and few chain hotels in these residential districts, but in keeping with the neighborhoods' chic, independent reputation, there are boutique properties and bed-and-breakfasts. There is also a smattering of budget hotels, even in the best locations.

Coyoacán and San Ángel

Mexico City's southern neighborhoods are cleaner, greener, and more peaceful than its urban heart. Yet with few businesses headquartered in the area and zoning restrictions making it more difficult to build, the south of the city has very few hotel options. Travelers can find a few options along Insurgentes Sur, though most will end up staying in the city center and visiting Coyoacán and San Ángel during day trips.

Near the Airport

There are decent hotels near the airport (including a few built directly into the airport itself) but unless you have a very brief layover, you'll be much better off staying near the city center, even if it means taking a taxi there and back.

ALTERNATIVE LODGING OPTIONS

Mexico City has a robust presence on Airbnb. In many central neighborhoods, including the Roma, hotels will often beat the prices of an apartment rental. In the southern neighborhoods, however, like Coyoacán and San Ángel, where there are few nice accommodations, Airbnb can be a good option.

Suites-only hotels cater to long stays with in-room kitchenettes and sitting areas. Some bed-and-breakfasts also offer these types of accommodations.

Centro Histórico   Map 1

✪ Downtown Hotel $$

This 17-room hotel in a stunning 17th-century palace makes wonderful use of its historic architecture through a simple yet elegant design scheme that emphasizes the amazingly high ceilings and old stone walls of the original building. While there's no lobby, the hotel shares the palace with several restaurants and a lovely Mexican-design-centric shopping center, and the awesome rooftop bar and swimming pool are enviably cool places to relax.

MAP 1: Isabel la Católica 30, 55/5130-6850, www.downtownmexico.com; Metro: Zócalo

Downtown Hotel

Gran Hotel de la Ciudad de México $$

Replete with tiered balconies and old steel-cage elevators, the art nouveau lobby at the Gran Hotel de la Ciudad is crowned by a vaulted Tiffany glass ceiling, made in Paris in 1908. Guest rooms, arranged around the central atrium, have an ultra-romantic vibe, with floral bedspreads and TVs hidden from view behind white-and-gold cabinets. Rooms overlooking the Zócalo are the most coveted; keep in mind that they can be noisy, too.

MAP 1: 16 de Septiembre 82, 55/5255-1083, www. granhoteldelaciudaddemexico.com.mx; Metro: Zócalo

NH Centro Histórico $$

In the heart of the Centro Histórico, this Spanish-owned hotel doesn't take many design cues from its historic surroundings. Rather, the atmosphere is clean and thoroughly modern, adhering to a dark, neutral color scheme throughout the building. Though not especially spacious, the 100-plus well-priced guest rooms are comfortable and totally functional, with clean bathrooms, cable TV, in-room safes, free Wi-Fi, and air-conditioning.

MAP 1: Palma 42, 55/5130-1850, www. nh-hoteles.es; Metro: Zócalo

Zócalo Central $$

On the northeast corner of the Zócalo, this reasonably priced, contemporary hotel (formerly the Holiday Inn) has a perfect central location, with a bank of rooms looking directly over the Zócalo. Guest rooms are clean and comfortable, with a conservative dark color scheme and marble baths, and the staff is notably accommodating and friendly. The same hotelier operates another similar property, Histórico Central (Bolívar 28, 55/5521-2121), just a few blocks away, in a 300-plus-year-old building on Bolívar.

MAP 1: Cinco de Mayo 61, 55/5130-5138, www.centralhoteles.com; Metro: Zócalo

Downtown Beds $

At this hostel, hotelier Grupo Hábita mixes its signature design sense with low-key backpacker charm. Both dorms and private rooms are simple but sufficiently stylish, with white-washed walls and brick ceilings. Amenities include an on-site movie-screening room, an inexpensive patio bar, and bike rental. Plus, guests can use the posh rooftop pool at the Downtown Hotel upstairs (with a minimum purchase at the bar).

MAP 1: Isabel la Católica 30, 55/5130-6855, www.downtownbeds.com; Metro: Zócalo

Hostal Centro Histórico Regina $

Located in an 18th-century mansion, this hostel offers the perfect trio of great location, low nightly price, and a cool, youthful atmosphere. Dorm rooms, though a bit crowded, are clean and pretty, with parquet floors, high ceilings, and French windows overlooking the street below. Right on the Regina pedestrian corridor, it's a quick stumble from several neighborhood bars to the dorm, though you may be tempted to spend the evening "in" at the hostel's rooftop bar.

MAP 1: 5 de Febrero 58 at Regina, 55/5709-4192, www. hostalcentrohistoricoregina.com; Metro: Isabel la Católica

Hostel Mundo Joven Catedral $

Just behind the cathedral, this popular hostel has dozens of dorm-style rooms with wood floors, in-room lockers,

HOTEL BARS WITH A VIEW

Just because you aren't staying in a hotel doesn't mean you can't enjoy some of its amenities. As in many big cosmopolitan cities, some of the capital's nicest bars are located in its upscale hotels. Here are five top-notch places with awesome views.

THE ROOFTOP BAR AT THE DOWNTOWN HOTEL

While taking a break from a tour around the Centro (or waiting for a table at Azul Histórico downstairs), head up to the shaded rooftop bar in the **Downtown Hotel** (page 218), where you can drink a cold margarita while looking out over the Porfiriato-era facade of the Casino Español across the street.

TERRAZA AT THE GRAN HOTEL DE LA CIUDAD DE MÉXICO

At the bar and restaurant in the **Gran Hotel de la Ciudad de México** (page 219), the attraction is the view of the Zócalo (and the chance to walk through the Gran Hotel's gorgeous lobby). It offers a full menu and a buffet brunch on the weekends, but you can come for drinks in the afternoon.

CIELO DE CORTÉS AT HOTEL DE CORTÉS

Lounge furniture and umbrellas beckon from the roof deck of the **Hotel de Cortés** (page 222), with great views of the church spires and rooftops surrounding the Alameda Central. In the evenings, it's a hot spot with a boisterous crowd, often with live DJs. The house specialty is creative martinis.

KING COLE BAR AT THE ST. REGIS

Even if you aren't staying at the super-luxe **St. Regis** (page 223), you can experience the pleasures of being a guest at their King Cole Bar (daily 10am-2am), which serves the hotel's world-famous Bloody Marys. The decor is formal and elegant, and a terrace overlooks the Paseo de la Reforma.

LA TERRAZA AT CONDESA DF

It's no wonder the rooftop bar and sushi restaurant at the boutique **Condesa DF** (page 227) is frequented by Condesa locals: The views of leafy treetops in Parque España, the open-air terrace, and top-notch sushi make it the perfect place to unwind with a drink in the evening.

and clean bunk beds. A handful of private rooms have views of the Catedral Metropolitana (though note that street-facing rooms also get more ambient noise than interiors). Downstairs, there's a patio restaurant. On the top floor is a picturesque terrace bar, where guests often convene to swap travel tips and snap photos of the back of the cathedral. It is best to reserve ahead for dorm beds and necessary for private rooms, which book well in advance.

MAP 1: República de Guatemala 4, 55/5518-1726, www.mundojovenhostels.com; Metro: Zócalo

✪ Hotel Catedral $

Located right between the Zócalo and the Plaza Santo Domingo, Hotel Catedral is a great value, combining a wonderfully central location with comfortable modern guest rooms and genuinely affable service. The accommodating staff is always willing to call a taxi or give directions. It's popular with Mexican families, business travelers, and a smattering of tourists, and there's always a pleasant buzz in the lobby.

MAP 1: Donceles 95, 55/5518-5232, www.hotelcatedral.com; Metro: Zócalo

Hotel Gillow $

Run by the same owners as the Hotel Catedral, the Gillow is, like its sibling, a friendly and well-priced hotel in the heart of the Centro. Its crowning feature is a wholly perfect location, just a few blocks from the Zócalo and right between the pedestrian street Madero and bustling Cinco de Mayo. Exterior rooms with balconies, though slightly noisier, have beautiful views of the Centro's colonial palaces.

MAP 1: Isabel la Católica 17, 55/5510-2636, www.hotelgillow.com; Metro: Zócalo

✪ Hotel Isabel $

This rambling five-story hotel has long been a favorite with budget travelers, offering ramshackle charm at a low nightly rate. The 74 guest rooms vary widely in character (ask to see another if you don't like the accommodations you were assigned), though all have a scruffy old-fashioned feeling, with creaky wood furniture and high ceilings. You can shave a bit off the nightly price if you are willing to stay in a room with shared bath.

MAP 1: Isabel la Católica 63, 55/5518-1213, www.hotel-isabel.com.mx; Metro: Isabel la Católica

Hotel Principal $

The friendly Hotel Principal is a budget-traveler favorite, offering small but clean rooms with a touch of charming colonial influence. Though the lobby is old-fashioned and dim, guest rooms are organized around four stories of bright, plant-filled courtyards. Double doors open onto each bedroom—though note that they have no windows and can get a bit stuffy during the warmest months. Short of staying in a hostel, this hotel is one of the most inexpensive options in the Centro.

MAP 1: Bolívar 29, 55/5521-1333, www.hotelprincipal.com.mx; Metro: Allende

Hotel Ritz Ciudad de México $

Though not nearly as fancy inside as the Porfiriato-era building in which it's housed, the Ritz is still a good low-cost choice in the Centro, with 120 clean rooms with carpets, cable TV, fans, free local phone calls and Wi-Fi, bathtubs, and lock boxes. Decor is dated but homey. Particularly nice are the street-facing rooms, which have windows opening over Madero, the pedestrian corridor in the heart of the Centro. The decent rooftop terrace restaurant also offers room service.

MAP 1: Madero 30, 55/5130-0169, www.hotelritz.mx; Metro: Allende

Hotel Zamora $

One of the best parts of this downtown hotel is its enviable location on the pedestrian street Madero. Rooms with a small balcony and street views are decidedly the best option at this basic hotel, which has long been popular with backpackers. The 36 rooms are organized around a pretty interior patio, but don't expect luxury at this price; here simplicity reigns. Rooms with private baths are a bit more expensive.

MAP 1: Cinco de Mayo 50, 55/5512-1832; Metro: Allende

THE WAITING GAME

Mexico City has a multitude of hotels, and those on the road or who don't like to plan ahead can generally count on finding an open room in their price range—particularly in the budget category. The benefit of waiting to book is having a chance to see the hotel, as well as the room they are offering you, before you commit to a night. Budget travelers will find the most options in the Centro Histórico, where many hotels are within walking distance of each other, so it isn't out of the question to hoof it to another spot if you aren't happy with your first choice. Popular budget hotels can fill up, though, so if you have your heart set on a certain place, make a reservation.

Even on the higher end of the spectrum, most of Mexico City's larger hotels rarely reach capacity, and some run same-day specials. That said, you can often score much better deals by booking ahead at larger establishments via the Internet or through airline-and-hotel packages. Most important, popular boutique hotels and bed-and-breakfasts (especially those that get a lot of press in magazines and travel blogs) will fill up far in advance. If you definitely want to stay in a smaller place, it's worth making a reservation with as much anticipation as possible.

Alameda Central   Map 2

Hilton Mexico City Reforma $$$
A high-rise hotel overlooking the Alameda Central, the Hilton is popular with business travelers, though tourists can also get good deals by booking rooms in advance. Accommodations are clean and modern, with the muted, rather corporate style you'd expect from a large luxury hotel chain. Request a room on a higher floor for wonderful views of the city (and less traffic noise from the street below).
MAP 2: Av. Juárez 70, 55/5130-5300, www.hilton.com; Metro: Juárez

Chaya B&B $$
Occupying the top floor of the art deco Barrio Alameda building, this bed-and-breakfast has 11 simple yet stylish guest rooms opening onto a central patio, each with charming views of the urban cityscape. The best vistas belong to the pretty front-facing suites, which look directly onto the Alameda Central. A full breakfast is served daily in the shared breakfast room, which also overlooks the park. Well-behaved pets are welcome. Note that the building lacks an elevator.
MAP 2: Barrio Alameda, Doctor Mora 9, 55/5512-9074, www.chayabnb.com; Metro: Juárez

Hotel de Cortés $$
History recommends this boutique hotel: The striking early-colonial-era building, likely constructed in the 17th century, became a hotel in 1780 and has been in operation as a guesthouse ever since. It has been upgraded to a boutique property, and rooms are now thoroughly modern, with wood floors, a soothing white-and-tan color scheme, and pretty tiled baths with skylights above the showers. Each room overlooks the main covered courtyard, where the hotel's fusion restaurant serves breakfast, lunch, and dinner.
MAP 2: Av. Hidalgo 85, 55/5518-2181, www.boutiquehoteldecortes.com; Metro: Hidalgo

Hotel Fleming $

This low-cost hotel several blocks south of the Alameda is a good value for its price, with 80 spotlessly clean and relatively spacious rooms with satellite TV and free Wi-Fi. Rooms overlooking the courtyard are quieter than the street-view rooms. For those not used to an urban environment, the neighborhood can feel a bit rough after hours, but for the price, this is a nice, central place to stay.

MAP 2: Revillagigedo 35, 55/5510-4530, www.hotelfleming.com.mx; Metro: Juárez

Paseo de la Reforma   Map 3

Four Seasons Hotel $$$

The stately Four Seasons, near the main entrance to Chapultepec, has long been known as the premier high-end choice for international travelers in Mexico City, consistently receiving high ratings in top travel magazines for its attentive service and top-notch amenities. The eight-story hotel's guest rooms are elegant yet cozy, filled with armchairs, lamps, and writing desks; some have French doors opening onto the pretty central garden.

MAP 3: Paseo de la Reforma 500, 55/5230-1818, toll-free in Mexico 800/906-7500, www.fourseasons.com/mexico; Metro: Sevilla

St. Regis $$$

Every detail has been carefully considered at this five-star luxury hotel on the Paseo de la Reforma, a branch of the famed New York City establishment. This towering skyscraper, open since 2009, boasts breathtaking views of the city, which get better the higher you go. Rooms are subdued and elegant, with luxury bed linens and spacious baths. As in New York, you can find the King Cole Bar in the lobby, complete with its famous line of Bloody Marys.

MAP 3: Paseo de la Reforma 439, 55/5228-1818, www.starwoodhotels.com; Metro: Sevilla

St. Regis

✪ El Patio 77 $$

This small guesthouse is located in a renovated mansion in the Colonia San Rafael, a turn-of-the-20th-century neighborhood that is still largely off the beaten track for most tourists. Guest rooms are individually decorated yet consistently beautiful; color palettes are muted, and furnishings are a mix of antique and hand-crafted. The suites are spacious, with

223

light-filled bathrooms and street-facing balconies; there are also several reasonably priced rooms with shared bath. The ecofriendly hotel collects rainwater, recycles gray water, and heats showers with solar power.

MAP 3: Icazbalceta 77, 55/5592-8452, www.elpatio77.com; Metro: San Cosme

✪ Hotel Carlota $$

In the spring of 2015, Hotel Carlota opened in what was formerly a family-friendly budget hotel, reinventing the space as a floor-to-ceiling showcase of contemporary Mexican design, with interiors and architecture by well-known Mexico City firms. There is original art in every room, and a hot in-house restaurant, Carlota, overlooks the sun-kissed central patio and glass-walled pool. Just a block from the Paseo de la Reforma, it's a central, chic place to stay.

MAP 3: Río Amazonas 73, 55/5511-6300, www.hotelcarlota.com; Metro: Insurgentes, Metrobús: Reforma

Hotel Geneve $$

Hotel Geneve seems trapped in time, from its pink facade to its turn-of-the-20th-century lobby, filled with overstuffed furniture, dark-wood bookshelves, and globe lamps. Guest rooms are not as opulent as the hotel's beautiful common areas suggest, lacking the polish and modernity of higher-end accommodations; however, they maintain a pleasantly old-fashioned feeling. Given the location and history, the rack rate isn't particularly high, but prices can drop much lower if you book ahead.

MAP 3: Londres 130, 55/50080-0800, www.hotelgeneve.com.mx; Metro: Insurgentes

Hotel Imperial Reforma $$

One of the most recognizable buildings on the Paseo de la Reforma, this old, wedge-shaped hotel, with a gold dome on the roof, has balconied guest-room windows overlooking the street. The interior of the hotel isn't quite as beautiful as the Old World exterior, but the 60 carpeted guest rooms are spacious and comfortable, if a tiny bit worn. The location on one of the city's iconic thoroughfares, close to the Centro, is convenient and charming.

MAP 3: Paseo de la Reforma 64, 55/5705-4911 or 800/714-2909, www.hotelimperial.com.mx; Metro: Juárez or Hidalgo

Room Mate Valentina $$

Part of the Spanish-owned Room Mate group, this friendly hotel is an excellent value, with clean, spacious rooms, each equipped with a sitting area, desk, and big bathroom. The white-on-white color scheme and ultra-minimalist look feel a bit austere, but amenities are plentiful, including Wi-Fi and flat-screen TVs. Best of all, the hotel is in the heart of the Zona Rosa, a safe, always-bustling location, and the service is outgoing and friendly.

MAP 3: Amberes 27, 55/5080-4500, http://valentina.room-matehotels.com; Metro: Insurgentes

Suites del Ángel $$

This quiet all-suites establishment near the Ángel de la Independencia is nice choice for families or business travelers looking for a bit more space and privacy than what you'd find at a typical hotel. Every suite includes a sitting area with a sofa bed, a private bath and bedroom, and a small kitchenette, with a refrigerator and microwave.

Given the space and central location, the hotel is surprisingly affordable, with no extra charge for children.
MAP 3: Rio Lerma 162, 55/5242-9500, www.hotelesdelangel.com.mx; Metro: Insurgentes

✪ Casa de los Amigos $

A guesthouse and social-justice organization, Casa de los Amigos offers basic dorm accommodations and private rooms with shared bath. As part of its mission, Casa de los Amigos houses and acclimates political refugees, so you may be sleeping next to someone who's come to Mexico from very far away (in addition to meeting the long-term volunteers, who live on-site). A shared kitchen serves as an informal gathering spot, while the peaceful upstairs library was once the studio of muralist José Clemente Orozco, the home's former owner.
MAP 3: Ignacio Mariscal 132, 55/5705-0521, www.casadelosamigos.org; Metro: Revolución

Casa González $

Close to the U.S. and British embassies in the central Cuauhtémoc neighborhood, this friendly family-run guesthouse has 22 cheerful private bedrooms located in several buildings that share a plant-filled central courtyard. Bedrooms are reasonably priced, but cute and clean, some with private patios. Just a few steps from Paseo de la Reforma, the hotel is perfectly central and an all-around good value.
MAP 3: Río Sena 69 at Río Lerma, 55/5514-3302, www.hotelcasagonzalez.com; Metro: Insurgentes

Hotel Del Principado $

Conveniently located near the Zona Rosa and Paseo de la Reforma, the Principado has 50 modern rooms decorated in a rather bland but functional style. If you aren't looking for frills, the hotel is a good value. (Book on a third-party website for the lowest prices, which can drop below US$50). Management is efficient and helpful, and there is an on-site restaurant with a big, inexpensive breakfast buffet.
MAP 3: Londres 42, 55/5533-2944, www.hoteldelprincipado.com.mx; Metro: Insurgentes

Hotel Manalba $

A comfortable, friendly, and inexpensive hotel near the Monumento a la Revolución Mexicana, this modern spot has Mayan-themed decor in the lobby and clean, small, modern rooms equipped with TVs, wireless Internet, and loud bedspreads. Some rooms have interior windows, which can be a bit dark, though very quiet; for the price and comfort, it's a good-value spot.
MAP 3: Antonio Caso 23, 55/5566-6066, www.hotelmanalba.com.mx; Metro: Revolución

Hotel María Cristina $

In a lovely four-story colonial-style building just off the Paseo de la Reforma, the long-standing María Cristina delivers a bit of Old World ambience without breaking the bank. The attractive lobby is filled with dark-wood furniture and iron chandeliers, and guest rooms surround the lovely interior gardens. The decor is rather dated, and some rooms feel more worn than others, but overall it's quaint and comfortable, best suited to those looking for a non-corporate, low-key hotel experience.
MAP 3: Río Lerma 31, 55/5566-9688, www.hotelmariacristina.com.mx; Metro: Insurgentes

Chapultepec and Polanco Map 4

✪ Camino Real Mexico City $$$

One of the most original architectural concepts in Mexico City, the Ricardo Legorreta-designed Camino Real is a marvel of mid-20th-century design, from its pink sculptural wall at the entryway to the unique circular fountain in the courtyard. On top of that, the Camino Real is a full luxury establishment, well known for its excellent service and amenities. It has three swimming pools, rooftop tennis courts, and numerous in-house eateries, including a branch of the world-famous restaurant Morimoto.

MAP 4: Av. Mariano Escobedo 700, 55/5263-8888, U.S./Canada 800/722-6466, www.caminoreal.com/mexico; Metro: Chapultepec

Hotel Hábita $$$

This boutique hotel is considered one of the chicest places to stay in the city. Behind its unusual frosted-glass facade, the 36 guest rooms are elegantly minimalist, with classic modern furniture in dark neutral tones, long glass desks, and, in most, small terraces. It features a cool lobby restaurant and a glassed-in exercise room upstairs; the signature establishment, however, is the popular rooftop nightclub and bar.

MAP 4: Av. Presidente Mazaryk 201, 55/5282-3100, www.hotelhabita.com; Metro: Polanco

JW Marriott $$$

The JW Marriott is one of the "big three" hotels rising over the Bosque de Chapultepec from Campos Eliseos, and it's the favored choice of many travelers for its genial service. The hotel's comfortable rooms were renovated in 2013, and they have a homey feeling, with wood furnishings, lamps, and carpeting, though no major emphasis on design. Most impressive are the views, which get better the higher up you go.

MAP 4: Andrés Bello 29, 55/5999-0000, U.S./Canada 888/813-2776, www.marriott.com; Metro: Auditorio

✪ Las Alcobas $$$

In the heart of Polanco, this boutique hotel has enough style to warrant its chic zip code, but its intimate size distinguishes it from nearby establishments. The 35 elegant guest rooms are warm and modern, with rosewood furniture and huge plate-glass windows allowing in ample natural light (but, fortunately, not much sound from the street below; the glass is double-paned). Details are taken seriously: Beds are dressed in Italian linens, flat-screens are equipped with home-theater sound systems, and marble baths have rain showers stocked with handmade soaps.

MAP 4: Presidente Masaryk 390A, 55/3300-3900, www.lasalcobas.com; Metro: Polanco

InterContinental Presidente Mexico City $$$

The InterContinental Presidente is the oldest of the grand park hotels, originally built in 1977. Its multistory pyramid lobby, topped with an immense skylight, is impressive, though the 660 rooms are more modern and subdued. The hotel is known for its dining, with six restaurants and a bar, including Au Pied de Cochon French restaurant, open daily 24 hours, and the Balmoral tea room, with English-style afternoon tea and snacks.

MAP 4: Campos Eliseos 218, 55/5327-7700, U.S./Canada 800/327-0200, www.interconti.com; Metro: Auditorio

W Mexico City $$$

The W Mexico City underwent a massive renovation in 2015, reopening with an artsy new design that includes an ultra-modern cocktail bar in the lobby. The bold new look extends to the guest rooms, which have splashy colors and white polished floors. Fortunately, some things haven't changed: Most bedrooms have remarkable views of the surrounding city or Chapultepec park, and the in-house bar retains the buzzy atmosphere that made the W hotel chain famous worldwide.

MAP 4: Campos Eliseos 252, 55/9138-1800, www.starwoodhotels.com; Metro: Auditorio

Wyndham Garden Polanco $$

This hotel typically attracts business travelers, but the price and quality make it a good choice for any visitor to the city. Rooms are modern and functional, though a bit nondescript; on the higher floors, however, you'll have lovely views of the park. For those who like the Polanco neighborhood, it's a good alternative to the pricier hotels that dominate the skyline along the Bosque de Chapultepec.

MAP 4: Tolstoi 22, 55/5262-0848 or 800/900-4672, www.wyndhampolanco.com; Metro: Chapultepec

Roma and Condesa   Map 5

Condesa DF $$$

Located in a fine triangular mansion overlooking the tree-filled Parque España, this design-centric boutique hotel is beloved by bloggers, neighborhood hipsters, and chic travelers who place equal value on comfort and aesthetics. Here, 24 beautifully modern guest rooms and 16 suites surround a central atrium with an in-house restaurant and lobby, stylishly decorated with globe lamps, an eclectic mix of tables and chairs, and an aqua-and-white color scheme.

MAP 5: Av. Veracruz 102, 55/5241-2600, www.condesadf.com; Metro: Sevilla

Hippodrome Hotel $$$

This discreet 16-room hotel is in the Edificio Tehuacan, a lovingly restored 1930s art deco building a half block from Parque España in the Condesa. The rooms are quite small by Mexico City standards, but the interiors were carefully chosen to complement the building's inherent charms, with art deco finishes in the bedrooms and period-style furnishings; flat-screen TVs, 600-thread-count sheets, goose-down pillows, and other modern luxuries are nonetheless abundant. Top-floor suites have gorgeous, plant-filled terraces overlooking architectural landmark Edificio Balmori.

MAP 5: Av. México 188, 55/6798-3974, www.hippodromehotel.mx; Metro: Sevilla, Metrobús: Sonora

Casa de la Condesa $$

It's hard to imagine a more perfect location than at the Casa de la Condesa, a small hotel overlooking the trees and fountains of the Plaza Luis Cabrera in the Roma. While guest rooms aren't particularly contemporary, they are plenty spacious, and they all include a kitchenette. That said, you may never do more than heat your morning coffee here: The hotel is smack dab in the middle of the Roma's many dining and nightlife options.

MAP 5: Plaza Luis Cabrera 16, 55/5584-3089, www.casadelacondesa. net; Metro: Insurgentes, Metrobús: Álvaro Obregón

Condesa Haus $$

On a quiet residential street in the southeastern Condesa, a beautiful old mansion has been turned into a bed-and-breakfast that offers plenty of modern comforts while ably preserving the building's historic ambience, from original ceramic-tile floors to the soaring ceilings in the lobby. Each room is individually decorated around a theme, like the lovely Porfirio room, which takes its cues from late-19th-century Mexico, with a claw-foot tub, Juliet balconies, and a decorative iron headboard on the queen-size bed.

MAP 5: Cuernavaca 142, 81/1769-2769, www.condesahaus.com; Metro: Patriotismo

La Casona $$

In a residential area of the Roma neighborhood, convenient to Reforma, Polanco, and the Condesa but on a quiet side street, La Casona is housed in a lovingly refurbished late-19th-century mansion. The small but luxurious hotel contains a very good café-restaurant, a gym, services for business travelers, and 30 rooms filled with wooden writing desks and lacy curtains.

MAP 5: Durango 280, 55/5286-3001, www.hotellacasona.com.mx; Metro: Sevilla

✪ Red Tree House $$

A lovely bed-and-breakfast in the heart of the Condesa, Red Tree House occupies a converted family home, with comfy guest rooms opening onto the central garden. The relaxed atmosphere—which is plenty stylish but still cozy—seems to instill a sense of community among guests, who often gather in the common areas or enjoy a glass of wine together during complimentary afternoon happy hours. With its genuinely friendly staff and can't-be-beat location, it's one of the best spots in the capital.

MAP 5: Culiacan 6, 55/5584-3829, http://theredtreehouse.com; Metro: Chilpancingo

Villa Condesa $$

This discreet boutique hotel occupies a lovely old mansion on a tree-filled residential street, just a block away from the Parque España. Rooms are warmly decorated, some with romantic private balconies and French doors. There's no nightclub or buzzy rooftop bar (though there is a restaurant for hotel guests, where some in-the-know locals drop in), but that's exactly the charm of this little spot: It's a tucked-away, quiet place to stay, with no sign on the door or flashy lobby.

MAP 5: Colima 428, 55/5211-4892, www.villacondesa.com.mx; Metro: Sevilla

Distrito Condesa $

A pleasant and affordable little inn in a converted family home, Distrito Condesa has an enviable location, just blocks from Parque México and a stone's throw from the neighborhood's many nightlife and dining options. With its friendly staff and low price, it's a good choice for independent travelers who are looking for a convenient place to stay, with small but attractive rooms with wood floors and modern baths.

MAP 5: Cholula 62, 81/1769-2769 or 55/6303-1357, www.distritocondesa.com; Metro: Patriotismo

Hostal La Buena Vida $

Billing itself as the first "boutique hostel" in Mexico City, Buena Vida offers perks you don't often find in dormitory-style accommodations: There is a shared bathroom in each room (rather than a shared bath on each floor, as is more common in hostels), as well as daily cleaning and towel service, free Wi-Fi, and breakfast included in the nightly cost. The decor also surpasses typical backpacker style, as you'll notice from the hostel's geometric pink facade.

MAP 5: Mazatlán 190, 55/5271-9799, www.hostallabuenavida.com; Metro: Patriotismo

Hotel Embassy $

This basic hotel has an ideal north Roma location, clean and comfortable rooms, and a super-low nightly price, though a retro turquoise-and-purple color scheme dominates most of the carpeted bedrooms. At the intersection of Orizaba and Puebla, it's a quick walk to Metro Insurgentes and just a few blocks to the Plaza Río de Janeiro in the heart of the Roma. For couples, staying here may actually be cheaper than a hostel: A double room runs under US$30.

MAP 5: Puebla 115, 55/5208-0859, www. hotelembassymx.com; Metro: Insurgentes

Hotel Milan $

The Milan has long been a favorite with visitors for its surprisingly nice rooms and undeniably awesome location, right on the Roma's main corridor, Álvaro Obregón. Rooms have TVs and Wi-Fi. There is room service from the downstairs restaurant, which has long maintained a good reputation in the neighborhood (you'll see plenty of locals lunching there midweek). Street-facing rooms are more atmospheric, but you'll have to deal with some ambient noise. Rooms with queen-size beds ring in under US$50.

MAP 5: Álvaro Obregón 94, 55/5584-0222, www.hotelmilan.com.mx; Metro: Insurgentes

Hotel Stanza $

At the easternmost end of Álvaro Obregón, this nice midrange hotel has spacious, quiet, carpeted guest rooms. In many rooms, the dark color scheme and oversize furnishings aren't the most contemporary look, but there are plenty of comforts, including large baths, flat-screen TVs, and writing desks. Though it's a step up in price from the budget hotels in the area, Stanza delivers an overall nicer environment and better service than many of its neighbors.

MAP 5: Álvaro Obregón 13, 55/5208-0052, http://stanzahotel.com; Metro: Niños Héroes or Insurgentes

Coyoacán Map 6

La Casita del Patio Verde $$

There are only three rooms in this itty-bitty bed-and-breakfast, located on a charming cobblestone street in residential Coyoacán. The largest room is in its own detached cottage, with two double beds and a fireplace. In the main house, there are two considerably smaller but lovely bedrooms on the second floor. For those who want to experience life in this quiet neighborhood, La Casita is one of the few options—and fortunately, it's a lovely choice.

MAP 6: Callejón de la Escondida 41, 55/4170-3523, www.bbmexicocity.com; Metro: Coyoacán

San Ángel Map 6

City Express Insurgentes Sur $

City Express is a small Mexican-owned chain of pod-style hotels, which are designed for convenience and low cost. Rooms are very small, with everything, from the showers to the TVs, in reduced sizes. It caters principally to business travelers, though tourists can also get good deals here. This branch is close to the Teatro Insurgentes, putting UNAM and San Ángel within striking distance.

MAP 6: Av. Insurgentes Sur 1581, 55/5482-0280, http://cityexpress. hotelescity.com; Metro: Barranca del Muerto, Metrobús: Teatro Insurgentes

Greater Mexico City Map 7

Airport Hilton $$$

This Hilton is built on top of the international terminal—take the elevator up to the fourth floor, and you will be in the lobby. The hotel's rooms all have 24-hour housekeeping, minibars, and free wireless Internet. Carlos' Place Bar is a good place to sip a drink, watch planes take off, and keep track of incoming flights if you are waiting for someone. It's pricey for what you get, but that's to be expected for the convenience of staying in the airport terminal.

MAP 7: Benito Juárez International Airport Terminal 1, Capitan Carlos León and Blvd. Puerto Aérea, tel./fax 55/5133-0505, www. hilton.com; Metro: Terminal Aéreo

Camino Real Aeropuerto $$$

Connected to the domestic terminal via a pedestrian bridge, the Camino Real is a large, comfortable hotel. Amenities include a health club and pool, several good restaurants, and friendly service. Rooms are nothing special for the price, but they're more spacious than the Hilton's rooms and about the best available around the airport. Though it's the same hotel chain as the famous Camino Real in Polanco, this branch is more about comfort and convenience than high-end luxury.

MAP 7: Puerto México 80, 55/3003-0033, www.caminoreal.com; Metro: Terminal Aéreo

NH Hotel Aeropuerto $$

The only hotel in the newly constructed Terminal 2 at Benito Juárez International Airport, the NH has almost 300 rooms, with hardwood floors, a clean, modern design, and enough amenities to justify its decent nightly price. Its chief attraction, however, is its proximity to the airport. For those flying Aeroméxico, Delta, or other airlines that leave from the new wing, it couldn't be more convenient: There is an entrance directly inside the terminal.

MAP 7: Benito Juárez International Airport Terminal 2, Eje 1 Nte. and Blvd. Puerto Aérea, 55/5786-5750, www.nh-hotels.com; Metro: Terminal Aéreo

El Diplomatico $

There are few nice places to stay in Mexico City's quiet, cleaner southern neighborhoods. This glass-fronted hotel, on the southern stretch of Avenida Insurgentes, is an exception. Rooms are impeccably clean and spacious, all equipped with Wi-Fi, coffeemakers, air conditioning, and cable TV. Though a bit off the beaten path for most visitors, it's closer to San Ángel and Coyoacán, and a quick ride on Insurgentes Metrobús if you want to head downtown.

MAP 7: Av. Insurgentes Sur 1105, Col. Noche Buena, 55/5563-6066, www. eldiplomatico.com.mx; Metro: San Antonio, Metrobús: Parque Hundido

DAY TRIPS

Mexico City is propitiously located in one of the most densely populated and diverse regions in the country. From the capital, you're within a few hours of impressive ancient ruins, snowcapped volcanoes, enchanting small towns, and bustling colonial-era cities. With efficient buses and well-maintained highways radiating out from the city in every direction, it's easy to plan a change of scenery.

Iglesia Santa Prisca, Taxco

For most first-time visitors to Mexico City, a day-trip to the pyramids at Teotihuacán is a must. Just an hour east of the city, Teotihuacán is the most visited archaeological site in Mexico, an awe-inspiring example of city planning in 5th century Mesoamerica. Those with a strong interest in pre-Columbian history, however, will find a number of remarkable destinations in and around the Valley of Mexico, including the well-preserved fortified city of Xochicalco near Cuernavaca. In some cases, beautiful archaeological sites are adjoined by charming small towns; such is the case in Tepoztlán, a popular weekend destination that boasts pre-Columbian ruins in addition to lovely colonial architecture and abundant natural beauty.

Puebla is one of the most rewarding destinations near the capital, just 90 minutes south. Boasting a gorgeous *centro histórico,* Puebla is also known throughout Mexico for its inventive cuisine and its traditions in handicrafts, particularly Talavera pottery. For a quieter colonial experience, visit the silver city of Taxco, a picturesque community spread over a hillside and known for its stunning central church.

✪ **CLOSEST TO THE GODS:** For its scale and beauty, the ancient city of Teotihuacán was named "place of gods" by the Nahuatl-speaking people in the Valley of Mexico. Get sweeping views of this divine archaeological site from the top of the 75-meter-high **Pirámide del Sol,** the most iconic structure in Teotihuacán (page 239).

✪ **BEST PLACE TO START THE DAY:** The heart of Puebla's gorgeous colonial downtown, the **Zócalo** is adjoined by the city's impressive cathedral and surrounded by sidewalk cafés, perfect for sipping a coffee while planning your walking tour of the city's Centro Histórico (page 244).

✪ **MOST IMPRESSIVE REGIONAL MUSEUM:** There is an excellent collection of pre-Columbian art along with interesting temporary exhibits at Puebla's top-notch **Museo Amparo** (page 245).

✪ **MOST PERFECTLY PRESERVED COLONIAL CHURCH:** Built with the spoils of the silver trade, the remarkably pristine **Iglesia Santa Prisca** is Taxco's crown jewel, a lavish baroque church perched above the city (page 253).

✪ **BEST EARLY-COLONIAL MONUMENT:** An early Spanish settlement and former home of Hernán Cortés, Cuernavaca has many impressive early-colonial-era buildings, of which the austere and beautiful 16th-century **Catedral de la Asunción** is a must-see (page 255).

✪ **MOST INSPIRING LOOKOUT:** Ascend through lush forests to the pre-Columbian **Pirámide de Tepozteco,** on a bluff overlooking the tiny town of Tepoztlán, Morelos. The views of the valley below, together with the adrenaline of the climb, will take your breath away (page 262).

Day Trips

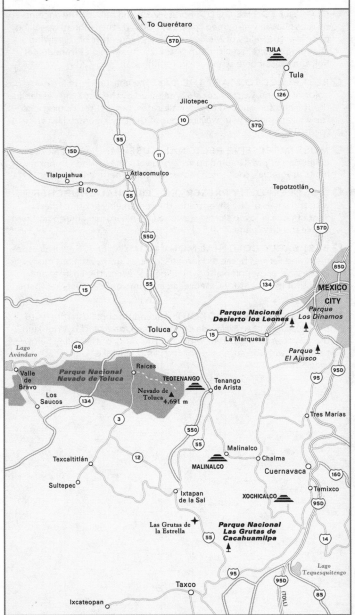

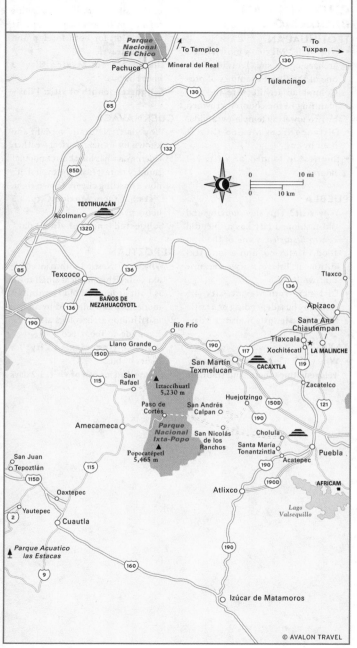

Parque
Nacional
El Chico

To Tampico

Pachuca   Mineral del Real

To
Tuxpan →

130

Tulancingo

85

130

132

85D

0   10 mi

0   10 km

TEOTIHUACÁN

Acolman

132D

85

Texcoco

136

136

Tlaxco

BAÑOS DE
NEZAHUACÓYOTL

136

Apizaco

Santa Ana
Chiautempan

190

Río Frío

Tlaxcala   ★ LA MALINCHE

117

Xochitécatl

119

Llano Grande

150D

190

San Martín
Texmelucan

CACAXTLA

Zacatelco

115

San
Rafael

Iztaccíhuatl
5,230 m

Huejotzingo

150D

121

Paso de
Cortés

San Andrés
Calpan

190

Amecameca

Parque
Nacional
Ixta-Popo

San Nicolás
de los
Ranchos

Cholula

San Juan
Tepoztlán

Popocatépetl
5,465 m

Santa María
Tonantzintla

Puebla

115D

Acatepec

AFRICAM

Oaxtepec

115

190

Yautepec

190D

2

Atlixco

Lago
Valsequillo

Cuautla

Parque Acuatico
las Estacas

190

9

160

Izúcar de Matamoros

© AVALON TRAVEL

235

CHOOSING AN EXCURSION

TEOTIHUACÁN

- **Why visit?** Mexico's most-visited archaeological site, Teotihuacán is one of the finest examples of pre-Columbian architecture and city planning in the country, crowned by two towering temple-pyramids.
- **Distance from Mexico City:** 1 hour by bus
- **Suggested length of visit:** 2-4 hours

PUEBLA

- **Why visit?** This slow-moving and old-fashioned city has a splendid *centro histórico,* some of the best food in Mexico, and a long tradition of Talavera-style ceramic craftwork.
- **Distance from Mexico City:** 1.5 hours by bus, depending on traffic
- **Suggested length of visit:** 1-3 days

TAXCO

- **Why visit?** The unique topography, relaxed atmosphere, and tradition of fine silverwork have made this former mining town a popular destination for both foreign and national travelers.
- **Distance from Mexico City:** 3 hours by bus
- **Suggested length of visit:** 1 day

CUERNAVACA

- **Why visit?** Naturally verdant and known for its near-perfect weather, Cuernavaca has long been a popular country retreat from the capital. It's now a bustling city in its own right.
- **Distance from Mexico City:** 1.5 hours by bus
- **Suggested length of visit:** 1 day

TEPOZTLÁN

- **Why visit?** Nestled within an emerald valley, this magical small town is built around an old Dominican monastery and adjoined by an unusual hilltop archaeological site, the Pirámide de Tepozteco.
- **Distance from Mexico City:** 1.5 hours by bus
- **Suggested length of visit:** 1-2 days

Teotihuacán

Little is known about the people who built the ancient city of Teotihuacán in the northern Valley of Mexico. The name itself, which means "the place of gods" in Nahuatl, was given to the ancient city several centuries later. What the people of Teotihuacán called their city, what language they spoke, or what ethnic heritage they came from remains unknown. One of the largest archaeological sites in the Americas, Teotihuacán is known today for its towering temple-pyramids, as well as for its impressive city planning and architecture.

Though the area in the northern Valley of Mexico was inhabited long before Teotihuacán was settled, construction of the major buildings in Teotihuacán took place between 100 BC and AD 250. The population grew rapidly as the city-state grew powerful; by the 4th century, Teotihuacán's cultural hegemony was evident in cities throughout Mesoamerica. Anthropologists estimate that, at its height, Teotihuacán was home to as many as 150,000 people and covered over 20 square kilometers, forming the largest city in the Western Hemisphere at the time. Under unknown circumstances, Teotihuacán began to decline in the 7th century AD, possibly under attack from nearby tribes; the city was largely abandoned, leaving only 30,000 residents through the Late Classic period. By 900, the city was almost entirely empty.

Teotihuacán

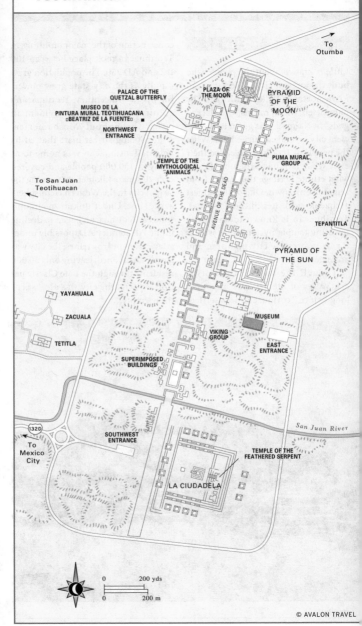

Teotihuacán

To Otumba

PALACE OF THE
QUETZAL BUTTERFLY

PLAZA OF
THE MOON

PYRAMID
OF THE
MOON

MUSEO DE LA
PINTURA MURAL TEOTIHUACANA
BEATRIZ DE LA FUENTE

NORTHWEST
ENTRANCE

PUMA MURAL
GROUP

TEMPLE OF THE
MYTHOLOGICAL
ANIMALS

To San Juan
Teotihuacan

AVENUE OF THE DEAD

TEPANTITLA

PYRAMID
OF THE
SUN

YAYAHUALA

ZACUALA

MUSEUM

TETITLA

VIKING
GROUP

EAST
ENTRANCE

SUPERIMPOSED
BUILDINGS

132D

SOUTHWEST
ENTRANCE

San Juan River

To
Mexico
City

TEMPLE OF THE
FEATHERED SERPENT

LA CIUDADELA

0   200 yds

0   200 m

© AVALON TRAVEL

With its impressive architecture and proximity to Mexico City, it's not surprising that Teotihuacán is the most visited archaeological site in Mexico. It is particularly popular on the spring equinox, when thousands of people assemble at the ruins to absorb the special energy of the sun.

SIGHTS

Calzada de los Muertos (Avenue of the Dead)

Teotihuacán's principal artery, the Calzada de los Muertos, runs two kilometers south to north between La Ciudadela and the Pyramid of the Moon. The avenue is impressive at its current scale, but archaeological evidence suggests it originally ran another kilometer farther south during Teotihuacán's height. It's flanked on either side by pyramid-shaped residences.

La Ciudadela (The Citadel)

On the south end of the Avenue of the Dead, there is a large, fortresslike enclosure, once located at the geographic center of the city. Archaeologists surmise that this area, called the Main Plaza, was where ritual performances took place. At the southeast end of the plaza is the impressive Templo de Quetzalcóatl (Temple of Quetzalcóatl or, as it is sometimes called, the Temple of the Feathered Serpent), which is decorated with elaborate stone carvings of serpents' heads protruding from the facade.

The remains of more than 200 men and women were found buried here. Evidence suggests they were sacrificed during the construction of the pyramid. The corpses were placed in pits with thousands of pieces of worked shell and numerous obsidian blades and points, suggesting that they may

have been Teotihuacano warriors, rather than prisoners from neighboring tribes.

Museo del Sitio de la Cultura Teotihuacana

Just beside the Pirámide del Sol, the Museo del Sitio de la Cultura Teotihuacana (Site Museum) contains a collection of artifacts excavated from the site (though the best collection of art and artifacts from Teotihuacán is in the Museo Nacional de Antropología in Mexico City). The building also has a snack bar, a bookshop, and restrooms, as well as a small but nicely tended botanical garden, right beside the Pyramid of the Sun. Admission is included in the cost of your ticket, and the museum is open the same hours as the archaeological site.

Museo de la Pintura Mural Teotihuacana "Beatriz de la Fuente"

Opened in 2001, this small museum contains interesting murals excavated from the archaeological site, as well as anthropological exhibits detailing religion and customs in the ancient city. Admission is free with your ticket to the ruins; it operates daily 8am-5pm.

✪ Pirámide del Sol (Pyramid of the Sun)

One of the largest, most impressive pyramids in the world, the Pirámide del Sol measures just under 70 meters in height. The climb to the top is steep and can be exhausting on warm, sunny days in the valley. Take your time, but be prepared for some fantastic views on a clear day.

In 1971, a long stairway was discovered that ended in a four-chamber lava cave, 100 meters long, under

WALMART AND TEOTIHUACÁN

In 2004, Walmart de México, the largest subsidiary of the massive U.S. retail outlet Walmart (and the biggest private employer in Mexico), began construction on a new mega-supermarket in the community of San Juan Teotihuacán. The supermarket, part of Walmart's Bodega Aurrerá chain, was about a kilometer from the great ruins of Teotihuacán. INAH, the National Anthropology Institute, officially stated that the construction would not affect the ancient site, despite its location within the outer limits of a protected zone, and Walmart appeared to have legal paperwork to support the new construction. People of the town, however, were outraged at not only the proximity of the new store to the ruins but the way their small-business-based community would be affected by the giant retailer. When a little pre-Columbian altar and some artifacts were discovered in what is now Bodega Aurrerá's parking lot, it helped galvanize opposition to the project.

Townspeople accused the local authorities of corruption for allowing construction on protected lands, and pointed fingers at INAH for jeopardizing a historic monument. Showing fierce pride in the ruins, as well as in their community, Teotihuacán locals organized months of protests against the megastore, and their efforts were eventually joined by high-profile Mexican intellectuals, including Oaxacan painter Francisco Toledo and essayist Elena Poniatowska. At one point, several protesters went on a weeklong hunger strike.

Although the protests received a great deal of national and international press, Walmart prevailed: The Bodega Aurrerá opened in 2005, and it hasn't lacked clients. However, the people of San Juan Teotihuacán weren't far off the mark: An exhaustive 2012 investigation by the *New York Times* uncovered more than US$200,000 in bribes paid to Teotihuacán's mayor and other government authorities to make concessions on laws and alter the town's zoning map; according to the *Times* report, it is part of a larger trend within the company to offer payouts for building permits in Mexico. Investigations into the case are ongoing.

the pyramid. Archaeologists surmise that the cave was considered by the city's builders to be a sacred entryway to another world, which is why they chose the location to build their largest pyramid.

Pirámide de la Luna (Pyramid of the Moon)

At the north end of the Calzada de los Muertos is the beautiful Pyramid of the Moon, centered on the Plaza of the Moon, which along with the Main Plaza at the Ciudadela was one of the principal ritual areas in the city. Built later than the other principal monuments in the city, the Pyramid of the Moon is 46 meters high and not as steep a climb as the Pyramid of the Sun, but the views over the city and surrounding countryside are still great. When approaching the pyramid along the Avenida de los Muertos, note

how the outline of the structure mirrors that of Cerro Gordo, the mountain behind it.

Palace of Quetzalpapalotl and Patio of the Jaguars

Just to the west of the Pirámide de la Luna, the impressive Palacio de Quetzalpapalotl is far more ornate than other dwellings in the city and was likely the home of a ruler or priest of Teotihuacán. In the main patio, principally excavated in the 1960s, there are beautiful stone columns carved with bas-relief butterflies and birds in profile. The roof was partially reconstructed by anthropologists in a style thought to be consistent with Teotihuacán's original architecture.

Just behind the palace, the Patio of the Jaguars is a small rectangular room that still retains its original red-tinted frescos, depicting jaguars with conch shells in their mouths.

RESTAURANTS

Of the few places to eat around the ruin site, the most distinctive is undoubtedly La Gruta (55/5531-4877 or 594/956-0127, http://lagruta.mx; daily 11am-7pm). The menu covers Mexican basics, from *sopa de tortilla* (tortilla soup) to grilled meats, as well as daily specials. The setting, however, is the real attraction: It's in an underground cave, lit by candles, just behind the Pirámide del Sol. Come for a snack and a beer to enjoy the unique ambience.

PRACTICALITIES

The Teotihuacán archaeological zone (Ecatepec Pirámides km 22 + 600, Municipio de Teotihuacán, Estado de México, 594/956-0276, www.teotihuacan.inah.gob.mx; daily 9am-5pm, US$5, children under 13, students, teachers, seniors, and people with disabilities free) has five entrances to the site, three on the west side and two on the east. They are each adjoined by a parking lot (US$4 per car), and they all have public restrooms. Unless you don't want to do a lot of walking, the best place to start your tour is at the southern entrance (no. 1), visiting the Citadel before heading north along the Calzada de los Muertos to the pyramids. Buses will drop you off here. For a shorter tour, the second entrance is just in front of the Pirámide del Sol.

Wear good walking shoes for exploring the site. A hat, sunblock, and water are musts to carry with you. If you want to experience the site in relative peace, arrive early, when the ticket-takers open the gate. The tour buses start arriving around 10am. Weekends are the busiest, especially on Sunday, when admission is free for nationals.

GETTING THERE AND AWAY

The ruins lie about 50 kilometers northeast of Mexico City. Autobuses Teotihuacán (55/5767-3573, www.autobusesteotihuacan.com.mx) buses depart the Terminal Central del Norte (Eje Central Lázaro Cárdenas 4907, www.centraldelnorte.com) every 15 minutes 6am-2pm and return every 15 minutes from the ruins to the terminal until 8pm. The trip to Teotihuacán takes about an hour. Ask for the bus to Los Pirámides, not Teotihuacán (or you may end up in the town of the same name). It costs about US$6 roundtrip.

Most travelers will prefer the flexibility of taking the bus to Teotihuacán on their own. However, for those who want to skip the hassle of going to the bus station, Turibus (800/280-8887, www.turibus.com.mx, $70) operates daily tours to Teotihuacán, departing from the Zócalo at 9am every morning. (This company also offers the double-decker sight-seeing rides around Mexico City.) The tour bus stops at the Basílica de Santa María de Guadalupe before heading to the pyramids; the cost includes guide service (in Spanish), admission to the archaeological site, and lunch.

Puebla and Vicinity

Though the city of Puebla is a popular day-trip from the capital, it is nonetheless surprising that this big and beautiful metropolis remains largely off the beaten track for most foreign visitors, despite its fine architecture, celebrated cuisine, and wonderful traditions in art and craftwork. Though close to Mexico City, it has a very different ambience than its neighbor to the north. It's mellower and more old-fashioned, with a family-oriented downtown district filled with funky small businesses, a more visibly Catholic population, and air clean enough to provide intermittent glimpses of the volcano Popocatépetl rising to the west.

Many people come to Puebla to eat, and with good reason. Though famous *poblano* dishes like *chiles en nogada* and *tinga* are prepared throughout the country, they rarely reach the sublime perfection they achieve in their native home, and street snacks here, though perhaps less ubiquitous than in the capital, are both uniquely prepared and utterly delicious. At the same time, many visitors will find the city's architecture and history to be just as rich and enthralling as its culinary traditions. Puebla has a long and important history in Mexico, founded in the early colonial era. It's one of the few cities in Mexico that weren't built directly atop an existing native community, and its beautifully preserved historic center is filled with some of the most impressive colonial churches, palaces, and ex-convents in the country, replete with ornate gold-leaf trimmings,

downtown Puebla

242

Downtown Puebla

To Av Juárez
Bravo
Paseo de
Parque

CALLE 13 SUR
CALLE 11 SUR
AV 3 PONIENTE
AV 3 SUR

CALLE 13 NORTE
CALLE 11 NORTE
CALLE 9 NORTE
CALLE 7 NORTE
CALLE 5 NORTE
CALLE 3 NORTE
CALLE 2 NORTE
CALLE 4 NORTE
CALLE 6 NORTE

AV REFORMA
AV 2 PONIENTE
AV 4 PONIENTE
AV 6 PONIENTE
AV 8 PONIENTE
AV 10 PONIENTE
AV 12 PONIENTE
AV 14 PONIENTE

AV 9 SUR
AV 7 SUR
AV 5 SUR
AV 5 PONIENTE
AV 7 PONIENTE
AV 9 PONIENTE

CALLE 9 SUR
CALLE 7 SUR
CALLE 5 SUR
CALLE 3 SUR

FONDA DE SANTA CLARA
URIARTE TALAVERA
MUSEO BELLO
LAS RANAS
EL MURAL DE LOS PLABNOS
CASA DE LA CULTURA AND BIBLIOTECA PALAFOXIANA
MUSEO AMPARO
CATEDRAL
CAFÉ DE LOS PORTALES/ HOTEL ROYALTY
Zócalo
AV 16 DE SEPTIEMBRE
AV 3 ORIENTE
AV 5 ORIENTE
AV 7 ORIENTE
AV 9 ORIENTE

IGLESIA DE SANTO DOMINGO DE GUZMÁN
MUSEO DE ARTE VIRREINAL SAN PEDRO
MUNICIPAL TOURIST OFFICE
TOURISM OFFICE
CASA DE LOS MUÑECOS
HOTEL SAN LEONARDO
HOTEL COLONIAL
CALLE 2 SUR
CALLE 4 SUR

AV 5 DE MAYO
AV 2 ORIENTE
AV 4 ORIENTE
AV 6 ORIENTE
AV 8 ORIENTE
AV 10 ORIENTE
AV 12 ORIENTE
AV 14 ORIENTE

CALLE DEL SAPO
CALLEJÓN DE LOS SAPOS
LA PASITA
MESÓN SACRISTÍA
EL CONVENTO DE LAS CAROLINAS
POST OFFICE
POZOLERÍA MATAMOROS
EL PARIAN

HOTEL IMPERIAL
RESTAURANT BAR CASA REAL
LA GRAN FAMA
MUSEO DEL ESTADO
TEATRO PRINCIPAL

BLVD HÉROES DEL 5 DE MAYO
AV PALAFOXY MENDOZA
AV 2 ORIENTE

To Iglesia de San José and Museo de Arte Religioso Santa Mónica

TEMPLO DEL TERCER ORDEN Y EX-CONVENTO DE SAN FRANCISCO

0   200 yds
0   200 m

© AVALON TRAVEL

243

ON THE ROAD TO PUEBLA: TWIN PEAKS

Twin volcanoes rising between Puebla and Mexico City, Popocatépetl and Iztaccíhuatl are the most recognizable and striking natural landmarks in the region. Often shortened to Popo and Izta, the volcanoes' Nahuatl names mean "the smoking mountain" and "the white woman," respectively, and they were the subject of great fascination and various legends in pre-Columbian Mexico. Today, these beautiful peaks are the crown jewels of a national park, Parque Nacional Izta-Popo, a surprising refuge of natural beauty located in the middle of the most densely populated region in Mexico.

A symmetrical cone and the second-highest peak in Mexico, Popo has become all the more picturesque, but perhaps a touch more troublesome, since it woke from a decades-long slumber in 1994. In the year 2000, the largest eruption in 1,200 years occurred on the mountain, and it remains one of Mexico's most active volcanoes, frequently spewing smoke and ash into the air. Craterless Izta, just 16 kilometers north, lies dormant beside it.

Both Popo and Izta have permanent glaciers at their peaks, a rarity in Mexico (only the country's highest mountain, the Pico de Orizaba, also claims them), though they are blanketed with pine and oak forests, as well as alpine prairie, at lower elevations. The wilderness surrounding the volcanoes was among the earliest designated nature preserves in the country, receiving national park status from President Lázaro Cárdenas in 1935. Occupying a unique place right between Mexico's great plateau and the subtropical southern states, the Izta-Popo National Park extends into the states of Mexico, Morelos, Puebla, and Tlaxcala. It is home to at least 48 types of mammals and more than 150 bird species, as well as a multitude of plants and mushrooms (many of which are edible and popular for soups and quesadillas in the pueblos that surround the volcanoes). Several endemic species inhabit the park, including the rather charming zacatuche, or volcano rabbit, which was named for its habitat amid the zacates, or tall grasses, of the park.

---

magnificent stonework, and Puebla's distinct signature, Talavera tile.

SIGHTS

✪ Zócalo

The Zócalo (Palafox y Mendoza and Av. 5 de Mayo) is Puebla's main public plaza, facing the cathedral and bordered on three sides by 16th-century *portales* (arcades). Once a bustling marketplace, it is today a nice park, with shady trees and park benches, surrounded by sidewalk cafés, restaurants, shops, and newspaper stands. It's always bustling with activity and a great place for sipping a coffee or simply enjoying quality people-watching.

Catedral de la Inmaculada Concepción

On the south side of the Zócalo, Puebla's Catedral de la Inmaculada Concepción (Av. 16 de Septiembre, 222/232-2316, daily 8am-7:30pm, free) is one of the most beautiful churches in Mexico, first begun in 1575 by Francisco Becerra and completed almost a century later, in 1664. The tile-domed facade, adjoined by the two highest church towers in the country, is a mix of medieval, Renaissance, and baroque styles, and inside, you'll even notice a few neo-classical touches in Manuel Tolsá's marble and onyx altar.

Casa de la Cultura and Biblioteca Palafoxiana

Formerly the archbishop's palace, the Casa de la Cultura (Av. 5 Ote. 5, 222/246-3186, Mon.-Fri. 9am-8pm, Sat.-Sun. 10am-5pm, free) was originally built in 1597. Today, the building is a cultural center with exhibition spaces, a cinema, and a café, as well as the home of the Biblioteca Palafoxiana (Tues.-Sun. 10am-5pm), one of the oldest libraries in the Americas. In 1646, Bishop Juan Palafox y Mendoza donated the first 5,000 volumes, including works of philosophy, theology, and history, some printed as early as the 15th century.

Iglesia de Santo Domingo de Guzmán

Three blocks north of the plaza on Cinco de Mayo lies what remains of the fine baroque Dominican monastery Iglesia de Santo Domingo de Guzmán (5 de Mayo and Av. 6 Ote., 222/268-7232, daily 8am-2pm and 4:30pm-8pm, free), constructed in the mid-16th century and consecrated in 1690. Inside the spacious, highly ornamented church, the exceptional Capilla del Rosario stands out, with walls that are covered with gilded floor-to-ceiling carvings, tiles, and cherubs.

Iglesia de San Cristóbal

Constructed in the 17th century, the Iglesia de San Cristóbal (4 Norte at Av. 6 Oriente, 222/235-9645, daily 7am-2pm and 4pm-8pm, free) is another wonderful example of baroque architecture in Puebla, with a beautifully carved sandstone facade and an interior filled with elaborate relief figures (though not, as in many churches, gilded).

✪ Museo Amparo

The Museo Amparo (Calle 2 Sur 708, 222/229-3850, www.museoamparo. com, Wed.-Mon. 10am-6pm, Sat. 10am-9pm, US$3) is an excellent anthropology and art museum with a gorgeous rooftop café located in two adjoining colonial-era buildings three blocks from the Zócalo. The museum's permanent collection contains more than 2,000 pieces of pre-Columbian and colonial art, including outstanding artifacts from the Maya, Olmec, Zapotec, and Mixtec cultures, as well as paintings, pottery, crafts, and

furniture created in Puebla during the viceroyalty. Though best known for its permanent collection, the museum also hosts nice temporary exhibits, often exploring themes in modern and contemporary art.

Museo de Arte Religioso Santa Mónica

Museo de Arte Religioso Santa Mónica (Av. 18 Pte. 103 at 5 de Mayo, 222/232-0178, Tues.-Sun. 10am-5pm, US$3) was founded as a convent in 1610. The building was converted to a religious-art museum and taken over by INAH in 1940, exhibiting work by many well-known colonial-era artists divided over two stories of exhibition spaces. Just as interesting, the museum offers a look at the living quarters and daily life of the nuns who once lived here.

Museo José Luis Bello y Zetina

José Luis Bello, a wealthy poblano businessman, spent his riches on elegant furnishings and art from Mexico, Europe, and Asia, including porcelain, glass, Talavera ceramics, wrought iron, religious vestments, and clothing. Today, the Museo José Luis Bello y Zetina (Av. 3 Pte. 302, 222/232-4720, www.museobello.org, Tues.-Sun. 10am-4pm, free) displays that massive collection in a historic building that was once part of Puebla's large Dominican convent.

Museo Universitario Casa de los Muñecos

An unusual colonial-era building, the Casa de los Muñecos (2 Norte 2, 222/229-5500, http://museobuap.mx, Mon.-Fri. 10am-5pm, Sat.-Sun. 10am-6pm, free) is famous for its brick facade, which, according to legend, is adorned with satirical portraits of the town's fathers, who wouldn't let the owner construct a third floor (though he eventually gained permission to do so). Today, it houses a small museum with a permanent collection of colonial-era oil paintings, vintage scientific tools and musical instruments, prints, and other historic artifacts owned by the Universidad Autónoma de Puebla.

Museo del Estado Casa de Alfeñique

The intricate baroque facade of Museo del Estado Casa de Alfeñique (Av. 4 Ote. 416, 222/232-0458, Tues.-Sun. 10am-3pm, US$2) is a classic example of *alfeñique* architectural style, named for a white sugar candy made in Puebla. Built in 1790, it now houses the state museum, with old manuscripts related to Puebla history, ethnography on different indigenous groups in the state, and colonial clothing. It's worth the entrance fee to see the beautiful interiors.

Plaza Cívica and Fuerte Loreto

To the north of the *centro histórico*, Puebla's civic center is adjoined by the historic military Fuerte Loreto and the Museo de la No Intervención (Calz. de los Fuertes s/n, Centro Cívico 5 de Mayo, Zona Histórica de los Fuertes, 222/234-8513, Tues.-Sun. 10am-4:30pm; US$3, free Sun.), located on the site of the famous Battle of Puebla, in which local troops defeated French invaders, celebrated annually on May 5—or, as it is better known, Cinco de Mayo. The fort is a lovely place to spend an afternoon, with a coffee shop on-site, plenty of public spaces, and great views of the city below.

Parque Conmemorativo del 150 Aniversario de la Batalla de Puebla

Though it is a bit outside the Centro, those interested in contemporary design will want to walk a few extra blocks to see the Parque Conmemorativo del 150 Aniversario de la Batalla de Puebla (Centro Cívico 5 de Mayo, Av. Ejército de Oriente, free), an innovative new park and monument designed by famed Mexico City architect Enrique Norten in 2012, as part of a larger renovation of Puebla's Plaza Cívica and the historic Fort Loreto and Fort Guadalupe. The unusual public space is composed of undulating wood decks with lovely views of the surrounding city.

RESTAURANTS

Start your food tour at one of Puebla's oldest markets, the Mercado Melchor Ocampo El Carmen (21 Oriente 209, daily 7am-7pm). This is the place to try *cemitas,* Puebla's version of the *torta,* or sandwich, filled with meat and often garnished with the fragrant herb *pápalo.* The market is packed during the lunch hour.

Another quick bite, *tacos árabes* are a fusion of Mexican and Middle Eastern traditions, and they are another specialty in Puebla: crispy spit-roasted pork served in a pita, sometimes with *jocoque,* an acidic strained-yogurt spread. One of the tastiest and most popular places to try *tacos árabes* is at the always-packed Las Ranas (2 Poniente 105, 222/232-1946, Mon.-Sat. noon-8:30pm, Sun. 2pm-8:30pm). Accompany them with an order of delicious *frijoles charros* (stewed beans).

PUEBLA: A CULINARY CAPITAL

Puebla has a remarkable culinary tradition, noted for its complex flavors and for its use of centuries-old heirloom recipes. Uniting pre-Columbian and Spanish ingredients and preparations with a touch of French and Middle Eastern influence, food in Puebla is delicious, and very much a part of the cultural experience of visiting the city.

Moles—thick, heavily spiced sauces (often served over poultry)—are prepared throughout the country, with many famous versions produced in the state of Oaxaca. According to legend, however, mole was first created by the nuns of the Convento de Santa Rosa in Puebla, during the 16th century.

Puebla's signature version of the dish, **mole poblano,** usually combines dozens of ingredients, including chocolate, dried chile peppers, onion, garlic, peanuts, raisins, cinnamon, coriander, peppercorns, and sesame seeds. In Puebla, you'll find mole piled onto sandwiches, slathered over turkey, or stuffed into tamales.

Variations on mole are served in restaurants throughout the city. **Pipián,** sometimes called *mole verde,* is a flavorful sauce made with green pumpkin seeds and spices, ground till smooth; it is also considered a specialty in Puebla, though you'll see it prepared in the traditional cuisine of other regions, like Yucatán. *Pipián rojo* is a variation, made with tomatoes and dried chiles.

Popular throughout Mexico, **chiles en nogada** are a highly distinctive *poblano* creation. Traditionally prepared during the fall harvest season and served as a part of the Independence Day holidays in September, a *chile en nogada* is a large green poblano pepper stuffed with beef or pork, almonds, fruit, and spices, which is then bathed in a creamy walnut sauce and showered with pomegranate seeds. Another rich regional dish, **tinga poblana** is slow-cooked shredded pork in a stew of chipotle chiles and vegetables. It is usually served with tortillas and rolled into tacos.

Some wonderful quick bites and street foods are also typical to Puebla. A popular appetizer or snack, **chalupas** are small, handmade corn tortillas that are deep fried in *manteca* (lard) or hot oil, then doused in spicy salsa and topped with shredded pork and onions. Puebla's version of the *torta* is the **cemita,** a sandwich made on a sesame-studded roll also called a *cemita. Cemitas* are piled with meat, string cheese, lettuce, tomato, and onion, then garnished with *pápalo,* a fragrant Mexican herb. Another *poblano* sandwich, the **pelona** is served on a soft, lightly fried bun, layered with beans, meat, and cheese. **Tacos árabes** are a Middle Eastern-inspired taco made with spit-roasted meat served in a warm pita and topped with lime and chipotle salsa.

Puebla is also famous throughout the country for its traditional *dulces* (sweets). On the highways outside town, vendors sell bags of the city's famous candy to motorists idling at the tollbooths. Among the most typical sweets in Puebla are starchy treats made with **camote** (sweet potato). Sweet potatoes are cooked, sweetened, and flavored, theny rolled into soft, cigar-shaped tubes. Also typical to Puebla are **macarrones,** a type of *dulce de leche* (milk candy), and **mueganos,** a fudgelike cake made with flour, egg, butter, and unrefined sugar. Sweets made with pumpkin seeds are a regional specialty; try **tortitas de Santa Clara,** a small cookie topped with pumpkin-seed cream, and **jamoncillo,** a fudgelike treat garnished with nuts. Many of these sweets (like much of Puebla's famous food) were originally created by nuns, who sold candies and eggnog (*rompope*) to support their convents, as they continue to do today.

If you'd like to do more than taste, there are cooking classes at the **Mesón Sacristia** boutique hotel and restaurant (6 Sur 304, 222/232-4513, http://mesones-sacristia.com).

Simple yet remarkably good, the **Pozolería Matamoros** (Palafox y Mendoza 6, 222/237-6365, Thurs.-Tues. 2pm-10pm) is just a few blocks from the main square. The namesake dish, a rich hominy soup called pozole, is excellent, but the menu also includes a number of *poblano* specialties, like *chalupas* (hand-rolled corn cakes

topped with red or green salsa, shredded chicken, and diced onions). Head to the more spacious upstairs dining room, where you can order a beer and enjoy a leisurely lunch.

One of the nicest places in town for a traditional meal is the lobby restaurant in the **Hotel Colonial** (Calle 4 Sur 105, 222/246-4612, daily 7am-10pm), which offers a daily three-course *comida* (lunch special) for a reasonable price. The menu changes daily but almost always includes the option of ordering the restaurant's excellent *mole poblano* with chicken breast or thigh. The pretty dining room, illuminated by skylight, is popular with local families and can get quite crowded on the weekends.

The legendary Fonda de Santa Clara (Av. 3 Pte. 307, 222/242-2659, and Av. 3 Pte. 920, 222/246-1952, www.fondadesantaclara.com, daily 8am-10pm) is a classic *poblano* restaurant serving regional food, like *mixiotes, tingas,* and mole in a delightfully old-fashioned dining room decorated with Puebla's famous Talavera tile. Many people come here to try the *chiles en nogada*, one of Puebla's signature dishes.

A sophisticated, upscale spot preparing inspired *poblano* cuisine, El Mural de los Poblanos (16 de Septiembre 506, 777/242-0503, www.elmuraldelospoblanos.com, Sun.-Thurs. 8am-noon and 1pm-11pm, Fri.-Sat. 8am-noon and 1pm-11:30pm) serves regional dishes made with local ingredients. Everything on the menu, from the creative soups to the range of heirloom moles, is served with unique style and pretty, inventive presentations. Appropriately, they also have a great list of small-batch mezcal and Mexican artisanal beer.

SHOPS

The city and surrounding state of Puebla is well known for its fine artisan products and craftwork, which include sculpted onyx, *papel amate* (handmade bark paper), *papel picado* (decorative cut-paper flags), handmade furniture, wool rugs, silverwork, and, most famously, Talavera pottery,

which is principally elaborated in the city of Puebla and nearby Cholula.

To browse a selection of handicrafts from Puebla and beyond, stroll the outdoor market El Parian (Calle 8 Nte. between Av. 2 and Av. 6 Ote.), where rows of craft shops are housed in a former 18th-century clothing warehouse. Just a few blocks from the Zócalo, the market's specialty is Talavera, and there are numerous stalls selling colorful painted wares of varying quality and prices, from huge urns to little keepsakes and tiles.

Perhaps the most famous—and certainly the most historic—Talavera shop in Puebla is Uriarte (Av. 4 Pte. 911, 222/232-1598, http://uriartetalavera.com.mx, daily 10am-7pm), originally founded in 1824. Uriarte's delicately painted pottery, including dishes, trays, tea sets, urns, tiles, and more, is all handmade and very high quality; if you buy more than you can pack in your suitcase, they can help arrange shipping.

You'll have to travel a bit outside of the central area to visit the factory store of Talavera de la Reyna (Lateral Sur Recta a Cholula 3510, 222/225-4058, http://talaveradelareyna.com.mx, Mon.-Fri. 9am-7pm, Sat. 9am-3pm, Sun. 11am-3pm), another very high quality artisan producer of Talavera. At their Cholula-based factory, these artisan producers sculpt, glaze, and paint everything by hand, creating gorgeous traditional as well as more modern designs.

Puebla is famous throughout the country for its traditional handmade candies. In the Centro, old-fashioned sweet shops, or *dulcerías,* line Calle 6 Oriente between 5 de Mayo and 4 Norte. One of the most historic spots is Dulcería La Gran Fama (6 Ote. 208, 222/242-3316, www.lagranfama.

com, Mon.-Sat. 9am-2:30pm and 5pm-8pm, Sun. 10am-6pm), which carries traditional sweets from the region, including *camotes* (a flavored sweet-potato candy), *tortitas de Santa Clara* (a round pumpkin-seed-cream-topped cookie), *dulce de leche* (milk candy), and much more. Many of these unique treats have been made in Puebla since the colonial era.

Puebla is also well known as a place for hunting antiques, with some very interesting vintage pieces (and occasionally some priceless antiques) showing up in the weekend flea market along the street Callejón de los Sapos (Av. 7 Ote. and Calle 4 Sur, Sat.-Sun. 10am-5pm). Here you'll find everything from old maps and silverwork to jewelry and vintage magazines, as well as the occasional religious artifact or saint (which will come with a hefty price tag). The numerous permanent shops along the alleyway offer some very nice collections of Mexican antiques.

Near Los Sapos, the tiny, folkloric shop La Pasita (Calle 5 Ote. 602, Fri.-Wed. 1pm-6pm) sells bottles and serves shots of housemade liqueurs in flavors like almond, coconut, and fancifully named *sangre de la bruja,* or witch's blood (blackberry and hibiscus). The drink of the house is the sweet, dark raisin liqueur *pasita,* served in a shot glass with a piece of cheese on a toothpick floating inside.

HOTELS

There are plenty of accommodations in Puebla's *centro histórico,* though many in the budget category are somewhat sad and dank. A well-priced option in the center of town, the Hotel Imperial (Av. 3 Pte. 721, 222/242-4860, www.hotelimperialpuebla.mx, US$55-65) has spacious rooms with TVs, telephones, and private baths. Amenities include a restaurant, pool table, parking lot, hot water all day, and bicycles for free use.

A block from the plaza and across from a picturesque little square, the surprisingly well-priced Hotel Colonial (Calle 4 Sur 105, 222/246-4612 or 800/013-0000, www.colonial. com.mx, US$70-80) is very convenient for exploring downtown and has, as the name suggests, a really lovely historic colonial ambience. The rooms are fairly large and comfortable, and some have balconies, wood floors, and tile baths. It's a popular spot with European travelers.

The Hotel San Leonardo (Av. 2 Ote. 211, 222/223-6600, www.hotel-sanleonardo.com.mx, US$70-175) has comfortable, clean, remodeled rooms, some with stunning views of the volcanoes outside Puebla (though note that rooms with views cost quite a bit more than interior accommodations). The real highlight of this hotel is the elegant old French-colonial building in which it's housed, decorated with antiques and Oriental rugs, and only a few steps from the Zócalo.

A charming option on a quiet street in the Centro, the Mesón Sacristía de la Compañía (Calle 6 Sur 304, 222/246-6084, www.mesones-sacristia.com, US$120) has just eight rooms, each carefully decorated with antiques and collectibles. An antiques store, the excellent Restaurante Sacristía, and Bar El Confesionario are all within the 18th-century building that houses the hotel.

Puebla's chicest accommodations are at La Purificadora (Callejón de la 10 Nte. 802, Paseo San Francisco, Barrio Alto, 222/309-1920, www.

lapurificadora.com, US$100-130), a hotel from the same group that operates Hotel Hábita, Downtown Hotel, and Condesa DF in Mexico City. Blending 19th-century architecture with modern design, the guest rooms have wood floors, fluffy white bed linens, and lots of natural light.

INFORMATION AND SERVICES

The Puebla state tourism office (5 Oriente 3, 222/122-1100 ext. 6418, www.puebla.travel, daily 10am-6pm) in the Zócalo can offer maps and information on upcoming festivals, art exhibits, and other municipal goings-on in Puebla city and state.

GETTING THERE AND AWAY

First- and second-class buses depart Mexico City's Terminal TAPO (Calz. Ignacio Zaragoza 200) almost constantly, all day and night, with lines ADO, Cristóbal Colón, and Estrella Roja offering first-class service to CAPU, a large bus terminal north of the city center in Puebla (Calle 11 Nte. and Blvd. Atlixco). The trip takes about 90 minutes and runs around US$5, depending on bus line and service class. Estrella Roja (www.estrellaroja.com.mx, 222/273-8300) runs the express bus direct from the Mexico City airport to CAPU hourly.

NEAR PUEBLA
ZONA ARQUEOLÓGICA DE CHOLULA

What appears to be a large church-topped hill in the center of Cholula is actually the largest pyramid in the continent by volume, with a base measuring 450 meters on each side. Construction on this massive structure began in the 3rd century BC and continued for almost a thousand years. The pyramid was first thoroughly explored in 1931, revealing altars with offerings, floors, walls, and buried human remains. You can visit the pyramid and part of the excavation site at the Zona Arqueológica de Cholula (Av. 8 Nte. 2, San Andrés Cholula, 222/247-9081, daily 9am-6pm, US$3). To get to the beautifully gilded Capilla de la Virgen de los Remedios (daily 8am-4pm), first built in 1594 and rebuilt after an earthquake in the mid-19th century, follow the steep path to the top of the hill. On clear days, views of Popocatépetl are spectacular.

Estrella Roja operates direct buses (US$9-11) between Mexico City's TAPO and the Cholula bus terminal four times a day, though it's generally most convenient to get to Cholula via Puebla. Minibuses leave central Puebla from Avenida 2 Poniente at Calle 3 Sur. The trip costs about US$2. A taxi from the *centro* costs around US$10 and takes about 15 minutes.

Taxco

The silver city of Taxco was the site of one of the most important mines during the colonial era, a boon to Spanish settlers who dreamed of finding mineral wealth amid Mexico's craggy peaks. Unlike the great silver cities to the north of the capital, Taxco remained sparsely populated during the viceroyalty, though evidence of the great wealth produced by the silver mines is amply displayed in the city's breathtaking central church, Santa Prisca, erected and paid for by local silver magnate José de la Borda.

Though no longer a mining town, Taxco is still closely associated with silver. Many of Mexico's finest silverwork is produced in the area, including at the former workshop of the great American jewelry designer William Spratling, just outside the city. Many people visit Taxco to browse the local jewelry shops, but many more simply come to enjoy the unique atmosphere. A place of blue skies and postcard-worthy vistas, Taxco was built along the peaks and valleys of several adjoining hillsides, where baroque churches and whitewashed houses are organized along a maze of cobblestone streets. Built long before automobiles, central Taxco retains the atmosphere of another era— and, in fact, you need to watch your step when exploring this city on foot, as there's barely room for both cars and pedestrians on the steep, windy streets.

Taxco

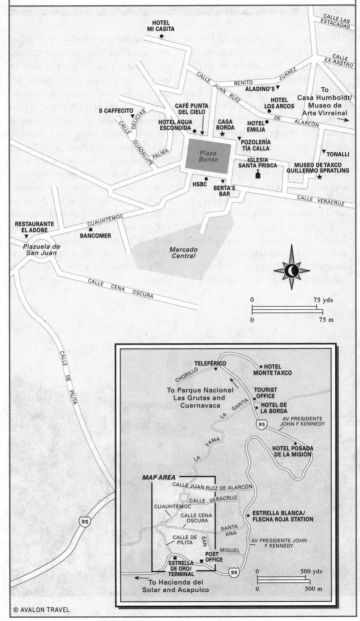

Taxco

HOTEL MI CASITA

CALLE LAS ESTACADAS

CALLE EX-RASTRO

CALLE JUAN RUIZ

BENITO JUAREZ

ALADINO'S

HOTEL LOS ARCOS

To Casa Humboldt/ Museo de Arte Virreinal

DE ALARCÓN

S CAFFECITO

CAFÉ PUNTA DEL CIELO

HOTEL AGUA ESCONDIDA

CASA BORDA

HOTEL EMILIA

POZOLERÍA TÍA CALLA

TONALLI

CALLE DELICIAS

CALLE GUADALUPE PALMA

Plaza Borda

IGLESIA SANTA PRISCA

MUSEO DE TAXCO GUILLERMO SPRATLING

HSBC

BERTA'S BAR

CALLE VERACRUZ

RESTAURANTE EL ADOBE

CUAUHTÉMOC

BANCOMER

Plazuela de San Juan

Mercado Central

CALLE CENA OSCURA

0   75 yds
0   75 m

CALLE DE PILITA

TELEFÉRICO

HOTEL MONTE TAXCO

CHORRILLO

To Parque Nacional Las Grutas and Cuernavaca

LA GARITA

TOURIST OFFICE

HOTEL DE LA BORDA

95

AV PRESIDENTE JOHN F KENNEDY

LA FAMA

HOTEL POSADA DE LA MISIÓN

MAP AREA

CALLE JUAN RUIZ DE ALARCÓN

CALLE VERACRUZ

CUAUHTÉMOC

CALLE CENA OSCURA

SANTA ANA

ESTRELLA BLANCA/ FLECHA ROJA STATION

95

CALLE DE PILITA

SAN MIGUEL

AV PRESIDENTE JOHN F KENNEDY

POST OFFICE

95

ESTRELLA DE ORO/ TERMINAL

To Hacienda del Solar and Acapulco

0   500 yds
0   500 m

© AVALON TRAVEL

252

SIGHTS

⊕ Iglesia Santa Prisca

One of the most stunning and well-preserved baroque churches in Mexico, the Iglesia Santa Prisca (Jardín Borda, 762/622-0183, daily Tues.-Sat. 10am-1pm and 5pm-8pm, Sun. 10am-2pm, free) is not only a fine example of churrigueresque architecture and art, but testimony to the massive wealth of the colonial silver trade. Financed by colonial-era mining magnate José de la Borda, this gorgeous church took just seven years to complete (lightning fast, considering both the era and the elaborateness of the design), which accounts for the its harmonious, unified style. Inside, the 12 magnificent altars of hand-carved wood are covered with 22-carat gold leaf and expressive saints.

Mercado Central

Beside the Iglesia Santa Prisca, Taxco's wonderful, rambling Mercado Central (Plaza Borda, daily 7am-8pm) is chockablock with stalls hawking all manner of food, herbal remedies, and clothes. It's easy—but entirely pleasant—to get lost amid its labyrinthine passageways.

Museo de Arte Virreinal

Originally built in the late 18th century as a private home, the impressive Museo de Arte Virreinal (Calle Juan Ruiz de Alarcón 6, 1.5 blocks from the plaza, 762/622-5501, Tues.-Sat. 10am-6pm, US$1.50) served as a guesthouse in later years and reputedly was where Baron Alexander Von Humboldt stayed when he came through Taxco in the 19th century (the building is also known as the Casa Humboldt). Now it's an interesting religious art museum, with exhibits dedicated to the history of Taxco and the central Santa Prisca church.

Museo Guillermo Spratling

American William Spratling was a writer, intellectual, and innovative designer who lived in Taxco from the 1930s till his death in 1967. He became an influential producer of beautiful silver jewelry and tableware that combined modern aesthetics and pre-Columbian designs. The Museo Guillermo Spratling (Delgado 1, 762/622-1660, Tues.-Sat. 9am-6pm, Sun. 9am-3pm, US$3), just behind Santa Prisca on Plazuela Juan Ruiz de Alarcón, houses Spratling's own small collection of pre-Hispanic art from Guerrero and central Mexico.

Plaza Borda

A shady spot under ancient laurel trees, Plaza Borda (between Cuauhtémoc and Tolsá) is the quiet, old-fashioned central plaza in the heart of Taxco, bordered by gift shops and restaurants. You may not have your best meal here, but you can certainly enjoy the lovely views. On the east side of the plaza, the towering stone mansion Casa Borda was built for the Borda family in the mid-18th century and now holds a small cultural center.

The *Teleférico* (Cable Car)

From Avenida de Los Plateros and Chorrillo in the northern Los Arcos neighborhood, a Swiss-built cable car (Sun.-Thurs. 8am-7pm, Fri.-Sat. 8am-10pm, US$8) takes passengers up 173 vertical meters to the top of a bluff overlooking the city. Views are, of course, spectacular. At the top you'll find the old-school Hotel Monte Taxco, where you can enjoy the view longer with a drink in one of the in-house bars.

Rancho Spratling

Visiting Rancho Spratling (Carr. Taxco-Iguala, Taxco El Viejo), the ranch and former workshop of William Spratling, is well worth the half-hour trip south of town. You can see the workshop where fine silver is still crafted by artisans using Spratling's famous designs, a museum depicting Spratling's life, and a showroom of work. Though the ranch is open to visitors, it is necessary to make an appointment beforehand; you can get information at S Caffecito (Delicias 23, Taxco, 762/627-6177, Tues.-Sat. 9am-6pm), a restaurant managed by the same family that runs the Spratling estate.

RESTAURANTS

Though it's not a culinary capital, there are some nice places to eat in Taxco, and, thanks to the city's hilly geography, even very casual eateries often have spectacular views of the city. One such low-key spot for a snack is Tonalli (Humboldt 3, 762/622-4720, Tues.-Sun. 8:30am-7pm), just next door to the Museo Guillermo Spratling, where you can get an inexpensive and well-prepared plate of guacamole, quesadillas, tacos, or tostadas while enjoying panoramic views of surrounding Taxco and the back of Santa Prisca from the casual roof deck.

The rich hominy soup pozole is a specialty of the state of Guerrero, and the Pozolería Tía Calla (Plaza Borda 1, 762/622-5602, Wed.-Mon. 1:30pm-10pm) is one of the best eateries in town, in business since the 1950s. In addition to the huge, inexpensive bowls of green, red, or white

pozole, you can choose from authentic Mexican fare, like crispy *taquitos* and guacamole, served at friendly prices. Cash only.

The beautiful Caffecito (Delicias 23, 762/627-6177, Tues.-Sat. 9am-6pm) is one of the nicest options in town. The restaurant is set in William Spratling's former home and garden (where a friendly basset hound will greet you at the door). The kitchen serves both Mexican and Italian food (and occasional fusions of the two cuisines), like lasagna, salads, and enchiladas, made with fresh, local ingredients. Breakfasts are also fantastic, served with freshly baked bread and housemade jam.

Restaurant El Adobe (Plazuela de San Juan 13, 762/622-1416, Mon.-Thurs. 8am-11pm, Fri.-Sat. 8am-midnight, Sun. 8am-10:30pm) serves classic Mexican dishes, meats, and seafood in a cozy atmosphere, with tile floors, hanging lamps, and wood furniture, as well as some balcony tables with views.

HOTELS

A popular weekend trip from Mexico City, tiny Taxco is brimming with hotels. Though there aren't many shoestring crash pads here, you'll find plenty of good value accommodations, including some fun old-school resorts with pools and gardens. If visiting on the weekend, it's a good idea to make reservations, as rooms can sometimes be scarce.

One of the most popular spots in Taxco, the Hotel Agua Escondida (Plaza Borda 4, 762/622-1166 or 800/504-0311, www.aguaescondida. com, US$65-100) has a pleasingly historic ambience to go with its prime location in the historic center of Taxco. The guest rooms are done up with tile floors and old wood headboards. Amenities include a rooftop bar (open to the public) with lovely views of Santa Prisca and a pool for hotel guests. Expect a crowd on weekends.

Tucked away along a little pedestrian alley just a block from the main square, **Hotel Mi Casita** (Altos de Redondo 1, 762/627-17777, www.hotelmicasita.com, US$55-75) is a comfortable, friendly, and well-priced hotel with lovely, spacious guest rooms with tile floors, TVs, and French doors opening onto open-air arcades, some with views of Santa Prisca.

Hotel de la Borda (Cerro del Pedregal 2, opposite the junction of Av. Kennedy and Calle La Garita, 762/622-0025, www.hotelborda.com, US$70-150) is where JFK and Jackie stayed when they visited Taxco. You can request the First Couple's room, though many boast equally panoramic views of the city below. With its beautiful, old-fashioned atmosphere, large clean rooms, and sparkling pool with a view of Taxco, it's a unique spot.

GETTING THERE AND AWAY

Estrella de Oro (800/900-0105, www.estrelladeoro.com.mx) and **Costa Line** (800/003-7635, www.costaline.com.mx) offer first-class and luxury service from Mexico City's Central Terminal del Sur Taxqueña (Av. Taxqueña 1320). It takes about three hours by bus to get to Taxco from the capital, and the trip costs roughly US$15-20 each way.

Cuernavaca

An easy drive an hour south of Mexico City, Cuernavaca shares many cultural similarities with the capital, and it has long been a favored retreat for harried big-city residents. With its verdant vegetation and temperate climate, Cuernavaca has attracted many of Mexico's most powerful politicians and businesspeople, who built luxury villas here for their weekend getaways. In fact, Cortés was the first of many Mexico City residents to keep a vacation home in Cuernavaca; his was built out of the ruins of the city pyramid. Since the 1980s, many Mexico City residents have made the move permanently, giving this medium-sized metropolis a pleasant, cosmopolitan atmosphere. Unfortunately, *chilangos* have brought some of their problems with them: crime, traffic, and air pollution are now common in Cuernavaca.

SIGHTS

✪ Catedral de la Asunción

Cuernavaca's keynote sight is the austere **Catedral de la Asunción** (Hidalgo at Juan Ruiz de Alarcón, 777/312-1290, daily 8am-8pm, free). Surviving since the very early colonies, it was part of a Franciscan monastery originally founded in 1526. Inside, note the wonderful early-colonial murals in the main nave depicting the martyrdom of Mexican saint San Felipe de Jesús in Nagasaki, Japan, in 1597. The murals were rediscovered during the cathedral's 1957 renovation, though they likely date from the 17th century. Within the same complex, the **Templo del Tercer Orden** has a highly ornate, 18th-century gilded altarpiece, which has been remarkably well preserved.

Jardín Borda

The owner of Taxco's great silver mines, José de la Borda, built a luxurious hacienda in Cuernavaca in the 18th century, which later his son Manuel converted into an extensive garden filled with footpaths, fish ponds, and fountains, today known as Jardín Borda (Av. Morelos 271, 777/318-1050, www.jardinborda.com, Tues.-Sun. 10am-5:30pm, US$3 adults, free Sun.). Showing off Cuernavaca's natural fecundity, the gardens are lush and green, providing a much-needed respite from the city's traffic-clogged streets.

Plaza de Armas and Jardín Juárez

Cuernavaca's two central plazas (bordered by Blvd. Benito Juárez, Miguel Hidalgo, Ignacio Rayon, and Galeana) are filled with trees and often bustling with locals buying newspapers, getting their shoes shined, relaxing on benches, or chatting. Plaza de Armas is the larger of the two, adjoined by the Jardín Juárez, with its late-19th-century kiosk supposedly designed by French architect Alexandre Gustave Eiffel. The majority of buildings surrounding these two plazas are modern, so they lack a bit of the colonial charm of many central squares in the region.

Museo Casa Robert Brady

The Museo Casa Robert Brady (Netzahualcóyotl 4, 777/318-8554, Tues.-Sun. 10am-6pm, US$3) is a charming little museum containing the collection of art, antiques, and furniture of American Robert Brady at his former home in Cuernavaca. The house, known as Casa de la Torre, is still largely decorated as it was when

chapel in Cuernavaca

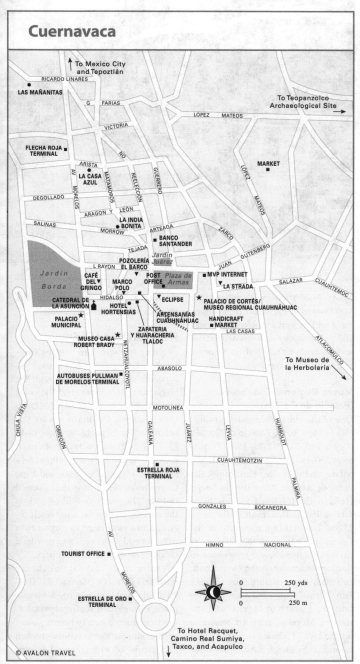

Cuernavaca

To Mexico City and Tepoztlán

RICARDO LINARES
LAS MAÑANITAS

G FARIAS

To Teopanzolco Archaeological Site

LÓPEZ MATEOS

VICTORIA

FLECHA ROJA TERMINAL

ARISTA

NO

MARKET

LA CASA AZUL

MATAMOROS

GUERRERO

REELECCIÓN

MORELOS

AV

DEGOLLADO

ARAGON Y LEÓN

LÓPEZ MATEOS

SALINAS

LA INDIA BONITA

MORROW

ARTEAGA

ZARCO

TEJADA

BANCO SANTANDER

JUAN GUTENBERG

POZOLERÍA EL BARCO

L RAYON

Jardín Juárez

Jardín Borda

CAFÉ DEL GRINGO

MARCO POLO

POST OFFICE

Plaza de Armas

MVP INTERNET

SALAZAR

CUAUHTEMOC

LA STRADA

CATEDRAL DE LA ASUNCIÓN

HIDALGO

ECLIPSE

PALACIO DE CORTÉS/ MUSEO REGIONAL CUAUHNÁHUAC

HOTEL HORTENSIAS

ARTESANÍAS CUAUHNÁHUAC

HANDICRAFT MARKET

PALACIO MUNICIPAL

ZAPATERÍA Y HUARACHERÍA TLALOC

LAS CASAS

MUSEO CASA ROBERT BRADY

NETZAHUALCOYOTL

ATLACOMULCO

ABASOLO

To Museo de la Herbolaria

AUTOBUSES PULLMAN DE MORELOS TERMINAL

CHULA VISTA

MOTOLINEA

OBREGÓN

GALEANA

JUÁREZ

LEYVA

HUMBOLDT

CUAUHTEMOTZIN

ESTRELLA ROJA TERMINAL

PALMIRA

GONZALES

BOCANEGRA

HIMNO

NACIONAL

TOURIST OFFICE

AV MORELOS

ESTRELLA DE ORO TERMINAL

0   250 yds
0   250 m

To Hotel Racquet, Camino Real Sumiya, Taxco, and Acapulco

© AVALON TRAVEL

Jardín Juárez

Brady lived there, with more than 1,000 works of native art from across the world, as well as colonial antiques and paintings by well-known artists such as Frida Kahlo, Rufino Tamayo, and Miguel Covarrubias.

Museo Regional Cuauhnáhuac (Palacio de Cortés)

One of the oldest colonial-era buildings in Mexico, the Palacio de Cortés (Leyva 100, 777/312-8171 or 777/312-6996, Tues.-Sun. 9am-7pm, US$4 palace and museum) runs along the Plaza de Armas. After the conquest, Hernán Cortés lived in this huge fortresslike palace, built in the early 1520s. The building remained in the Cortés family through 1629. Today, the palace contains the attractive Museo Regional Cuauhnáhuac (www.inah. gob.mx/paseos/cuauhnahuac, Tues.-Sun. 10am-5pm), a museum that details the history of Mexico and the state of Morelos, with an emphasis on the local Tlahuica people, as well as murals by Diego Rivera that trace

the history of Cuernavaca from the Spanish invasion to the present.

RESTAURANTS

Catering to locals and visiting *capitaleños,* Cuernavaca has a nice assortment of places to eat, though the restaurants here don't rival the color and diversity of the food in Mexico City. Close to the main square, La India Bonita (Dwight Morrow 15-B, 777/312-5021, www.laindiabonita. com.mx, Sun.-Thurs. 8am-10pm, Fri.-Sat. 9am-11pm) is a classic old-time Cuernavaca restaurant that opened in 1933. The pretty, tree-filled patio is the perfect setting for a top-shelf tequila and a plate of *sopes* (round corn cakes topped with beans and shredded chicken) or stuffed chile peppers.

For a more casual meal, try Pozolería El Barco (Rayón 3, 777/314-1020, daily 11am-10pm), a simple place with garden seating specializing in pozole, a hearty hominy soup served with pork or shredded chicken and garnished with chopped onions, oregano, radishes, and chiles. Pozole is a specialty of the state of Guerrero, served in three different styles here (red, green, or white), each seasoned differently. They also serve tacos, *chalupas* (thick corn cakes topped with meat and salsa), and pig's-feet tostadas, among other dishes.

A lovely setting for a fancy meal, the hotel Las Mañanitas (Ricardo Linares 107, 777/314-1466, www.lasmananitas. com.mx, daily noon-5pm and 7pm-11pm) serves upscale Mexican food and cocktails on a very relaxing terrace overlooking the hotel gardens, though you can also have drinks and snacks in the bar area, if you don't want to commit to a full meal. It always has a fresh seafood meal of the day, as well as other specials.

Marco Polo (Hidalgo 30, 777/312-3484 or 777/318-4032, www.marco-polo.com.mx, daily 1pm-10pm) is a popular Italian restaurant. The upstairs dining room is always packed with customers, often foreigners, enjoying the relaxed ambience and decent food. It serves a good cappuccino to top off your meal.

HOTELS

As a longtime holiday city, Cuernavaca has a wide range of hotel options, from modest-but-decent rooms near the plaza to luxury spreads on the outskirts of town. For those traveling on a budget, the Hotel Hortensias (Hidalgo 13, 777/318-5265, www.hotelhortensias.com, US$30) is a small, family-run hotel set around a pretty, plant-filled interior garden. The decor in both the guest rooms and common areas is amusingly dated, but it's a good deal right in the center of town.

A newer boutique hotel near the city center, La Casa Azul (C. Gral Mariano Arista 17, 777/314-2141, www.hotelcasaazul.com.mx, US$100-200) is a good pick if you plan to do some sightseeing but also want to paddle around in a pool and relax with a book in one of Cuernavaca's famous gardens. The common areas are beautiful, and rooms are cleanly decorated in neutral colors and tasteful crafts, with soft, white bedding and clean bathrooms.

If you've come to Cuernavaca to escape the city, there are old-fashioned family-style resort-hotels where you can spend the weekend floating in the pool, as they did in mid-20th-century Mexico. One of these is the Hotel Racquet (Av. Francisco Villa 100, 777/101-0350 or 800/002-5425, www.hotelracquet.com, US$120 and over) in the pretty Rancho Cortés neighborhood, which originally opened in 1939. It features tennis and racquetball courts, a pool, several restaurants and bars, and an on-site spa.

For modern luxury, the Camino Real Sumiya (Col. José Parras, in Jiutepec, near the highway exit to Tepoztlán and Cuautla, 777/329-9888, www.caminoreal.com, US$140-160) was originally constructed as a residence by American heiress Barbara Hutton, who designed the space with Japanese-style interiors, verdant gardens, and walking paths. Rooms are clean and comfortable, also with an Asian theme, and equipped with flat-screen TVs and Wi-Fi.

Las Mañanitas (Ricardo Linares 107, 777/314-1466, www.lasmananitas. com.mx, US$250 and up), a 15-minute walk from the city center, is a super luxe place to stay, with resident peacocks and flamingos roaming the tropical gardens, an elegant swimming pool, and on-site spa. Rooms are cleanly decorated yet charming, and some have private terraces.

Around the grounds, there are plenty of intimate nooks to sit and enjoy the ambience.

GETTING THERE AND AWAY

Cuernavaca is on the Acapulco-México highway, south of Mexico City. On the toll road, it takes less than an hour to get there, if there's no traffic. If you're driving to Cuernavaca, take Insurgentes Sur all the way south until it departs the city, following signs for the Cuernavaca *cuota* (toll road). Cuernavaca is about an hour south on the highway.

From Mexico City, buses to Cuernavaca depart from the Taxqueña bus terminal (Av. Taxqueña 1320). With buses every 15 minutes from about 5:30am to 7pm, Autobuses Pullman de Morelos (55/5445-0100, www.pullman.mx) runs buses into two terminals, Cuernavaca Centro (Abasolo 12, 777/312-6001) and Cuernavaca Casino (Plan de Ayala 102, 777/318-9205). You can also take Estrella de Oro (www.estrelladeoro.com.mx, 800/900-0105) to Cuernavaca. It takes about an hour and a half to get there by bus and costs roughly US$8-10 each way.

NEAR CUERNAVACA

Zona Arqueológica Xochicalco

After the decline of Classic Zapotec and Mayan cities to the south, the population in Mesoamerica largely dispersed, creating both competition and instability throughout the region and giving rise to great fortified settlements in central Mexico. Located on a natural hilltop southwest of Cuernavaca, the remarkably well-preserved ruins at the Zona Arqueológica Xochicalco (Carr. Federal Xochicalco-Tetlama, Xochicalco, Miacatlán, 737/374-3090, daily 9am-5:30pm, US$4) were a fortress city and ceremonial center. Xochicalco's extensive systems of defense, which included walls, trenches, and moats, helped it maintain and protect trade routes as it grew to prominence in the 7th century.

Xochicalco is one of the most densely built pre-Columbian cities in Mexico, and among the many temples and pyramids at this site, perhaps the most outstanding structure is the Pyramid of the Plumed Serpent, its sloped base decorated with intricate geometric patterns and stone reliefs of sinuous serpents and men with plumed headpieces. On the back side of the main acropolis is a tunnel leading to a manmade cave, first used to mine rock and later used by the priests of Xochicalco as a subterranean observatory; a long vertical shaft dug by hand let full sunlight into the cave at midday, which could be used to fix dates.

Autobuses Pullman de Morelos (www.pullman.mx) offers buses from its Cuernavaca Centro terminal (Abasolo 12, 777/312-6001), as well as from Mexico City's Taxqueña terminal (Av. Taxqueña 1320), to Xochicalco, though it is often more convenient to hire a taxi from Cuernavaca to the ruins.

Tepoztlán

Tucked into a lush valley bordered by a dramatic wall of cliffs, Tepoztlán is a ruggedly beautiful little town just outside Cuernavaca. Adjoined by an unusual mountaintop archaeological site, it is the mythical birthplace of the Mesoamerican god Quetzalcóatl, and even today, older residents still speak Nahuatl.

For centuries a sleepy little village, Tepoztlán has become a favorite weekend getaway for Mexico City residents, as well as a bit of an artist community with a hippie sensibility. Although the people of Tepoztlán (frequently shortened to "Tepoz") seem content enough with all the cafés, art shops, and weekend visitors, they keep tourism on their own terms, and the town retains an old-fashioned, easygoing atmosphere.

SIGHTS

Museo de Arte Prehispánico Colección Carlos Pellicer

The small Museo de Arte Prehispánico Colección Carlos Pellicer (Pablo González 2, 739/395-1098, Tues.-Sun. 10am-6pm, US$1), just behind the Templo de la Natividad, houses a nice collection of pre-Hispanic pottery from Totonac, Maya, Zapotec, and Olmec cultures, from the collection of poet Carlos Pellicer, who lived in Tepoztlán. Take note of the fine Mexica statue of the god Ometochtli.

Tepoztlán

☯ Pirámide de Tepozteco

Perched on a ledge in the hills 400 meters above Tepóztlán (and over 2,000 meters above sea level), the **Pirámide de Tepozteco** (Cerro del Tepozteco, via Avenida del Tepozteco), dedicated to Ometochtli, the Mesoamerican god of plenty and the legendary creator of pulque, occupies one of the most spectacular spots in the region. The pyramid itself is not much to see, but the chance to hike up into the hills and catch views of the Tepoztlán valley below makes it worth the rigorous hike to the top.

From the town square it's an ascent of about two kilometers to the pyramid (daily 9:30am-6pm, US$3.50). To find the start of the trail, just follow the Camino del Tepozteco directly north from the main square and you'll hit the bluffs. Although plenty of nonathletes make their way up to the top, be prepared for a good hour's workout. Wear sturdy shoes and avoid weekends, or you'll feel as though you're hiking up with the entire population of Mexico City.

Weekend Market

The town center of Tepoztlán turns into one big market on weekends. The many shops in the center of town sell jewelry, art, and clothing from around the world, while locals sell Mexican handicrafts in outdoor stalls on the streets and in front of the church. If you don't make it to Tepoz on a Saturday or Sunday, there is a smaller artisan market just east of the Capilla de Nuestra Señora de la Asunción, selling jewelry, textiles, leather goods, and other handicrafts every day of the week.

Templo y Ex-Convento de la Natividad

Tepoztlán's **Templo y Ex-Convento de la Natividad** (Plaza Municipal, Revolución and Pablo González, 739/395-0255, Tues.-Sun. 10am-6pm.), a commanding stone church with adjacent Dominican monastery, was built 1555-1580 and was declared a World Heritage Site by the United Nations in 1994, along with other historic convents dotting the state of Morelos. Although it is simply decorated inside, the church is nonetheless a moving space, with a giant stone baptismal fountain at the entrance and soaring ceilings. Throughout the complex, you'll find remnants of frescos with Dominican themes on the walls.

Templo y Ex-Convento de la Natividad

The adjoining **Museo Ex-Convento de Tepoztlán** (739/395-0255, Tues.-Sun. 10am-5pm, free) has been restored and now serves as a regional museum where you can visit the former library, accommodations, and baths used by the Dominican friars during the colonial era.

OFF THE BEATEN TRACK: MALINALCO

Set amid dramatic scenery in a remote corner of the mountains between Toluca and Cuernavaca, Malinalco was once off the beaten path for most tourists. Today, it's become a weekend destination for Mexico City residents and a smattering of foreigners, but nonetheless it retains an authentic small-town atmosphere. In addition to enjoying the rural setting, there are a few sights worth visiting here: the 16th-century convent at the heart of Malinalco and the impressive archaeological site on a hill just outside the town.

At the heart of Malinalco, the impressive Augustinian monastery **Ex-Convento Agustino** (Plaza Central, Tues.-Sun. 10am-5pm, free) dates from the 1540s. Similar in style to the convent in Tepoztlán, the main **church** (El Templo del Divino Salvador) is largely unadorned yet imposing, while the cloister to the side is divided into two levels and surrounds an open garden. Decorating the walls of the cloister are beautiful murals of flowers and animals. Note an obviously pre-Columbian carved rock sitting on a stump in front of the church. On Wednesday an **open-air market** takes over the center of town. Vendors arrive in Malinalco from the surrounding communities, selling everything from tamales and handmade tortillas to clay pots and wood utensils.

The **Zona Arqueológica de Malinalco** (Amajac s/n, Col. Santa Monica, 722/215-7080, Tues.-Sun. 9am-5:30pm, US$4) sits on a bluff about one kilometer west of the town of Malinalco, all uphill on a dirt road. The small but impressive site, also known as Cuauhtinchan or Cerro de los Idolos, was built in the Late Classic period. The six monuments are carved directly out of the mountain rock, the only place in central Mexico where the Mexica used this technique. The post was a tribute to Malinalxochitl, the Mexica goddess and sister of Huitzilopochtli. The long stairway up to the ruins is a bit of a slog, but it's broken up with interesting write-ups (in three languages: English, Spanish, and Nahuatl) on the site itself and local history, culture, and environment. Views from the ruins across the town and surrounding countryside are magnificent.

RESTAURANTS

Located in a lush agricultural region, Tepoztlán is blessed with wonderful fresh foods, which you can get a taste of at the **Mercado de la Plaza Municipal** (Plaza Municipal, between Revolución and Envila, daily 8am-7pm). In this picturesque outdoor market, myriad stalls sell excellent *barbacoa* (slow-cooked lamb) and set-price *comidas corridas* (lunch specials), though it's particularly worth trying the popular regional snack called *itacate,* a thick, toasted, wedge-shaped corn cake stuffed with meat or veggie fillings. Vegetarians will want to seek out **Fonda Silvia,** where many of the delicious daily options are made without meat, dairy, or eggs.

One of Tepoztlán's most famous spots is the colorful scoop shop **Tepoznieves** (Av. 5 de Mayo 21, 739/395-4839, www.tepoznieves.mx, daily 8:30am-9:30pm), which sells traditional Mexican *nieves* (similar to a sorbet or ice milk) in a staggering array of flavors, like coconut, corn, tequila, strawberry, walnut, pistachio, and more. There are now branches of Tepoznieves in Mexico City, Cuernavaca, and other Mexican cities, but the original spot still does robust business in central Tepoztlán.

At the end of Avenida del Tepozteco, in a house set amid a jungle of plants, **Axitla** (Av. del Tepozteco 50, 739/395-0519, Wed.-Sun. 10am-7pm) is worth the 10-minute walk from the square for the ambience, as well as the menu of tasty, reasonably priced meals, both Mexican and international. Specialties include *chile jaral,* a wide chile pepper stuffed with shredded beef and raisins, and lamb cooked in a zucchini sauce. You can dine either alfresco or in the pink high-ceilinged dining room overlooking the trees and river.

An elegant restaurant right in the center of town, **El Ciruelo** (Zaragoza 17, 739/395-1203 or 739/395-1037, www.elciruelo.com.mx, Mon.-Thurs. 1pm-6pm, Fri.-Sat. 1pm-11pm, Sun. 1pm-7pm) features an outdoor patio with views of the mountains and creative cuisine, with dishes like *enchiladas de pato* (duck enchiladas), chicken breast in mole and plum sauce, and beef fajitas with nopal (prickly pear cactus).

HOTELS

So close to the capital and Cuernavaca, Tepoztlán is a hugely popular weekend destination. During the week it's usually no problem to show up without reservations, but you'll want to book ahead if you're staying on a Friday or Saturday night.

A good low-budget choice is the small and friendly Posada Mahe (Paraíso 12, 739/395-3292, US$35), on a cobbled street just above the town center. Quiet and clean, it has cozy, hand-painted rooms with tile floors and teeny but nice private bathrooms.

One of the nicest hotels in town is the enchanting Posada del Tepozteco (Paraíso 3, 739/395-0010, www.posadadeltepozteco.com.mx, US$180 and up). It's perched just above the main square, and from the gardens and guest rooms, there are breathtaking views overlooking the town and valley, as well as the towering bluffs to the north. The garden patio is a supremely pleasant place to sip a drink, and there's a pretty pool where you can swim on warm days. Accommodations are full of old-fashioned Mexican charm, with tiled walls and vintage wooden furnishings.

A great place to soak up the positive energy that abounds in Tepoztlán, La Buena Vibra (San Lorenzo 7, 739/395-1491, www.hotelbuenavibra. com, US$200 and up) is a bit out of the center of town, but the point of staying here is precisely to get away from it all. Overlooking the bluffs of El Tepozteco, the ultra-relaxing grounds and gardens include a pool, a meditation room, and a spa. Beautiful guest rooms are designed with a bit of Eastern aesthetic, including Buddha statues.

GETTING THERE AND AWAY

Autobuses Pullman de Morelos (Av. 5 de Mayo, 739/395-0520 or 55/5549-3505, www.pullman.mx, US$7) and Omnibuses Cristóbal Colón (operated by ADO, www.ado.com.mx, US$10) run regular buses every 30 minutes 6:30am-9:30pm to and from the Taxqueña terminal in Mexico City (Av. Taxqueña 1320). The trip takes about 1.5 hours.

BACKGROUND

The Landscape

GEOLOGY

Mexico City is located in the Valle de México, an alpine basin surrounded by volcanic mountains, which measures a considerable 2,200 meters at its lowest point. The valley is on the southern edge of a great plateau known as the Mexican Altiplano, which extends from the United States border to the Trans-Mexican Volcanic Belt, just south of Mexico City. Several of Mexico's highest peaks—including the famous twin volcanoes of Popocatépetl (5,465 meters) and Iztaccíhuatl (5,230 meters)—rim the valley to the south and southeast.

The Popocatépetl volcano rises above Mexico City.

The Valle de México was once covered by a series of broad, shallow lakes, which have been largely drained in the past 500 years; today, much of the city is built atop spongy dry lakebed. The unstable earth makes the city more susceptible to damage during seismic tremors. Earthquakes are frequent throughout the region, largely generated by the subduction of the Cocos tectonic plate beneath the North American plate, on Mexico's Pacific Coast. Because of the interaction between earthquake wave movement and the valley's weak subsoil, Mexico City sometimes feels the effects of a coastal quake more than places closer to the quake's actual epicenter. Such was the case in the deadly 1985 earthquake, the epicenter of which was more than 160 kilometers away.

Contributing to seismic activity, the Trans-Mexican Volcanic Belt remains active, with eruptions from nearby volcanoes sending tremors (as well as toxic dust) through the capital. The main culprit is Popocatépetl, the most active

265

THE GREAT QUAKE

At 7:18am on September 19, 1985, Mexico City trembled violently for more than three full minutes, as an 8.1 magnitude earthquake rippled across central Mexico. Though the epicenter of the quake was located off the Pacific Coast, its force was so great that it was felt as far away as Guatemala City and Houston, Texas. There was some damage along the coast, but Mexico City sustained the most astounding devastation. In the capital, the water-rich sediment atop which the city had been built is highly susceptible to movement, amplifying the force of the tremor. The ground moved so violently that it led to soil liquefaction, creating waves of movement that were, ominously, particularly traumatic to taller buildings.

In those three minutes, hundreds of buildings came crashing to the ground while drainage pipes and gas mains burst beneath the streets, contaminating the water supply and causing fires and explosions throughout the city. The death toll was massive, though never definitively determined, with estimates ranging from at least 10,000 to more than 35,000. Tens of thousands more were injured and over 100,000 left homeless. Exacerbating the situation, important medical centers were among the 3,000-plus buildings that were seriously damaged during the quake. Just a day later, a massive aftershock of almost equal magnitude amplified the destruction.

The federal and municipal governments were overwhelmed by the scale of the tragedy, and the people of Mexico City became important first responders, with regular civilians risking their lives to dig through the rubble for trapped victims. Citywide, and with uncharacteristic disregard for social divisions, people offered homes to neighbors, distributed food, and helped to bring order to the devastated city.

Several books have been published about the events of September 19, 1985, and their aftermath, including *No Sin Nosotros* (*Not Without Us*), by beloved essayist Carlos Monsiváis, and *Nada, Nadie: Las Voces del Temblor* (*Nothing, No One: The Voices of the Earthquake*), by Elena Poniatowska—both in Spanish. The memory of the tragedy still looms in the popular consciousness (as well as in the modern cityscape, where some buildings have remained abandoned since the quake). In 2010, the city commemorated the event's 25th anniversary in a ceremony overseen by Mayor Marcelo Ebrard and President Felipe Calderón. They dedicated a plaque to the victims along the Alameda Central, where the venerable old Hotel Regis stood before crashing to the ground during the earthquake.

Mexico City remains vulnerable to tragedies of this kind. In the wake of the '85 quake, building codes were updated and many unsafe structures were demolished. However, central neighborhoods of the city remain particularly weak, still standing atop the dry lakebed and its sandy, water-saturated soil. As fault lines continue to tremble along the Pacific Coast, most city residents live in fear of another earthquake.

volcano in the region, which has had several notable eruptions since the 1990s, requiring the evacuation of people living in its foothills. In July 2013, the volcano spewed enough dust and ash that airlines had to cancel their flights for 24 hours.

HYDROLOGY

Before the Mexica arrived in the Valley of Mexico and began the centuries-long projects of damming its lakes, the water level fluctuated dramatically throughout the year, depending on rainfall. In the late 15th century, Nezahualcóyotl, the poet-king of Texcoco, oversaw the construction of a massive dike dividing Lake Texcoco into two halves, one salty and one fresh, as a means of controlling floods. In Tenochtitlán, a system of canals was built for drainage control and transportation, while fresh water was brought in by aqueduct from Chapultepec.

As part of his final assault on the Mexica in 1521, Cortés ordered the breaching of Tenochtitlán's dams in an attempt to destroy the city. After the Mexica defeat, the Spaniards left the dike in ruins when they rebuilt the city, and as a result saw their new colonial capital flooded repeatedly. It was not until 1900, with the construction of the Gran Canal de Desagüe (Great Drainage Canal) under President Porfirio Díaz, that the waters of Lago de Texcoco were finally emptied.

Currently the only major bodies of water in the valley are small tracts of Lake Xochimilco in the south, the lakes in Chapultepec, and the remnants of Lake Texcoco northeast of the city, in the state of Mexico. The rivers that once flowed into the valley from the western mountains—such as Río Mixcoac, Río de la Piedad, Río Tacubaya, and Río Churubusco—still exist but are canalized and sealed under major avenues, eventually draining into one of the five canals on the east side of the city, which in turn flow out of the valley to the northeast.

The soggy earth below the city has contributed to the capital's rapid sinking: In the Centro Histórico, you may notice old stone buildings are cracked or tilting, some to the point of becoming uninhabitable. Some neighborhoods have dropped an estimated 7.5 meters in the last century alone! Air quality is also affected; the dried lakebeds in the northeast part of the valley create swirling clouds of dust that are swept up into the atmosphere and moved to the southwest, directly across the city, by the prevailing winds, worsening the air pollution.

CLIMATE

Altitude tempers Mexico City's tropical location, creating a remarkably pleasant climate year-round. During the spring and fall, daytime temperatures generally hover 22-23°C (72-73°F), dropping to 10-12°C (50-54°F) in the evening. The short winter season usually runs between December and February, and the weather is cooler throughout those months, especially at night. April, May, and early June are typically the warmest months, when the temperature slowly climbs until the rainy season begins.

As in most of central Mexico, Mexico City's climate can be divided into two distinct seasons: the dry season, which runs from November to May, and the shorter rainy season, from June to October. During the rainy season, flash floods, furious downpours, and even hailstorms pummel the capital, bringing everything to a halt. In most cases, these storms rarely last longer than an hour or two, and they help moderate the heat of the summer.

ENVIRONMENTAL ISSUES

Mexico City's 20-million-plus population has had a substantial impact on the environment in the Valle de México. There is a growing environmental consciousness in the capital, and there have been some modest improvements in recent decades, but environmental problems remain one of the most substantial issues facing the city.

AIR QUALITY

A semi-opaque haze of yellowish smog lingers above Mexico City most days, blocking the view of the surrounding mountains. The city's well-publicized air-pollution problems hit an all-time high in the late 1980s and early 1990s; though the city has made progress in improving the environment, air quality is an ongoing problem in the capital. The winter months are the worst, when there are fewer and lighter air currents.

SEEING GREEN IN MEXICO CITY

Mexico City faces a multitude of environmental problems, from air pollution and acid rain to water shortages and deforestation. For a long time, it looked as if the city would continue to grow without regard for its natural environment, but a new green awareness has taken root. The administration of former mayor Marcelo Ebrard made environmental issues a top priority with its Plan Verde (Green Plan), which helped reduce air pollution and promote new transport alternatives. Small businesses, restaurants, and designers are also taking a proactive environmental stance. Trendy restaurants like **Quintonil** (page 123) and **Máximo Bistrot Local** (page 133) emphasize native products, while organic grocery stores like the **Green Corner** (page 132) sell local fare. Here are a few of the interesting green projects underway:

EL MERCADO DEL TRUEQUE

Mexico City produces 12,000 tons of garbage daily, but much of what goes to the dump isn't waste. To promote recycling, the Secretaría del Medio Ambiente (SMA, Environmental Secretariat) introduced the **Mercado del Trueque.** Held on the second Sunday of each month, the market allows you to trade recyclables for fresh food. City residents can turn in up to 10 kilos of aluminum, glass, plastic, paper and cardboard, computers, used cellular phones, and other recyclable refuse, for which they receive credit for purchases at the on-site food market. All the market's food vendors hail from the local region. Locations change; check the monthly calendar at the SMA's website (www.sma.df.gob.mx/mercadodetrueque).

CYCLING

People of all stripes are now riding through town on cherry-red bicycles from Mexico City's incredibly popular **Ecobici bike-share program** (page 187). The government has also taken steps to encourage cycling in the capital by designing new bike lanes and closing off automobile traffic on the Paseo de la Reforma on Sundays.

MERCADO EL 100

This market in the Roma neighborhood is called the **Mercado El 100** (page 207) to signify that nothing sold here comes from farther than 100 miles (or about 160 kilometers) away. Set up every Saturday in the Plaza del Lanzador, it's a colorful place to browse jars of local honey, unusual lettuces, fresh cheese, and homemade sweets.

VERTICAL GARDENS

A nonprofit environmental-design organization, VerdMX (www.verdmx.org) has helped build a number of vertical gardens in the city, including the leafy blanket along the wall of the **Shops at Downtown** (page 197) in the Centro Histórico and a unique modern sculpture covered in leafy greens along the Avenida Chapultepec. Many other private architects are helping to equip the city with green rooftops and vertical gardens, a beautiful and oxygen-giving addition to the urban jungle.

CASA DEL AGUA

In a city with a serious water shortage, **Casa del Agua** (Puebla 242, www.casadelagua.com.mx) has an interesting proposition. Here, rainwater is collected on-site and purified, then sold in reusable glass bottles. The shop also sells bottled herbal infusions, which you can sip on their pretty roof deck.

Automobile traffic is the number-one contributor to air-quality problems in the greater Mexico City metropolitan region. To help address air quality, the local government has implemented several programs, including tighter vehicle emissions checks, reforestation projects, and a program to restrict driving, called "Hoy No Circula," which restricts the number of cars on the road.

Mexico City surveys its Metropolitan Air Quality Index (Índice Metropolitana de Calidad de Aire, or IMECA) every day, measuring the city's levels of ozone, carbon monoxide, carbon dioxide, lead, sulfur, and other contaminants. You can track the daily IMECA readings in most local newspapers or online or at the website maintained by the Mexico City Secretaría de Medio Ambiente (Environment Secretariat) at www.sma.df.gob.mx.

WATER
Mexico City consumes 3.5 million cubic meters of water every day, twice the level of many industrialized countries. Poor infrastructure is an unfortunate contributor to usage; it is estimated that a quarter (or more!) of the city's water supply is lost through leaky pipes before it reaches household taps.

Because of the dwindling aquifers, about 20 to 30 percent of the city's water is pumped uphill 1,000 meters from the Lerma and Cutzamala Rivers, 100 kilometers to the west. As a result, not only is the Mexico City water table dropping, but water shortages are increasing all around central Mexico to supply the thirsty capital.

A reforestation program along the banks of the dwindling Lago de Texcoco has helped to cut back on dust and to recycle carbon dioxide, and it may also speed efforts to reclaim more rainwater in the lake basin. More creative, low-tech measures begun include digging 600 absorption wells in the southern mountain parts of Tlalpan, Milpa Alta, Xochimilco, Magdalena Contreras, and Cuajimalpa *delegaciones*. These will collect rainwater and funnel it underground, which will both reduce the risk of flooding and help replenish the subterranean aquifers.

History

PRE-COLUMBIAN HISTORY
EARLY CIVILIZATIONS
More than 30,000 years ago, the majority of the North American continent was covered in sheets of ice. Amid this forbidding landscape, the first human settlers are believed to have migrated from Siberia to North America via a narrow land bridge across the Bering Strait. These first people were followed by another wave of migrants, likely of Asian descent, who eventually migrated to the southern reaches of the Andes Mountains of South America.

Eventually, tribes of hunter-gatherers began to organize into communities—there is evidence of living sites dating back over 20,000 years—in a region known as Mesoamerica, a culturally linked swath of territory that covers southern Mexico, Belize, Guatemala, Honduras, El Salvador, and Nicaragua. Although the American population was now physically isolated from Eurasia, they independently developed farming techniques, with maize cultivation dating back 9,000 years.

THE FIRST INHABITANTS OF THE VALLEY
Groups of nomads arrived in the Valle de México sometime around 20,000 BC. Over the next several thousand years, the valley's population grew to rely on gathering fruits and grains,

NEZAHUALCÓYOTL: THE POET, THE CITY

When the city of Tenochtitlán rose to power during the 15th century, the Mexica formed a strategic alliance with the Nahuatl-speaking people of Tlacopan and Texcoco on either side of their island city. At that time, the great King Nezahualcóyotl ruled the Acolhua people of Texcoco. As *tlatoani* (monarch), Nezahualcóyotl was a visionary city planner and engineer, responsible for designing the massive dam in Lake Texcoco that prevented the annual flooding in Tenochtitlán, as well as the aqueduct that brought fresh water to the city from Chapultepec. He was a reputed to be a great lover of nature, and some of the oldest *ahuehuetes* (cypresses) in the Bosque de Chapultepec were said to have been planted by Nezahualcóyotl during his lifetime. He is also remembered, perhaps most reverently, as a great poet and philosopher. Much of the classic Nahuatl verse has been attributed to him, often ruminations on war, the divine, and the ephemeral nature of human life. Many of Nezahualcóyotl's moving *cantos* (songs) have been etched into the stone patio at the Museo Nacional de Antropología.

Today, not far from where he once ruled the Acolhua, a massive urban settlement bears the poet-king's name. Ciudad Nezahualcóyotl, located on the southeast fringe of the Mexico City, was built atop the drained bed of Lake Texcoco in the early 20th century, right after the Xochiaca Dam was built, exposing new dry land for development. Urban services were slow to arrive in the area, but people were not. Even without electricity, by the 1950s the suburban community had a population of 40,000, comprising mostly poor immigrants from the rural countryside. Despite ongoing problems with land titles in the area, Ciudad Neza continued to grow unchecked throughout the 20th century, finally garnering some public services like paved roads and potable water when it became an official municipality in the 1960s, though even these basic services weren't a given.

Ironically, King Nezahualcóyotl is a symbol of high-mindedness and visionary leadership, while the city that bears his name characterizes the modern metropolis's failures in urban planning. In Ciudad Neza, massive immigration and a lack of city services gave way to slumlike conditions for many residents during the late half of the 20th century. With a population of well over a million people, it is now one of Mexico's biggest cities (though considered part of the greater Mexico City metropolitan region), but it has long been plagued by poverty, extortion, drugs, and gang wars. In recent decades, Neza has begun to modernize, and there is new industry in the area, but it remains a place largely representative of the massive and uncontrolled settlement of the city.

especially maize, until agricultural societies established themselves in the third millennium BC.

The agricultural revolution created profound changes in social organization. Between 1500 and 650 BC, the villages around the valley's lakes grew. The first full-fledged city to develop was Cuicuilco, centered around a pyramid site located at what is now the junction of Insurgentes Sur and Periférico Sur. By 100 BC a second city was growing at Teotihuacán in the north. Cuicuilco had already begun to decline when its existence was dramatically cut short when Volcán Xitle exploded and covered Cuicuilco with beds of lava.

TEOTIHUACÁN AND THE CLASSIC PERIOD

Characterized as an era of great human advancement, the Classic period in Mesoamerica began about AD 250-300. During the early Classic period, an unknown people founded the city of Teotihuacán in the Valley of Mexico. Teotihuacán's largest structure, the 70-meter Pyramid of the Sun, was completed around AD 100, though the city reached its peak several hundred years later. With an estimated population reaching 150,000 (and possibly more), Teotihuacán's influence reached throughout Mesoamerica. It was overtaken and destroyed around AD 800, though its lofty pyramids remain standing today.

As Teotihuacán declined, the great Maya and Zapotec people flourished in the south of Mexico, from AD 200 to 1000. Though their city-states and vast empires had little direct influence on the Valley of Mexico, the Maya aesthetic and philosophical legacy, as well as their skill in astronomy and mathematics, had a notable impact throughout the region.

THE TOLTECS AND THE POST-CLASSIC

After AD 1000, Maya and Zapotec cities began to decline, as new tribes descended from the north. Among these, a bellicose people known as the Toltec dominated central Mexico about AD 800-1000, controlling trade routes from the huge city-state of Tollan, now called Tula, in present-day Hidalgo. The Toltecs controlled the Valley of Mexico, though their reach extended as far north as Zacatecas and as far south as Guatemala. Similarities in the architecture of post-Classic Maya cities and Tula have also prompted debate about the interaction between these peoples, suggesting that the Toltec may have been involved in the building of great post-Classic cities like Chichen Itzá.

The Toltec civilization never reached the heights achieved by Teotihuacán and began to decline after AD 1200. After suffering successive invasions from the Chichimeca tribes to the north, Tula was eventually abandoned.

THE MEXICA AND EL GRAN TENOCHTITLÁN

After the decline of Tula, there was increased migration into the Valley of Mexico. In 1250, the powerful cities of Azcapotzalco, Culhuacan, and Texcoco controlled much of the area when a nomadic northern tribe known as the Mexica (pronounced meh-SHEE-ka) arrived in the valley. According to legend, these people originally came from the city of Aztlán, thought to be on the coast of modern-day Nayarit; for that reason, historians began calling them the Aztecs, though the Mexica people never used that name.

After years of enslavement and attacks on their settlements, the Mexica eventually founded a city on an uninhabited island not far from the shore in Lake Texcoco, which they named Tenochtitlán. According to legend, the Mexica knew that they were meant to settle the island when they saw an eagle perched on a cactus with a snake in its beak (a rendering of that vision is at the center of the Mexican flag). Courageous warriors, the Mexica eventually gained dominance over the valley, vanquishing their chief rivals, the Tepanecs, with the assistance of King Nezahualcóyotl of Texcoco, and establishing a strategic triple alliance with the cities of Texcoco and Tlacopan under their fourth emperor, Itzcóatl.

In the generations following Itzcóatl's rule, the Mexica started to rewrite their own history, identifying the Toltecs as their spiritual ancestors and downplaying their nomadic past. Moctezuma I, who took power in 1440 after Itzcóatl's death, embarked on an expansionist program that brought much of the Valley of Oaxaca and the Gulf Coast regions under Mexica control. During the next generations of Mexica rulers, almost all of central Mexico fell under their sway, with the exception of a few regions that maintained their independence, notably the Tlaxcaltecas and Chollulans to the east. By the time Moctezuma

Xocoyotzin, or Moctezuma II, took power, in 1502, the Mexica were the ruling power in Mesoamerica.

As the center of the empire, the city-state of Tenochtitlán grew rich and splendid, demanding lavish tributes of food, clothing, tools, and jewelry from the hundreds of cities it controlled. Upper-class Mexica dressed in embroidered tunics decorated with feathers, and their boys were sent to schools called *calmécac* (children of regular civilians were also sent to vocational schools, to learn the craft of their community, in addition to natural history and religion). Adjacent to Tenochtitlán, and eventually linked to it by continual landfill projects, the smaller island of Tlatelolco was the empire's principal market center, ruled by its own line of kings.

Tenochtitlán itself was large, orderly, and clean. Laid out in an organized grid pattern, it was crisscrossed by a system of canals, which allowed for drainage during the flood season and also provided the principal means of transportation to and from the mainland via canoe. At the center of the city was a stepped pyramid-temple, today called the Templo Mayor, which was the principal religious monument in the city. Indeed, religion was central to life in Tenochtitlán. Huitzilopochtli, the god of war, and Tlaloc, the god of rain, were central figures in their pantheon. The Mexica fed Huitzilopochtli's favor by performing human sacrifices in their temples—a practice common throughout Mesoamerica but brought to new heights in Tenochtitlán. The Mexica often sacrificed prisoners of war brought home from their many battles, with massive sacrifices taking place on festival days.

SPANISH CONQUEST AND THE COLONIAL ERA
THE CONQUEST

After Christopher Columbus's 1492 voyage to the Indies, Iberian conquest of the Americas swiftly began. The Spaniards first took control of several Caribbean islands, principally Hispaniola and Cuba, where the native population was enslaved and largely died out after a few generations, owing to disease and depression. During that time, several Spanish envoys discovered the existence of richer "islands" to the east, populated by civilizations more advanced than those in the Indies. Rushing to gain control of these new territories, Cuban governor Diego Velázquez chose a young Spaniard named Hernán Cortés from Medellín, Spain, to lead a reconnaissance expedition to the Mexican coast.

Cortés accepted the post, amassing a huge group of volunteers to accompany him on the voyage. Sensing Cortés's growing power and insubordination, Velázquez attempted to cancel Cortés's appointment, but Cortés sailed anyway, bringing 11 ships and close to 500 men with him. He landed first in Cozumel, then touched down along the Gulf Coast, where he battled local Chontol Maya people, who didn't comply with Cortés's repeated demands for food and gold. It was here that Cortés first heard of the Mexica and Emperor Moctezuma.

After destroying his boats (thereby forcing dissenting Spanish soldiers to join the conquest), Cortés made his way to Tenochtitlán, gathering Mexica enemies as his allies along the way. Emperor Moctezuma had already received detailed reports about the Spanish arrival, and descriptions had led him to fear Cortés was the embodiment of the god Quetzalcóatl. When the Spanish arrived in Tenochtitlán, Moctezuma allowed them to enter the city as protected guests.

Several weeks went by without event, but tensions brewed. When Cortés returned to the Gulf Coast to fight off a brigade of soldiers sent by Velázquez, Pedro de Alvarado was left in charge, and he led a misguided massacre of 200 Mexica nobles at the festival of Tóxcatl. Cortés returned, but the situation between the Spanish and the Mexica was now irreparable. During this time, Moctezuma was also killed under unresolved circumstances, while being held hostage by the Spanish. Trying to escape under the cover of darkness and in possession of as much gold and jewelry as they could carry, the Spanish lost hundreds of soldiers to angry Mexica attackers while trying to flee the city in a massacre remembered as the Noche Triste (Night of Sorrows).

Playing on the widespread resentment of the Mexica throughout the region, the Spanish recruited help from many tribes near Tenochtitlán and regrouped their forces. The Spanish were further assisted by the smallpox virus, which they had unwittingly introduced to the Americas. In a matter of weeks, thousands of native people fell sick and died, including Moctezuma's successor, Emperor Cuitláhuac.

After months of preparation, the Spanish launched a waterborne attack on Tenochtitlán in January 1521. Months of conflict ensued, concluding with a siege of the city. Led by Moctezuma's cousin, Cuauhtémoc, the Mexica resisted the Spanish, even as they ran low on both food and water

supplies. Finally, Cortés and his military forced the Mexica to flee to the adjoining community of Tlatelolco, where they were overcome. The Spanish razed Tenochtitlán and built a new city on its ruins. Victorious, the Spanish named their new city Mexico, capital of New Spain.

NEW SPAIN

Under the direction of Alonso García Bravo, a new Spanish city was built, borrowing much from Tenochtitlán's highly organized street plan. As they worked, the Spanish built a temporary capital in the community of Coyoacán, which had been an ally during their siege of Tenochtitlán. The first viceroy (governor) of Mexico, Don Antonio de Mendoza, took his post in 1535.

The conquest and colonization were brutal for native people, both physically and culturally. Where they encountered resistance, the Spanish used ruthless tactics to subdue native tribes. Many indigenous people were enslaved, while others succumbed to foreign disease. As a result of these changes, the native population dropped significantly during the early years of New Spain.

Fifteenth-century Spain was a deeply Catholic place, entrenched in the Inquisition at the time Cortés conquered Tenochtitlán. Converting the native population to Catholicism was a top priority for the Spanish crown (and a justification for colonization), and as early as the mid-1520s, missionaries had founded settlements in Mexico City and in the surrounding communities.

In addition to seeking converts, the Spanish came to the New World in search of wealth and fortune. To encourage settlement, the crown doled out land grants throughout the territories, and Spanish families established large haciendas, clearing the native land for agriculture and cattle grazing. Having admired the gold and silver jewelry worn by Mexica nobles, the Spanish aggressively sought precious metals within the craggy Sierra Madre. Fortuitously, a Spanish expedition discovered a large silver vein outside the modern-day city of Zacatecas in 1546. Several more bountiful silver veins were discovered shortly thereafter.

The discovery of silver changed the power dynamic in the colonies, giving the New World massive trading power with the Old World. All of the immense quantities of silver mined in New Spain passed through Mexico City, where merchants had an official monopoly on all trading in the colony. As a result of these advantages, the city grew immensely wealthy and came to be known throughout Europe as *la ciudad de los palacios* (the city of palaces). With the decline of the silver industry in the late 17th and early 18th centuries, Mexico City's economy stagnated, though the last decades of the 18th century saw a burst of reformist zeal under the new Bourbon kings.

Throughout the colonial era, society was highly stratified: Spaniards born in Spain were afforded the highest place in society, and were consistently appointed to all of the most important political posts. Mexican-born people of Spanish heritage were referred to as *criollos* and, despite their common heritage, had a lower social and political standing. *Mestizo* people of mixed ethnic heritage held a far lower place in society, only better than the abysmal position of indigenous workers and slaves.

INDEPENDENT MEXICO
THE WAR OF INDEPENDENCE

After close to 250 years of Spanish rule in the New World, Bourbon king Charles III ascended the Spanish throne. A believer in "enlightened absolutism," he made dramatic changes to the governance of New Spain. Undermining the colony's economic autonomy, he established royal monopolies on seminal industries like tobacco, gunpowder, and mercury (needed for silver extraction). He also forbade church loans, which were a major source of credit within Mexican communities. Finally, he expelled the highly popular Jesuit order from Mexico. For many Mexicans—especially those who had already come to resent the colony's strict hierarchies and distant authority—these changes bred deep resentment.

Mexico's struggle for independence began on September 16, 1810, when Padre Miguel Hidalgo y Costilla gave his famous *grito de la independencia* (cry of independence) from a church in Dolores, Guanajuato, where he and a group of *criollos* led the insurrection. After Hidalgo's capture and assassination, José María Morelos took charge of the army. He in turn was captured and executed. The battles continued for almost a decade until the government of Ferdinand VII was overthrown in Spain. As a result of the change in Spanish governance, Colonel Agustín de Iturbide, a fierce royalist, switched sides to join the Mexican army. With Iturbide at the helm, Mexico achieved independence with the Treaty of Córdoba in 1821. Mexico City, home of wealthy nobles, remained a royalist holdout during the struggle, firmly opposed to independence.

EARLY INDEPENDENT MEXICO

The end of the war was the beginning of a century of political unrest and instability in Mexico. After signing the Treaty of Córdoba, Mexico took its first steps toward establishing autonomy. Twenty-four states were named in the First Mexican Empire, with independence leader Agustín de Iturbide crowning himself emperor of Mexico. In 1824, Mexico City was officially designated the seat of the federal government.

Just eight months after Iturbide took control of the government, Vicente Guerrero and Antonio López de Santa Anna led a successful revolt against the government. They established the first Mexican republic, and another hero of the War of Independence, Guadalupe Victoria, became the country's first president. Amid turmoil, Vicente Guerrero assumed the post of president when Guadalupe Victoria stepped down, though the conservative forces of General Anastasio Bustamante quickly ousted him.

MEXICAN-AMERICAN WAR

In 1831, Antonio López de Santa Anna was elected president. During this time, the United States was aggressively expanding westward, and U.S. citizens had begun to settle in Texas. When Mexico's constitution centralized power and abolished slavery in 1835, Texas declared independence. In response, Santa Anna sent troops to Texas. He sustained a major victory at the Alamo, but the brutality of the fighting galvanized Texans against the Mexican president. After numerous confrontations, the Texan army overpowered Santa Anna's forces.

On June 16, 1845, the United States annexed Texas, though the state's independence was never formally recognized by the Mexican government. When a skirmish broke out between Mexican forces and the U.S. military along the Texas border, President James Polk asked the Congress to declare war. Aggressively recruiting new soldiers to join the effort, the United States advanced into Mexico under General Winfred Scott. After battles through the north, the army captured the important central city of Puebla, from which Scott's army launched an offensive on the capital. After numerous battles, Scott took control of Mexico City during the Battle of Chapultepec, when American forces invaded the castle on the Cerro de Chapultepec and raised their flag over the city.

The capital of Mexico was temporarily relocated to Querétaro, where Santa Anna signed the infamous Treaty of Guadalupe, which ceded half of Mexico's territory to the United States, including California, New Mexico, Arizona, Texas, Colorado, and Nevada.

REFORM AND FRENCH RULE

Santa Anna returned to power after the war, but he was overthrown in 1855 by a Zapotec lawyer named Benito Juárez. Among his most significant acts, Juárez abolished church property and amended the constitution to officially recognize freedom of religion. Juárez's presidency was repeatedly threatened by conservative and royalist forces, though he is remembered today as one of Mexico's most just and visionary presidents.

Juárez had a great impact on the layout and power structures in Mexico City. When he took the presidency, much of the Centro Histórico was controlled by large convents, including San Agustín, San Francisco, Santo Domingo, and La Merced. After seizing church properties under the Reform laws, city officials demolished large parts of these religious compounds and repossessed their land. Remnants of the old convents still stand, but none are fully intact today.

Failing to oust liberals from power, conservative leaders conspired with the government of France to overthrow Juárez's government. France invaded Mexico under Napoleon III and, after a disastrous defeat in Puebla, came back to successfully overwhelm Juárez's forces. The French established the Second Mexican Empire, placing Emperor Maximilian I of Austria in charge. During his brief rule, Maximilian and his wife, Carlota, claimed the Castillo de Chapultepec as their residence, redesigning it in a grand European style. To link the new palace with downtown, the Paseo de la Reforma (originally the Paseo de la Emperatriz), now the city's broadest boulevard, was laid out.

In 1867, there was yet another successful uprising by the liberals; Maximilian was executed in Querétaro. Benito Juárez returned to the presidency, and he remained in power until his death in 1872.

MODERN MEXICO CITY
THE PORFIRIATO

Not long after Juárez's successor, Sebastián Lerdo de Tejada, had won his second election, army general Porfirio Díaz took office in a coup. A hero in the war against the French, Porfirio Díaz was a liberal from Oaxaca, but his politics changed in office. He became a powerful and conservative political leader with a strong military outlook. Fascinated by European aesthetics, he spent lavishly on city infrastructure and architecture in the European style.

Under Díaz, Mexico City began to expand beyond the Centro Histórico. The first neighborhoods established outside downtown were Guerrero and San Rafael, north and west of the Alameda, in the 1850s and 1860s, followed by the development of San Cosme and Santa María la Ribera farther west, and later Juárez and Cuauhtémoc on either side of the newly chic Paseo de la Reforma. The Colonia Roma, just to the south, followed.

Díaz held the presidency for 26 consecutive years, a period known as the Porfiriato. Under Díaz's dictatorship, Mexico entered into an era of relative stability, though the regime's despotic tendencies did not play out positively for the majority of Mexicans. While the country's wealth increased, social conditions for the poor worsened under Díaz's iron-fisted control.

THE MEXICAN REVOLUTION

After almost 30 years of the Porfiriato, wealthy politician Francisco I. Madero announced his presidential candidacy, in opposition to Díaz. President Díaz jailed him, and in return, Madero declared a revolt against the Díaz government on November 20, 1910, now remembered as the Day of the Revolution.

The Mexican Revolution was helmed by some of Mexico's most colorful personalities. Leading the *división del norte* (northern division), the wily and charismatic bandit Pancho Villa recruited thousands to the revolutionary cause. From the state of Morelos, Emiliano Zapata was a middle-class landowner who joined the revolution to promote land reform among peasants. Zapata rode to war dressed as a traditional Mexican *charro* (cowboy), with a wide-brim sombrero and thick moustache. He is still revered for his populist politics and his strong commitment to rural people and land rights.

Within six months, the people's army defeated Díaz's military. Madero initially took the presidency, but Victoriano Huerta ousted Madero in a coup. In response, Venustiano Carranza, Álvaro Obregón, Pancho Villa, and Emiliano Zapata led yet another revolt against Huerta's government. Villa and Zapata toppled Huerta's regime in August 1914.

Venustiano Carranza made a bid for the presidency, initially opposed by both Villa and Zapata. However, Carranza was able to win a broad base of support by promising constitutional reform. He oversaw the writing of the Constitution of 1917, which included land, law, and labor reforms. Carranza was eventually forced out of power by General Álvaro Obregón.

POST-REVOLUTIONARY MEXICO CITY

The post-revolutionary period was a time of great progress, culture, and intellectual achievement in Mexico. During Obregón's presidency, José Vasconcelos served as the Secretary of Public Education, overseeing the establishment of the National Symphonic Orchestra as well as the famed Mexican mural program. Music and cinema flourished during the 1930s and 1940s, with Mexican movies outselling Hollywood films during World War II. During and after the Spanish Civil War, many European intellectuals took up residence in Mexico, adding to the thriving art and cultural community. Always the center of the republic, Mexico City was at the heart of this cultural movement, its artists, writers, thinkers, musicians, and actors gaining national and worldwide fame.

In a watershed moment in Mexican politics, Lázaro Cárdenas was elected to the presidency in 1937. Unlike his predecessors, Cárdenas enacted land reform and redistribution as laid out in the Constitution of 1917. In a move that would serve as a model for other oil-rich nations, Cárdenas expropriated oil reserves from the private companies that had been running them. He established Petróleos Mexicanos (Pemex), concurrently founding the National Polytechnic Institute to ensure a sufficient engineering force in the country.

EXPANSION AND POST-WORLD WAR II BOOM

Mexico City's population exploded during the 20th century. In 20 years alone, the population doubled, from 906,000 in 1920 to 1,757,000 in 1940. To cope with its new residents, the city expanded in all directions, with little planning. The government turned a blind eye to the impromptu settlements set up by rural immigrants, which would eventually become entire cities in their own right, and freely gave out permits to build new, upscale neighborhoods for the wealthy.

The construction of the new national university complex in the early 1950s, along with the expansion of Avenida Insurgentes to connect it to the city center, led to the buildup of the entire southwestern quadrant of the city in just a few short years. Wide-open fields south of Roma were quickly converted into the Del Valle and Nápoles neighborhoods. In the early postwar years the formerly out-lying villages of Mixoac, San Ángel, Tacuba, Tacubaya, and Coyoacán were formally incorporated into the city limits. To the north, the industrial areas grew quickly. When the middle-class suburb Ciudad Satelite was built with great optimism in the late 1950s, it was surrounded by open land; in the years that followed, the city swallowed it completely.

The poor, rural immigrants flood-ing into the city didn't have money to buy property or houses, and so they simply erected shantytowns in the less desirable, eastern side of the valley, once under the waters of Lake Texcoco. Over the years, these *ciudades perdi-das* (lost cities) have become perma-nent cities. The classic *ciudad perdida* is Ciudad Nezahualcóyotl, which saw its population increase from 65,000 in 1960 to 650,000 in 1970 to over a mil-lion by the 1990s, making it one of the largest cities in the country.

THE 1960S AND THE TLATELOLCO MASSACRE

Mexico City was selected to host the Olympic Games in 1968. For Mexico's government, the Olympic Games were a major financial investment, as well as an important opportunity to boost the nation's economy and bring Mexico to the world stage. Mexican students saw the international pub-licity as an opportunity to draw at-tention to Mexico's one-party-rule government. There were widespread protests against the government in the months preceding the opening cere-mony, many drawing tens of thou-sands of protestors.

Ten days before the Olympic Games were set to begin, thousands of stu-dents marched in protest to the Plaza de las Tres Culturas in Tlatelolco. The gathering was meant to be peaceful, but armed military troops were sent in, firing indiscriminately on the crowd. While the government stated that only four students had been killed, eyewitnesses saw hundreds of bodies. The official events were never fully uncovered, yet the massacre per-manently tarnished the government's reputation with the people of Mexico City.

ECONOMIC CRISIS, NAFTA, AND THE ZAPATISTA MOVEMENT

In the early 1980s, falling oil prices and high worldwide interest rates cre-ated a massive recession in Mexico. President Miguel de la Madrid was forced to drastically cut government spending, the economy stagnated, and unemployment soared. Recovery was incredibly slow, with the GDP grow-ing just 0.1 percent per year until 1988. The situation worsened for the capital after a massive earthquake on September 19, 1985. Measuring an 8.1 on the Richter scale, the quake shook Mexico City for three full min-utes, during which time hundreds of buildings collapsed to the ground and around 10,000 people were killed (though some estimates put the num-ber of fatalities much higher). There was major damage to infrastructure, leaving tens of thousands without po-table water and hospitals inoperable.

Economic recovery began under the next president, Carlos Salinas de Gortari, who renegotiated the coun-try's external debts and embarked on a policy of trade liberalization. By 1994, Mexico was economically stable enough to sign as a member of the North American Free Trade

Agreement (NAFTA). However, shortly after PRI president Ernesto Zedillo was sworn into office, Mexico's currency collapsed and recession returned. The U.S. Treasury and the International Monetary Fund put together a massive financial bailout. Under NAFTA, Mexico's economy has continued to grow annually, and trade between NAFTA nations has more than tripled.

The same morning that NAFTA went into effect, a small indigenous army called the Ejército Zapatista de Liberación Nacional (Zapatista Army of National Liberation), or EZLN, took armed control of several cities in the southernmost state of Chiapas, including the historic capital of San Cristóbal de las Casas. Known as the Zapatistas (in a nod to Revolution hero Emiliano Zapata), this small but well-organized group of largely indigenous revolutionaries declared war on the Mexican government, citing the years of poverty and oppression suffered by the country's native people. In response to the uprising, the Mexican government quickly dispatched thousands of troops to Chiapas, pursuing the EZLN as they retreated into the southern jungles, where the rebel army suffered heavy casualties.

This rebellion was small in scope but wide-reaching in consequences, inspiring support for indigenous causes throughout Mexico—and throughout the world. The army's unofficial leader, Subcommandante Marcos, became a national spokesman for the indigenous cause and, along with a convoy of EZLN leadership, met repeatedly with Mexican government leaders. In 2000, they marched peaceably to Mexico City, where they met with the federal government and were greeted by thousands of supporters.

PRI OPPOSITION: THE PRD AND THE PAN

In 1988, leftist politician Cuauhtémoc Cárdenas, son of post-Revolution president Lázaro Cárdenas, split from the ruling PRI party and announced his candidacy for president against Carlos Salinas de Gortari. Cárdenas was defeated in a highly suspect election, during which the voting systems failed to function for several hours. He lost another race against the PRI in 1994 but was elected mayor of Mexico City two years later, bolstering the notion that Mexico was ready for a change from the one-party system that had ruled since the early 20th century.

In the meantime, the conservative Partido Acción Nacional (PAN) had made inroads into politics. In the elections of 2000, popular support began to rally around the tall, mustachioed Vicente Fox Quesada, a former Coca-Cola executive. Campaigning on a ticket of change, Fox won a much celebrated victory over PRI candidate Francisco Labastida. The PAN did not control the Congress, however, and Fox's presidency was marked by inefficiency. Fox's PAN successor, President Felipe Calderón, was elected in 2006, taking the office after winning by just one percentage point over the Party of the Democratic Revolution (Partido de la Revolución Democrática; PRD) candidate, Andrés Manuel López Obrador.

During his presidency, Calderón declared a war on drugs, and a major spike in drug-related violence plagued much of northern Mexico, causing widespread instability and fear along the border with the United States, among other areas. Capitalizing on dissatisfaction with the PAN and the violence in Mexico, the PRI regained control of the executive branch with the election of Enrique Peña Nieto to the presidency. Like his predecessor, Peña Nieto won over PRD candidate López Obrador, and protests against his legitimacy, though less widespread, were also fierce.

Government and Economy

GOVERNMENT
THE FEDERAL REPUBLIC

As laid out in the Constitution of 1917, Mexico is a democratic republic. It is divided into 31 individually governed states, plus one *distrito federal* (federal district) in Mexico City. The federal government is divided into three branches: executive, legislative, and judicial. State governments are similarly divided into three branches and are elected locally.

THE DISTRITO FEDERAL, A.K.A. CIUDAD DE MÉXICO

After independence, Mexico City was declared the seat of the national government. Though technically federal land, the Distrito Federal was divided into independent *municipios* throughout the post-Independence era. President Álvaro Obregón abolished the *municipios* altogether, dividing the city into *delegaciones* and uniting political power into a single body run by the federal government. Thereafter, the mayor of Mexico City was appointed directly by the president of the Mexican republic.

After seven decades as a badly managed appendage of the federal government, Mexico City's political reform began in 1989 with the birth of the Asamblea de Representantes del Distrito Federal (Legislative Assembly), housed in the old federal Congress in the Centro. After

arduous negotiations, the city took its first step in modern democracy by voting for the first full elections of the assembly and *jefe del gobierno* (mayor) on July 6, 1997.

In Mexico City's first open elections for governor of the city, Cuauhtémoc Cárdenas won 47 percent of the vote. On top of that, Cárdenas's leftist Partido de la Revolución Democrática (PRD) swept every single assembly district in direct vote. The PRI, PAN, and the smaller parties were able to capture seats only by proportional representation. Two years later, Cárdenas stepped down to pursue a run for the presidency and was followed in the mayoralty by another leftist PRD politician, Andrés Manuel López Obrador.

Since the beginning of elections for *jefe del gobierno* in Mexico City, the post has always been filled by PRD politicians. Though they are not without controversy, the party's progressive, populist politics have made some notable changes to the Distrito Federal, such as the introduction of the new aboveground bus system called Metrobús; the development of a financial-assistance program for single mothers and other vulnerable groups; and the restoration of much of the Centro Histórico. The PRD is also known for its socially progressive positions, which have led to the legalization of both same-sex marriage and abortion in the past decade.

In early 2016, the government announced that the Distrito Federal would now officially be named Ciudad de México, and that the city would be granted greater autonomy and more state-like powers, including the creation of a local congress and the drafting of a city constitution.

POLITICAL PARTIES
Partido Revolucionario Institucional (PRI)
Although the Institutional Revolutionary Party no longer maintains unilateral power in Mexican politics, it remains one of the most important political parties in the country. After its losses in 2000, it regained majority in the legislature in 2003 and retook the presidency in 2012. The PRI was traditionally considered a leftist party, espousing many of the socialist viewpoints common to Latin American governments. Over time, it has become more centrist, especially in its new role as an opposition party.

Partido Acción Nacional (PAN)
The National Action Party is a traditionally conservative party, established in the 1930s to protect the rights of the Catholic church. Economically, the PAN generally supports a market economy and free trade, and socially, they also toe a traditionally conservative line, opposing both same-sex marriage and abortion. The PAN grew strong among conservative voters in northern Mexico, and PAN candidates won the national presidency in 2000 and 2006.

Partido de la Revolución Democrática (PRD)
The Party of the Democratic Revolution is the most leftist of the three major political parties in Mexico, and it's associated with the organization Socialist International. The PRD grew out of the leftist opposition to the PRI, originally led by Cuauhtémoc Cárdenas. The party maintains an important presence throughout the country for its recent leadership in Mexico City's government, where PRD mayors have instituted strong urban-planning programs.

Other Parties
Aside from the three major political organizations, smaller parties in Mexico include the Labor Party and the Green Party, which also have representation in the Congress. In many cases, these smaller political organizations will work together with one of the three major parties to back a candidate. In 2005, the Labor Party officially backed PRD presidential candidate Andrés Manuel López Obrador. In 2000 the Green Party joined the PAN in supporting the president, Vicente Fox Quesada.

ECONOMY
Mexico City produces over 20 percent of Mexico's entire gross domestic product. Since the 1950s, Monterrey and Guadalajara have been developing industrial bases of their own, and in more recent decades, cities such as Puebla, Querétaro, Aguascalientes, Tijuana, and Toluca have been rapidly industrializing as well. But Mexico City completely controls the financial sector, as it's home to Bolsa Mexicana de Valores (the Mexican stock exchange) and all major banks and insurance companies. It also plays a big

role in the service economy and is the headquarters of all of the dominant media and communications conglomerates.

THE INFORMAL ECONOMY

As they have for generations, many new immigrants to the city begin their new urban lives hawking their modest wares from any street corner not already occupied by another seller. Driven in part by a desire to clean up the downtown area, city authorities have begun regular patrols to evict unlicensed vendors in the city's central districts. In addition to *ambulantes,* there are thousands of housekeepers, nannies, cooks, chauffeurs, and other household employees employed throughout the city as a part of the informal economy.

POVERTY

Mexico is a wealthy nation with abundant natural resources. Yet wealth is poorly distributed throughout the population, and vast extremes in the standard of living define the modern social landscape. Mexico City resident Carlos Slim was named the world's wealthiest person by *Forbes* magazine in 2010, yet 10 percent of Mexicans do not have access to sufficient food or medical care. According to government figures, more than 40 percent of Mexico's population lives below the poverty line. Mexico City, like the rest of the country, is a place of great extremes. You will see fashionable people dining in restaurants on a Monday afternoon, while children beg for change at a nearby traffic stop.

People and Culture

POPULATION

Accurate population statistics for Mexico City are difficult to obtain. According to the official 2010 census conducted by the National Institute of Statistics and Geography (Instituto Nacional de Estadística y Geografía; INEGI), there are 8,851,080 people living in Mexico City. If you extend the range to the entire metropolitan zone (which includes many densely populated areas of the state of Mexico adjacent the city, like the million-plus municipalities of Ciudad Nezahualcóyotl and Ecatepec de Morelos), INEGI counted 20.1 million inhabitants of Mexico City. Many estimates put the actual number much higher.

Mexico City's growth has slowed considerably since the 1970s, when its population was expanding at an average rate of 4.5 percent per annum. Throughout the 2000s, the city's population grew negligibly (and more slowly than the countrywide growth rate of 1 percent), and the most recent census numbers even show more people emigrating from the city than immigrating to it. In general, the population growth of the past 30 years has been in the outer edges of Mexico City, while the population of the inner core has been declining steadily.

CLASS AND ETHNICITY

A large, multiethnic country, Mexico has suffered from racial and class divisions throughout most of its history. In the colonial era, Mexican society was highly stratified: The most privileged class was that of the *peninsulares,* pure-blooded Spaniards born in Spain, followed by *criollos,* pure-blooded Spaniards born in Mexico. *Mestizos,* of mixed Indian-Spanish heritage, and *indios* (indigenous people) were afforded a lower social status and little political power.

Today, the vast majority of Mexicans are *mestizo,* or mixed race. Genetic studies have confirmed that most Mexicans are predominantly a mix of Spanish and indigenous American heritage; however, *mestizo* implies a mixed ethnic background, and it may include other ethnicities. To a much smaller extent than in the United States or the Caribbean, some African slaves were brought to New Spain during the colonial era, and they also mixed with the population. White Mexicans, comprising about 10 percent or less of the population, are generally Spanish descendants, though there have also been other waves of European migrants to Mexico over the course of the country's history, including Irish, German, and French, among others.

In the country at large, about 8-10 percent of the population identifies as indigenous, with around 6 percent speaking a native language. Nahuatl, the language spoken by the Mexica and many other people in the Valley of Mexico and the surrounding regions, is the most widely spoken indigenous language in Mexico. Nonetheless, it's been more or less erased in the capital; fewer than 2 percent of people in Mexico City speak a native language.

Today, social stratifications are not entirely inalienable, but social mobility is highly limited. In Mexico, your economic class will determine a great deal about your possibilities in life.

Lack of opportunities and hard economic realities make it far more difficult for the rural or urban poor to improve their economic situation.

INDIGENOUS PEOPLE AND CULTURES

An estimated 30 million people were living in Mesoamerica when the Spanish arrived in the 15th century. Immediately following the conquest, the native population was drastically reduced, both through violence and through diseases introduced by European settlers. Though many ethnic groups disappeared entirely, a significant indigenous population has survived to the present day, with the largest communities living in Oaxaca, Chiapas, Yucatán, Quintana Roo, Hidalgo, Puebla, and Morelos. About 6,700,000 people in Mexico speak an indigenous language, and many communities in remote or rural areas have maintained native customs, craftwork, and dress.

Mexico City draws a large number of indigenous immigrants, though their presence is largely subdued. You will rarely see people dressed in traditional clothing or speaking native languages, though there are some historic Nahuatl-speaking communities in the state of Mexico, as well in some of the small towns to the south of the city. For more information about Mexico City's indigenous communities, the Asamblea de Migrantes Indígenas de la Ciudad de México (Assembly for Indigenous Migrants to Mexico City) hosts educational events, cosponsors conferences, and gives workshops, including classes in native languages, in support of native people living in the capital (www.indigenasdf.org.mx).

While most Mexicans are fiercely proud of the advanced societies of pre-Columbian Mexico, native people have been highly marginalized since the beginning of the colonial era. Today, predominantly indigenous communities suffer from a lack of basic resources, education, and infrastructure. They are at a further disadvantage from a deeply embedded racism that has been perpetuated since the colonial area. Today, 75 percent of indigenous people live below the poverty line.

WOMEN

In Mexico, women and men share equality under the law. Second-wave feminism arrived in Mexico in the 1960s, and there are numerous nonprofit organizations working to improve conditions for women, socially and politically. In 1994, the EZLN's rebel army included male and female soldiers and commanders, and listed women's rights within its agenda for social justice. At the same time, the feminist movement in Mexico has never received a wide base of support.

There has traditionally been a large gender gap in Mexico's workforce, as many women leave school early in order to help out at home. In today's Mexico, economic realities, social changes, and increased education have changed women's relationship to the workforce, with women taking jobs in all sectors of society, from the small entrepreneur who cleans homes to the high-ranking political leader, as you'll see amply illustrated in Mexico City's workforce. At the same time, women earn less than men, across the board, and continue to play a larger role in the household.

HOMOSEXUALITY

Mexico is a generally accepting society, and most people are unlikely to raise a fuss about someone else's business. At the same time, the Catholic church has traditionally opposed gay and lesbian relationships, making it less acceptable for homosexuals to come out within conservative Catholic households. Today, as in many aspects of society, Mexican attitudes towards homosexuality are becoming more liberal. In the capital, gay marriage was legalized in 2008, and gay couples may legally adopt children. Popular support for same-sex marriage is split, with about half the country supporting it.

Generally speaking, the gay community is more visible and comfortably accepted in Mexico City than in most parts of Mexico. More and more, it is common to see same-sex couples holding hands while walking down the street or snuggling on a park bench.

RELIGION

After Cortés vanquished the city of Tenochtitlán, the Spanish razed the Mexica temples and built Catholic churches atop their remains. Coming from a deeply religious atmosphere in Spain (where the Inquisition was in full effect), colonial missionaries were active throughout New Spain, establishing an abundance of churches, Catholic schools, and hospitals. Throughout Spanish rule of Mexico, the Catholic church was one of the country's biggest landowners and a major player in politics. There were massive conversions among the indigenous population to Catholicism, which are said to have spiked after the apparition of the Virgin of Guadalupe in Mexico City in 1531. Today, according to INEGI, close to 85 percent of Mexicans identify as Catholic.

The Catholic church continues to hold a very important place in

Mexican society, even for those who aren't actively religious. Throughout the country, Catholic schools are among the best and most popular options in private education, while Catholic mass is the traditional celebration for life's milestones: baptism, important birthdays, marriage, and death. Catholic holidays are widely and exuberantly celebrated, with the entire country taking a vacation for the Holy Week and the Easter holidays.

One religious icon common to all of Mexico is the Virgin of Guadalupe. Worship of the image began in the early colonial era, after Juan Diego Cuauhtlatoatzin was said to have witnessed a dark-skinned Virgin Mary in a series of three visions at Tepeyac, a hill in northern Mexico City. Today, many Mexican churches are named for Our Lady of Guadalupe, who has become fused with Mexican identity. The official feast day for Guadalupe, December 12, is widely celebrated in Mexico City and throughout the country. After years of controversy, Juan Diego, the Mexica man who saw the vision of the Virgen de Guadalupe, was declared a saint in 2002.

OTHER RELIGIOUS GROUPS

Mexicans who don't identify as Catholic are generally Protestants and Evangelicals, who number at about 7.5 percent of the population. The country also has a small historic Jewish community. The majority of Jewish immigrants arrived in Mexico from Syria, the Balkans, and Eastern Europe at the end of the 19th century to the beginning of the 20th century. Today, an estimated 90 percent of the 40,000-50,000 Mexican Jews live in Mexico City, with notable communities in Condesa, Polanco, and Santa Fe, among other areas. The Comite Central Israelita de México (www.tribuna.org.mx) is the best source of news, information, and statistics about Mexico City's Jewish community.

LANGUAGE

Mexico is the largest Spanish-speaking country in the world. The type of Spanish spoken in Mexico is usually referred to as Latin American Spanish, in contrast to the Castilian Spanish spoken in Spain. Still, the Spanish here differs significantly from that of even other Spanish-speaking countries in the Western Hemisphere. While English is widely spoken in the service industry, first-time visitors are often surprised by how little English one hears in Mexico City compared to what might be encountered at popular beach resorts in Mexico. Visitors should take the time to learn at least enough Spanish to conduct everyday transactions, like ordering food in restaurants or paying for a bus ticket.

Mexican Spanish, and especially Mexico City Spanish, is extremely rich with slang expressions, unique tones of voice, and hilarious wordplay, and it is immediately recognizable to any other Spanish speaker, both because of its distinct character and also because of the prevalence of Mexican television and movies throughout Latin America. Many Anglicisms have crept into the Mexican language. For example, the common Latin American Spanish term for car is *coche,* but in Mexico you'll often hear *carro.*

Another distinctive aspect of Mexican Spanish is the great number of words incorporated from indigenous Mexican tongues, particularly Nahuatl, the language spoken by the Mexica. Among notable examples, the word *chocolate* comes from the Nahuatl word *chocolatl. Coyote* is a derivation of the term *coyotl*, also from the Nahuatl. (Both of these words have also been transferred from Nahuatl to English.) In Mexico, many indigenous plants or animals, like the *guajolote* (wild turkey) and *mapache* (raccoon), are still more commonly referred to by their indigenous names. In addition, Mexico retained many indigenous place-names after the conquest. Oaxaca, Guanajuato, Tlaxcala, and Cancún are a few of the many cities that have Castellan versions of the Nahuatl place-name—not to mention the name México itself, which took its name from the Mexica people of Tenochtitlán.

FESTIVALS AND EVENTS
JANUARY
Día de los Reyes Magos
On January 6, El Día de los Reyes Magos (Three Kings' Day), Mexican families exchange gifts and share a *rosca de reyes,* a wreath-shaped sweet bread topped with crystallized fruit. Reyes Magos is celebrated throughout the city, where you'll notice traditional bakeries selling hundreds of *roscas de reyes* in the days leading up to January 6.

FEBRUARY
Día de la Candelaria
On the Día de la Candelaria, celebrated annually on February 2, families dress up the baby Jesus from their nativity scene, then take him to church to be blessed before being stored till the next Christmas season. Whoever found the baby figurine in the *rosca de reyes* on Día de los Reyes Magos is responsible for taking the figure to church, as well as for inviting friends and family to their home for a party with tamales and *atole*. (While La Candelaria is a Catholic tradition, the tamales and *atole* may be related to a pre-Columbian festival to the rain god Tlaloc.) The feast is most enthusiastically celebrated in the neighborhood of Tacubaya, where all sorts of sweets, as well as myriad costumes for the baby Jesus figurines, are sold around the church Nuestra Señora de la Purificación, known locally as the Candelaria.

Zsona MACO
Since 2004, Mexico City has been home to a prestigious five-day contemporary-art fair known as Zsona MACO (México Arte Contemporáneo), with a roster of exhibitors coming from both the surrounding city and overseas, including some well-known names from New York and Europe. It's a high-quality and well-attended event, held in early February at the Palacio de Cultura Banamex in the Lomas de Sotelo neighborhood. Complete visitor information is available on the website (www.zsonamaco.com).

MARCH AND APRIL
Feria de la Flor Más Bella del Ejido
The southern neighborhood of Xochimilco celebrates the arts and floriculture with a weeklong festival every spring. Events include music and dance performances, a contest for the best-decorated *trajinera* (the traditional rafts used in Xochimilco's canals), and a local beauty pageant. Dates vary.

Festival del Centro Histórico de la Ciudad de México
This two-week cultural celebration has become one of the most high-profile artistic events in the country, held in public plazas, museums, and concert

venues across the Centro Histórico every March and April. The lineup includes concerts, theater performances, art exhibits, seminars, dance, culinary events, and activities for children, held in theaters, palaces, public squares, and museums downtown. Check out the lineup online (http://festival.org.mx).

Semana Santa

Easter week, or Holy Week, is one of the most important religious holidays of the year in Mexico. It is celebrated with enormous solemnity, tradition, and pageantry throughout the country, including in Mexico City—though many *capitaleños* also take advantage of the break in work or school to spend the week outside the city, at the beach or in the country.

The celebrations (and vacations) officially begin on Domingo de Ramos, or Palm Sunday, when hand-woven palm crosses and other adornments are sold outside the city's churches. The following Friday, Viernes Santo (Good Friday) is the single most important day of the season. (In fact, it's more likely that a restaurant or a shop will close on Good Friday than on Easter Sunday.) In Iztapalapa, a working-class neighborhood in southeast Mexico City, a very solemn and dramatic Passion Play is performed, with literally thousands of participants and even more spectators.

Unless you are planning to visit Iztapalapa, the main reason to visit Mexico City during the Easter holidays is to experience a notably quieter metropolis. Traffic is subdued, museums are close to empty, and you'll rarely need a reservation at a restaurant—though you'll often find restaurant and bar owners close up shop for the week, too.

MAY
Cinco de Mayo

This festival commemorates the defeat of an attempted French attack on Puebla, east of Mexico City, on May 5, 1862, by an improvised Mexican defense, including a Zacapoaxtla indigenous regiment, which fought with particular ferocity. The French invasion eventually succeeded, but the successful battle is celebrated with music, dance, food, and other cultural events, particularly in Puebla.

JUNE
Marcha Nacional de Orgullo LGBTTTI (National LGBTTTI Pride March)

The massively attended Marcha del Orgullo Lésbico, Gay, Bisexual, Travesti, Transexual, Transgénero e Intersexual (LGBTTTI) along the Paseo de la Reforma is usually held on the same weekend as New York City's pride festivities, in remembrance of the events at Stonewall Inn. The crowd gets as glammed up as the marchers, and the party continues late in the evening (and into the next day), especially in the Zona Rosa. More information is available at online (www.marchaorgullomexico.com.mx).

JULY
La Feria de Flores and La Fiesta de la Virgen del Carmen

The annual Feria de Flores is celebrated in San Ángel's Parque de la Bombilla every July, when the plaza is filled with hundreds of flower vendors, as well as food and crafts stands. The fair was initially linked to the neighborhood's annual celebrations for the Virgen del Carmen, which take place every July 16, in the Ex-Convento del Carmen.

SEPTEMBER
Día de la Independencia

Mexico celebrates its independence from Spain rule in 1810 on September 16. In Mexico City, the president of the republic appears on the balcony in the Palacio Nacional at 11pm on September 15, reenacting independence hero Miguel Hidalgo's cry for independence, "Viva México!"— also known as El Grito—to a crowd of thousands in the Zócalo below. There is a military parade through the Centro and along the Paseo de la Reforma the following day.

OCTOBER
Design Week Mexico

Established in 2009 with the objective to promote homegrown architects and industrial, graphic, and interior designers, Design Week Mexico has expanded tremendously since its inception, now attracting many international visitors to the program of artist talks, exhibitions, and public installations. In 2015, the Museo de Arte Moderno mounted an exhibition dedicated to influential midcentury architect Pedro Ramírez Vázquez, while dozens of local designers showed their work in a temporary "pavilion" made of shipping containers in Parque Lincoln in Polanco, among other events.

NOVEMBER
Día de Muertos

Día de Muertos, or Day of the Dead, is one of Mexico's most famous holidays, unique the world around. The name is actually a bit of a misnomer, as it is actually celebrated on two days: November 1 and November 2. In the days leading up to Día de Muertos, it is common to build altars in the family home, though you'll also see them in the lobbies of hotels, storefronts, restaurants, and other public places. In the Zócalo, massive altars are constructed by different nonprofit and cultural groups. On November 1 and 2, families gather at the municipal cemeteries to clean gravesites and leave flowers at the headstones of their deceased relatives.

The best-known Día de Muertos celebration in Mexico City is held in the village of San Andrés Mixquic, in the hills in the south of the city. Here, villagers prepare elaborate shrines and leave their doors open for two days so that friends, family, and passersby will visit. In culmination, at 8pm on November 2, the cemetery is lit up with candles in a beautiful event called La Alumbrada.

Día de la Revolución

The anniversary of the Revolution of 1910, November 20, is a national holiday. In Mexico City, there is a parade through the Centro commemorating the Revolution, including traditional shows of horsemanship and dance.

DECEMBER
Día de Nuestra Señora de Guadalupe

The feast day of the Virgin of Guadalupe, December 12, is one of the most important holidays across Mexico. On the days and weeks leading up to the 12th, groups of pilgrims can be seen walking toward the Basílica de Santa María de Guadalupe in northern Mexico City, often setting off noisy fireworks as they go. Special masses are held throughout Mexico, and in Mexico City, the area around the basilica is packed with thousands of pilgrims.

Las Posadas

Beginning on December 16, Mexicans hold nightly posadas—candlelight processions terminating at elaborate, community-built nativity scenes—in commemoration of Mary and Joseph's search for lodging. The processions continue for nine consecutive nights.

Navidad

The week between Christmas and New Year's Day is a quiet time in the Mexico City, when many residents leave the city for the holidays and restaurants, bars, and other businesses take advantage of the break to remodel or rest. Still, it can be a lovely and festive time to visit. The palaces around the Zócalo are beautifully decorated, and there is a massive, free ice-skating rink installed in the plaza during December.

The Arts

Mexico has rich and varied traditions in music, literature, visual arts, architecture, and film, as well as robust traditions in popular art, textiles, craft, and clothing. Both traditional and contemporary forms are celebrated in Mexico City, with fine art museums, popular art museums, concert halls, galleries, and festivals enthusiastically attended by locals.

FILM

Though Mexicans have been making films since the genre was invented, the 1930s and 1940s are known as the Golden Age of Mexican cinema. During this era, Mexican directors prolifically produced feature films, even surpassing Hollywood in international success during World War II. The glamorous and charismatic film stars of the Golden Age—Mario Moreno Cantiflas, Tin-Tan, Dolores del Rio, Pedro Infante, and Maria Felix, among others—are some of the country's most beloved personalities. In the 1940s and 1950s, Spanish filmmaker Luis Buñuel made many of his most celebrated films in Mexico, including *Los Olvidados*. Mexican film output began to decline by the mid-century, though a few experimental young filmmakers contributed to the canon, including Arturo Ripstein and Mexico-based Chilean-French filmmaker Alejandro Jodorowsky.

In the 21st century, Mexican film and filmmakers have made a prominent resurgence. In 2000, Alejandro González Iñárritu's widely acclaimed *Amores Perros* was heralded as the beginning of a new era in Mexican filmmaking, focused on gritty modern themes. The following year, Alfonso Cuarón's film *Y Tu Mamá También* was nominated for several Golden Globes and Academy Awards. Cuarón and González Iñárritu, like many of Mexico's filmmakers and actors, work extensively in Hollywood; González won Best Director at Cannes for his 2006 release, *Babel, while Cuarón took home the same prize for Gravity, in 2014.* Another lauded director from Mexico, horror film director Guillermo del Toro, won major accolades for his 2008 release, *El Laberinto del Fauno (Pan's Labyrinth)*.

POPULAR ART AND CRAFTS

Mexico has celebrated traditions in popular art and handicrafts, or *arte-sanía*. Most Mexican craftwork relies on centuries-old techniques that unite pre-Hispanic and Spanish aesthetics. Among other disciplines, Mexico is famous for textiles, weaving, embroidery, ceramics and pottery, blown glass, baskets, woodworking, toy-making, hammered tin, lacquered wood, shoemaking, and tooled leather.

Like most aspects of Mexican culture, traditional handicrafts are highly specific to the region in which they are produced. In Puebla, for example, the Spanish introduced tin-glazes and kiln-firing to skilled indigenous potters. The resulting blend of traditions created a New World version of Spain's decorative Talavera ceramics, but with more color and whimsy. In Tonalá, Jalisco, artisans create an entirely different line of burnished and painted pottery, much of which can be used for cooking.

LITERATURE

Elaborate hieroglyphic books and a priest-dominated literary tradition existed in the New World before the arrival of the Spaniards. Writing in the beautiful Nahuatl language, the poet-king of Texcoco, Nezahualcóyotl, was a prolific writer of verse, with many poems written by or attributed to him surviving today.

The fantastic chronicles of Spanish soldiers, explorers, and priests in the Americas show early expression of many enduring Mexican themes. Two examples of this genre, widely available in English translation, make for compelling reading. Bernal Díaz del Castillo's *Conquest of New Spain* is the memoir of a foot soldier in Cortés's military campaign against the Mexica empire. A very different view can be found in Bartolomé de las Casas's *Brevísima relación de la destrucción de las Indias* (Brief Account of the Devastation of the Indies), which details the astounding brutality that the invaders visited upon the people of what was then called the New World. De las Casas, a priest who accompanied many expeditions, raised the first voice of protest against Spanish destruction of native peoples and cultures.

After the conquest, Mexican-born writers continued to make a distinguished contribution to literature in Spanish. Baroque dramatist Juan Ruiz de Alarcón and writer Carlos de Sigüenza y Góngora were two important literary figures during the colonial era, but they are both surpassed in reputation by the beloved baroque poet Sor Juana Inez de la Cruz. *Respuesta a Sor Filotea* (Reply to Sister Philotea), in which she defends a woman's right to devote herself to the arts and poetry, has become a feminist classic.

During the 20th century, Mexico's national character was more strongly reflected in its literary traditions. Writers like Rosario Castellano and Juan Rulfo began to describe a distinctly Mexican environment, exploring the country's identity and consciousness. In the 1990s, Mexican poet and essayist Octavio Paz received the Nobel Prize in literature. His meditation on the Mexican people, *The Labyrinth of Solitude,* is his most famous work, though he is also remembered as an able poet. Another excellent observer of Mexican character and society is Carlos Monsiváis, whose *Rituales del Caos* is a collection of essays on life in Mexico City; it's available in Spanish only.

Two Colombian writers, Gabriel García Marquéz and Álvaro Mútis, garnered international acclaim for their fiction, which was set in Latin American locales and imbued with a distinctly Latin perspective. The fact that these two literary stars chose to live and write in Mexico City says much about the capital's intellectual environment. Another novel by a Latin American literary star that takes place mainly in Mexico City is *Los Detectives Salvajes,* by Chilean expatriate Roberto Bolaño. It offers a surprisingly accurate portrait of the city's subcultures.

MUSIC AND DANCE

Native Mesoamerican, African, and European musical traditions all contributed to development of unique New World music and dance. In Mexico, folk musical styles, or *sones,* developed in various regions, with diverse rhythms and instrumentation. From these *sones,* various genres of Mexican music flourished. Such song forms, like *huapango* from the Huasteca region, are still very popular throughout the country, though not often heard in Mexico City.

Mariachi, Mexico's most well-known musical ensemble, is a derivation of *son jarocho,* the musical genre from the state of Jalisco. Mariachi is characterized by its brassy sound and robust vocal style, as well as its impressive visual presentation. Dressed in formal *charro* suits and large sombreros, mariachi bands usually feature a lineup of violins, trumpets, guitars, bass guitars, and *jaranas* (a slightly larger five-string guitar). Mariachi music is a fixture at special events, like weddings or birthday parties, throughout Mexico.

Mariachis often play *rancheras,* traditional Mexican ballads, often covering nostalgic or patriotic themes. This song style became very popular in the late 19th and early 20th centuries, and again flourished in the 1940s and 1950s with popular *trío* bands such as Los Panchos and Los Diamantes.

One of Mexico's most popular and distinctive genres, *norteño* music grew out of the traditional *conjunto norteño,* an ensemble noted for its inclusion of the *bajo sexto* (a 12-string guitar) and the button accordion, an instrument that was introduced by German immigrants to northern Mexico. European styles, like polka and waltz, also influenced *norteño* music. Similar to *norteño,* the popular *banda* style incorporates more brass sounds. *Norteño* and *banda* groups, like the world-famous Los Tigres del Norte, have a massively popular following in both Mexico and the United States.

VISUAL ART AND ARCHITECTURE

Though most pre-Columbian cities were abandoned or destroyed by the 16th century, their ruins offer a glimpse into the accomplished architecture, city planning techniques, and artistic achievements of early Mesoamerica. The most distinctive features of Mesoamerican cities are the stepped temple-pyramids, seen in the Valley of Mexico at sites like Teotihuacán, which are often surrounded by wide public plazas and palaces.

As the Spanish began to colonize the Americas, they built new cities in the European style. Catholic missionaries and Jesuit educators were active throughout the country, and wealthy benefactors helped support their efforts by funding massive religious projects. Baroque art and design, which originated in Italy, was the dominant aesthetic during the colonial era. Inside chapels, religious oil paintings and elaborate retablos (altarpieces) show enormous creativity and skill on the part of Mexican artists. Among the most famous names of the era, indigenous artist Miguel Cabrera contributed hundreds of religious paintings to chapels in Mexico City, Guanajuato, and other colonial capitals.

The French occupation and the ensuing dictatorship of Porfirio Díaz also left a mark on the country's architecture, especially in the capital. Emperor Maximilian oversaw the construction of the Paseo de la Reforma in Mexico City, a large and central avenue that was designed to resemble a Parisian boulevard. During his decades of presidency, Porfirio Díaz followed in the emperor's footsteps, investing in buildings, monuments, and sculptures that would transform Mexico City into a European-style capital, which also included neoclassical buildings.

At the same time President Díaz was constructing marble monuments, a new and more national strain of art was emerging in Mexico. The wildly original printmaker José Guadalupe Posada produced political and social satire in lithography, woodcut, and linocut for local publications, often depicting Mexican aristocrats as *calaveras* (skeletons). His wry wit and whimsical aesthetic would become synonymous with Mexico, and today, his pieces are often used as illustration during Day of the Dead.

After the Revolution of 1910, art, culture, and intellectual thought flourished in Mexico. Through progressive movements in government, the folk arts began to receive institutional support, while a new, government-sponsored public murals program brought artists Diego Rivera, José Clemente Orozco, and David Alfaro Siqueiros to a greater public and international fame. American photographer Edward Weston spent extensive time living and working in Mexico, not long before Manuel Álvarez Bravo began photographing nationalistic scenes in Mexico, rising to international prominence. A fixture in Mexico City's political circles, Frida Kahlo was another expressive oil painter of the post-revolutionary era; she became internationally renowned for a series of powerful self-portraits.

Today, Mexico has a vibrant and growing contemporary art scene. Mexico's most celebrated international artist, Gabriel Orozco, presented a massive retrospective at the New York Museum of Modern Art in 2009, not long after he opened the gallery Kurimanzutto in the capital with a team of partners. The wildly famous British artist Damien Hirst lives part-time on the Mexican coast (and has exhibited in Mexico City), while Belgian genius Francis Alÿs lives and works in Mexico City. Collectors have also been important in stimulating Mexico's art scene, particularly Eugenio López Alonso, the owner of the Colección Jumex, a vast and important collection of Latin American and contemporary art.

ESSENTIALS

Getting There

AIR

AEROPUERTO INTERNACIONAL BENITO JUÁREZ

The Aeropuerto Internacional Benito Juárez (55/2482-2424, 55/2482-2400, www.aicm.com. mx) is on the east side of the city near the highway to Puebla. Both domestic and international flights leave from either of two main wings, Terminal 1 and Terminal 2, each used exclusively by different airlines. A light rail track connects the terminals in case you end up on the incorrect side of the airport, though they are fairly distant; before leaving for the airport, check with your carrier to see which terminal your airline operates from.

Though it rarely gets much attention, inside the "Sala B" in Terminal 1, there is a mural by Mexican artist Juan O'Gorman illustrating the history of flight, from a Mexica nobleman eyeing the wings of a bat with curiosity to the Wright brothers and Charles Lindbergh.

Mexico City's airport

ALTERNATIVE AIRPORTS

In some cases, you can save a little bit of money by traveling to an airport near the capital, rather than flying directly into Mexico City itself. Notably, the international airport in Toluca (www.vuelatoluca.com) has become a popular inexpensive alternative for travelers heading to Mexico City from national destinations like Cancún, Acapulco, Guadalajara, and Los Cabos. You may also be able to find international flights to and from the city of Puebla on major carriers, though they are rarely much cheaper than flights directly to the capital.

GETTING TO AND FROM AEROPUERTO INTERNACIONAL BENITO JUÁREZ

Taxi

Registered taxis operate out of the airport, with service 24 hours a day, 365 days a year. Official airport taxis are more expensive than regular cabs, but they are the only legal option available (non-airport taxis are not allowed to pick up passengers within the terminals).

There are several safe, registered taxi companies that operate out of the domestic and international wings in Terminal 1 and in Terminal 2, which offer flat-rate prices to destinations throughout the city. There is little difference between one airport taxi company and another. Buy a ticket from one of the booths inside the airport terminal, then take your ticket curbside to the queue of waiting taxis, where attendants will take you to a car and help you load your luggage (it's customary to offer a small tip to the porters). Generally, taxis costs about US$15-20 to most central neighborhoods, and several dollars more if heading south to Coyoacán or San Ángel.

Metro and Metrobús

If you're arriving in Mexico City between 6am and midnight and don't have a lot of baggage, you can take the

Metrobús

Metro into town from the Terminal Aéreo station, on Line 5. The station is just outside Terminal 1, on the Boulevard Puerto Aéreo, at the corner of Avenida Capitán Carlos León González. (Follow the signs for the Metro out of the airport; they look like a stylized letter *M*.)

The Metrobús also connects to the airport via an extension of Line 4. There are stops for the Metrobús heading into the city center at door 7 in Terminal 1 and at door 2 in Terminal 2. The first major hub on Metrobús Line 4 is the San Lázaro station, which connects to the Terminal Central del Norte bus station, as well as to the Metro. You can also continue on Line 4 to the Buenavista train terminal, which offers connecting service to the Metro, to Metrobús Line 1, or to the suburban trains to the state of Mexico. Metrobús operates roughly from 5am to midnight.

Intercity Bus

Several bus companies offer direct routes from the airport to the nearby cities of Toluca, Pachuca, Puebla, Cuernavaca, and Querétaro. They depart from both the international wing of Terminal 1 and from the ground floor of Terminal 2. Follow the signs to the ticket counters. Most buses run every half hour or hour throughout the day, with more limited but continuing service at night. Rates and schedules are available on the airport's website (www.aicm.com.mx).

Driving

The airport is just off the eastern side of the Circuito Interior, an intercity highway that is easily accessible from most major neighborhoods in the center, west, and south of the city. The best route from most central neighborhoods is via the Viaducto, a highway that cuts east to west across the center of the city; just south of the airport, there is a left-hand exit onto the Circuito. Once on the Circuito, the airport exit is clearly marked, but follow signs to make it to the correct terminal and wing. There are parking lots in the domestic and international wing of Terminal 1 and in Terminal 2, with rates of about US$4 per hour and US$25 for 24 hours.

BUS

For both visitors and Mexicans, buses are the most popular and economical way to travel around Mexico. Dozens of private companies offer service to almost every corner of the country, with literally hundreds of buses leaving from and arriving in Mexico City every hour.

Unless you are going a very short distance, first-class or executive-class bus service is generally faster and more comfortable than second-class service. First-class buses have more comfortable seats, fewer stops, and in-cabin bathrooms—some even offer snacks and drinks for the ride. Second-class buses are 20 to 40 percent cheaper than first-class buses, and they are generally comfortable and safe. The disadvantage of second-class buses is that they rarely offer direct service

between two cities. Instead, they stop at rural towns along their route to pick up and drop off passengers, adding considerably to travel time.

That said, second-class buses can be more convenient for shorter trips, with many bus lines offering frequent and inexpensive service between neighboring towns. In some cases, they are the only option to a more off-the-beaten path destination.

INTERCITY BUS STATIONS

There are four major bus terminals in Mexico City, located at the four major exits from the city. Each is accessible by Metro, and some by Metrobús.

For northern destinations, including Querétaro, San Miguel de Allende, Guanajuato, Zacatecas, Chihuahua, Monterrey, and Tijuana, buses depart from the **Terminal Central del Norte** (Eje Central Lázaro Cárdenas 4907, www.centraldelnorte.com), also called **Los Cien Metros.** The Terminal Central del Norte is accessible via the Autobuses del Norte station on Metro Line 5.

Terminal Central Sur "Taxqueña" (Av. Taxqueña 1320) is a smaller station serving southern destinations, like Cuernavaca, Acapulco, and Taxco, accessible via Metro Line 2 Tasqueña station. Taxqueña also connects to the Tren Ligero (light rail) to the southern neighborhoods of the city.

Terminal de Autobuses de Pasajeros de Oriente, better known as "TAPO" (Calz. Ignacio Zaragoza 200), offers service to eastern and southeastern cities, like Oaxaca and Puebla. To get there, take Metro Line 1 or Metrobús Line 4 to the San Lázaro station.

Terminal Centro Poniente (Av. Sur 122) has departures to Toluca, Valle de Bravo, Morelia, Guadalajara, and Puerto Vallarta, and is connected to the Observatorio Metro station on Line 1.

When arriving by bus, all stations have authorized taxi services operating in the terminal. Only authorized taxis are legally permitted to pick up passengers at a bus station, and it's always better to take an authorized taxi anyway; bus stations are prime scouting sites for taxi thieves.

BOOKING BUS TICKETS

For trips to major cities nearby (such as Puebla, Toluca, or Cuernavaca), buses depart from Mexico City every 20-30 minutes throughout the day, so it's generally unnecessary to make advance reservations. If you are going to destinations with less frequent service or are traveling during the holidays, it's best to get your ticket beforehand. Contact ADO (800/702-8000, www. ado.com.mx) for Oaxaca, Puebla, Chiapas, Veracruz, Yucatán, and other southern destinations. Autobuses Pullman de Morelos (55/5445-0100, www.pullman.mx) runs buses to Cuernavaca and Acapulco. For northern destinations, including Tepozotlán, Guadalajara, San Miguel de Allende, Guanajuato, Zacatecas, Puerto Vallarta, and more, use ETN (800/800-0386, www.etn.com.mx) or Primera Plus (800/375-7587, www. primeraplus.com.mx).

DRIVING
DRIVING TO AND FROM QUERÉTARO AND POINTS NORTH

Take Paseo de la Reforma west past Chapultepec to the Periférico, turn north on the Periférico, and follow it all the way past Ciudad Satélite and Tlalnepantla, keeping an eye out for Querétaro signs. It's also possible to follow the Eje Central north from downtown, but this is sometimes more complicated and with more traffic. Returning to the city, stay on the Periférico around the northwest side of the city and either get off at Paseo de la Reforma (for Polanco, the Zona Rosa, and the Centro) or continue farther south on the Periférico for San Ángel and Coyoacán.

DRIVING TO AND FROM TOLUCA AND VALLE DEL BRAVO

Paseo de la Reforma and Avenida Constituyentes (a major avenue parallel to Reforma but farther south) both lead directly to free and toll highways to Toluca. The toll road costs US$5 for the 16-kilometer stretch to La Marquesa (one of the most expensive tolls in the country for the distance), where it meets back up with the free road. Coming in from Toluca, keep an eye out for signs directing you to Reforma (for Polanco, Paseo de la Reforma, or the Centro Histórico) or Constituyentes (for Condesa, Roma, or anywhere in the south of the city).

DRIVING TO AND FROM CUERNAVACA AND ACAPULCO

Both Avenida Insurgentes and Calzado Tlalpan (the southern extension of Pino Suárez, the road on the east side of the Zócalo) lead directly to both the free and toll highways to Cuernavaca. Tlalpan is usually faster as there are more lanes and fewer stoplights, but Insurgentes is simpler. Follow signs for the *cuota* or toll road; it costs about US$8, bypassing the scenic yet incredibly slow and somewhat dangerous free highway.

DRIVING TO AND FROM PUEBLA AND OAXACA

The easiest way to get to the exit to Puebla is to take Pino Suárez and Tlalpan south, turn off on the Viaducto Miguel Alemán heading east, and follow the signs to Puebla. Returning to the city, paradoxically, it's a bit of a trick to find the entrance to the Viaducto, whereas following Izazaga and then Fray Servando into the city center is fairly straightforward. The toll road to Puebla costs US$5 and allows you to avoid all the curves and slow trucks on the free highway.

DRIVING TO AND FROM TEOTIHUACÁN

Getting out on the highway to the ruins northeast of Mexico City is simple: Take Avenida Insurgentes north and keep going straight. At the first tollbooth, Pachuca drivers stay to the left, while those going to Teotihuacán stay to the right.

Getting Around

Depending on where you're going, there are ample transport options, including buses, microbuses, taxis, Uber, Metro, Metrobús, and light rail. Getting around Mexico City on public transportation is cheap, efficient, and generally safe. Within each neighborhood, walking is the best way to see everything.

METRO

Mexico City's extensive underground Metro system (www.metro.df.gob.mx) is a reliable, ultra-cheap, and safe way to travel both short and long distances. Almost all of the city's central districts have at least one Metro stop in the vicinity, and daytime service on most lines is frequent, with one train arriving minutes after another has departed the station.

Mexico City's Metro is incredibly easy to use. The system's 11 color-coded lines run in a web across the city, intersecting at key points, with each stop marked by a visual icon as well as a name. In the station, signs marked Correspondencia indicate the walking route to transfer train lines; to know where to go, look for the name of the final station in the direction you are going.

You buy individual tickets for each ride on the Metro at in-station *taquillas* (ticket counters). At a cost of US$0.25 per ticket, it is the most inexpensive major urban subway in the world, and the second-busiest, after Tokyo. It runs 5am-midnight on weekdays, 6am-midnight on Saturday, and 7am-midnight on Sunday.

PEAK HOURS

Riding the Metro can be considerably more difficult when the trains are full. Peak hours vary by line, but most tend to get shockingly crowded at centrally located stations at the beginning and the end of the workday. Sometimes, it can be close to impossible to board, and the crowds of waiting passengers on the platform simply watch a series of full-to-the-brim trains pass by. In general, riding the Metro is particularly challenging during the weekday morning rush hour, 7am-9:30am, and in the evenings 5:30pm-7:30pm.

CUSTOMS AND SAFETY

Unfortunately, getting on and off a train is a bit of a free-for-all, especially during rush hour. Riders are not known for their courtesy when boarding crowded cars, so you need to be proactive if you want to exit; most people will not make space for you to pass. Pickpockets are also not unknown on the Metro. Keep an eye on your belongings.

WOMEN'S CARS

Women traveling alone, both foreign and Mexican, may receive unwanted attention on the Metro. Particularly disturbing, some women are groped on crowded subway cars. To avoid these problems there are train cars specially designated for women and children only, which operate during peak hours on some Metro lines, generally located at the rear of the train.

METROBÚS

Metrobús (www.metrobus.cdmx.gob.mx) is a high-speed bus service that runs on dedicated lanes along major city avenues. For destinations along Insurgentes, including Roma, Condesa, San Ángel, and UNAM, the Metrobús can be a far more convenient option than the Metro.

The first line of the Metrobús opened on Avenida Insurgentes in 2005. There are five more Metrobús lines, which may come in handy if traveling beyond the regular central neighborhoods. Particularly, the circular route that runs between the TAPO bus station and the Buenavista train station passes a number of popular attractions on its way through the Centro Histórico and past the Alameda Central.

Note that in order to service the most popular stations along these routes, not every bus that runs along a Metrobús line covers the full route. Along Insurgentes, for example, some buses will only go as far as the Glorieta Insurgentes or the Buenavista train station before returning south. Look for the bus's end point posted above the windshield.

Most Metrobús lines operate 5am-midnight Monday-Friday and 6am-midnight on the weekends, though hours vary slightly by route. Like the Metro, the Metrobús can become intolerably packed during peak hours. Though it is slightly less hectic than the below-ground free-for-all, it is nonetheless more comfortable to avoid the Metrobús 7am-9am and 5:30pm-7:30pm.

The fare for Metrobús is about US$0.50 flat rate, with free transfer between lines. Unlike for the Metro, you do not buy individual tickets for each ride but a prepaid electronic Metrobús card, which you fill up with credit and then scan at the entrance. There are machines where you can buy or refill a Metrobús card in each station.

SUBURBAN LIGHT RAIL

Some outlying neighborhoods in the north and south are serviced by light-rail lines. In the south, the Tren Ligero (www.ste.df.gob.mx) departs from the Tasqueña Metro station, running to Estadio Azteca and Huichapan 6am-7pm Monday-Saturday, 7am-8pm Sunday, and from Tasqueña to Xochimilco 6am-11pm Monday-Saturday, 7am-11pm on Sunday.

The Ferrocarril Suburbano de la Zona Metropolitana (Estación

Terminal Buenavista, Av. Insurgentes Norte and Eje 1 Norte, 55/1946-0790, www.fsuburbanos.com) offers frequent passenger-train service to the Valley of Mexico, to points between Cuautitlán and the Buenavista train terminal, located at Avenida Insurgentes Norte in Colonia Buenavista (and accessible via Metro Buenavista).

Volkswagen taxi

TAXI

There are three types of taxis in Mexico City: roving taxis *libres,* hailed on the street; *sitio* taxis, which are based at a fixed station; and radio taxis, reached by telephone. By law, all taxis (except for private car services, which sometimes operate from high-end hotels) are equipped with *taxímetros* (taximeters).

TAXIS LIBRES

Metered *taxis libres* roam the street picking up passengers. Most are painted white and pink, per city regulation, though you'll still see some red-and-gold (the previous color scheme) sedans circulating the streets. Taxis hailed on the street in Mexico City have a bad reputation, with good reason. Though not particularly common, there have been many armed muggings in taxis, for both foreigners and locals. In almost any circumstance, it

is better to take a registered taxi, either a *sitio* or a radio taxi.

In the case that you do take a street taxi, check that the driver has a taxi-meter and *tarjetón* (identification card) in the window with a license number, keep the window rolled up and doors locked (most robberies involve an accomplice), and give clear directional instructions to the driver. Be sure the driver turns on the meter as soon as you start driving.

Street taxis charge US$0.80 (about 9 pesos) as a base rate, then about a peso per 250 meters or 45 seconds—roughly US$0.40 per kilometer. After 11pm and until 6am, taxis are legally allowed to charge an additional 20 percent on the fare. Most have special meters with a night setting. If it's late, taxi drivers may refuse to turn on their meter and will instead want to negotiate a price. Although this is technically illegal, it's common practice.

SITIO, RADIO, AND HOTEL TAXIS

Safer alternatives to street cabs are the city's abundant *sitio* (pronounced SEE-tee-yoh) taxis and radio taxis, which operate with a fleet of registered drivers. You'll find *sitios* all over the city, except in the Centro Histórico. *Sitios* often have a curbside kiosk nearby where dispatchers log the taxis in and out, though some do not. *Sitios* are legally allowed to charge a slightly higher price than *libres,* with a base fare of about US$1.50 and an additional US$0.50 per kilometer. There are *sitios* at all four major bus terminals in Mexico City, as well as a number of *sitios* operating at Benito Juárez International Airport. Radio-dispatched *sitios,* or radio taxis, reached by telephone, with service to and from anywhere in the city, are

SITIOS AND RADIO TAXIS

It's always safer to take registered or *sitio* taxis than to hail cabs on the street in Mexico City. Like regular taxis, *sitios* and radio taxis run on a metered rate, with a base cost and per-kilometer charge that is slightly more expensive than the regular cabs circulating in the street. Where can you find a *sitio*?

Sitios operate at Benito Juárez International Airport and inside each of the four major bus stations. At the airport and bus stations, you buy your ticket and pre-pay for the ride before heading to the queue on the street, where you will be escorted to a taxi. Within the city, you can always ask a hotel or restaurant to call you a secure taxi; most have a company they use often and trust. Alternatively, you can go directly to a *sitio* or call a cab yourself. (Note that there are few *sitios* in the Centro Histórico, so it's best to ask a hotel or restaurant to call you a car.)

SITIOS
ZONA ROSA
Taxis Genova
Liverpool at Genova, 55/5207-4751

POLANCO
Taxis Moliere
Moliere at Horacio, 55/5280-9153

ROMA
Taxi Radio Mex
Merida at Guanajuato, 55/5574-3368 or 55/5574-3520

CONDESA
Servi Taxis
Parque España at Veracruz, 55/5516-6020
Sitio Parque México
Michoacán at Avenida México, 55/5286-7129 or 55/5286-7164

DEL VALLE/NAPOLES
Sitio Parque Hundido
Porfirio Díaz at Insurgentes, 55/5598-8000 or 55/5598-1019

RADIO TAXIS
Radio Union
55/5514-2850 or 55/5514-8074
www.taxisradiounion.com.mx

considered the safest way to travel. Radio taxis charge a base rate of about US$2.50 and about US$0.60 per kilometer or 45 seconds.

In addition to city-licensed taxis, most high-end hotels work with private-car services; these are the most expensive cabs by far, usually charging a flat rate between destinations, though they are safe and can be very comfortable. The cars are usually unmarked, four-door sedans, and the drivers often speak some English.

Some are licensed tour guides as well, who will offer a flat rate for a day trip to places like Teotihuacán or Xochimilco with tour services included.

UBER

Uber operates in Mexico City, and is generally a safe, pleasant, and inexpensive way to get around. Uber charges a flat rate between destinations, and often arrives within minutes. In order to use the service, you need to use the

Uber app on your phone, which is connected to a credit card. Download it, and make sure you have roaming capabilities on your phone.

BUS

In addition to the Metro and Metrobús, there are several types of buses in the city, from large city buses to smaller microbuses called *peseros*. In general, visitors to the city will not need to use regular city buses to reach destinations in the central districts, but they can come in handy if you are traveling to La Villa or other destinations in greater Mexico City.

To find the right bus for your destination, start by looking at the placards posted in the front window. Usually, only the end of the route is listed (along with, in some cases, major destinations along the way), so you most likely will have to ask drivers where they stop. At the end of each Metro line, huge corrals of *peseros* and smaller VW-bus *combis* depart for destinations around the edge of the city.

CAR

Driving in Mexico City can be a challenge at first, particularly because of the city's size and circuitous topography. Not to mention, maddening traffic jams can halt your progress for hours on end. Fortunately, *chilangos,* though perhaps a little heavy-footed on the gas, aren't particularly reckless drivers. Armored cars, city buses, and taxis can occasionally be aggressive (practice defensive driving!), but those who have driven in other large, chaotic cities will find Mexico City negotiable with the proper maps or GPS navigator in tow.

One essential factor to peaceful driving in the city is to choose your hours carefully. Mornings (8am-10am) can be very congested, while midday traffic is usually reasonable until around 4pm. During the week, late afternoon and early evening are the worst, particularly on the main commuter routes in and out of the city and in the Centro. Traffic begins to dissipate around 9pm, or earlier in the city center. The worst traffic of all is Friday afternoon, and even worse still if it's a *viernes quincena,* a Friday that coincides with the twice-monthly payday. Unpredictable demonstrations in various parts of the city—but particularly on Paseo de la Reforma, on Paseo Bucareli, and in the city center—also regularly tie up traffic.

NAVIGATION

As might be expected, learning your way around an urban area of several million inhabitants can be a bit confusing, but being familiar with a couple of major avenues can help you stay oriented. Avenida Insurgentes is the longest boulevard in the city and is a major north-south route crossing Mexico City. To the northeast, Insurgentes takes you to the exit for Pachuca and Teotihuacán, while to the south it continues past San Ángel to UNAM and the exit to Cuernavaca and Acapulco. Paseo de la Reforma is a broad avenue punctuated by large traffic circles (called *glorietas*) running northeast-southwest from the exit to Toluca to the Basílica de Santa María de Guadalupe.

The city is circled by two ring highways, the inner Circuito Interior and the outer Periférico. The Circuito makes a complete loop, although it changes names (Río Churubusco, Patriotismo, Revolución, and Circuito Interior) along the way. There are no freeways passing through the center of town, so the city has developed a system of *ejes viales* (axes), major thoroughfares that cross the city, with traffic lights (somewhat) timed, either east-west or north-south. *Ejes* are numbered and given a reference of *norte* (north), *sur* (south), *oriente* (east), or *poniente* (west). Other important roads that are not technically *ejes* are the east-west Viaducto Miguel Alemán and the south-to-center Avenida Tlalpan, both of which are major two-way arteries.

In addition to a good GPS system, the best tool for drivers is the *Guía Roji,* a bright-red book of maps and indexes of the city. It can be found in Sanborns department stores, as well as at many street corner newsstands, for about US$20.

HOY NO CIRCULA

Mexico City's "Hoy No Circula" ("Don't Drive Today") program has made major strides in reducing automobile emissions in the Valley of Mexico. Both the capital and Mexico state participate in the program, which prohibits cars from circulating on certain days of the week, based on the last letter of their license plate. Foreign-registered cars are not exempt from the program, nor are cars from other states of the republic. Failure to comply can result in hefty fines and even towing and impoundment of your car. Even for foreigners, there is no opportunity to claim ignorance; every driver has the responsibility to comply with the restrictions.

In 2016, the government extended restrictions, including Sunday for the first time. Be sure to check www.sedema.df.gob.mx for updated information.

The schedule is as follows:

- **Monday:** No driving if final digit is 5 or 6.
- **Tuesday:** No driving if final digit is 7 or 8.
- **Wednesday:** No driving if final digit is 3 or 4.
- **Thursday:** No driving if final digit is 1 or 2.
- **Friday:** No driving if final digit is 9 or 0.
- **Saturday:** First Saturday of the month, no driving if final digit is 5 or 6. Second Saturday of the month, no driving if final digit is 7 or 8. Third Saturday of the month, no driving if final digit is 3 or 4. Fourth Saturday of the month, no driving if final digit is 1 or 2. Fifth Saturday of the month (if applicable), no driving if final digit is 9 or 0.
- **Sunday:** In most cases, all vehicles may drive. Check www.sedema. df.gob.mx for updated information.

Local cars are required to have a decal bearing either a 0, 1, or 2. A 0 or 00 means the car is exempt from any days off, regardless of the license number, because it has passed emissions tests. A 1 requires the car to not circulate on one day, regardless of the conditions; and a 2 means the car cannot circulate on two days of the week during a pollution alert.

For cars with foreign plates, or for cars registered in states other than the state of Mexico or Mexico City, there are additional restrictions. The rules are as follows:

- Cars with license plates ending in 1 or 2: No driving 5am-10pm on Thursday.
- Cars with license plates ending in 3 or 4: No driving 5am-10pm on Wednesday.
- Cars with license plates ending

in 5 or 6: No driving 5am-10pm on Monday or 5am-11am Monday-Thursday.

- Cars with license plates ending in 7 or 8: No driving 5am-10pm on Tuesday or 5am-11am Monday and Wednesday-Friday.
- Cars with license plates ending in 0 or 9: No driving 5am-10pm on Friday or 5am-11am Monday, Tuesday, Thursday, and Friday.

Foreign-registered cars are not required to have decals, though like local cars, they may apply for exemption from the Hoy No Circula rules by passing emissions tests and receiving a "0" or "00" hologram from Centros de Verificación (Verification Center) run by the Secretaría del Medio Ambiente del Gobierno (the Environment Secretariat).

On rare occasions (such as for Christmas holidays), cars from outside Mexico City may be exempt from the circulation rules. Other times, when pollution levels are high, additional restrictions may be added to the program. Full schedules and rules are available (in Spanish) at the Environmental Secretariat's website: www.sedema.df.gob.mx.

OFFICIALS

Traffic cops, or *transitos,* respond to traffic accidents and issue citations for moving violations. When you're driving in Mexico, the transit cops may stop you. However, if your car is in Mexico legally, the papers are in order, and you haven't broken the law, it should be a fairly easy interaction. If you did break the traffic rules in some way, you will be issued a citation and fine, which you will pay in the transit office.

In addition to city police, there are *policía federal,* or federal police,

patrolling the intracity highways. Federal police can be helpful in the case of a roadside emergency or accident. If pulled over by a federal officer, you should have little problem if you have all your paperwork in order.

Another official service on the streets of the city is Apoyo Vial (Road Support), men and women in bright-yellow uniforms driving motor scooters. Funded jointly by the city and federal governments, Apoyo Vial helps out with emergency breakdowns, traffic accidents, and directing traffic in congested areas. Their services are free.

BRIBES

Mexico has developed a bad and not undeserved reputation for police corruption. The famous *mordida,* or bribe, has become so legendary that many foreigners reach for their wallet as soon as they see flashing lights in their rearview mirror. In reality, not every interaction with a traffic cop will necessarily end in extortion. In some cases, you will just receive a warning, and in others, a legal citation.

That said, extortion does happen. If you have committed a traffic violation, you may find yourself threatened with going to the *delegación,* the precinct house, if you don't pay a "fine" there and then—in other words, paying off the cop instead of dealing with the paperwork of an actual moving violation. If you find yourself in this position, you can simply insist on following proper legal channels and go to the *delegación* with the cop, or you can pay the bribe and go on your way. If you are confident of having done nothing wrong and insist on being taken to the *delegación,* there is a chance the cop will give up and allow you to go without any fine.

If you did do something wrong, you can still insist on doing everything by the books, though going down to the *delegación* is a several-hour ordeal. In general, do not offer bribes to federal police officers.

CAR RENTALS

There are many car-rental offices throughout the city and in the airport, as well as in the lobbies of some of the bigger hotels. In general, rental car prices are much more expensive in Mexico than in the United States. Mandatory insurance packages (which you are required to buy when you go to pick up the keys, even if they don't appear in an online booking) can triple the price of the rental. All told, a small car with unlimited mileage will run US$50-80 a day, sometimes less if you shop around. International companies operating in Mexico include Avis (www.avis.com.mx), Budget (www.budget.com.mx), and Dollar (www.dollar.com).

Many local rental agencies offer cars at lower prices than the U.S. agencies. A good option is Casanova Renta de Automoviles (Chapultepec 442, 55/5514-0449 or 55/5207-6007, Mon.-Fri. 8am-6:30pm, Sat. 8am-1:30pm; Patriotismo 735, Col. Mixcoac, 55/5563-7606, Mon.-Fri. 8am-6:30pm, Sat. 8am-1:30pm; www.casanovarent.com.mx), offering no-frills cars for 20-30 percent cheaper than big car-rental companies. Be sure to reserve ahead of time, as their good prices mean that they often sell out of options.

Visas and Officialdom

TOURIST PERMITS AND VISAS

Immigration paperwork is fairly straightforward for residents of most countries, whether they are planning a short-term or long-term stay in Mexico. For more detailed information, visit the website of the Secretaría de Relaciones Exteriores (www.sre.gob.mx/en) or the Instituto Nacional de Migración (www.inm.gob.mx).

ENTRY REQUIREMENTS

No advance permission or visa for travel to Mexico is required for the citizens of about 40 countries, including the United States, Canada, most of Europe and Latin America, New Zealand, and Australia. Citizens of these countries need only a valid passport to enter Mexico.

TOURIST PERMITS

Visitors who do not require a visa to visit Mexico are granted a six-month travel permit, officially known as the *forma migratoria multiple* (FMM) but unofficially referred to as a "tourist card," at the airport or border. If arriving by air, you'll receive the paperwork on the plane and your card will be ratified at the immigration desk when you land. If driving, stop at the immigration office at the border to get a tourist card.

Tourist cards are valid for travel in Mexico for up to 180 days. In most cases, the immigration official will automatically award you 90 or 180 days when you enter (you can request the full 180, if you need it). If you only get 90 days and need to extend your time, you can do so free of charge at any immigration office.

If you lose your tourist card while you are in Mexico, you can report it at an immigration office and pay a fine to replace it, or you can wait and pay the fine at the airport. If you choose to do the latter, leave ample extra time to check in and visit immigration before your flight.

CHILDREN TRAVELING ALONE OR WITH ONE PARENT

Children under the age of 18 entering Mexico unaccompanied by either parent must present a letter translated into Spanish and notarized by a Mexican embassy or consulate that gives the consent of both parents for the trip. The letter should include the dates of travel, the reason for the trip, airline information, and the name of the child's official guardian. The U.S. State Department further recommends that unaccompanied minors travel with a copy of their birth certificate or other documents that prove their relationship. In cases of divorce, separation, or death, the minor should carry notarized papers documenting the situation.

Rules regarding minors were originally established to help combat human trafficking and are therefore rather strict. Current information on minors traveling to Mexico can be obtained from the Mexican Embassy in the United States (http://embamex.sre. gob.mx/eua).

TOURIST VISAS

If you do not live in one of the 40 countries exempt from visa requirements, it is necessary to apply for a tourist visa in advance of arrival in Mexico. If you apply in person at a Mexican consulate, you usually can obtain a tourist visa on the day of application,

although for some countries it can take a couple of weeks. Legal permanent residents of the United States, regardless of nationality, do not need visas to visit Mexico for tourism.

BUSINESS VISAS

Citizens of Mexico's NAFTA (North American Free Trade Agreement) partners, the United States and Canada, are not required to obtain a visa to visit Mexico for business purposes. Instead you can receive a free NAFTA business permit (*forma migratoria NAFTA*, or FMN), which is similar to a tourist card, at the point of entry; it's valid for 30 days. To ratify your FMN, you must present proof of nationality (a valid passport or original birth certificate, plus a photo identification or voter registration card) and proof that you are traveling for "international business activities," usually interpreted to mean a letter from the company you represent, even if it's your own enterprise. Those who arrive with the FMN and wish to stay over the authorized period of 30 days must replace their FMN with an FM3 form at an immigration office in Mexico.

Citizens of non-NAFTA countries who are visiting for business purposes must obtain an FM3 visa endorsed for business travel, which is valid for one year. Visitors to Mexico coming as part of human rights delegations, as aid workers, or as international observers should check with a Mexican embassy about current regulations.

OVERSTAYS

If you overstay your visa, the usual penalty is a fine of about US$50 for overstays up to a month. After that the penalties become more severe. When crossing a land border, it's rare that a Mexican border official asks to see your FMT or visa. The best policy is to stay up to date in spite of any laxity of enforcement.

NON-IMMIGRANT VISAS (FM3)

Far and away the most popular visa option for foreign residents of Mexico is the *forma migratoria 3*, or FM3. There are several categories of FM3, but all of them classify holders as non-immigrant residents of Mexico. FM3s are the type of visa issued to most retirees, employees, and business owners. The benefit of an FM3 is that it allows you to come and go from Mexico as you please, and there is no minimum residency requirement.

You must apply for an FM3 at the Mexican consulate in your home country. The applicant must submit a proof of citizenship (passport), proof of residence, three months of bank statements, five color photos measuring 2.3 by 3 centimeters (three looking directly at the camera and two in profile), and a proof of income.

STUDENT VISAS

Students who will be in Mexico for fewer than six months can use a tourist visa for the length of their stay. No special visa is required. Those planning to study in Mexico for a longer period of time may need to apply for a student visa, which is a variation of the FM3 (application procedures are roughly analogous).

CUSTOMS
BASIC ALLOWANCES

Customs, or *aduana*, allows visitors to Mexico to enter the country with personal items needed for their trip, as well as duty-free gifts valued at no more than US$500. Personal effects may include two photographic or video cameras and up to 12 rolls of film, up to three cellular phones, and one laptop computer. The full list of permitted items is available at the Customs Administration, or La Administración General de Aduanas (www.aduanas.gob.mx). Most animal-derived food products are not permitted, including homemade foods, pet food or dog treats, fresh or canned meat, soil, or hay. Other food products are permitted.

If you are arriving by air, you will be given a customs declaration form on the airplane and will pass through the customs checkpoint right after immigration. Customs checks are performed by random selection. After collecting your luggage, you will be directed to a stoplight and asked to press a button. If you get a green light, you can pass. If you receive a red light, customs officials will open your luggage to inspect its contents. In larger airports, luggage is often passed through an X-ray machine, and passengers may be detained if a possible contraband item is detected.

There are severe penalties for carrying firearms to Mexico. Also note that narcotics are heavily regulated in Mexico, so if you have a prescription for painkillers or other controlled substances, carry what you'll need for personal use, along with an official note from your doctor. Sudafed and all pseudoephedrine-based decongestants are illegal in Mexico, so leave those at home.

Customs regulations can change at any time, so if you want to verify the regulations on a purchase before risking duties or confiscation at the border, check with a consulate in Mexico before crossing, or look on the customs website (in Spanish): www.aduanas.sat.gob.mx.

PETS

Mexico, the United States, and Canada share land borders, and therefore, as long as a cat or dog is in good health, there are no quarantine requirements between those countries. If you are bringing a cat or dog to Mexico, the animal must be accompanied by a certificate of health, issued by a licensed international veterinarian no more than 10 days before arrival in Mexico, and proof of a current rabies vaccination. Further, rabies vaccinations must be issued at least 15 days before entry but can be no more than a year old. If you're not coming from the United States or Canada, you must also present proof that the animal has been treated for worms and parasites. Bring a copy of your pet's vaccination record; customs officials may request it. If your pet does not meet health standards, it may be detained at the airport.

EMBASSIES AND CONSULATES

Most foreign embassies are located near the city center, with the majority of embassies concentrated in the Polanco and Cuauhtémoc neighborhoods, including the United States Embassy (Paseo de la Reforma 305, Col. Cuauhtémoc, 55/5080-2000, http://mexico.usembassy.gov), the Canadian Embassy (Schiller 529, Col. Bosque de Chapultepec, 55/5724-7900, www.canadainternational.gc.ca), Australian Embassy (Ruben

United States Embassy

Dario 55, Col. Polanco, 55/1101-2200, www.mexico.embassy.gov.au), and the British Embassy (Río Lerma 71, Col. Cuauhtémoc, 55/1670-3200, www.gov.uk/government/world/mexico). If you have trouble with the law while you are in Mexico, or your citizenship papers have been lost or stolen, you should contact your embassy right away.

POLICE

Officers in blue fatigues patrolling streets or parks are a part of the Protección Civil (Civil Protection), the local police force. In Mexico City, they are generally around to keep the peace in public spaces, as well as to respond to emergencies, break-ins, or other complaints. The police officers stationed in the Centro Histórico or along the Paseo de la Reforma are generally happy to answer questions or give directions to tourists as well.

Conduct and Customs

BUSINESS AND ETIQUETTE
TERMS OF ADDRESS

Mexicans are generally polite and formal when interacting with people they do not know well. When speaking to an elder or to someone with whom you will have a professional relationship, it is customary to use the formal pronoun *usted* instead of the informal *tú*. If you are unsure which pronoun a situation requires, you can always err on the side of caution by using *usted* with anyone you've just met.

It is also common practice to speak to someone you've just met using a polite title, such as *señor* for a man, *señora* for a married or older woman, and *señorita* for a young woman. When speaking with a professional, Mexicans may also use the person's professional title, such as *doctor/doctora* (doctor), *arquitecto/arquitecta* (architect), or *ingeniero/ingeniera* (engineer).

GREETINGS

When greeting someone in Mexico, it is customary to make physical contact, rather than simply saying "hello." A handshake is the most common form of greeting between strangers, though friends will usually greet each other with a single kiss on the cheek. The same physical gestures are repeated when you say good-bye. When greeting a group of people, it is necessary to greet and shake hands with each person individually, rather than address the group together.

If you need to squeeze past someone on a bus or reach over their shoulder at the market, it is customary to say *"con permiso"* (with your permission).

If you accidentally bump into someone (or do anything else that warrants a mild apology), say *"perdón"* (sorry).

TIME AND APPOINTMENTS

Mexico has a well-earned reputation for running on a slower clock. Certainly, there is less urgency in Mexico, and it is not considered excessively rude to arrive tardy to a social engagement. In fact, guests are usually expected to run about a half hour (or more) late for a party at a friend's home. However, when it comes to doctor's appointments, business meetings, bus schedules, or any other official event, punctuality is just as important in Mexico as it is anywhere else.

It should also be noted that, when it comes to social engagements, Mexicans will typically accept an invitation rather than decline, even if they don't plan to attend. Some Mexicans feel more self-conscious refusing an invitation than not showing up later.

TABLE MANNERS

When you are sharing a meal, it is customary to wish other diners *"buen provecho"* before you start eating. *Buen provecho* is similar to the well-known French expression *bon appetite*. If you need to leave a meal early, you should excuse yourself and again wish everyone at the table *"buen provecho."* Charmingly, many people will also wish other diners in a restaurant *"buen provecho"* on their way out. As in most countries, when sharing a meal, it is customary to wait for everyone to be served before starting to eat.

When dining out with friends or acquaintances, Mexicans rarely split the bill. Usually, one of the parties will treat the others. If you were the one to invite a friend or business associate to a meal, you should also plan to treat. Usually, whoever you've treated will pick up the tab the next time.

TIPPING

In a restaurant, wait staff receive a tip of 10-15 percent on the bill, though foreigners are generally expected to tip on the higher end of the scale. In bars, a 10 percent tip is standard.

Tipping of chambermaids is optional according to Mexican custom—some guests tip, and some don't, and it is less common in budget hotels. Remember that these folks typically earn minimum wage; even a small tip can be helpful. It is customary to tip porters at an airport or hotel several dollars per bag, or about US$5-10, depending on how far you are going and the size of your load. In nicer hotels, it is necessary to give a higher tip.

In most cases, it is not necessary to tip a taxi driver when traveling within city limits, though tips are always graciously welcomed, even if it's just a few pesos. At service stations, a small tip of about 5-10 percent is customary for gas station attendants (all gas stations are full service in Mexico).

SMOKING

Smoking tobacco (including electronic cigarettes) is prohibited in restaurants and bars throughout Mexico City. Though many people still smoke, they are required by law to smoke outside (patios, sidewalk seating, and open-air terraces located inside restaurants are all places where smoking is permitted). When the anti-smoking laws first went into effect, tough fines on establishments violating the policy helped ensure its widespread adoption throughout the city. However, as time passed, many establishments opened open-roofed segments of their restaurants or allowed patrons to smoke near entryways, leading to more lax rules.

DRESS

Mexicans are not particularly concerned with how visitors dress, but you will probably feel more comfortable if you conform to some basic standards. In Mexico City almost no one ever wears shorts; although this is mainly because of the cool year-round climate, it also demonstrates that *capitalinos* tend to be more formal in dress than Mexicans in other cities, especially those on the coast. Upon entering a church or chapel in Mexico, visitors are expected to remove their hats.

BUSINESS HOURS

Standard business hours are 8am to 6pm Monday through Friday, with lunch breaks taken between 1 and 3pm. Banks are usually open from 9am to 5pm Monday through Friday, though hours may be longer and include Saturdays at some branches. Though lunch breaks are common in a corporate environment, many small business owners will work in their shop from morning to night, without so much as a coffee break.

No matter what hours are posted for small businesses, the actual opening and closing times may vary with the whims of the proprietors. This is also true for tourist information offices. Banks usually follow their posted hours to the minute.

Health and Safety

FOOD AND WATER
FOOD SAFETY

Many first-time visitors to Mexico are particularly concerned with food safety. Getting sick from a serious food-borne illness or parasite isn't particularly common in Mexico City, especially if you use common sense when eating. However, a number of travelers do experience gastrointestinal distress or diarrhea while visiting Mexico.

Some visitors experience diarrhea or stomach upset during their time in Mexico City (or right after coming home). Changes in the food you eat and the water you drink, changes in your eating and drinking habits, and a new overall environment can cause unpleasant diarrhea, nausea, and vomiting. Because it often affects Mexico newcomers, gastrointestinal distress is called *turista* (tourist) in Mexico, and "traveler's diarrhea" in English. In many cases, *turista* can be effectively treated with a few days of rest, liquids, and anti-diarrhea medication, such as Pepto Bismol, Kaopectate, or Imodium.

To avoid turista, eat and drink with moderation, and go easy on foods offered by outdoor street vendors or market stands, because this is where you're most likely to suffer from unsanitary conditions. One rule of thumb is to eat street food only where you see a lot of other clients, which is a good indication of quality and also means there's a lot of turnover, so the food is fresh. Some people consume street food with no incident; others become ill after eating in markets or on the street. Use your discretion.

If the symptoms are unusually severe or persist for more than a few days, see a doctor. It could be a case of amoebic or bacterial dysentery. Most hotels can arrange a doctor's visit.

WATER QUALITY

Mexican tap water is treated and potable, yet it is generally considered unsafe for drinking, in part because of the unknown condition of most buildings' plumbing and water tanks. Hotels and restaurants serve only purified drinking water and ice. Bottled water, like all bottled beverages, is readily available and safe for drinking. You can also make tap water safe for drinking by boiling it for several minutes to kill any bacteria or parasites.

ALTITUDE SICKNESS

Some visitors who fly into the 2,240-meter (7,347-foot) Mexico City airport experience mild altitude sickness shortly after arrival. Symptoms include headache, shaky stomach, breathlessness, and general malaise. The body needs time to acclimate to the change in barometric pressure and lesser amounts of oxygen, and the air pollution can exacerbate the symptoms. If you feel ill, take it easy for a while: no running, no climbing pyramids, no alcohol. Some people find it takes them two or three days to fully adjust to the elevation when flying in from places at or near sea level.

DEHYDRATION

At a high altitude, it's important to drink plenty of water and other fluids to avoid dehydration. Alcohol and caffeine increase your potential for dehydration. Symptoms of dehydration include darker-than-usual urine or inability to urinate, flushed face, profuse sweating or an unusual lack thereof, and sometimes a headache, dizziness, and general feeling of malaise.

INFECTIOUS DISEASE

No vaccines are required for travel to Mexico City, though it's always a good idea to be up to date on routine vaccines. Some doctors recommend the hepatitis A vaccine for travel to Mexico. Hepatitis A affects the liver and is contracted from contaminated food or water. Symptoms may resemble the flu, though they are severe and may last several months. Typhoid is also contracted through contaminated food or water, though it's more of a concern in rural areas.

H1N1, or swine flu, was a major health concern in Mexico City in the spring of 2008. You may still notice hand sanitizers at the entryway in restaurants, and, of course, it is always best practice to wash your hands before eating. However, swine flu is no longer a major health concern in Mexico.

To date, the mosquito that carries the Zika virus is not found in Mexico City, owing to the city's high altitude.

MEDICAL ASSISTANCE

The quality of basic medical treatment, including dentistry, is high in Mexico City. Large hotels usually have a doctor on staff or a list of recommended physicians in the neighborhood. Polanco is the best area for private medical clinics, where a consultation will run US$25-60. Another good option is to call the Hospital ABC, which has a referral service for quality doctors of different specializations.

EMERGENCIES

In case of emergency, dial 911 from any telephone to reach an emergency dispatcher.

DOCTORS AND HOSPITALS

Hospital American British Cowdray (ABC) (Calle Sur 136, No. 116, 55/5230-8000 or 55/5230-8161, www.abchospital.com), at the corner of Avenida Observatorio, south of Bosque de Chapultepec in Colonia Las Américas, is considered one of the best hospitals in the city, and prices are accordingly high. Another well-regarded hospital is Hospital Español (Ejército Nacional 613, Polanco, 55/5255-9700 for ambulances and 55/5255-9600 general information, www.hespanol.com).

PRESCRIPTIONS AND PHARMACIES

Visitors to Mexico are permitted to carry prescription medication for pre-existing conditions among their personal effects. Generally, they can bring no more than a three-month supply of medicine with them, and it should be accompanied by documentation from a doctor. (There can be strict penalties, including incarceration, for tourists who are suspected of drug abuse.) Most common over-the-counter medication is available in Mexico. Drugs in Mexico are regulated and safe; there are also generic brands.

If you need to purchase prescription medication while you are in Mexico, you can visit a doctor, who will write you a prescription. Most Mexican pharmacies do not ask for prescriptions for the majority of medication, except for certain oft-abused substances. However, it is usually a better idea to get a prescription for medication, as the brands and dosages may differ in Mexico. If you'd like to take your meds home, rules for export depend on your home country.

There are pharmacies, or *farmacias,* throughout the city. Many are open 24 hours a day. All Sanborns department stores have an in-house pharmacy.

CRIME CONCERNS

Until the 1980s, Mexico City was known as one of the safest large cities in the Americas. The image suffered a reversal after the economic crisis of 1994-1995, when the peso plummeted, unemployment soared, and some urban residents began resorting to robbery and kidnapping. Since then, the city has maintained a poor image with regard to crime, which is not totally undeserved. Fortunately, the city has become much safer, and, with reasonable precautions, most visitors will feel entirely comfortable and safe throughout their stay.

PRECAUTIONS

In most cases, crime in Mexico City is economic—in other words, theft, break-ins, mugging, and pickpocketing are the most common problems. Crime can occur anywhere in Mexico City, even in affluent neighborhoods, but you can reduce the dangers by traveling by day or on well-lit roads, keeping an eye on your wallet and camera in crowded subway cars or busy markets, carrying a cell phone, and always taking registered taxis.

There have been rare but very troubling cases of taxi-related muggings and kidnappings, wherein taxi drivers shuffle unsuspecting passengers down dark side streets, where they are assaulted and robbed by organized gangs. To avoid taxi-related crimes, take registered taxis, called *sitios,* or Uber. There are safe registered taxi stands in the airport, in bus terminals,

and in every major neighborhood, and dozens of independent companies that will pick you up anywhere in the city.

After dark, you should be more cautious, especially when walking through unpopulated areas. The Centro Histórico is now patrolled by police officers in the evening, but it is best to stick to the areas to the west of the Zócalo, along the Alameda Central, or near the pedestrian street Regina if you are going out at night. After dark, avoid walking alone through the Doctores, Santa María la Ribera, Tabacalera, Guerrero, the areas around Plaza Garibaldi, and most of Juárez until you are better acquainted with the city. In the Roma, Condesa, and Polanco neighborhoods, there is less crime in the evening, especially in popular areas where crowds of diners and partygoers make the streets safe for walking. Nonetheless, it is wise to be on guard in the evenings, no matter where you are, and to avoid deserted streets or very late hours.

It's a good idea to carry limited cash and credit cards—no more than you need for an outing—when moving about the city, and don't wear ridiculously expensive-looking clothes or jewelry. Keep money and valuables secured, either in a hotel safe or safe deposit box, and lock the doors to your hotel room and vehicle.

When using ATMs as a source of cash, do so during the day or in well-lit, well-trafficked places. One reliable option is to use the Inbursa ATMs located inside Sanborns department stores. In general, don't change too much money at once.

Finally, if confronted by someone intent on robbing you, don't resist. Most Mexican thieves are simply out for quick cash. Violence is usually a problem only if you don't cooperate.

Travel Tips

STUDYING IN MEXICO
SPANISH LANGUAGE AND MEXICAN CULTURE

Mexico City is an excellent place to study Spanish, even if it hasn't traditionally been a popular choice with language learners. One of the major advantages of studying Spanish in Mexico City is having the opportunity to interact with a largely Spanish-speaking population on a daily basis. Here, using Spanish is a necessity in daily transactions, which is a huge asset to anyone with a serious drive to learn the language. There are also some excellent language-school options.

One of the best options is the prestigious Universidad Nacional Autónoma de México's Centro de Enseñanza Para Extranjeros (Center for Instruction for Foreigners), or CEPE, which offers blocks of intensive introductory, intermediate, and advanced Spanish-language classes, as well as culture and history courses. The programs enjoy a very good reputation and are divided among six departments: Spanish, Art History, History, Social Sciences, Literature, and Chicano Studies.

Universidad Nacional Autónoma de México (UNAM) also runs special training programs for teachers of Spanish as a Second Language (SSL). For all courses, tuition is reasonable, and CEPE can arrange housing either with local families or in dormitories. UNAM/CEPE also has a branch in Taxco (Ex Hacienda El Chorrillo s/n, Barrio del Chorrillo, Apartado Postal 70, Taxco, 762/622-0124, www.cepetaxco.unam.mx).

Universidad La Salle (Benjamin Franklin 65, Col. Condesa, 55/5728-0500, www.ulsa.edu.mx) offers good, inexpensive Spanish group classes and is closer to the center of the city than UNAM.

International House Mexico City is run by Language Link of Peoria, Illinois (U.S. 800/552-2051, fax 309/692-2926, www.langlink.com). Programs include classes in the Colonia Condesa and, if desired, homestays with a Mexican family.

ACCESS FOR TRAVELERS WITH DISABILITIES

Although the government has made some efforts to improve the situation, Mexico City is not an easy place for travelers with disabilities, particularly people with a limited range of movement. Many of the old, colonial-era structures that house hotels, restaurants, and museums do not have ramps or wheelchair access, nor do they have elevators inside the building. Using the Metro system can also be a challenge; currently only six stations (on Lines 3 and 9) have special platforms for people in wheelchairs. That said, there have been some positive developments in the city. The newer Metrobús system is a big improvement on the Metro, with ramps leading into all stations, audio-signaled pedestrian crossings, and information printed in Braille. Many public museums and cultural centers have added ramped entrances. With a little advance planning, visitors can also find a number of hotels and restaurants that have made special accommodations for visitors with disabilities.

TRAVELING WITH CHILDREN

Mexico City is a surprisingly kid-friendly, family-oriented place. There are plenty of great activities for kids in the city, from the wonderful children's museum in Chapultepec Park to the colorful Ballet Folklórico performances at the Palacio de Bellas Artes. Most restaurants welcome children, and you will see plenty of other kids touring museums and cultural centers with their parents. A few hotels do not allow children under a certain age, but others are more than happy to accommodate children with foldout beds in the rooms. Children under 5 ride for free on the Metrobús.

WOMEN TRAVELING ALONE

Women traveling alone will generally feel safe and comfortable in Mexico City, though they should take the same safety precautions they would take in any large city. Mexico is a social place, and unaccompanied women may be approached by men when dining alone at a restaurant or having a beer in a cantina—or even wandering through a museum. In

most cases, curiosity and the chance to flirt drives most of these interactions, and most would-be suitors will leave you alone if you aren't interested in chatting. That said, unaccompanied foreign women may also experience unwanted catcalling from men in the street. Generally, these interactions will not escalate, so the best tactic is to simply ignore the catcaller. In the rare case that you do feel unsafe, look for a nearby police officer or enter a well-lit restaurant or business.

GAY AND LESBIAN TRAVELERS

Gay and lesbian visitors will find a generally accepting, cosmopolitan environment in the capital. There is a large and relatively visible gay population in the city, with a particular concentration of gay bars and shops as well as expressly gay-friendly establishments in the Zona Rosa. Although many Mexico City residents are still relatively conservative Catholics, the attitude throughout the city is definitively one of tolerance; lately, it is not uncommon to see same-sex couples holding hands or kissing in public.

Information and Services

MONEY
CURRENCY

The unit of currency in Mexico is the peso, which comes in paper denominations of 20, 50, 100, 200, and 500. Coins are available in denominations of 5, 10, 20, and 50 centavos, and 1, 2, 5, 10, and 20 pesos. The $ symbol denotes prices in pesos. While it's highly unlikely you'll ever confuse dollar and

peso prices because of the differing values, you should ask when in doubt.

Paying in Dollars

A few commercial establishments in Mexico City will accept U.S. dollars as well as pesos. Paying with pesos, however, usually means a better deal when the price is fixed in pesos; if you pay in dollars for a purchase quoted in pesos, the vendor can determine the exchange rate.

Sales Tax

An *impuesto al valor agregado* (IVA, or value-added tax) of 16 percent is tacked onto all goods and services, including hotel and restaurant bills as well as international phone calls. Hotels may add a further 2 percent lodging tax. Most budget hotels include the IVA and hotel tax in their quoted prices.

CHANGING MONEY

In general, changing money is easy in Mexico City. The best way to get pesos is with an ATM card; they are accepted in *cajeros automático* (ATMs) in all Mexican and foreign-owned banks and invariably offer the best and most up-to-the-minute exchange rate. Some charge a rather hefty handling fee, however, so pay attention when clicking through the screens.

When using your ATM card, always choose an official bank (like Banamex, Santander, Scotiabank, Inbursa, Banorte, HSBC, or BBVA Bancomer). Recently, there have been reports that ATM and credit card numbers have been stolen and used for illicit withdrawals in Mexico. If you are dealing with an official bank rather than a standalone ATM, it will be easier to get the money credited back to your account in the unfortunate case that your number is used fraudulently.

Banks

Banks that handle foreign exchange generally accept a wide range of foreign currencies, including the euro, English pounds, Japanese yen, and Canadian dollars. Either cash or traveler's checks are accepted, though the latter usually guarantee a slightly better exchange rate. The main drawbacks with banks are the long lines and short hours—9am-3pm Monday-Friday, but the foreign-exchange service usually closes about noon-12:30pm.

Casas de Cambio

The second-best exchange rate, generally speaking, is found at the *casa de cambio*, or private money-changing office. Nowadays, these are far less common as most travelers carry ATM cards, but you can still see them in the airport. If you're going to change money at an exchange house, it pays to shop around for the best rates, as some places charge considerably more than others. The rates are usually posted; *compra*, always the lower figure, refers to the buying rate (how many pesos you'll receive per dollar or other foreign currency), while *vende* is the selling rate (how many pesos you must pay to receive a dollar or other unit of foreign currency).

The bank exchange booths at the Mexico City airport offer similar rates to banks and are open long hours (some stay open 24 hours), so the airport is a good place to change some money on arrival. You'll also find ATMs and *casas de cambio* in the airport.

MAPS AND TOURIST INFORMATION
MAPS

The government statistics institute, Instituto Estadísticas, Geografía e Información (INEGI) (Balderas 71, 55/5512-8331, Mon.-Fri. 9am-8pm; Patriotismo 711, 55/5278-1000; www.inegi.gob.mx), sells a variety of maps, as well as statistical yearbooks and other information resources. It also has a small store at the airport's domestic terminal.

Mexico City Maps

Most tourist-information kiosks offer small foldout maps of the city that point out noteworthy sites. You can pick them up for free at any tourist-information booth you see. For a highly accurate and detailed map of the city, the best option is the excellent *Ciudad de México Area Metropolitana,* a massive flipbook street atlas published by Guía Roji (www.guiaroji.com). It covers every corner of Mexico City and includes two complete indices, one by street name and one by *colonia* (neighborhood). You can buy the Guía Roji in many corner newsstands or in a Sanborns store, or order online from Mexico Maps (www.mexicomaps.com).

Highway Maps

Those planning to spend time on Mexico's back roads should buy a Mexican road atlas. The best available is the annual 127-page *Guía Roji por las Carreteras de México,* published in Mexico and available at newsstands and at Sanborns department stores. This atlas covers the entire country, including downtown maps of major city centers and a fairly complete network of unpaved roads, villages, and *ejidos* (communal farmlands).

TOURIST INFORMATION

Mexico City has its own tourist office, the Secretaría de Turismo de la Ciudad de México (Av. Nuevo León 56, 9th fl., Col. Hipódromo Condesa, 55/5286-9077, fax 55/5286-9022, www.mexicocity.gob.mx). For the most part this is an administrative office, so if it's information you need, you're better off visiting one of the several tourist suboffices (*módulos de información turística*) around the city and at the airport. These small offices usually stock a variety of free brochures, maps, hotel and restaurant lists, and information on local activities, and are staffed by Mexicans who are trained to handle visitor queries. Some speak very good English.

TIME, POWER, AND MEASUREMENTS

TIME

Mexico City time coincides with central standard time in the United States and is six hours ahead of Greenwich mean time (GMT -6). Between the first Sunday in April and the last Sunday in October each year, Mexico City changes by one hour to central daylight saving time.

Time in Mexico is commonly expressed according to the 24-hour clock, from 0001 to 2400 (one minute past midnight to midnight).

ELECTRICITY

Mexico's electrical system is the same as that in the United States and Canada: 110 volts, 60 cycles, alternating current (AC). Electrical outlets are of the American type, designed to work with appliances that have standard double-bladed plugs.

MEASUREMENTS

Mexico uses the metric system as the official system of weights and measures. This means the distance between Nogales and Mazatlán is measured in kilometers, cheese is weighed in grams or kilograms, a hot day in Monterrey is 32°C, gasoline is sold by the liter, and a big fish is two meters long.

COMMUNICATIONS AND MEDIA

POSTAL SERVICE

Correos de Mexico (www.correos-demexico.gob.mx), Mexico's national postal service, is known to be both erratic and slow. It can be reliable, if sluggish, for simple communications, like postcards. However, larger and more valuable items are at risk of loss or seizure. If they do arrive, months of delay are not uncommon. While it is certainly possible that the postal service will successfully deliver your package or letter, it isn't a particularly reliable way to communicate. If something absolutely must arrive in the hands of the recipient, you should pay more for a private service.

The Mexican post office offers a more reliable express-mail service called Mexpost. International rates are relatively high, but it is a good option for mailing communications within Mexico. The most atmospheric place to send a postcard is doubtlessly the grand old Palacio Postal (Tacuba 1, Mon.-Fri. 9am-6pm), which also has Mexpost services.

Palacio Postal

COURIER SERVICES AND SHIPPING COMPANIES

In most cases, you will have better luck shipping packages with private companies. They offer more reliable and fast (though also more expensive) ways to send letters and packages within Mexico and internationally. DHL, UPS, FedEx, and Mexican-owned Estafeta all offer national and international expedited shipping. In Mexico, DHL tends to be the most widely used and reliable service.

Though these companies have branches throughout the city, some convenient locations include DHL Internacional de México (Madero 70, Col. Centro, 55/5345-7000, www.dhl. com); Federal Express (República de Uruguay 17, Col. Centro, and Puebla 46, Col. Roma, 800/900-1100, www. fedex.com); and UPS de México (Paseo de la Reforma 34, Col. Juárez, 800/7433-877, www.ups.com).

The courier Estafeta Mexicana (Av. Insurgentes 105-9, Col. Juárez, 55/5511-0206) is an official agent of the U.S. postal service, which makes for reliable, lower-priced service to the United States.

TELEPHONE SERVICES

Ground lines are becoming increasingly uncommon in Mexico, as many people switch to the relative ease and lower upfront costs of cellular telephones. If you need to make local calls while you're visiting, many hotels will include calls to Mexico City landlines in the cost of a room. Because Mexico's cellular phone service operates on a different system, called El Que Llama Paga (Whoever Calls, Pays), calling a cell phone will incur an additional charge.

On the street, if you aren't using a cell phone, the best option is to use

DIALING

Making telephone calls in Mexico isn't always straightforward business. If your call won't go through, try adding a 1 or a 0 or an area code before the number you are trying to dial.

Here's a basic primer for dialing around the country and internationally. Area codes are called *lada* in Mexico.

LANDLINE TO LANDLINE IN MEXICO CITY
To dial from landline to landline within Mexico City, you need only to dial the eight-digit number, without an area code.

CALLING LAND LINES IN MEXICO CITY, GUADALAJARA, AND MONTERREY FROM ANOTHER CITY
Phone numbers in Mexico City are eight digits long, rather than the standard seven digits used throughout the rest of the country. However, the area code (55) is just two digits, so the full number is the standard ten digits long.

When dialing Mexico City from anywhere outside the city, you must mark the area code **55,** followed by the eight-digit number, for a total of ten digits. Guadalajara and Monterrey also have eight-digit numbers and two-digit area codes; their area codes are 33 and 81, respectively.

LANDLINE TO LANDLINE IN ANY OTHER CITY IN THE REPUBLIC
From the capital, to call a landline in another city, dial **01 + area code + seven-digit phone number.**

FROM LANDLINE TO CELL PHONE
To call a cellular phone from a landline in Mexico City, you must dial **044** before the phone number. If you are calling a cell phone in another city (in other words, long distance), put **045** before the number. If you are calling a cell phone from a payphone or from an international cell phone, you do not need to use any prefix.

FROM CELL PHONE TO LANDLINE
To call a landline from a cell phone, dial the **area code + phone number,** even if you are dialing from within the same city.

FROM CELL PHONE TO CELL PHONE
To call one cell phone from another, dial **1 + area code + phone number,** even if you are dialing from within the same city.

DIALING THE U.S. AND CANADA
To reach the United States or Canada, **dial 001 + area code + phone number.** (The country code is 1.)

DIALING ELSEWHERE INTERNATIONALLY
To call any country other than the United States or Canada dial **00 + country code + area code + phone number** for a total of 14 digits.

FROM OVERSEAS TO MEXICO
Mexico's country code is 52. To call Mexico from the United States or Canada, dial: **011 + 52 + area code + phone number.** If you are calling a Mexican cell phone from overseas, you usually must add a 1 before the area code and after the country code.

the public pay-phone service called **Ladatel** (an acronym for Larga Distancia Teléfono). Though they are increasingly going out of service, there are still plenty of Ladatel phones in the central districts. To use a Ladatel phone, you buy a card (for sale in pharmacies, stationery stores, bus terminals, supermarkets, or convenience stores) with prepaid credit, which you can then use at public phone booths.

International Calls

To direct-dial an international call via a landline, dial 00 plus the country code, area code, and number. Note that long-distance international calls are heavily taxed and cost more than equivalent international calls from the United States or Canada. Confirm prices with your hotel before dialing internationally.

The cheapest way to make long-distance international calls is via the Internet, using Skype or some other service, though most U.S. and Canadian carriers offer economical short-term service for visitors to Mexico.

FOREIGN CELL PHONES IN MEXICO

Considering the high costs of domestic telephones and cellular service, it is not surprising that roaming charges can be particularly high for foreign cell phones in Mexico. U.S. cell phones are generally locked to their carrier, so you will have to activate an international plan with your usual company if you want to use your U.S. cell phone in Mexico. If you plan to use Uber or navigation apps, be sure to purchase international data coverage as well.

Europeans and Canadians have the option of buying a Mexican SIM card for their unlocked phones. Once you have a Mexican chip, you can buy credit for your phone and make local calls. There are cell phone outlets throughout the city that will be happy to help you get it set up; they will sell you credit directly, or you can have credit charged directly to your phone at the register in OXXO or other convenience stores.

National Cell Phones

You can buy a new Mexican cell phone in Mexico City for about US$65, with call credit already on it—not an entirely unaffordable option if you're going to be making a lot of calls. When your credit expires, you can buy more credit at one of the thousands of cellphone outlets throughout the city or at the checkout counter at OXXO or another convenience store (you supply them with the number and pay, and they will immediately charge your phone with credit).

Note that Mexico's cellular phone service operates on a different system, called El Que Llama Paga (Whoever Calls, Pays). There are high surcharges for calling a cellular telephone, especially when you call a cellular phone in another city.

Email and Internet Access

Today, most hotels, coffee shops, and restaurants offer free wireless Internet connections to patrons. If you bring your computer, tablet, or smartphone, you should have no problem connecting it while you are in Mexico City.

If you'd prefer to travel without your laptop, cybercafés are an excellent and inexpensive alternative. Scattered throughout the city, these public computer terminals charge by-hour or by-minute rates to use the Internet on shared computers. It rarely comes to more than a few dollars an hour, and most have printing and scanning services.

MEDIA
Newspapers

Among the national Spanish-language dailies, *Reforma* and *El Universal* are the two most popular mainstream papers. *La Jornada* is a highly political, leftist paper, while *El Financiero* generally covers business and politics.

For local English-language news,

Mexico City-based newspaper *The News* is a tabloid-format paper covering national and international news, with a strong focus on the United States. It publishes stories from the news wires, in addition to its own reporting. Once a subsidiary of a Mexican newspaper, *Novedades,* it is now an independent publication.

Magazines

In Spanish, *Proceso* (www.proceso.com.mx) is a political magazine known for its crack reporting. Its stories on Mexican politics are often excellent. Two glossy weekly magazines are *Milenio,* which also has good international news stories, and *Cambio.*

International Publications

Newsstands in Mexico tend to be limited to national publications, though most airports and some bookshops will carry a wider range of imported titles like *Vanity Fair, Time, The Economist,* and other general interest magazines. The department-store chain Sanborns has a large newsstand, with dozens of national titles and many English-language titles as well.

Television

There are six broadcast networks in Mexico, four run by media conglomerate Televisa and two by TV Azteca. Channels run by Televisa and TV Azteca broadcast a mix of morning shows, news programs, sports, and American television series (usually dubbed into Spanish), as well as widely popular *telenovelas,* or soap operas, limited-run television dramas.

There are two excellent public television channels in Mexico City: the widely viewed Canal Once (Channel 11) and the Mexico City-based Canal 22 (Channel 22). These channels offer special programming on culture, politics, travel, and anthropology, in addition to airing high-quality movies and documentaries.

Radio

Mexico City has a long history of excellent radio and boasts hundreds of AM and FM stations. Radio Universidad, 96.1 FM and 860 AM, is run by UNAM and has excellent educational and musical programming. Another good radio station with news 24 hours a day is Formato 21, 790 AM.

RESOURCES

Glossary

abarrotes: grocery store
achiote: a seed used in traditional Yucatec cooking
adobado: a seasoned rub for meat
aduana: customs
aeropuerto: airport
agave: large Mexican succulent plant
agave azul: blue agave, used in tequila production
agua: water
aguas frescas or aguas de fruta: cold fruit drink
ahuehuete: cypress
almuerzo: meal eaten around midday
alquiler: rent
andador: pedestrian walkway
antigüedades: antiques
antojitos: snacks or appetizers
antropología: anthropology
antro: nightclub
arquitecto: architect
arte: art
artesanía: traditional handicraft
arrachera: Mexican skirt steak
atole: a sweet and hot beverage made with corn flour, often served with tamales
autobús: bus
autopista: highway
ayuntamiento: town council
azulejo: tile
bajo sexto: acoustic bass
banco: bank
baño: bathroom
barbacoa: pit-cooked lamb
barrio: neighborhood
biblioteca: library
billar: billiards, pool
birria: slow-roasted goat
boliche: bowling
bolillo: white roll
bomberos: firefighters
bosque: forest

botana: snack or appetizer, often served free with drinks at cantinas

buen provecho: an expression used to say "enjoy your meal"

café: coffee

café con leche: coffee with milk

café de chinos: traditional Chinese-run diner

café de olla: coffee prepared with unrefined sugar and cinnamon in a clay pot

cajero: cashier; automatic teller

caldo: broth

caldo de pollo: chicken broth

calle: street

callejón: alley

camion: bus, truck

canadiense: Canadian citizen

cantina: traditional bar or drinking establishment

capilla: chapel

capital: capital

capitaleño: capital resident (Mexico City resident)

carne: meat

carne asada: grilled meat

carnitas: braised pork

carretera: highway

casa: house

casa de cambio: currency exchange house

casita: small house

centavo: cent

centro historico: historic district

cempasuchil: marigold, a flower commonly used in Day of the Dead celebrations

cerveza: beer

ceviche: lime-cured fish

chapulín: grasshopper

charreada: traditional Mexican show of horsemanship and ranch skills, similar to rodeo in the United States

charro: traditional Mexican cowboy

chilacayote: figleaf gourd, a type of small squash

chilango: Mexico City resident

chilaquiles: fried tortilla strips bathed in salsa, cream, and cheese

chiles en nogada: poblano pepper stuffed with meat, dried fruit, and nuts, covered in creamed walnut sauce, and sprinkled with pomegranate seeds

chile relleno: stuffed chili pepper

chinicuiles: a caterpillar that inhabits the maguey cactus

chipotle: a smoky dried chili pepper, derived from fresh jalapeño pepper

churro: a tube-shaped sweet bread, deep fried and dusted in sugar

clínica: medical clinic

cochinita pibil: Yucatec-style pulled pork

cocina: kitchen

colectivo: shared taxi service

colegio: school (private)

colonia: neighborhood

comal: griddle

comedor: informal eatery

comida: the large midday meal in Mexico, typically eaten around 2pm

comida corrida: an economical, set-price lunch served in restaurants

comida yucateca: Yucatec food

convento: convent

consulado: consulate

correos: postal service

corrida de toros: bullfight

corrido: popular ballad

costo: cost

criollo: a term used in New Spain to describe a Mexican-born person of Spanish descent

Cruz Roja: Red Cross

cuarto: room (hotel)

cuarto doble: double room

cuarto sencillo: single room

cuenta, la: the bill, or check, at a restaurant

cultura: culture

cumbia: a traditional musical style from Colombia

curado: drink made with pulque, sweetener, and fresh fruit or other natural flavors

delegación: borough

depósito: deposit

desayuno: breakfast

Día del Amor y la Amistad: Valentine's Day

Día de Muertos: Day of the Dead

distrito: district

Distrito Federal: Federal District; former name for Mexico City

doctor, doctora: doctor

dulces: sweets

dulces típicos: traditional Mexican sweets

ejes vial: traffic axis, thoroughfare

ejido: communally owned land

elote: corn

embajada: embassy

entrada: appetizer

enviar: send (by mail)

escamoles: fire-ant eggs, a delicacy of pre-Columbian cooking

escuela: school

español: Spanish

esquites: corn on the cob, usually dressed with mayonnaise, grated cheese, and chile powder

estación: station

estacionamiento: parking

estadounidense: United States citizen

farmacia: pharmacy

feria: fair

ferrocarril: railroad

festival: festival

fideicomiso: bank trust

fiesta: party

fiesta brava: bullfighting

fiestas patrias: patriotic holidays

flan: egg custard dessert

flauta: deep fried and stuffed tortilla, topped with cream and salsa

flor de calabaza: squash flower

FM3: non-immigrant resident visa

FM2: immigrant visa

FMM: *forma migratoria multiple* (tourist card)

fonda: casual restaurant

fútbol: soccer

gachupín: Spanish person

galería: gallery

garnachas: snacks, street food

gordita: stuffed corn cake

gratis: free

gringa: a flour tortilla filled with melted cheese and meat

gringo: American

guayaba: guava

guayabera: a men's dress shirt from the Caribbean region

güero/a: light-colored; a fair-haired or fair-skinned person

guisado: stew or side dish

habitación: room (in hotel)

horchata: traditional drink made with ground rice, sugar, cinnamon, and water

huapango: a style of music typical to the Huasteca region

huarache: torpedo-shaped corn flatbread

huauzontle: a Mexican green vegetable

huésped: guest (as in a hotel)

huevo: egg

huevos a la mexicana: eggs scrambled with tomato, onion, and chili pepper

huevos rancheros: fried eggs in tomato-chili sauce

huipil: traditional women's tunic from southern Mexico

huitlacoche: corn fungus

iglesia: church

impuestos: taxes

indígena: indigenous person, or adj. indigenous

ingeniero: engineer

instituto: institute

IVA (impuesto al valor agregado): value added tax

jamaica: hibiscus

jarana: larger five-string guitar

jardín: garden

joyería: jewelry

lavandería: laundry

ley seca: dry law

libramiento: freeway

librería: bookstore

licuado: milkshake or fruit shake

limonada: limeade

llamada: call, phone call

llamada internacional: international phone call

llave: key

longaniza: a type of sausage

luchador: wrestler

lucha libre: wrestling

maciza: in *carnitas,* pork shoulder or leg

madre: mother

maestro: master; teacher

maguey: large succulent plant common in Mexico, used for making mezcal

majolica: tin-glazed pottery

mañana: tomorrow; morning

manta: lightweight cotton fabric frequently used in traditional Mexican clothing

manteca: lard

mariachi: a traditional Mexican music ensemble

masa: dough

mercado: market

mestizo: a person of mixed ethnic heritage

Metro: subway

Metrobús: high-speed bus service

mezcal: distilled spirit made from the maguey plant

mezcal de gusano: mezcal with the maguey worm inside the bottle

migración: immigration

mole: flavorful sauce made of ground nuts and spices.

mole negro: ground sauce made of chocolate, nuts, and spices, originally from the state of Oaxaca

mole poblano: ground sauce made of chocolate, nuts, and spices, originally from the city of Puelba

mollete: a *bolillo* topped with beans, cheese, and salsa

municipio: municipality

museo: museum

narcotraficante: drug dealer

navidad: Christmas

nevería: ice cream parlor

nieve: ice milk or ice cream

nopal: prickly pear cactus

noticias: news

padre: father

palacio: palace

pan: bread

pan árabe: pita

pan de dulce: sweet bread

papadzules: Yucatec tacos stuffed with hard-boiled egg

parada, parada de autobús: bus stop

parque: park

parroquia: parish

partido: political party

Partido Acción Nacional: National Action Party

Partido Revolucionario Institucional: Institutional Revolutionary Party

Partido de la Revolución Democrática: Party of the Democratic Revolution

pastor: taco preparation using chili pepper and spices

peatón: pedestrian

peninsular: colonial-era term for a person born in Spain

periodico: newspaper

pesero: small city bus

peso: Mexico's currency

picadillo: spiced ground beef

pico de gallo: salsa made of chopped tomatoes, onion, cilantro, and chili peppers

pipián: a sauce made of ground pumpkin seeds and spices

pirámide: pyramid

piso: floor

plata: silver

plaza: plaza or public square

plaza de toros: bullring

plazuela: small plaza

poblano: from the state or the city of Puebla

Porfiriato: historical period during the presidency of Porfirio Díaz

posada: inn

pozole: hominy soup

preparatoria: high school

presa: reservoir

presidente: president

priista: member of the PRI political party

primaria: primary school

propina: tip

Protección Civil: Civil Protection, or police

pueblo: small town

puesto: street stand or market stall

pulque: alcoholic drink made from fermented maguey

pulquería: traditional drinking establishment serving pulque

quelites: indigenous Mexican wild vegetables and greens

quesadilla: a warmed tortilla stuffed with cheese

queso: cheese

raicilla: a distilled spirit typical to the state of Jalisco

ranchera: musical style from northern Mexico

rebozo: shawl

receta: prescription

restaurante: restaurant

retablo: devotional painting or altarpiece

revista: magazine

rosca de reyes: a traditional fruitcake served on Three Kings' Day

ruinas: ruins

sangrita: a tomato-based chaser for tequila

santa escuela: a Jesuit school in the colonial era

salsa: sauce

salsa roja: condiment made with red tomatoes and chili peppers, or red chili peppers

salsa verde: condiment made with green tomatoes, chili peppers, and spices

sección amarilla: yellow pages

secretaría: secretary, secretariat

segundaria: secondary school

Semana Santa: Holy Week

señor: Mr. or mister; sir; man

señora: Mrs., madam; woman

señorita: Miss, young woman

siesta: nap

sitio: taxi stand

sombrero: hat

son: traditional musical styles

sopa: soup

sope: thick, round corn-based flatbread

sotol: a distilled spirit typical to northern Mexico

supermercado: supermarket

surtido: mixed

taco: seasoned meat or vegetables enclosed in a warm tortilla

tacos dorados: deep-fried tacos

tacos de guisado: tacos prepared with a variety of fillings

Talavera: hand-painted majolica-style pottery from Puebla, Mexico

tamal: tamale, or steamed corn cake (plural: tamales)

tamal oaxaqueño: tamale prepared in a banana-tree leaf in the Oaxacan style

taquilla: ticket counter

tarifa: fare

teatro: theater

telera: a flat, white bread roll used for *tortas*

templo: temple

tequila: a Mexican distilled spirit made from blue agave

tianguis: open-air market

tinga: a preparation of seasoned shredded meat

tintorería: dry cleaning

tlacoyo: diamond-shaped stuffed corn flatbread, a common street snack

tlayuda: a large Oaxacan tortilla stuffed with beans, cheese, meat, and salsa

torta: hot or cold sandwich served on a white *telera* roll

tortería: shop selling *tortas,* or hot or cold Mexican-style sandwiches

transito: transit

tranvía: trolley

Tren Ligero: light rail

tuna: prickly pear fruit
turismo: tourism
turista: tourist or traveler's diarrhea
universidad: university
vecindad: neighborhood
vendedor: seller
verano: summer
Viernes Santo: Good Friday
vino: wine
visa: yisa
xoconostle: sour prickly-pear fruit
zócalo: central square adjoined by a cathedral
zona arqueológica: archaeological zone

ABBREVIATIONS

Col.: *colonia* (neighborhood)

IMN: Instituto Nacional de Migración (National Institute of Immigration)
nte.: *norte* (north)
ote.: *oriente* (east)
PAN: Partido Acción Nacional (National Action Party)
PRD: Partido de la Revolución Democrática (Party of the Democratic Revolution)
PRI: Partido Revolucionario Institucional (Institutional Revolutionary Party)
prol.: *prolongación* (prolongation, usually of a city street)
pte.: *poniente* (west)
pp: *por persona* (per person)
s/n: *sin número* (without number, as in addresses)

Chilango Slang

The Spanish spoken in Mexico is lined with a rich vein of colloquialisms, slang expressions, and turns of phrase. Much Mexican slang used to come from working-class neighborhoods in the capital (especially Tepito), but nowadays there doesn't seem to be any particular neighborhood of origin. It remains, however, a singularly *chilango* (Mexico City) phenomenon, and is transmitted by the media to the rest of the country. In fact, because Mexican soap operas are by far the most popular in Latin America, people from other Spanish-speaking countries tend to understand a lot more Mexico City slang than would normally be expected.

A crucial aspect of understanding Mexican Spanish is the world of the *albur*, a sort of pun made at the expense of another. When a group of Mexican men are standing around talking, you'll notice one after the other is taking turns trying to twist someone's last phrase into some-

thing that will crack everyone else up. The trick is to make everyone laugh, but using clever phrasing, never just a straight insult or put-down.

As in Cockney English, another trick is to use words that sound similar to well-known swear words, thus making the meaning more acceptable, and more humorous, in polite company.

Rare is the foreigner who masters local slang enough to take part in this generally good-natured word competition, but it's entertaining to try. Just don't be surprised when suddenly everyone is laughing at you, and you're not quite sure why. Nothing to be done but laugh along with them.

aguafiestas: a spoilsport, a party pooper
aguas: watch out!
a huevo: definitely, for sure
antro: night spot, club
a toda madre: excellent
a todo dar: agreeable, wonderful
a todo mecate: similar to *a toda madre,*

but softer, as *madre* has a slightly vulgar connotation when used in this sense

banda: people, as in *mucha banda*, meaning a lot of people

bicla: bicycle

cabrón: a jerk, a mean person

caer gordo: dislike

caer el viente: to realize

cámara: same as *simón; cool*

cantar oaxaca: to vomit

carnal: good friend, literally "of the flesh"

chafa: poor quality

chale: multipurpose exclamatory interjection (such as "really?" "wow!" "no way!" "right on!"); often used as *"chale, mano"*

chamaco, chamaca: little boy, little girl

chamba: work

changarro: small business

chavo, chava: young man, young woman

chela: beer

chesco: soft drink

chido: cool, right on

chilango: someone from Mexico City

chingar: to "screw" somebody, in both meanings of the word

chingo: a whole lot

chingón: really excellent

choncho: big

chupar: to drink

colonia: neighborhood, in Mexico City (*barrio* is more common elsewhere in Latin America)

cotorrear: chat

cuaderno: friend (literally, notebook)

cuate: buddy, good friend

cuero: handsome, good-looking

dar el gatazo: looks right

de pelos: excellent

desmadre: a big mess, really screwed up

donas: two

dos tres: more or less

duques: two

en un ratón: in a while, a twist on *"en un rato"*

está cañón: a tough situation, a twist on

está cabrón, which means the same but is more vulgar

está del nabo: it sucks

está grueso: literally "it's fat," meaning "wow, heavy, that's serious"

fajar: to make out, to kiss

fresa: literally "strawberry," meaning a prissy, a snotty rich kid

gabacho: American

gachupín, gachupina: derogatory word for someone from Spain

guácala: gross

guacarear: to vomit

guapachoso: someone who likes tropical music

guarro, guarura: bodyguard

güero: fair-haired or fair-skinned

güey: dude, guy; common throughout Mexico, but used every other word by young *chilangos*, and even *chilangas*

hueva: a drag, something boring or tedious

jefe, jefa: father, mother

jetón: asleep

la chota: police

lana: literally "wool"; i.e., money

la neta: the best; also the truth, the real deal

la pura neta: even better

la puritita neta: better still

madral: many

mamón: stuck-up, arrogant person

mango: attractive

mano: short for *hermano* (brother) and the Mexican equivalent of "bro"

melón: 1,000,000 pesos

móchate: pass it along already, give me one, or give me some (often *móchate, güey* or *móchate, cabrón*)

naco: someone with bad taste

nave: literally boat, but slang for car

neta: the truth

ni madres: no way, not a chance

no canta mal las rancheras: isn't so bad himself/herself

no mames: vulgar, meaning "no way, get out"; invariably said as *no mames, güey*

no manches: means the same as *mames*, but twisted at the end to make it sound less crude

ojete: a strong, vulgar insult

órale: exclamation; "right on," "wow"

pachanga: big party

pachangear: to go partying

pacheco: stoned (i.e., smoking marijuana)

pedo: literally "fart," but meaning either "drunk" (*está bien pedo*) or a problem; i.e., *¿que pedo?* ("what's the problem?") or *no hay pedo* ("no problem")

pendejo: vulgar, insulting adjective, i.e., "idiot"

perro: as an adjective, something very difficult

perro: as a noun, a guy who sleeps around a lot

pinche: a vulgar adjective; e.g., *"¡Abre la pinche puerta!"* ("Open the @#! door!")

pitufos: literally "smurfs," meaning the blue-uniformed police

ponerse punk: to get mad, as in *no te pongas punk* ("don't get mad")

ponerse las pilas: literally "to insert batteries"; to motivate yourself

¿que hongo?: literally "what mushroom?," a play on *¿que onda?*

que mal viaje: what a drag, what a bad trip

¿que onda?: what's up?

que oso: literally "what a bear," but meaning "what a fool," as in, "what a ridiculous spectacle they're making of themselves"

¿que pasión?: twist on *¿que pasó?* ("what's happening?")

¿que pedo?: twist on *¿que pasó?* ("what's happening?")

que poca madre: "can you believe that?"

but with an indignant tone

¿que te picó?: literally, "what bit you?," meaning "what's the matter?" or "what's your problem?"

quiúbule: also "what's up?"; usually *"quiúbule, cabrón"* or *"quiúbule güey"*

rajar: a verb, meaning to back out of doing something, to bail

ratero: a thief (literally, "ratter")

rayarse: to be lucky

refinar: to eat

reventón: big party

rola: a tune, a song

se puso hasta atrás: he/she got thoroughly drunk

se puso hasta las chanclas: he/she got thoroughly drunk

simón: a play on the word *sí* (yes), but more hip and current; combination of "I agree" and "right on"

taco de ojo: someone attractive, nice to look at

tamarindos: the *tránsito* police, with brown uniforms

tirar la onda: try to hit on someone

tostón: 50 pesos

trancazo: a blow, a hard hit

tranzar: to deceive somebody

tripas: three

uñas: one

un milagro: 1,000 pesos

varos: pesos

vecindad: a grouping of apartments around a single courtyard, common in working-class Mexico City neighborhoods

vientos: "winds"; right on

vientos huracanados: "hurricane winds"; excellent

Spanish Phrasebook

Your Mexican adventure will be more fun if you use a little Spanish. Mexican folks, although they may smile at your funny accent, will appreciate your halting efforts to break the ice and transform yourself from a foreigner to a potential friend.

Spanish commonly uses 30 letters—the familiar English 26, plus four straight-forward additional consonants: ch, ll, ñ, and rr.

PRONUNCIATION

Once you learn them, Spanish pronunciation rules—in contrast to English—don't change. Spanish vowels generally sound softer than in English. (*Note:* The capitalized syllables below receive stronger accents.)

VOWELS

a like ah, as in "hah": *agua* AH-gooah (water), *pan* PAHN (bread), and *casa* CAH-sah (house)

e like ay, as in "may:" *mesa* MAY-sah (table), *tela* TAY-lah (cloth), and *de* DAY (of, from)

i like ee, as in "need": *diez* dee-AYZ (ten), *comida* ko-MEE-dah (meal), and *fin* FEEN (end)

o like oh, as in "go": *peso* PAY-soh (weight), *ocho* OH-choh (eight), and *poco* POH-koh (a bit)

u like oo, as in "cool": *uno* OO-noh (one), *cuarto* KOOAHR-toh (room), and *usted* oos-TAYD (you); when it follows a "q" the u is silent; when it follows an "h" or has an umlaut, it's pronounced like "w"

CONSONANTS

b, d, f, k, l, m, n, p, q, s, t, v, w, x, y, z, and ch pronounced almost as in

English; **h** occurs, but is silent—not pronounced at all

c like k as in "keep": *cuarto* KOOAR-toh (room), Tepic tay-PEEK (capital of Nayarit state); when it precedes "e" or "i," pronounce **c** like s, as in "sit": *cerveza* sayr-VAY-sah (beer), *encima* ayn-SEE-mah (atop)

g like g as in "gift" when it precedes "a," "o," "u," or a consonant: *gato* GAH-toh (cat), *hago* AH-goh (I do, make); otherwise, pronounce **g** like h as in "hat": *giro* HEE-roh (money order), *gente* HAYN-tay (people)

j like h, as in "has": *Jueves* HOOAY-vays (Thursday), *mejor* may-HOR (better)

ll like y, as in "yes": *toalla* toh-AH-yah (towel), *ellos* AY-yohs (they, them)

ñ like ny, as in "canyon": *año* AH-nyo (year), *señor* SAY-nyor (Mr., sir)

r is lightly trilled, with tongue at the roof of your mouth like a very light English d, as in "ready": *pero* PAY-doh (but), *tres* TDAYS (three), *cuatro* KOOAH-tdoh (four)

rr like a Spanish r, but with much more emphasis and trill. Let your tongue flap. Practice with *burro* (donkey), *carretera* (highway), and Carrillo (proper name), then really let go with *ferrocarril* (railroad)

Note: The single small but common exception to all of the above is the pronunciation of Spanish **y** when it's being used as the Spanish word for "and," as in "Ron y Kathy." In such case, pronounce it like the English ee, as in "keep": Ron "ee" Kathy (Ron and Kathy).

ACCENT

The rule for accent, the relative stress given to syllables within a given word, is straightforward. If a word ends in a vowel, an n, or an s, accent the next-to-last syllable; if not, accent the last syllable.

Pronounce *gracias* GRAH-seeahs (thank you), *orden* OHR-dayn (order), and *carretera* kah-ray-TAY-rah (highway) with stress on the next-to-last syllable.

Otherwise, accent the last syllable: *venir* vay-NEER (to come), *ferrocarril* fay-roh-cah-REEL (railroad), and *edad* ay-DAHD (age).

Exceptions to the accent rule are always marked with an accent sign: (á, é, í, ó, or ú), such as *teléfono* tay-LAY-foh-noh (telephone), *jabón* hah-BON (soap), and *rápido* RAH-pee-doh (rapid).

BASIC AND COURTEOUS EXPRESSIONS

Most Spanish-speaking people consider formalities important. Whenever approaching anyone for information or some other reason, do not forget the appropriate salutation—good morning, good evening, etc. Standing alone, the greeting *hola* (hello) can sound brusque.

Hello. *Hola.*
Good morning. *Buenos días.*
Good afternoon. *Buenas tardes.*
Good evening. *Buenas noches.*
How are you? *¿Cómo está usted?*
Very well, thank you. *Muy bien, gracias.*
Okay; good. *Bien.*
Not okay; bad. *Mal or feo.*
So-so. *Más o menos.*
And you? *¿Y usted?*
Thank you. *Gracias.*
Thank you very much. *Muchas gracias.*
You're very kind. *Muy amable.*
You're welcome. *De nada.*
Goodbye. *Adios.*
See you later. *Hasta luego.*
please *por favor*
yes *sí*
no *no*
I don't know. *No sé.*

Just a moment, please. *Momentito, por favor.*
Excuse me, please (when you're trying to get attention). *Disculpe* or *Con permiso.*
Excuse me (when you've made a boo-boo). *Lo siento.*
Pleased to meet you. *Mucho gusto.*
What is your name? *¿Cómo se llama usted?*
Do you speak English? *¿Habla usted inglés?*
Is English spoken here? (Does anyone here speak English?) *¿Se habla inglés?*
I don't speak Spanish well. *No hablo bien el español.*
I don't understand. *No entiendo.*
How do you say . . . in Spanish? *¿Cómo se dice … en español?*
My name is . . . *Me llamo…*
Would you like . . . *¿Quisiera usted…*
Let's go to . . . *Vamos a…*

TERMS OF ADDRESS

When in doubt, use the formal *usted* (you) as a form of address.

I *yo*
you (formal) *usted*
you (familiar) *tu*
he/him *él*
she/her *ella*
we/us *nosotros*
you (plural) *ustedes*
they/them *ellos* (all males or mixed gender); *ellas* (all females)
Mr., sir *señor*
Mrs., madam *señora*
miss, young lady *señorita*
wife *esposa*
husband *esposo*
friend *amigo* (male); *amiga* (female)
sweetheart *novio* (male); *novia* (female)
son; daughter *hijo; hija*
brother; sister *hermano; hermana*
father; mother *padre; madre*

grandfather; grandmother *abuelo; abuela*

TRANSPORTATION

Where is . . . ? *¿Dónde está . . . ?*
How far is it to . . . ? *¿A cuánto está . . . ?*
from . . . to . . . *de . . . a . . .*
How many blocks? *¿Cuántas cuadras?*
Where (Which) is the way to . . . ? *¿Dónde está el camino a . . . ?*
the bus station *la terminal de autobuses*
the bus stop *la parada de autobuses*
Where is this bus going? *¿Adónde va este autobús?*
the taxi stand *la parada de taxis*
the train station *la estación de ferrocarril*
the boat *el barco*
the launch *lancha; tiburonera*
the dock *el muelle*
the airport *el aeropuerto*
I'd like a ticket to . . . *Quisiera un boleto a . . .*
first (second) class *primera (segunda) clase*
round-trip *ida y vuelta*
reservation *reservación*
baggage *equipaje*
Stop here, please. *Pare aquí, por favor.*
the entrance *la entrada*
the exit *la salida*
the ticket office *la oficina de boletos*
(very) near; far *(muy) cerca; lejos*
to; toward *a*
by; through *por*
from *de*
the right *la derecha*
the left *la izquierda*
straight ahead *derecho; directo*
in front *en frente*
beside *al lado*
behind *atrás*
the corner *la esquina*
the stoplight *la semáforo*
a turn *una vuelta*
right here *aquí*

somewhere around here *por acá*
right there *allí*
somewhere around there *por allá*
road *el camino*
street; boulevard *calle; bulevar*
block *la cuadra*
highway *carretera*
kilometer *kilómetro*
bridge; toll *puente; cuota*
address *dirección*
north; south *norte; sur*
east; west *oriente (este); poniente (oeste)*

ACCOMMODATIONS

hotel *hotel*
Is there a room? *¿Hay cuarto?*
May I (may we) see it? *¿Puedo (podemos) verlo?*
What is the rate? *¿Cuál es el precio?*
Is that your best rate? *¿Es su mejor precio?*
Is there something cheaper? *¿Hay algo más económico?*
a single room *un cuarto sencillo*
a double room *un cuarto doble*
double bed *cama matrimonial*
twin beds *camas gemelas*
with private bath *con baño*
hot water *agua caliente*
shower *ducha*
towels *toallas*
soap *jabón*
toilet paper *papel higiénico*
blanket *frazada; manta*
sheets *sábanas*
air-conditioned *aire acondicionado*
fan *abanico; ventilador*
key *llave*
manager *gerente*

FOOD

I'm hungry. *Tengo hambre.*
I'm thirsty. *Tengo sed.*
menu *carta; menú*
order *orden*
glass *vaso*
fork *tenedor*

knife *cuchillo*
spoon *cuchara*
napkin *servilleta*
soft drink *refresco*
coffee *café*
tea *té*
drinking water *agua pura; agua potable*
bottled carbonated water *agua mineral*
bottled uncarbonated water *agua sin gas*
beer *cerveza*
wine *vino*
milk *leche*
juice *jugo*
cream *crema*
sugar *azúcar*
cheese *queso*
snack *antojo; botana*
breakfast *desayuno*
lunch *almuerzo*
daily lunch special *comida corrida* (or *el menú del día* depending on region)
dinner *comida* (often eaten in late afternoon); *cena* (a late-night snack)
the check *la cuenta*
eggs *huevos*
bread *pan*
salad *ensalada*
fruit *fruta*
mango *mango*
watermelon *sandía*
papaya *papaya*
banana *plátano*
apple *manzana*
orange *naranja*
lime *limón*
fish *pescado*
shellfish *mariscos*
shrimp *camarones*
meat (without) *(sin) carne*
chicken *pollo*
pork *puerco*
beef; steak *res; bistec*
bacon; ham *tocino; jamón*
fried *frito*

roasted *asada*
barbecue; barbecued *barbacoa; al carbón*

SHOPPING

money *dinero*
money-exchange bureau *casa de cambio*
I would like to exchange traveler's checks. *Quisiera cambiar cheques de viajero.*
What is the exchange rate? *¿Cuál es el tipo de cambio?*
How much is the commission? *¿Cuánto cuesta la comisión?*
Do you accept credit cards? *¿Aceptan tarjetas de crédito?*
money order *giro*
How much does it cost? *¿Cuánto cuesta?*
What is your final price? *¿Cuál es su último precio?*
expensive *caro*
cheap *barato; económico*
more *más*
less *menos*
a little *un poco*
too much *demasiado*

HEALTH

Help me please. *Ayúdeme por favor.*
I am ill. *Estoy enfermo.*
Call a doctor. *Llame un doctor.*
Take me to . . . *Lléveme a . . .*
hospital *hospital; sanatorio*
drugstore *farmacia*
pain *dolor*
fever *fiebre*
headache *dolor de cabeza*
stomach ache *dolor de estómago*
burn *quemadura*
cramp *calambre*
nausea *náusea*
vomiting *vomitar*
medicine *medicina*
antibiotic *antibiótico*

pill; tablet *pastilla*
aspirin *aspirina*
ointment; cream *pomada; crema*
bandage *venda*
cotton *algodón*
sanitary napkins use brand name, e.g., Kotex
birth control pills *pastillas anticonceptivas*
contraceptive foam *espuma anticonceptiva*
condoms *preservativos; condones*
toothbrush *cepilla dental*
dental floss *hilo dental*
toothpaste *crema dental*
dentist *dentista*
toothache *dolor de muelas*

POST OFFICE AND COMMUNICATIONS

long-distance telephone *teléfono larga distancia*
I would like to call . . . *Quisiera llamar a . . .*
collect *por cobrar*
station to station *a quien contesta*
person to person *persona a persona*
credit card *tarjeta de crédito*
post office *correo*
general delivery *lista de correo*
letter *carta*
stamp *estampilla, timbre*
postcard *tarjeta*
aerogram *aerograma*
air mail *correo aereo*
registered *registrado*
money order *giro*
package; box *paquete; caja*
string; tape *cuerda; cinta*

AT THE BORDER

border *frontera*
customs *aduana*
immigration *migración*
tourist card *tarjeta de turista*
inspection *inspección; revisión*
passport *pasaporte*

profession *profesión*
marital status *estado civil*
single *soltero*
married; divorced *casado; divorciado*
widowed *viudado*
insurance *seguros*
title *título*
driver's license *licencia de manejar*

AT THE GAS STATION

gas station *gasolinera*
gasoline *gasolina*
unleaded *sin plomo*
full, please *lleno, por favor*
tire *llanta*
tire repair shop *vulcanizadora*
air *aire*
water *agua*
oil (change) *aceite (cambio)*
grease *grasa*
My . . . doesn't work. *Mi . . . no sirve.*
battery *batería*
radiator *radiador*
alternator *alternador*
generator *generador*
tow truck *grúa*
repair shop *taller mecánico*
tune-up *afinación*
auto parts store *refaccionería*

VERBS

Verbs are the key to getting along in Spanish. They employ mostly predictable forms and come in three classes, which end in *ar, er,* and *ir,* respectively:
to buy *comprar*
I buy, you (he, she, it) buys *compro, compra*
we buy, you (they) buy *compramos, compran*
to eat *comer*
I eat, you (he, she, it) eats *como, come*
we eat, you (they) eat *comemos, comen*
to climb *subir*

I climb, you (he, she, it) climbs *subo, sube*

we climb, you (they) climb *subimos, suben*

Here are more (with irregularities indicated):

to do or make *hacer* (regular except for *hago*, I do or make)

to go *ir* (very irregular: *voy, va, vamos, van*)

to go (walk) *andar*

to love *amar*

to work *trabajar*

to want *desear, querer*

to need *necesitar*

to read *leer*

to write *escribir*

to repair *reparar*

to stop *parar*

to get off (the bus) *bajar*

to arrive *llegar*

to stay (remain) *quedar*

to stay (lodge) *hospedar*

to leave *salir* (regular except for *salgo*, I leave)

to look at *mirar*

to look for *buscar*

to give *dar* (regular except for *doy*, I give)

to carry *llevar*

to have *tener* (irregular but important: *tengo, tiene, tenemos, tienen*)

to come *venir* (similarly irregular: *vengo, viene, venimos, vienen*)

Spanish has two forms of "to be":

to be *estar* (regular except for *estoy*, I am)

to be *ser* (very irregular: *soy, es, somos, son*)

Use *estar* when speaking of location or a temporary state of being: "I am at home." *"Estoy en casa."* "I'm sick." *"Estoy enfermo."* Use *ser* for a permanent state of being: "I am a doctor." *"Soy doctora."*

NUMBERS

zero *cero*

one *uno*

two *dos*

three *tres*

four *cuatro*

five *cinco*

six *seis*

seven *siete*

eight *ocho*

nine *nueve*

10 *diez*

11 *once*

12 *doce*

13 *trece*

14 *catorce*

15 *quince*

16 *dieciseis*

17 *diecisiete*

18 *dieciocho*

19 *diecinueve*

20 *veinte*

21 *veinte y uno* or *veintiuno*

30 *treinta*

40 *cuarenta*

50 *cincuenta*

60 *sesenta*

70 *setenta*

80 *ochenta*

90 *noventa*

100 *ciento*

101 *ciento y uno* or *cientiuno*

200 *doscientos*

500 *quinientos*

1,000 *mil*

10,000 *diez mil*

100,000 *cien mil*

1,000,000 *millón*

one-half *medio*

one-third *un tercio*

one-fourth *un cuarto*

TIME

What time is it? *¿Qué hora es?*

It's one o'clock. *Es la una.*

It's three in the afternoon. *Son las tres de la tarde.*

It's 4am. *Son las cuatro de la mañana.*
six-thirty *seis y media*
a quarter till eleven *un cuarto para las once*
a quarter past five *las cinco y cuarto*
an hour *una hora*

DAYS AND MONTHS

Monday *lunes*
Tuesday *martes*
Wednesday *miércoles*
Thursday *jueves*
Friday *viernes*
Saturday *sábado*
Sunday *domingo*
today *hoy*
tomorrow *mañana*
yesterday *ayer*
January *enero*

February *febrero*
March *marzo*
April *abril*
May *mayo*
June *junio*
July *julio*
August *agosto*
September *septiembre*
October *octubre*
November *noviembre*
December *diciembre*
a week *una semana*
a month *un mes*
after *después*
before *antes*

(Courtesy of Bruce Whipperman, author of *Moon Pacific Mexico*.)

Suggested Reading

DESCRIPTION AND TRAVEL

Franz, Carl, and Lorena Havens. *The People's Guide to Mexico.* Berkeley: Avalon Travel, 2012. This guidebook to Mexico is really in a class by itself, a mix of wry observation, anecdotes, and hard-won travel advice. It's been republished countless times during its more than 40-year history in print.

Gerrard, A. Bryson. *Cassell's Colloquial Spanish: A Handbook of Idiomatic Usage.* New York: Macmillan, 1980. Not as out-of-date as the publication year might suggest, Cassell's explains common *vulgarismos* (slang) used in Mexico, Central America, and South America.

Hernandez, Daniel. *Down and Delirious in Mexico City.* New York: Scribner, 2011. An L.A.-based journalist chronicles his often-rowdy explorations into the underworld and counterculture of contemporary Mexico City.

Martinez, Ruben. *The Other Side: Notes from the New L.A., Mexico City, and Beyond.* New York: Vintage Books, 1993. A stimulating account of the growing pan-Latino culture extending from Los Angeles to El Salvador, with plenty of pop culture information on Mexico City.

Novo, Salvador. *Los Paseos de la Ciudad de México.* Mexico City: Fondo de Cultura Económica, 2005. This slim volume presents a mix of history, anecdotes, memories, and meditations on six iconic places in the capital, including the Alameda

Central and the street Bucareli. Spanish only.

FICTION

Bolaño, Roberto. *The Savage Detectives*. New York: Picador, 2008. The celebrated Chilean-born author lived for many years in Mexico, and this entertaining, thought-provoking novel is largely set in the capital city, capturing the metropolis's unique youth culture with surprising acuity.

Burroughs, William. *Queer*. New York: Penguin Books, 1987. Set mainly in Mexico City during the Beat era, this autobiographical novel fictionalizes Burroughs's flight to Mexico to avoid drug charges in the United States.

Fuentes, Carlos. *The Old Gringo*. New York: Farrar, Straus, Giroux, 1985. The most famous novel by celebrated writer Carlos Fuentes takes place during the Mexican Revolution.

Kerouac, Jack. *Mexico City Blues: 242 Choruses*. New York: Grove Press, 1990. Beat novelist and poet Kerouac lived intermittently in Mexico City during the 1950s, and he wrote parts of this seminal poem, as well as his novella *Tristessa*, in the capital.

Lida, David. *Travel Advisory*. New York: William Morrow & Company, 2000. A collection of 10 gritty short stories set in Mexico (several in Mexico City) from an American writer living in Mexico City.

Lowry, Malcolm. *Under the Volcano*. New York: Reynal & Hitchcock, 1990. Although it only sold two copies in two years when originally published in Canada in 1947, Lowry's tale of the alcoholic demise of a British consul in Cuernavaca has become a modern classic.

Poniatowska, Elena. *Tinisima*. Albuquerque: University of New Mexico Press, 2006. Using extensive historical research, Mexican essayist and intellectual Poniatowska reimagines the life of Italian-born film star, photographer, Edward Weston muse, and socialist revolutionary Tina Modotti in post-revolutionary Mexico in this moving book.

Taibo II, Paco Ignacio. *Return to the Same City*. New York: Mysterious Press, 1996. Mexico City's favorite eccentric mystery writer resurrects his detective protagonist, Héctor Belascoarán Shayne. The novel's 1993 predecessor, *No Happy Ending*, is also set in *la capital*.

FOOD

Adair, Marita. *The Hungry Traveler: Mexico*. Kansas City: Andrews McNeel Publishing, 1997. A pocket-sized Mexican culinary lexicon, with plenty of references to Mexico City and nearby states.

DeWitt, Dave, and Nancy Gerlach. *The Whole Chile Pepper Book*. Boston: Little, Brown and Co., 1990. Written by the editors of *Chile Pepper* magazine, this compendium of fact, lore, and recipes is the definitive culinary guide to chiles.

Gilman, Nicholas. *Good Food in Mexico City*. Bloomington: iUniverse, 2012. A listings-based guidebook to the city's taco stands, *fondas*, and restaurants by an American expatriate.

Muñoz Zurita, Ricardo. *Larousse Diccionario Enciclopédico de la Gastronomía Mexicana*. Mexico City: Larousse Mexico, 2013. An exhaustive reference book for cooks, covering Mexican ingredients, regions, and cooking techniques, written and researched by famed local chef Ricardo Muñoz Zurita. In Spanish.

Quintana, Patricia. *The Taste of Mexico*. New York: Stewart, Tabori & Chang, 1993. Written by one of Mexico City's most well-known chefs, this is an authentic Mexican cookbook, available in English.

HISTORY AND CULTURE

Bierhorst, John. *The Mythology of Mexico and Central America*. New York: William Morrow, 1990. A good introduction to Mexican mythology, particularly with regard to Mesoamerican cultures.

Caistor, Nick. *Mexico City: A Cultural and Literary Companion*. New York: Interlink Books, 2000. An interesting and extremely atmospheric account of different aspects of Mexico City history and culture, written by someone who is clearly fascinated with the city.

Coe, Michael D. *From the Olmecs to the Aztecs*. London: Thames and Hudson, 2008. Yale anthropologist Michael D. Coe has written extensively about Mesoamerican civilizations. In this volume, he introduces the great cultures of pre-Columbian Mexico.

Collier, George. *Basta: Land and the Zapatista Rebellion in Chiapas*. Oakland: Food First Books, 1994. An excellent introduction to indigenous communities and the 1994 Zapatista uprising in Chiapas.

De las Casas, Bartolomé. *Short Account of the Destruction of the Indies*. London: Penguin Books, 1992. A Dominican friar and humanitarian, de las Casas recounts his first-hand observations about Spanish colonization of the Americas.

Johns, Michael. *The City of Mexico in the Age of Díaz*. Austin: University of Texas Press, 1997. A well-written, well-researched, and ultimately fascinating chronicle of the capital during the rule of dictatorial president Porfirio Díaz.

Katz, Friedrich. *The Life and Times of Pancho Villa*. Stanford, California: Stanford University Press, 1998. The larger-than-life bandit revolutionary Villa is portrayed here in all his complexity in exhaustive detail.

Krauze, Enrique. *Biography of Power: A History of Modern Mexico, 1810-1996*. New York: HarperCollins Publishers, 1997. One of Mexico's most respected historians traces the course of Mexican history, principally through the actions of its leaders.

Lewis, Oscar. *The Children of Sanchez: Autobiography of a Mexican Family*. New York: Random House, 1979. A gritty anthropological account of the city, based on the lives of a family whose patriarch works as a waiter at the restaurant Café de Tacuba.

Lida, David. *First Stop in the New World: Mexico City, the Capital of the 21st Century*. New York: Riverhead, 2008. Lida, who is also a fiction writer and has worked as a journalist in Mexico City for years, put together a great selection of essays and reportages about all sorts of unique subcultures in the megalopolis in this volume.

Paz, Octavio. *The Labyrinth of Solitude: Life and Thought in Mexico*. New York: Grove Press, 1961. Paz has no peer when it comes to expositions of the Mexican psyche, and this is his best prose work.

Preston, Julia, and Sam Dillon. *Opening Mexico*. New York: Farrar, Straus, and Giroux, 2004. Preston and Dillon, former *New York Times* correspondents in Mexico, create an engrossing successor of sorts to Alan Riding's *Distant Neighbors*, starting in the mid-1980s but focusing principally on the *sexenio* of Ernesto Zedillo and the transition in 2000 with the victory of opposition candidate Vicente Fox.

Reed, John. *Insurgent Mexico*. New York: International Publishers, 1994. Famed American journalist Reed, of *Ten Days That Shook the World* fame, wrote this breathless, entertaining, and unabashedly biased first-hand account of time spent with Villa's troops in northern Mexico during the Mexican Revolution.

Riding, Alan. *Distant Neighbors: A Portrait of the Mexicans*. New York: Vintage Books, 1986. Riding was the *New York Times* correspondent in Mexico City for six years, and when he finished, he wrote this excellent exposition of Mexican culture and history.

Rodriguez, Jeanette. *Our Lady of Guadalupe: Faith and Empowerment among Mexican-American Women*. Austin: University of Texas Press, 1994. Explores the Guadalupe myth as the most powerful female icon in Mexican and Mexican American culture and as a symbol of liberation for Mexican Catholic women.

Thomas, Hugh. *Conquest: Montezuma, Cortés, and the Fall of Old Mexico*. New York: Simon & Schuster, 1995. An exhaustively researched and beautifully written account of one of the greatest events in history: the meeting of the New and Old Worlds in Mexico in 1519.

Womack, John. *Zapata and the Mexican Revolution*. New York: Knopf, 1970. This is considered the classic account of the legendary *caudillo del sur*, Zapata, and his role in the Mexican Revolution. A must for anyone interested in understanding Zapata's mythic status in the Mexican pantheon of heroes.

Index

N

OP

Restaurants Index

Nightlife Index

Shops Index

Hotels Index

Photo Credits

Acknowledgments

I received invaluable assistance from family, friends, and colleagues while writing and researching this edition of *Moon Mexico City*. I truly couldn't have done it alone. My deepest thanks to kind Gabriela Peña Garavito and her magical daughter, Emilia, for opening their home to me, keeping me cozy during summer rainstorms, and shuttling me around the city. More thanks are due to Lourdes Juárez Medrán for all the tasty meals and nice chats while I was there. A million *besos* and *abrazos* to my dear friend Carlos Pez, who takes generosity to a new level and loaned us the coolest crash pad in the city. Many thanks to Carlos Meade and Alfredo Lezama for their gracious hospitality, excellent nightlife and dining tips, and unfailing good company while eating out and exploring the city. You are the best. I am grateful for all the love (and opinions) I get from my Mexico family, particularly Ana Meade, Nico Ramos, Alicia Wilson, Melisa Valero, Carmen Meade, and Gabriela Gonzalez. Mom, Dad, and Amy, I wish you'd move to Mexico; I'm glad we stay so close, even when we're far away. Many thanks to Grace Fujimoto and everyone at Avalon Travel for giving me the opportunity to write this book and work with so many talented people. And, finally, my deepest thanks to my partner in life, Arturo Meade, whose opinions and spirit are infused throughout these pages, and to our *pequeño* Mariano, for joining us on the journey—and making it all a lot more fun.

CENTRO HISTÓRICO

CENTRO

SIGHTS

5	B2	Museo Nacional de Arte
6	B2	Palacio Postal
12	B4	Templo y Plaza de Santo Domingo
13	B4	Secretaría de Educación Pública
18	B4	Centro Cultural de España
20	B5	Antiguo Colegio de San Ildefonso
21	B5	Plaza Loreto
22	C2	Torre Latinoamericana
26	C3	Palacio de Cultura Banamex (Palacio de Iturbide)
47	C4	Museo del Templo Mayor
51	C4	Catedral Metropolitana
52	C4	Sagrario
53	C4	Museo de Arte de la SHCP (Antiguo Palacio del Arzobispado)
58	C4	The Zócalo
60	C4	Palacio Nacional
63	C5	Academia San Carlos
64	C6	Iglesia de la Santísima Trinidad
71	D3	Museo de la Cancillería (Oratorio de San Felipe Neri el Viejo)
73	D4	Museo de la Ciudad de México
77	E3	Templo y Convento de Regina Coeli
83	E3	Universidad del Claustro de Sor Juana
87	E6	Mercado de la Merced

RESTAURANTS

4	A4	Hostería Santo Domingo
7	B2	Bar La Ópera
10	B3	Limosneros
11	B3	Café de Tacuba
24	C2	Sanborns de los Azulejos
25	C2	Pastelería Ideal
31	C3	Café El Popular
33	C3	Salón Corona
35	C3	Casa del Pavo
38	C3	Casino Español
39	C3	Azul Histórico
48	C4	El Cardenal
49	C4	Balcón del Zócalo
65	D2	Churrería El Moro
66	D2	El Danubio
69	D3	Los Cocuyos
74	D5	El Ehden
75	D5	Productos Helús
76	D6	Roldán 37
78	E3	Zéfiro
79	E3	Coox Hanal
80	E3	Café Jekemir
85	E5	Al Andalus
86	E5	Restaurante Chon

NIGHTLIFE

2	A2	El Marrakech Salón
8	B3	La Purisima
14	B4	Salón España
23	C2	Miralto
29	C3	Zinco Jazz Club
34	C3	Pasagüero
67	D3	Mancera
68	D3	La Faena
82	E3	Hostería La Bota

ARTS AND CULTURE

9	B3	Teatro de la Ciudad de México, Esperanza Iris
17	B4	Galería de Arte de la SHCP
19	B4	Museo Archivo de la Fotografía
37	C3	Museo del Estanquillo
54	C4	Museo Mexicano de Diseño (MUMEDI)
61	C5	Ex-Teresa Arte Actual
62	C5	Casa de la Primera Imprenta de América
81	E3	Casa Vecina

SPORTS AND ACTIVITIES

| 3 | A3 | Arena Coliseo |
| 59 | C4 | Ice Skating in the Zócalo |

SHOPS

1	A2	La Hacienda
27	C2	Tienda-Librería del Palacio de Cultura Banamex
30	C3	Dulcería de Celaya
40	C3	Fábrica Social
41	C3	Remigio
42	C3	The Shops at Downtown
46	C4	Nacional Monte de Piedad
55	C4	MUMEDI Shop
56	C4	Sombreros Tardan
88	F6	Mercado Sonora

HOTELS

15	B4	Hotel Catedral
16	B4	Hostel Mundo Joven Catedral
28	C3	Hotel Ritz Ciudad de México
32	C3	Hotel Principal
36	C3	Hotel Gillow
43	C3	Downtown Hotel
44	C3	Downtown Beds
45	C4	Hotel Zamora
50	C4	Zócalo Central
57	C4	Gran Hotel de la Ciudad de Méx
70	D3	Hotel Isabel
72	D4	NH Centro His
84	E4	Hostal Centro Histórico Regin

Plaza Garibaldi

OBISPO

MINA

REPÚBLICA DE PERÚ

BELISARIO DOMÍNGUEZ

REPÚBLICA DE CU

DONCELES

Allende

5 DE MAYO

FRANCISCO

V. CARRANZA

REPÚBLICA DE URUG

SALVADOR

VIZCAÍNO

REGINA

SAN JERÓNIMO

JOSÉ MARÍA IZ

Isabel la Católica

Museo Nacional de Arte

Palacio Postal

Torre Latinoamericana

Palacio de Cultura Banamex (Palacio de Iturbide)

SEE MAP 2

Museo de la Cancill (Oratorio de San Fe Neri el Viejo)

Templo y Convento de Regina Coeli

Universidad del Claustro de Sor Juana

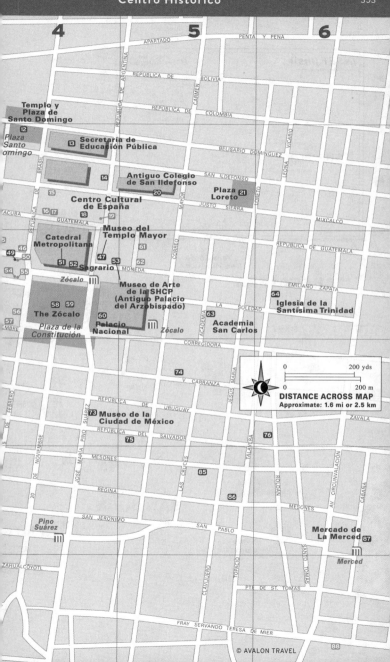

4

5

6

APARTADO

PENTA Y PENA

REPUBLICA DE BOLIVIA

REPUBLICA DE CARMEN

REPUBLICA DE COLOMBIA

**Templo y
Plaza de
Santo Domingo**

12

*Plaza
Santo
omingo*

13 **Secretaría de
Educación Pública**

BELISARIO DOMÍNGUEZ

VICARIO

14

SAN ILDEFONSO

LEONA

**Antiguo Colegio
de San Ildefonso**

20

**Plaza
Loreto** **21**

15

JUSTO SIERRA

LORETO

16 **17** **18** **19**

**Centro Cultural
de España**

MAYOR

MIXCALCO

ACUBA

GUATEMALA

**Museo del
Templo Mayor**

REPUBLICA DE GUATEMALA

**Catedral
Metropolitana**

61

49 **46**

47

CORREO

50

51 **52** **Sagrario** **53**

62

MONEDA

54 **55**

Zócalo

EMILIANO ZAPATA

**Museo de Arte
de la SHCP
(Antiguo Palacio
del Arzobispado)**

LA SOLEDAD

54

**Iglesia de la
Santísima Trinidad**

58 **59**

The Zócalo

56

60

**Palacio
Nacional**

Zócalo

63

**Academia
San Carlos**

ACADEMIA

57

*Plaza de la
Constitución*

SEMBRE

CORREGIDORA

74

V. CARRANZA

JESUS MARIA

0   200 yds

0   200 m

DISTANCE ACROSS MAP
Approximate: 1.6 mi or 2.5 km

REPUBLICA DE URUGUAY

SUAREZ

PINO

73 **Museo de la
Ciudad de México**

REPUBLICA DEL SALVADOR

75

TALAVERA

76

ZAVALA

MESONES

JOSE MARIA

REGINA

LAS CRUCES

85

ROLDAN

AV. CIRCUNVALACION

CABANA

DE NOVIEMBRE

86

MESONES

20

SAN JERONIMO

*Pino
Suárez*

SAN PABLO

**Mercado de
La Merced** **87**

ZAHUALCOYOTL

SANTO TOMAS

Merced

TOPACIO

PTE. DE ST. TOMAS

CLAVIJERO

FRAY SERVANDO TERESA DE MIER

88

© AVALON TRAVEL

INSET (Ins)

1

Plaza de
2 Tres Culturas

Zona
Arqueológica
3 Tlatelolco

4 Centro
Cultural
Universitario
Tlatelolco

GUERRERO

Garibaldi

Garibaldi

AV RICARDO FLORES MAGÓN

MARTE

ESTRELLA

ESTRELLA

HEROES

ZARCO

SOTO

LERDO

REAL PEDRO LUIS OGAZON

EJE CENTRAL LÁZARO CÁRDENAS

LUNA

SOL

GALEANA

PASEO DE LA REFORMA

ALLENDE

JAIME NUÑO

LIBERTAD

MOSQUETA

EJE 1 NORTE

Guerrero

MOSQUETA

GALEANA

ALAMEDA
CENTRAL

OBISP

PUENTE DE ALVARADO

Templo de 10
San Hipólito

REFORMA

11

PENSADOR MEXICANO

SANTA
VERACRUZ

19

20

TABACALERA

Hidalgo

AV HIDALGO

Plaza
Santa Veracruz

Bellas
Artes

DR MORA

DE

PASEO

12

13 14

15

16
17

18

Alameda
Central
21

Palacio
de Bellas
Artes

22

23

24

SEE MAP 3

26

AV JUÁREZ

35

A PIRANA

27 28

29 30

31

INDEPENDENCIA

HUMBOLDT

DONATO GUERRA

32 Juarez

36

37

AV MORELOS

25

DONATO GUERRA

Ministerio
33 Público

ARTICULO 123

DOLORES

LOPEZ

BUCARELI

34

VICTORIA

AYUNTAMIENTO

39

BALDERAS

Mercado
San Juan

Plaza de 43
San Juan

San J
de Let

EMILIO DONDE

Plaza José
Maria Morelos

ERNESTO

PUGIBET

41 40

42

44

45

EMILIO MARTINEZ

SAN JUAN

VIZCAIN

REVILLAGIGEDO

LUIS MOYA

BUEN

TONO

ARANDA

CENTR

Plaza de la
38 Ciudadela

ARCOS DE BELÉN

Salto
del Agu

Balderas

DR RAFAEL LUCIO

HEROES

NIÑOS

DR RIO DE LA LOZA

DR ANDRADE

EJE CENTRAL

LÁZARO CÁRDENAS SUR

46

SEE MAP 5

SEE MAP 1

SEE INSET

Lagunilla

SIGHTS

2	Ins	Plaza de Tres Culturas	9	B4	Plaza Garibaldi
3	Ins	Zona Arqueológica Tlatelolco	10	C2	Templo de San Hipólito
4	Ins	Centro Cultural Universitario Tlatelolco	21	C3	Alameda Central
			22	C3	Palacio de Bellas Artes
			42	E3	Plaza de San Juan

RESTAURANTS

25	D1	Café La Habana	37	D3	Fonda Santa Rita
27	D2	La Cervecería de Barrio	40	E3	Mercado San Juan
32	D2	Café 123	43	E3	El Huequito
34	D2	El Cuadrilatero	44	E3	El Caguamo

NIGHTLIFE

1	Ins	Salón Los Angeles	28	D2	Bósforo
6	B4	Salón Tenampa	36	D3	Cantina Tio Pepe
7	B4	Pulquería Hermosa Hortensia	45	E3	Pulquería Las Duelistas

ARTS AND CULTURE

8	B4	Museo del Tequila y El Mezcal	23	C3	Palacio de Bellas Artes
12	C2	Laboratorio Arte Alameda	29	D2	Museo de Arte Popular
13	C2	Museo Mural Diego Rivera	31	D2	Teatro Metropólitan
19	C3	Museo Franz Mayer	35	D3	Museo Memoria y Tolerancia
20	C3	Museo Nacional de la Estampa	38	E1	Centro de la Imagen

SPORTS AND ACTIVITIES

46	F1	Arena México	

SHOPS

5	A4	La Lagunilla	24	C3	Librería Educal
14	C2	Barrio Alameda	30	D2	Tienda MAP
15	C2	Navaja	39	E2	La Ciudadela Centro Artesanal
16	C2	Utilitario Mexicano	41	E3	Mercado San Juan
18	C2	FONART			

HOTELS

11	C2	Hotel de Cortés	26	D2	Hilton Mexico City Reforma
17	C2	Chaya B&B	33	D2	Hotel Fleming

Plaza Garibaldi

Secretaría de Educación Pública

Iglesia de la Enseñanza

Allende

Catedral Metropolitana

CENTRO HISTÓRICO

Plaza de la Constitución (The Zocalo)

Templo de Regina Coeli

Ex-convento de San Jerónimo

Isabel la Católica

Pino Suárez

0   200 yds

0   200 m

DISTANCE ACROSS MAP
Approximate: 2.1 mi or 3.3 km

© AVALON TRAVEL

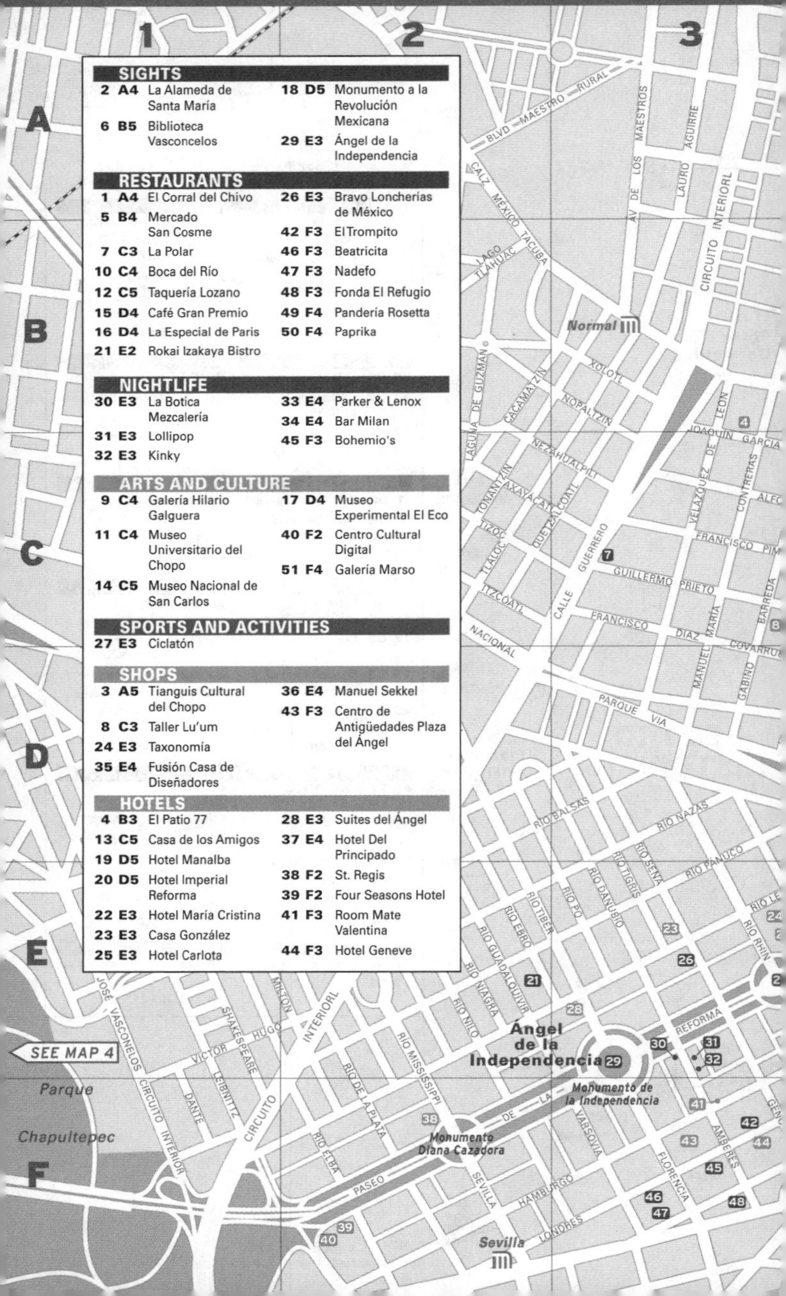

SEE MAP 4

Parque Chapultepec

Normal

Ángel de la Independencia 29

Monumento de la Independencia

Monumento Diana Cazadora

Sevilla

4

5

6

SALVADOR OTAZ MIRON

Alameda de Santa María

1

2 La Alameda de Santa María

ESTRELLA

LUNA

SOL

ZARCO

ANTA MARÍA
A RIBERA

JOSE ANTONIO ALZATE

EJE 1 NORTE

3

Buenavista

Biblioteca
Vasconcelos **6**

MARTINEZ DE LA TORRE   EJE 1 NORTE

JUANA INES DE LA CRUZ

Guerrero

AV JESUS GARCIA

MOCTEZUMA

CARLOS

MENESES

MAGNOLIA

San Cosme

RIBERA DE

SAN COSME

11

AMADO NERVO

PEDRO

MORENO

VIOLETA

12

HEROES

FERROCARRILEROS

MINA

Revolución

PUENTE DE ALVARADO

14

SAN RAFAEL

EDDISON

AV DE LA

13

SEE MAP 2

Hidalgo

Monumento a la
Revolución Mexicana

18

Plaza de la
República

REFORMA

Alameda
Central

REPUBLICA

AV JUAREZ

15

MAESTRO ANTONIO CASO

19

DE LA

TABACALERA

16

17

VIA

din
Arte

PASEO

DONATO GUERRA

AV MORELOS

Juárez

INDEPENDENCIA

ARTICULO 123

Monumento
de Colón

20

VICTORIA

Monumento
Cuauhtémoc

33

AYUNTAMIENTO

EMILIO DONDE

ERNESTO

PUGIBET

34

GRAL PRIM

Plaza José
María Morelos

ONA
ROSA

35 **36**

HAMBURGO

LONDRES

ABRAHAM GONZALEZ

37

BALDERAS

Balderas

51

Cuauhtémoc

Plaza de la
Ciudadela

ARCOS DE BELEN

49 **50**

MARSELLA

AV CHAPULTEPEC

TURIN

DR RIO DE LA LOZA

surgentes

PUEBLA

DURANGO

DR LICEAGA

0   300 yds

0   300 m

DISTANCE ACROSS MAP
Approximate: 2.7 mi or 4.3 km

SEE MAP 5

© AVALON TRAVEL

To ① Museo Soumaya ↗
② Museo Jumex

1 **2** AV EJERCITO NACIONAL **3**

POLANCO

LOS MORALES
SECC PALMAS

PALMITAS

Parque
América

Plaza
Mazaryk

Parque Linc...

SIGHTS
- **34 C5** Museo Nacional de Antropología
- **43 D6** Monumento a los Niños Héroes
- **44 D6** Castillo de Chapultepec and the Museo Nacional de Historia
- **45 D6** Baños de Moctezuma
- **53 F4** Casa Luis Barragán

RESTAURANTS
- **6 A5** Bimmy
- **7 A5** Pujol
- **8 A5** Eno
- **9 B2** Guzina Oaxaca
- **10 B2** Dawat
- **11 B2** El Turix
- **15 B3** Dulce Patria
- **19 B3** Non Solo Pasta
- **23 B4** Quintonil
- **25 B5** Mi Gusto Es
- **31 C4** Au Pied de Cochon
- **32 C4** Chapulín
- **37 C6** Los Panchos
- **46 E3** El Lago
- **55 F5** Café Zena
- **56 F5** Cancino
- **58 F5** La Poblanita de Tacubaya

NIGHTLIFE
- **3 A2** Joy Room
- **17 B3** Jules Basement
- **20 B4** Terraza at the Hotel Hábita

ARTS AND CULTURE
- **1 A1** Museo Soumaya
- **2 A1** Museo Jumex
- **5 A5** Luis Adelantado Mexico
- **26 B5** Museo Sala de Arte Público David Alfaro Siqueiros
- **29 C3** Auditorio Nacional
- **35 C6** Museo Rufino Tamayo
- **39 C6** Museo de Arte Moderno
- **41 D5** Casa del Lago Juan José Arreola
- **48 E5** Galería de Arte Mexicano
- **49 F2** Museo de Historia Natural and Museo Jardín del Agua
- **51 F4** Papalote Museo del Niño
- **52 F4** Archivo Diseño y Arquitectura
- **54 F4** Labor
- **57 F5** Kurimanzutto

SPORTS AND ACTIVITIES
- **40 D4** Bosque de Chapultepec
- **42 D5** Noches de Bici
- **47 E3** La Feria de Chapultepec
- **50 F3** Rancho del Charro Javier Rojo Gómez

SHOPS
- **4 A3** Studio Roca
- **12 B3** Pirwi
- **13 B3** Tane
- **16 B3** Common People
- **18 B3** El Péndulo
- **22 B4** Uriarte Talavera
- **24 B5** Talleres de los Ballesteros
- **30 C4** Pineda Covalín

HOTELS
- **14 B3** Las Alcobas
- **21 B4** Hotel Hábita
- **27 C3** JW Marriott
- **28 C3** W Mexico City
- **33 C4** InterContinental Presidente Mexico City
- **36 C6** Camino Real Mexico City
- **38 C6** Wyndham Garden Polanco

| 0 | 200 yds |
| 0 | 200 m |

DISTANCE ACROSS MAP
Approximate: 2.7 mi or 4.3 km

Lago
Mayor

Segun
Secci

Lago
Menor

To
50 Rancho del Charro
Javier Rojo Gomez

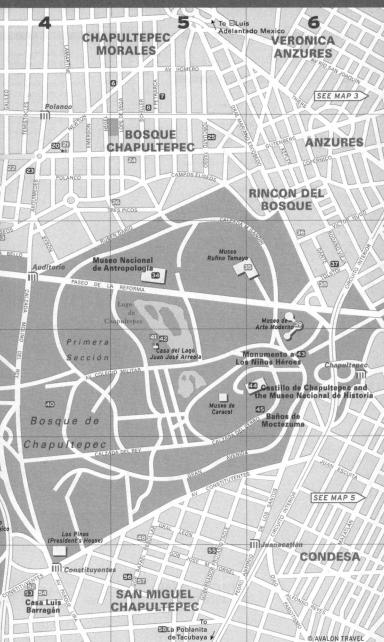

MAP 4

CHAPULTEPEC MORALES

To 5 Luis Adelantado Mexico

VERONICA ANZURES

6

AV HOMERO

LAMARTINE

Polanco

6

PETRARCA

7

SCHILLER

LOPE DE VEGA

HEGEL

EMERSON

NEWTON

TEMISTOCLES

GALILEO

AV RIO SAN JOAQUIN

THIERS

SEE MAP 3

GRAL MARIANO ESCOBEDO

ANZURES

GUTENBERG

KEPLER

COPERNICO

BOSQUE CHAPULTEPEC

25

TORCUATO TASSO

24

CAMPOS ELISEOS

20 21

22

23

ARQUIMEDES

POLANCO

26

TRES PICOS

RINCON DEL BOSQUE

CALZADA M. GANDHI

36

VICTOR HUGO

RUDANO VILLA

DANTE

TOLSTOI

CIRCUITO INTERIOR

RUBEN DARIO

BYRON

SEOS
33

A. BELLO

Auditorio

Museo Nacional de Antropología

34

Museo Rufino Tamayo

35

37

38

PASEO DE LA REFORMA

CALZADA MOLINO DEL REY

Lago de Chapultepec

Primera

Sección

41 42

Casa del Lago Juan José Arreola

AV. COLEGIO MILITAR

Museo de Arte Moderno 39

Monumento a 43 Los Niños Héroes

Chapultepec

Castillo de Chapultepec and the Museo Nacional de Historia

44

45 Baños de Moctezuma

40

Museo de Caracol

Bosque de

Chapultepec

CALZADA DEL REY

CALZADA DEL CERRO

AVENIDA

GRAN

AV. CONSTITUYENTES

JUAN ESCUTIA

MAZATLAN

SEE MAP 5

DE LOS SANTOS

CIRCUITO INTERIOR

PEDRO ANTONIO

gico

Los Pinos (President's House)

48

Juanacatlán

CONDESA

GRAL LEON

GDB

JOSE M TORNEL

GOBERNADOR PROTASIO TAGLE

55

DIAG

ALFONSO REYES

PAROTISIMO

Constituyentes

AV PARQUE LIRA

56

57

SAN MIGUEL CHAPULTEPEC

GRAL RAFAEL TEJOLLAR

CONSTITUYENTES

53 54

Casa Luis Barragán

52

To

58 La Poblanita de Tacubaya

© AVALON TRAVEL

SEE MAP 3

SIGHTS

4 A6 Templo San Francisco Javier and Plaza Romita	**9 B5** Plaza Río de Janeiro
	60 D3 Parque México

RESTAURANTS

13 B5 Rosetta	**61 D4** La Casa de la Tlayuda
23 C3 Contramar	**62 D4** Galanga
26 C4 Fonda Fina	**63 D4** Mercado Roma
27 C4 Yuban	**66 D4** El Parnita
28 C4 Huset	**67 D5** Máximo Bistrot Local
33 C4 Panadería Pancracia	**72 E2** Café La Gloria
36 C5 Peltre Lonchería	**76 E2** Taquería El Greco
38 C5 Sobrinos	**77 E2** Tacos El Güero (Tacos Hola)
41 C5 Café Paris	**78 E2** El Tizoncito
42 C5 Fournier Rousseau	**80 E3** Merotoro
46 C5 Cardinal	**82 E4** El Jarocho
47 C6 Romita Comedor	**85 F1** Neveria Roxy
48 C6 La Docena	**88 F2** Fonda Mayora
51 C6 Los Chamorros de Mérida	**89 F2** Tacos Gus
52 C6 Mog	**91 F2** El Califa
54 D1 The Green Corner	**92 F2** Taquería El Farolito
55 D2 El Pescadito	

NIGHTLIFE

1 A5 Patrick Miller	**50 C6** Félix
2 A5 Covadonga	**56 D2** Pata Negra
5 B4 Jardín Chapultepec	**57 D3** El Batáclan
6 B4 Rhodesia Club Social	**64 D4** Biergarten
7 B4 Pulquería Los Insurgentes	**65 D4** Mama Rumba
12 B5 Lucille	**68 D5** La Nuclear Pulquería
16 B6 Multiforo Alicia	**69 D6** M. N. Roy
22 C3 La Bodeguita en Medio	**73 E2** Centenario
25 C3 La Clandestina	**75 E2** Salón Malafama
40 C5 Licorería Limantour	**84 E5** Híbrido
	90 F2 Felina Bar

ROMA

PUEBLA

SALAMANCA

SINAI

VALLADOLID

DURANGO

CONDESA

Parque España

Plaza Popocatépetl

Parque México

HIPÓDROMO

HIPÓDROMO CONDESA

To 18 Foro Shakespeare
19 Sabrá Dios

ALVARO OBR

To 90 Felina Bar

SEE MAP 4

SEE MAP 6

© AVALON TRAVEL

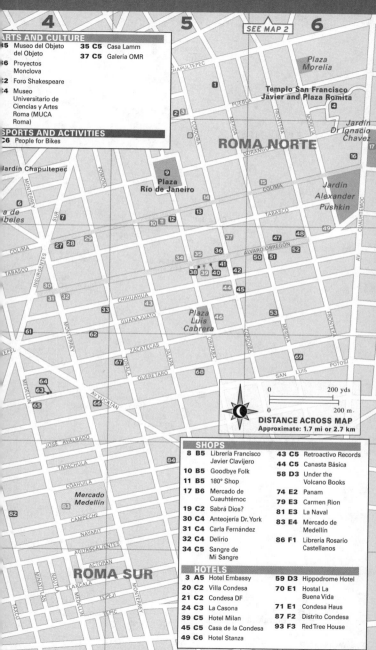

4 | **5** | SEE MAP 2 | **6**

Plaza Morelia

Templo San Francisco Javier and Plaza Romita

Jardín Dr Ignacio Chavez

ROMA NORTE

Jardín Chapultepec

Plaza Río de Janeiro

Jardín Alexander Pushkin

a de beles

Plaza Luis Cabrera

ROMA SUR

Mercado Medellín

DISTANCE ACROSS MAP
Approximate: 1.7 mi or 2.7 km

0   200 yds
0   200 m

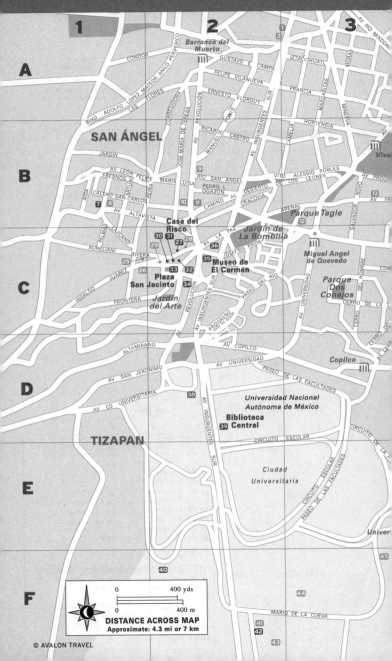

TETEPILCO

Cineteca Nacional

Panteón Xoco

Museo Frida Kahlo (Casa Azul)

Museo Casa León Trotsky

viveros de oacán

Plaza Santa Catarina

Plaza y Capilla de la Conchita

— SEE INSET —

COYOACÁN

PEDREGAL

Jardín Hidalgo and Antiguo Palacio del Ayuntamiento

Jardín Centenario

Parroquia y Ex-Convento de San Juan Bautista

INSET (Ins)

SIGHTS

6 A5	Museo Casa León Trotsky	
16 B4	Plaza Santa Catarina	
19 B4	Museo Frida Kahlo (Casa Azul)	
31 C2	Casa del Risco	
33 C2	Plaza San Jacinto	
35 C2	Museo de El Carmen	
37 C5	Plaza y Capilla de la Conchita	
39 D2	Biblioteca Central	
48 Ins	Jardín Hidalgo and Antiguo Palacio del Ayuntamiento	
51 Ins	Jardín Centenario	
54 Ins	Parroquia y Ex-Convento de San Juan Bautista	

RESTAURANTS

4 A4	Super Tacos Chupacabra	
7 B1	San Ángel Inn	
17 B4	Merendero Las Lupitas	
21 B4	Casa del Pan Papalotl	
23 B4	Mercado Coyoacán	
24 B5	El Beneficio	
27 C2	L'Encanto de Lola	
30 C2	Fonda San Ángel	
32 C2	La Camelia	
34 C2	Mercado Melchor Múzquiz de San Ángel	
36 C2	Cluny	
42 F2	Azul y Oro	
46 Ins	Café El Jarocho	
47 Ins	Fonda El Morral	
50 Ins	Corazón de Maguey	
52 Ins	Los Danzantes	
55 Ins	Pepe Coyotes	
59 Ins	Café Avellaneda	

NIGHTLIFE

5 A4	El Vicio	
22 B4	La Bipo	
57 Ins	La Coyoacana	
58 Ins	Mezcalero	

ARTS AND CULTURE

1 A3	Teatro de los Insurgentes	
3 A4	Cineteca Nacional	
8 B1	Museo Casa Estudio Diego Rivera	
9 B2	Teatro Helénico	
11 B2	Museo de Arte Carrillo Gil	
13 B3	Fonoteca Nacional	
41 F2	Museo Universitario Arte Contemporáneo	
43 F2	Sala Nezahualcóyotl	
44 F3	Espacio Escultórico de la UNAM	
45 F3	Filmoteca Unam	
56 Ins	Museo Nacional de Culturas Populares	

SPORTS AND ACTIVITIES

15 B4	Viveros de Coyoacán	
38 D2	Estadio Olímpico	
40 F2	Jardín Botánico del Instituto de Biología	
53 Ins	Equal Bicigratis	

SHOPS

10 B2	Mundo Gourmet	
12 B3	Librería Gandhi	
14 B3	Barricas Don Tiburcio	
20 B4	Taller Experimental de Cerámica	
25 C1	Casa del Obispo	
26 C1	Caracol Púrpura	
28 C2	Ecobutik	
29 C2	Bazaar Sábado	
49 Ins	Bazar Artesanal Mexicano de Coyoacán	

HOTELS

2 A2	City Express Insurgentes Sur	
18 B4	La Casita del Patio Verde	

Labels on map:

AUTOPISTA MÉXICO-PACHUCA

VIA MORELOS

85 D

AV HANK GONZÁLEZ

Lago Regulador

AV CENTRAL

Jardines del Tepeyac

Valle de Aragón

San Juan de Aragón

Aeropuerto Internacional Benito Juárez

Parque Nacional El Tepeyac

CALZ SAN JUAN DE ARAGÓN

Basílica de Santa María de Guadalupe

Federal

DE GUADALUPE

CALZ

Morelos

DR VÉRTIZ

RAYON

Centro Histórico

FERROCARRIL HIDALGO

AV TERESA

LÁZARO CÁRDENAS

TICOMÁN

EJE CENTRAL LÁZARA CÁRDENAS

CALZ. VALLEJO

CIRCUITO INTERIOR

MOSQUETA

Santa María la Ribera

Roma

AV SANTA CECILIA

AV J. REYES HEROLES

Nueva Santa María

PASEO DE LA REFORMA

CHAPULTEPEC

Tlalnepantla

Azcapotzalco

Tezozomoc

Polanco

RIO SAN JOAQUÍN

Bosque de Chapultepec

AV E. NACIONAL

ANILLO PERIFÉRICO

3

Lomas de Chapultepec Chapultepec

Condesa

SIGHTS

2 B5 Basílica de Santa María de Guadalupe
15 D4 Poliforum Siqueiros
19 E3 Cuicuilco
25 F4 Tlalpan
27 F5 Canals at Xochimilco

RESTAURANTS

16 D4 Fonda Margarita
24 F4 Arroyo

ARTS AND CULTURE

4 C4 Museo del Juguete Antiguo México
6 C5 Palacio de los Deportes
20 E4 Museo Anahuacalli
26 F5 Museo Dolores Olmedo

SPORTS AND ACTIVITIES

1 A3 Arena Ciudad de México
3 C3 Hipódromo de las Américas
7 C5 Foro Sol
8 C5 Autódromo Hermanos Rodríguez
12 D3 Estadio Azul
14 D3 Parque Hundido
18 E1 Desierto de los Leones
21 E4 Estadio Azteca
23 E5 Parque Ecológico de Xochimilco (PEX)

SHOPS

5 C5 Mercado de Jamaica
17 D5 Central de Abasto de la Ciudad de México
22 E5 Mercado de Plantas y Flores Cuemanco

HOTELS

9 C5 Camino Real Aeropuerto
10 C6 Airport Hilton
11 C6 NH Hotel Aeropuerto
13 D3 El Diplomatico

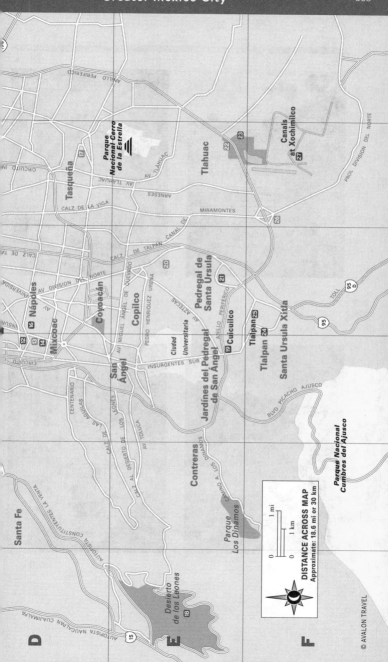

ANILLO PERIFERICO

CIRCUITO INT

Parque
Nacional Cerro
de la Estrella

AV TLAHUAC

AV TLAHUAC

Canals
at Xochimilco

27

PROL DIVISION DEL NORTE

Tasqueña

17

Tlahuac

22   23

ARNESES

CALZ DE LA VIGA

MIRAMONTES

26

CALZ DE TAL

CALZ DE TALPAN   CANAL DE

Nápoles

AV DIVISION DEL NORTE

20

Pedregal de
Santa Ursula

AV MIGUEL ANGEL DE QUEVEDO

Coyoacán

Copilco

21

16

Mixcoac

12
13
14

PEDRO HENRIQUEZ UREÑA

AV AZTECAS

ANILLO PERIFERICO

Cuicuilco

19

Tlalpan

25

Santa Ursula Xitla

CIRCUITO

San Angel

Ciudad
Universitaria

INSURGENTES SUR

Jardines del Pedregal
de San Angel

Tlalpan

24

95
D

95

TOLL

CENTENARIO

CALZ DE LOS LEONES

CALZ AL DESIERTO DE LOS

AV TOLUCA

Contreras

DINAMOS

BLVD PICACHO AJUSCO

CAMINO A LOS

Parque Nacional
Cumbres del Ajusco

Santa Fe

AUTOPISTA CONSTITUYENTES LA VENTA

Parque
Los Dínamos

Desierto
de los Leones

18

15

AUTOPISTA NAUCALPAN CUAJIMALPA

DISTANCE ACROSS MAP
Approximate: 18.6 mi or 30 km

0   1 mi

0   1 km

© AVALON TRAVEL

D

E

F

Also Available

MOON

CANCÚN & COZUMEL

Including Playa del Carmen, Tulum & the Riviera Maya

GARY CHANDLER & LIZA PRADO

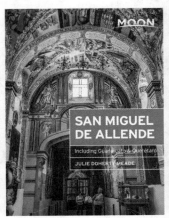

MOON

SAN MIGUEL DE ALLENDE

Including Guanajuato & Querétaro

JULIE DOHERTY MEADE

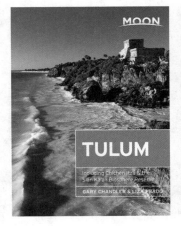

MOON

TULUM

Including Chichén Itzá & the Sian Ka'an Biosphere Reserve

GARY CHANDLER & LIZA PRADO

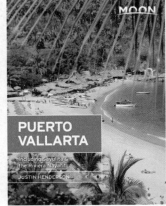

MOON

PUERTO VALLARTA

Including Sayulita & the Riviera Nayarit

JUSTIN HENDERSON

MAP SYMBOLS

■	Sights	⊛	National Capital	▲	Mountain	═══		Major Hwy
■	Restaurants	⊛	State Capital	✛	Natural Feature			Road/Hwy
■	Nightlife	○	City/Town	🗲	Waterfall	·········		Pedestrian Friendly
■	Arts and Culture	★	Point of Interest	♨	Park	- - - - -		Trail
■	Sports and Activities	•	Accommodation	⏚	Archaeological Site	▪▪▪▪▪▪		Stairs
■	Shops	▼	Restaurant/Bar	🄷	Trailhead	············		Ferry
■	Hotels	▪	Other Location	🄿	Parking Area	━ ━ ━		Railroad

CONVERSION TABLES

°C = (°F - 32) / 1.8
°F = (°C x 1.8) + 32
1 inch = 2.54 centimeters (cm)
1 foot = 0.304 meters (m)
1 yard = 0.914 meters
1 mile = 1.6093 kilometers (km)
1 km = 0.6214 miles
1 fathom = 1.8288 m
1 chain = 20.1168 m
1 furlong = 201.168 m
1 acre = 0.4047 hectares
1 sq km = 100 hectares
1 sq mile = 2.59 square km
1 ounce = 28.35 grams
1 pound = 0.4536 kilograms
1 short ton = 0.90718 metric ton
1 short ton = 2,000 pounds
1 long ton = 1.016 metric tons
1 long ton = 2,240 pounds
1 metric ton = 1,000 kilograms
1 quart = 0.94635 liters
1 US gallon = 3.7854 liters
1 Imperial gallon = 4.5459 liters
1 nautical mile = 1.852 km

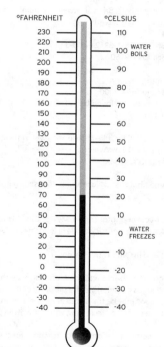

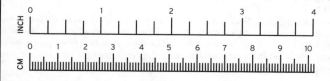

MOON MEXICO CITY
Avalon Travel
An imprint of Perseus Books
A Hachette Book Group company
1700 Fourth Street
Berkeley, CA 94710, USA
www.moon.com

Editors: Nikki Ioakimedes, Rachel Feldman, Erin Raber
Series Manager: Leah Gordon
Copy Editor: Deana Shields
Graphics Coordinator: Rue Flaherty
Production Coordinator: Rue Flaherty
Cover Design: Faceout Studios, Charles Brock
Interior Design: Megan Jones Design
Moon Logo: Tim McGrath
Map Editor: Kat Bennett
Cartographers: Brian Shotwell, Stephanie Poulain, Kat Bennett
Indexer: Greg Jewett

ISBN-13: 978-1-63121-408-0
ISSN: 1541-9150

Printing History
1st Edition — 2000
6th Edition — November 2016
5 4 3 2